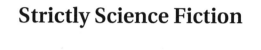

Strictly Science Fiction

Genreflecting Advisory Series

Diana Tixier Herald, Series Editor

Genreflecting: A Guide to Reading Interests in Genre Fiction, 5th Edition
   By Diana Tixier Herald

Teen Genreflecting
   By Diana Tixier Herald

Romance Fiction: A Guide to the Genre
   By Kristin Ramsdell

Fluent in Fantasy: A Guide to Reading Interests
   By Diana Tixier Herald

Now Read This: A Guide to Mainstream Fiction, 1978–1998
   By Nancy Pearl with assistance from Martha Knappe and Chris Higashi

Now Read This II: A Guide to Mainstream Fiction, 1990–2001
   By Nancy Pearl

Hooked on Horror: A Guide to Reading Interests in Horror Fiction
   By Anthony J. Fonseca and June Michele Pulliam

Junior Genreflecting: A Guide to Good Reads and Series Fiction for Children
   By Bridget Dealy Volz, Lynda Blackburn Welborn, and Cheryl Perkins Scheer

Christian Fiction: A Guide to the Genre
   By John Mort

Strictly Science Fiction: A Guide to Reading Interests
   By Diana Tixier Herald and Bonnie Kunzel

Strictly Science Fiction

A Guide to Reading Interests

Diana Tixier Herald
Bonnie Kunzel

2002
LIBRARIES UNLIMITED
A Division of Greenwood Publishing Group, Inc.
Greenwood Village, Colorado

LIBRARIES UNLIMITED
A Division of Greenwood Publishing Group, Inc.
7730 E. Belleview Avenue, Suite A200
Greenwood Village, CO 80111
1-800-225-5800
www.lu.com

Library of Congress Cataloging-in-Publication Data

Herald, Diana Tixier.
    Strictly science fiction : a guide to reading interests / by Diana
Tixier Herald and Bonnie Kunzel.
        p. cm. -- (Genreflecting advisory series)
    Includes bibliographical references and index.
    ISBN 1-56308-893-2
    1. Libraries--United States--Special collections--Science fiction. 2.
Readers' advisory services--United States. 3. Reading interests--United
States. 4. Fiction in libraries--United States. 5. Science
fiction--Bibliography. I. Kunzel, Bonnie, 1944- II. Title. III. Series.

    Z688.S32 H47 2002
    028'.9--dc21
                                                    2002003186

This book is dedicated to our families, without whose loving support and understanding this work could never have been started—much less completed. Thanks to husbands who cooked for us, grown children who put up with us, and everyone's faith in our eventual success—which kept us going, and going, and going. We couldn't have done it without you, gang, so here it is—this one's for you.

To Rick Herald, my son Nathan Herald and his wife Melissa, my daughter Chani and her husband Tanner Lewis, my grandson Jack Sundance Herald, who at age two lives science fiction adventure, and all the fosterlings. *DTH*

To George Kunzel, my son Derek Kunzel, and my daughter Erin, my new son-in-law Michael Turner, and his daughter, my grandchild Alexis—who is already well on her way (at the age of seven) to developing a true appreciation of the wonders to be found in science fiction! *BK*

Contents

Acknowledgments

Libraries Unlimited is grateful to NoveList (of EBSCO Publishing) for their permission to adapt and use images from their program throughout the Genreflecting Advisory Series.

This work could not have been done without the suggestions and recommendations of science fiction readers who freely shared favorite titles and authors with us.

Barbara Ittner, Acquisitions Editor, Libraries Unlimited, provided great insight and direction while trying to keep us grounded in this world. Her gentle suggestions and advice have made this a much better book than it would have been without her guidance.

Happy reading.

Introduction

What Is Science Fiction?

> Critical works pose science fiction as the most philosophi-
> cal, poetical, intellectual, and religious of the genre fictions.
> It is concerned with the mystery of the universe, man's place
> in it, and man's ultimate destiny: the continuation of human-
> kind in its basic nature and humanity. Science fiction ex-
> presses faith in human ingenuity, human intelligence, and
> the human spirit. Technology is considered in terms of ser-
> vice to mankind and the natural world. The biological sci-
> ences are considered as they might heighten or increase the
> capacity and quality of the human mind. Religion is viewed
> as a means of salvation. The end is to augment the quality of
> life. Science fiction has been labeled a fiction of questions:
> What if . . . ? If only . . . ? If this goes on . . .

So stated the late Betty Rosenberg in her first edition of *Genreflecting,* published nearly two decades ago. Some might challenge specific points of this description, but the essence of Rosenberg's comments remains true. Science fiction could certainly be described as the literature of "what if?" What if there were life on other planets? What if someone were to travel faster than light? What if there were people who lived inside a world rather than on its surface? What if all the men on a planet were to die off? What if one could enter a world created by a computer program? What if . . . ? The possibilities of science fiction are as endless as the human imagination. Indeed, it is a literature of possibilities.

But what really *is* science fiction? What or who defines it, and what factors help determine whether a particular title is labeled "science fiction"? Is SF merely a marketing device of the publishing industry? Do SF writers determine what the genre encompasses? Or is it ultimately up to readers and fans? Perhaps it is not really a genre at all. Certainly a case could be made for each of these possibilities. But our purpose here is one of practicality. So, rather than entering the philosophical and scholarly debate about what defines SF, let's try to achieve a general understanding of the genre and its readers.

Science fiction is a thoroughly discussed and highly analyzed genre, and definitions abound. Stanley Schmidt, the editor of *Analog,* defines science fiction stories as those "in which some aspect of future science or technology is so integral to the plot that, if that aspect were removed, the story would collapse." And John Clute, in *Science Fiction: The Illustrated Encyclopedia* (DK Publishing, 1995), says that SF (the accepted acronym for the genre) "is any story that argues the case for a changed world that has not yet come into being. SF is about worlds. . . and is a literature of possible world-changes, however unlikely they may appear; possible continuations of history over the sand-reefs of the Millennium, into brave new centuries." In the essay "On Science and Science Fiction" in *The Ascent of*

Wonder: The Evolution of Hard SF (Tor, 1994), Kathryn Cramer explains that "SF allows us to understand and experience our past, present, and future in terms of an imagined future." Peter Nichols, in his article on the history of SF in *The Encyclopedia of Science Fiction,* elaborates: "SF proper requires a consciousness of the scientific outlook, and it probably also requires a sense of the possibilities of change." A broader and simpler definition can be found in *Webster's Dictionary,* which states that science fiction is "fiction dealing principally with the impact of actual or imagined science on a society or individuals or having a scientific factor as an essential component" (*Merriam Webster's Collegiate Dictionary*, 10th ed., 1994).

In this genre just about anything can happen—as long as science or technology rather than magic or the fantastic is involved. In science fiction we can fly on the backs of fire-breathing dragons—but only if they are genetically created. This is the genre that explores the inner space of psi powers and such superhuman abilities as mental telepathy, teleportation, and telekinesis; it also explores the outer space of other planets and other galaxies, taking the reader to the far reaches of the imagination. Science fiction takes us backward and forward in time as well as across barriers between our world and alternate worlds. It investigates the world of computers from the outside—through the programs that are created, through the activities of hackers, and through the consequences of our dependence on them—and from the inside, where virtual reality experiences may become all-too-frighteningly real.

Science fiction can be optimistic, depicting utopia and irresistible realms of wonder, or it can be pessimistic, drawing us into dire worlds of social and ecological disaster. In science fiction stories BEMs, or bug-eyed monsters (the term applied to aliens in the early days of science fiction) may loom threateningly on the horizon, or aliens might travel to Earth on a mission of hope. Then again, extraterrestrials may come and treat humankind with much the same regard as uncaring gods. First contact can bring us infinite rewards or the horrors of invasion and destruction (if there's anything left after what we do to ourselves and our ecosystem).

In terms of content, science fiction can be "hard"—probing the ramifications of scientific theories and practical applications of quantum physics, bioengineering, or mathematics, or it can be "soft"—concentrating on psychology and social sciences and exploring relationships, the underpinnings of society, or even what it means to be human.

The characters, settings, and topics covered in science fiction are equally diverse. Stories may focus on a human hero or on a race of extraterrestrial creatures. Some stories are set in a near future, with highly plausible scenarios. Others are set so far in the future or in the past that they seem well-nigh impossible. Romance, mystery, war, plagues, robots, ecology—all provide springboards into the worlds of science fiction.

Some claim that science fiction is merely a subgenre of fantasy fiction. It is not our intention to argue the finer and philosophical points of the definition or to defend our treatment of SF as a genre. The purpose of this work is practical, and in terms of practicability, a separate treatment is warranted for readers' advisors. After all, taken to the extreme, one could argue that all fiction is fantasy. For the purposes of this guide, we adhere to Clute's definition of science fiction, but we exclude the closely allied genres of straight fantasy and horror. It is important to note that these three genres are often grouped together as "literature of the imagination," "literature of the strange," "speculative fiction," or "fantastic literature." Indeed, many authors write across these genres, and it is frequently difficult to pigeonhole a title into one of the genres. Often a specific title fits just as well in horror as it does in science fiction, and often a novel will incorporate aspects of horror or fantasy into the science fiction milieu. Then again, to readers not sophisticated in the realms of science and technology, science may seem like magic. The ability to construct a computer from scratch can appear as mysterious and unlikely as the ability to transmute lead into gold.

Another reason that SF, fantasy, and horror are so closely entwined is that organizations, journals, publishers, award committees, and even bookstores treat them as a cohesive group. For example, *Locus* magazine, "the newspaper of the science fiction field" covers all three genres; the Nebula award for best novel has been bestowed on books in all three genres; and bookstores often shelve SF and fantasy together.

Science fiction, a combination of science and fiction, can be seen as a marriage between knowledge and the imagination. The progenies of this union are seemingly endless—even without its companion genres of horror and fantasy. This book seeks to examine a number of the diverse titles contained within the parameters of the genre.

Why This Book?

As stated, science fiction is a much-discussed and highly analyzed genre. There are numerous guides to science fiction, including print journals, online resources, databases, encyclopedias, and bibliographies. Many of these guides are thoroughly researched and informative. Some of the resources that are more helpful to readers' advisors are listed in Chapter 8, "Resources for Librarians and Readers." These guides go into great depth on the history and evolution of the genre, categorizing titles into a multitude of subjects and types and discussing the literary abilities and accomplishments of particular SF authors. But in terms of finding an enjoyable book for a specific reading taste, these guides fall short. They fall short because they are not organized in a way that reflects or caters to reader interests.

This volume endeavors to fill that need. Its purpose is to put readers together with the books they want to read. It seeks to map the genre, grouping titles with similar qualities and appeal together so that readers (and those who advise readers) can easily locate books that are similar to others they have enjoyed. Thus, readers' advisors in libraries and bookstores can respond appropriately to the ubiquitous "what do you have that's similar to . . . ?" The arrangement helps the reader to find a starting place, and the annotations and icons help the user zero in on particular books. Because of the organization of titles and the detailed indexes, this book may also be useful with readers who recall a single element of a book—e.g., a character type or "what it was about"—but not other details.

Collection development specialists will find this approach helpful in ensuring breadth of coverage and locating important authors and their works. Those who are developing curriculum for science fiction literature classes may wish to refer to the guide for similar reasons. Finally, the book can be used by individuals who want to build their knowledge of the genre by sampling diverse titles. Thus, readers' advisory librarians, booksellers, collection development librarians, teachers, students, and science fiction aficionados will all hopefully find something of value in this resource.

The more than 900 titles described in this guide span the entire history of the genre—from Mary Wollstonecraft Shelley's 1818 *Frankenstein* to Lois McMaster Bujold's *Diplomatic Immunity* published in 2002. Our focus is on books that are currently in print or likely to be in library collections. The majority of the titles have been published in the past ten years, but popular older and classic works are also included. Publication dates listed with the titles are the dates of first publication. Because so many titles are re-issued in different formats and at different times, it should not be assumed that an older publication date indicates that a book is no longer available for purchase. (Nor should it be assumed that older titles are no longer of interest to SF readers.) In determining which titles to cover, we consulted a number of library catalogs. Several were examined in detail, including Princeton Public Library, Albuquerque Public Library, San Antonio Public Library, and Prospector: The Colorado Unified Catalog. We also based our selections on our experiences as frontline readers' advisors and devoted SF fans.

Organization

It is, perhaps, ironic that the genre of science fiction eludes scientific classification and that, unlike other genres, science fiction does not easily fall into neat subgenres, each appealing to a particular subset of readers. True, a good deal of classic science fiction has grown out of the heroic adventure tradition, and much of science fiction today can be cast as variations on the adventure story. However, the development of the genre over time has resulted in so many variations that appeal to such a diversity of readers that for readers' advisors, other approaches and access points are necessary.

Many readers are enticed by the adventurous aspects of science fiction—compelling stories with a fast pace and thrilling action—while others revel in situations and solutions, or scientific and technological possibilities. Some readers are enthralled by interactions between people, whether human or extraterrestrial. The conundrums posed by changing events through traveling in time or the "what ifs?" had historical events occurred differently are the unifying theme that others look for in SF.

This guide begins with a chapter based on the popular SF subgenre "Action Adventure." In this chapter you'll find the important sub-subgenre "space opera," as well as a number of type-, motif-, or theme-based sections, and finally a section on the SF format "shared worlds." From there we move into chapters based on other important types and themes for readers: technology, strange worlds, and "Us and Them" (Chapters 2 through 4). We have included Chapter 5 on "Genreblending," which covers SF titles with strong elements of other genres: romance, mystery, fantasy, horror, and so forth. We have also created a chapter (Chapter 7) that focuses on formats (short stories), and still another (Chapter 6) that highlights titles for a specific audience (young adults). These chapters reflect groups of readers and their preferences, and they group titles together in ways that readers most often approach the literature.

We have placed titles according to what we have determined to be their dominant features. Naturally, many SF titles fit into more than one of these overlapping categories. Therefore they are cross-referenced, and users should also consult the indexes to locate specific titles and authors. Of course, as each reader is an individual, not all groupings will work equally well for all readers, but we believe most science fiction fans will find appealing categories and groups of titles specific to their tastes. Some categories of science fiction, such as hard science fiction or cyberpunk, do not appear as entire chapters, but can be accessed through the keyword tagging or the subject index.

To further inform readers and readers' advisors, we have given brief annotations for most titles. In addition, we have created icons that identify important features of the books—e.g., classics, titles made into movies, award winners, and various other themes and qualities. The purpose of the icons is to give users "at-a-glance" information about the titles.

The icons are as follows:

 = Award winner

★ = Classic

🎬 = Film

YA = Young adult

The appendixes list award winners as well as a compilation of generally recognized "best of" titles. Further access is provided through author/title and subject indexes. It is always important for readers' advisors to listen to their readers, ask questions, and familiarize themselves with the literature. In the case of science fiction, this point cannot be stressed enough. Because of its thematic approach, we strongly recommend that you familiarize yourself with this book's various themes, types, and organizational components. We also suggest that you read a sampling of SF titles from diverse categories. One way to accomplish this is by reading anthologies or short stories from collections. (Refer to Chapter 7 for short story collections.) It is also important for readers' advisors, in particular, to customize their services to individual reading tastes. To successfully accomplish this, it is important to get to know the reader.

Who Is the Science Fiction Reader?

The stereotype of the SF reader is a brainy but nerdish young male. In reality, today's SF readers (like today's SF writers) can be either gender or any age. A readers' advisor is just as likely to work with a grandmother who reads (or writes) SF as with an SF reader who is the president of the local high school computer club. All it takes to enjoy reading science fiction is an ability and willingness to suspend disbelief and a questioning mind.

From our experience in working with readers, we might say that most science fiction readers are intelligent and informed. We can also say that like romance readers, they tend to fall into two camps: purists who are experts in the genre and general readers who welcome advice. Through purists, the readers' advisor can often discover new authors and titles, since this type of reader tends to be very knowledgeable about the genre and will often readily provide a wealth of information. Although unlikely to seek assistance in selecting books, purists will often place reserves on new titles or place interlibrary loan requests. They will notice and may comment on gaps in the collection. They are usually best served by passive readers' advisory resources, including book displays and bibliographies. On the other hand, the general reader who enjoys science fiction will usually benefit more from interaction with a readers' advisor. Some SF readers latch onto a single author and wish to read every book written by that person. Others may resonate with particular characters, worlds, or themes. Science fiction readers generally thrive on sequels, trilogies, and series, a fact that is reflected in SF publishing. And it is important to note that although SF generally focuses on the future, its readers treasure the history of the genre. So it should not be assumed that older titles are passé.

Readers' advisory is more of an art than a science. It is possibly the best way librarians can cement the importance of libraries in the hearts of taxpayers and the community served by the library. For decades readers' advisory has taken a back seat in the realm of library services, but in the twenty-first century it is moving into the forefront. Several library schools have added coursework, and many consortia and library organizations have featured workshops and programs on the topic. Joyce Saricks and Nancy Brown's *Readers' Advisory in the Public Library* (American Library Association, 1997), now in its second edition, should be required reading for all readers' advisors. The *Readers' Advisor's Companion* (Libraries Unlimited, 2002), edited by Kenneth Shearer and Robert Burgin, features sixteen timely and insightful articles on the subject by leaders in the field. Kenneth Shearer also edited *Guiding the Reader to the Next Book* (Neal-Schuman, 1996), which offers a wealth of information on the topic. Duncan Smith, the creator of *NoveList,* is another active advocate who gives readers' advisory workshops and training nationwide. One thing all these experts agree upon is the importance of listening to the reader and familiarizing yourself with the literature.

A Brief History of Science Fiction

Science fiction has been the subject of many scholarly studies. Many of the critical works delve into the history of the genre. John Clute's *Science Fiction: The Illustrated Encyclopedia* (DK Publishing, 1995) depicts the history of science fiction in relation to the surrounding world situation. The decade-by-decade charts relate important events in science fiction, film, radio, television, magazines, and world events, making it one of the most accessible historical treatments available. In Chapter 8 of this book you will find a list of some of the more important and useful titles for learning about the history of SF. Although this guide in no way intends to serve as a history of science fiction, the origins and evolution of the genre do shed some light on its appeal and readership. The brief summary that follows is an encapsulated history; its purpose is to give readers' advisors a glimpse of the origins and development of the genre.

Although there were precursors of science fiction in the eighteenth century and even earlier, Mary Wollstonecraft Shelley has been identified by many as "the mother of science fiction" for her creation of *Frankenstein,* written when she was still in her teens and published in 1818. Later in the nineteenth century, other pioneering works were written by Edgar Allan Poe, Jules Verne, and H. G. Wells, although at the time they were not called "science fiction." Some historians draw a connection between the birth of SF and the onset of the Industrial Revolution. Certainly scientific breakthroughs in transportation, weaponry, and factory production inspired many of the early SF writers. Darwin's theory of evolution and social revolutions also informed early works.

In the early part of the twentieth century, popular magazines featured serialized SF novels and short stories, and science fiction became a mainstay, although the term was still not widely used. Most early science fiction focused on the mechanical and on how machines would change the world. Technology was the essence, with characterization and plot taking a back seat. This was the era that brought the works of Stapledon, van Vogt, and Williamson to popularity. It was also the time when the early works of Heinlein, Asimov, and Clarke were published.

In the 1950s, as space exploration began and people began to wonder who was "out there," an interest in alien contact developed. This gave rise to the now mostly forgotten BEM (bug-eyed monster) stories that appeared regularly in the magazines of the era. In the 1960s science fiction began to delve into non-mechanical sciences, and many of the novels written in that era dealt with psychology, sociology, and how humans relate to their world and to change, heralding what was called a "New Wave" of science fiction. Philip K. Dick, Brian Aldiss, Frank Herbert, Samuel R. Delaney, and Kate Wilhelm made their mark.

The women's movement heralded the entry of females into SF's ranks, both as writers and as strong characters. Joanna Russ, Anne McCaffrey, and Ursula K. Le Guin did not have to hide behind the pseudonyms, androgynous names, or initials that disguised the gender of earlier women writers. Along with the rise of female authors, female and ethnically diverse protagonists began to be more prominently featured in 1970s SF. Gay, lesbian, physically disabled, and senior heroes have also appeared. But then, so have beings that change their sex entirely. The tremendous wave of popularity of science fiction's sister genre, fantasy, in the 1970s was reflected in SF with a number of epic tales set in such a distant time or place that Earth was all but forgotten and abilities forged by science in a distant past acquired seemingly magical attributes. C. J. Cherryh, Alan Dean Foster, Octavia E. Butler, and John Varley rose to popularity.

Cyberpunk, in which technology was portrayed as being perhaps not all that it had been cracked up to be, began to appear in the 1980s. William Gibson was probably the best known of the cyberpunk authors, but Bruce Sterling emerged as the spokesman for the subgenre. In the 1990s scientific advances in nanotechnology, artificial intelligence, and bioengineering became a visible force in the field. Authors such as Greg Bear, Nancy Kress, Kathleen Ann Goonan, Neal Stephenson, and Kim Stanley Robinson were writing on these topics. It is hard to predict the trends that will prevail in the current decade. *Ventus,* by Karl Schroeder, continues exploring the nanotechnology and artificial intelligence popular at the end of the 1990s. *Wheelers,* by Ian Stewart and Jack Cohen, introduces aliens so different that they never conceived the idea that life could evolve on a planet as obviously inimical to it as Earth. Authors to watch include Nalo Hopkinson, Jack McDevitt, Catherine Asaro, and Robert J. Sawyer.

It is interesting to note that SF was one of the first genres to spawn a devoted and organized fan presence. One might even go so far as to say that there is a SF subculture. Fans attend conventions, publish newsletters, and even write stories set in worlds created by favorite authors. (Sharyn McCrumb portrays the world of SF fandom in two wry tongue-in-cheek mysteries, *Bimbos of the Death Sun* and *Zombies of the Gene Pool.*) Contemporary fandom is an obvious presence on the World Wide Web, with newsgroups such as rec.arts.sfwritten providing a busy forum for fans, authors, editors, and publishers to discuss the genre on a daily basis.

Science fiction fans read SF magazines and watch SF on television and at the movies. In fact, throughout its history, science fiction has remained as inextricably rooted in popular culture and mass media as it is in scientific development. The immense popularity of SF films (e.g., *Star Wars, E.T., Jurassic Park*) is matched by the devotion of thousands of "trekkies" or "trekkers" to the television *Star Trek* series in all of its iterations.

Science fiction remains popular today—not only in the thousands of novels published annually but also in comics, graphic novels, games, television, and film. Readers of the genre seem to welcome new technologies, a fact that is now boosting audio book and e-book sales. In whatever shape or form it will take, it seems that SF is a genre that is here to stay.

A Word About Diversity in SF

In the world of science fiction, the term *diversity* takes on new dimensions. The major divisions between humans and alien life forms render insignificant such minor differences as skin color. Planet of origin becomes the point of identification, and just as people of all races came together in the United States after the September 2001 terrorist attacks, in science fiction the common bond of humanity holds people together in light of alien intrusions and interstellar explorations. We all remember the globally integrated crew of *Star Trek*'s U.S.S. *Enterprise*; that scenario captures the spirit of many SF stories. But issues of race and gender are not unknown in science fiction. Ursula K. Le Guin explored race issues (among others) in *The Lathe of Heaven,* and the James Tiptree Jr. Award is given to works that explore gender issues. In science fiction, only the approach to these issues is different. Problems of race, sex, physical disability, and age are approached with solutions—scientific, technological solutions.

Science fiction readers are often unaware of an author's race, ethnicity, and even gender. However, there are a number of minority authors, among them Octavia E. Butler, Stephen Barnes, Nalo Hopkinson, and Samuel L. Delany. An anthology of authors of the African diaspora, *Dark Matter*, edited by Sheree R. Thomas, was published in 2000.

Classic Science Fiction

Much of science fiction's history is distilled in the classic novels of the genre. Groundbreaking titles often invite mimicry and may even spawn whole movements or new subgenres. Within the classics, readers can also easily find "quality" or "literary" works because they are the titles that have withstood the test of time in a genre rich with memorable books. Orb and British publisher Orion have recently begun releasing classic reprints, bringing many long-out-of-print titles back into availability.

Although SF usually focuses on the future, its readers prize the history of the genre, as can be seen by perusing lists of favorites like those at "The Internet Top 100 SF/Fantasy List" (http://www.geocities.com/Area51/Cavern/6113/top100.html) and the "Locus All Time Best SF Poll from 1987" (http://www.sff.net/locus/poll/list87.html#ALLT1), where decades-old and out-of-print titles still linger.

The following classics are arranged by date of publication. Annotations for these works appear in subsequent chapters grouped with other like titles.

1818. Shelley, Mary Wollstonecraft. Frankenstein; Or, the Modern Prometheus.

1865. Verne, Jules. From the Earth to the Moon.

1870. Verne, Jules. Twenty Thousand Leagues Under the Sea.

1895. Wells, H. G. The Time Machine.

1896. Wells, H. G. The Island of Dr. Moreau.

1897. Wells, H. G. The Invisible Man.

1898. Wells, H. G. The War of the Worlds.

1901. Wells, H. G. The First Men in the Moon.

1912. Doyle, Sir Arthur Conan. The Lost World.

Burroughs, Edgar Rice. Mars Series.

> *1917. A Princess of Mars. (Originally published in 1912 in All-Story Magazine with the title "Under the Moons of Mars.")*

> *1918. The Gods of Mars.*

> *1919. The Warlord of Mars.*

> *1920. Thuvia, Maid of Mars.*

> *1922. The Chessmen of Mars.*

1923. Capek, Karel. R. U. R.

1930. Stapledon, Olaf. Last and First Men.

1932. Huxley, Aldous. Brave New World.

1933. Wylie, Philip and Edwin Balmer. When Worlds Collide.

1937. Stapledon, Olaf. Star Maker.

1941. Asimov, Isaac. "Nightfall." Astounding Science Fiction magazine.

Lewis, C. S. Perelandra Trilogy.

> *1943. Out of the Silent Planet.*

> *1943. Perelandra.*

> *1945. That Hideous Strength.*

1946. Van Vogt, A. E. Slan.

1949. Orwell, George. 1984.

1948. Van Vogt, A. E. The World of Null A.

1949. DeCamp, L. Sprague. Lest Darkness Fall.

1949. Stewart, George R. Earth Abides.

1949. Williamson, Jack. The Humanoids.

1950. Asimov, Isaac. Pebble in the Sky.

1950. Bradbury, Ray. Martian Chronicles.

1950. Leiber, Fritz. Gather, Darkness.

Asimov, Isaac. Foundation Series. A prequel is annotated on page 74 and a trilogy of sequels written by Greg Bear, David Brin, and Gregory Benford is annotated on page 57.

> *1951. Foundation.*

> *1952. Foundation and Empire.*

> *1952. Second Foundation.*

1952. Simak, Clifford D. City.

1953. Bester, Alfred. The Demolished Man. Reissued in 1996.

1953. Bradbury, Ray. Fahrenheit 451.

1953. Brown, Frederic. The Lights in the Sky Are Stars.

1953. Sturgeon, Theodore. More Than Human.

1954. Clement, Hal. Mission of Gravity.

1955. Asimov, Isaac. The End of Eternity.

1955. Brown, Frederic. Martians Go Home.

1955. Clifton, Mark and Frank Riley. The Forever Machine.

Norton, Andre. Solar Queen Series.

    1955. Sargasso of Space.

    1956. Plague Ship.

    1959. Voodoo Planet.

    1969. Postmarked the Stars.

1956. Bester, Alfred. The Stars My Destination.

1956. Heinlein, Robert A. Double Star.

1958. Blish, James. A Case of Conscience.

1958. Budrys, Algis. Who?

Norton, Andre. Time Traders Series.

    1958. The Time Traders.

    1959. Galactic Derelict.

    1962. The Defiant Agents.

    1963. Key Out of Time.

1959. Heinlein, Robert A. Starship Troopers.

1960. Budrys, Algis. Rogue Moon.

1961. Heinlein, Robert A. Stranger in a Strange Land.

1961. Leiber, Fritz. The Big Time.

1961. Miller, Walter M., Jr. A Canticle for Leibowitz.

1962. Burgess, Anthony. A Clockwork Orange.

1962. Dick, Philip K. The Man in the High Castle.

1962. L'Engle, Madeleine. A Wrinkle in Time.

1963. Simak, Clifford D. Way Station.

1964. Dick, Philip K. Martian Time-Slip.

Williamson, Jack, and Frederik Pohl. The Starchild Trilogy.

    1964. The Reefs of Space.

    1965. Starchild.

    1969. Rogue Star.

1965. Herbert, Frank. Dune.

1965. Leiber, Fritz. The Wanderer.

1965. Zelazny, Roger. . . . And Call Me Conrad. (Published first as a short story.)
   This Immortal. (Alternate title)

1966. Ballard, J. G. The Crystal World.

1966. Delany, Samuel R. Babel-17.

1966. Harrison, Harry. Make Room! Make Room!

1966. Heinlein, Robert A. The Moon Is a Harsh Mistress.

1966. Keyes, Daniel. Flowers For Algernon.

1967. Delany, Samuel R. The Einstein Intersection.

1967. Ellison, Harlan, ed. Dangerous Visions.

1967. Ellison, Harlan. I Have No Mouth and I Must Scream: Stories.

1968. Brunner, John. Stand on Zanzibar.

1968. Clarke, Arthur C. 2001: A Space Odyssey.

1968. Panshin, Alexei. Rite of Passage.

1968. Vonnegut, Kurt. Slaughterhouse Five or, The Children's Crusade: A Duty-Dance with Death.

1968. Zelazny, Roger. Lord of Light.

1969. Aldiss, Brian. Barefoot in the Head.

1969. Dick, Philip K. Galactic Pot-Healer.

1969. Le Guin, Ursula K. The Left Hand of Darkness.

1969. McCaffrey, Anne. The Ship Who Sang.

1970. Ballard, J. G. Love and Napalm.

1970. Blish, James. Cities in Flight.

1970. Niven, Larry. Ringworld.

1971. Delany, Samuel R. Driftglass.

1971. Farmer, Philip Jose. To Your Scattered Bodies Go.

1971. Silverberg, Robert. A Time of Changes.

1972. Asimov, Isaac. The Gods Themselves.

1972. Brunner, John. The Sheep Look Up.

1972. Ellison, Harlan, ed. Again, Dangerous Visions.

1973. Clarke, Arthur C. Rendezvous with Rama.

1974. Dick, Philip K. Flow My Tears, the Policeman Said.

1974. Le Guin, Ursula K. The Dispossessed.

1974. Niven, Larry and Jerry Pournelle. The Mote in God's Eye.

1975. Haldeman, Joe. The Forever War.

1975. Pohl, Frederik. Man Plus.

1975. Russ, Joanna. The Female Man.

1976. Wilhelm, Kate. Where Late the Sweet Birds Sang.

1977. Brown, Frederic. The Best of Frederic Brown.

1978. McIntyre, Vonda. Dreamsnake

1979. Clarke, Arthur C. The Fountains of Paradise.

1980. Vinge, Joan D. The Snow Queen.

1981. Adams, Douglas. The Hitchhiker's Guide to the Galaxy.

1981. Bishop, Michael. No Enemy But Time.

1984. Gibson, William Neuromancer.

1985. Card, Orson Scott. Ender's Game.

1986. Card, Orson Scott. Speaker for the Dead.

1988. Cherryh, C. J. Cyteen.

We have refrained from declaring publications of the last decade to be classics, although there are undoubtedly classics among them, because it is simply too early to tell which of the newer titles will withstand the test of time. But now let us take a closer look at the literature.

Chapter 1

Action Adventure

Science fiction is rooted in the traditions of the heroic adventure story, or "the hero's journey," and many of the early classics clearly fall within these parameters. The works of Jules Verne, H. G. Wells, and Edgar Rice Burroughs contain all the elements of a good adventure story. These are compelling tales with clearly defined conflicts between forces of good and evil. Action, usually physical and often fast-paced, must be taken to meet a challenge, overcome an obstacle, or accomplish a mission. In science fiction (SF) adventure, this action usually takes place in an alien setting or on a somehow threatening terrain. Those who dare to fight or fly are the characters who venture forth in adventure science fiction. In many of the stories, a single hero figures prominently. In others, a group of characters—a team or military contingent—may be involved. Philosophical implications and ponderings are put aside in this subgenre, and endings will likely provide tangible resolution to the conflict.

Science fiction adventure is the largest and probably the most popular subgenre of SF, as demonstrated by the success of such films as *Star Trek* and *Star Wars*. In its many variations, it is also the subgenre that snares young readers, creating many lifelong fans of science fiction. Readers who enjoy adventure science fiction and want to explore other genres may also enjoy political espionage novels and techno-thrillers.

This chapter begins with a list of general SF adventure stories, then covers the many titles in the ever-popular "space opera" sub-subgenre. Following that, titles are arranged thematically, according to broad areas of interest. Concluding the chapter is a list of titles that represent a distinct format, that of "shared worlds." As all of these titles are adventures, readers who enjoy one section may also be interested in others.

Science Fiction Adventure Subgenres

General Science Fiction Adventure

Aldiss, Brian. Helliconia Trilogy. Life on a planet where winter lasts for centuries, a year lasts a thousand Earth years, and humanity cycles through emergence to decline, is replete with adventures.

Helliconia Spring. 1982. With the end of winter, civilization reawakens on the planet Helliconia.

Helliconia Summer. 1983. Because a season on Helliconia lasts approximately 200 years, so much time has passed since the events in the first book that they have become the stuff of legends, if they are remembered at all. Court intrigue, suspense, and the slow heating of the planet are the backdrop for what happens to one group of people over a period of ten years now that summer has come.

Helliconia Winter. 1985. The trilogy began with everything waking up because spring had come. Now, with the approach of winter, it is time for this world to return to its somnolent state.

Anthony, Piers. *Killobyte.* 1993. Baal Curran, a depressed high school senior and juvenile diabetic, and Walter Toland, an ex-policeman and paraplegic, became friends while playing the game *Kill-o-byte*, a virtual reality game that lets the players experience the realities of death over and over again. Now Phone Phreak, a psychotic teenage hacker, has left Baal trapped in the game, sinking into a diabetic coma and dependent on the helpless Walter to come to her rescue.

Anthony, Piers. *Prostho Plus.* 1973. Annotated on page 145.

Anthony, Piers. *Total Recall.* 1989. Illusion battles with reality when the protagonist purchases implanted memories of a vacation to Mars and discovers that some of his true memories are now being hidden from him. A novelization of the movie based on the short story "We Can Remember It for You Wholesale," by Philip K. Dick.

Asimov, Isaac. *Nemesis.* 1989. On Earth a scientist tries to build a starship, while in space his young daughter grows up on a space habitat. Now that habitat, Rotar, which has traveled to a red dwarf star named Nemesis, and Earth are both being quickly and inescapably drawn toward disaster.

Bester, Alfred. *The Stars My Destination.* 1956. In the twenty-fourth century, Gully Foyle is a man with a mission. He was abandoned by the owner of his ship and left to die in space, but he survived. Now he wants revenge. This novel was also called *Tiger! Tiger!* (which the author preferred).

Brin, David. *Glory Season.* 1993. Annotated on page 100.

Brin, David. *The Postman*. 1985. After surviving the wars that destroyed civilization, Gordon leaves the shattered East behind and heads West, hoping to make a new life for himself. Attacked by bandits, he flees and comes across an abandoned jeep with a dead postman in it. Relieving the skeleton of its coat, hat, and leather bag, which are still serviceable after all these years, he continues his journey through what has become a wilderness of despair. Gordon has become "The Postman" and he must ultimately live up to this legend by carrying messages between previously isolated communities and spreading hope in a Restored United States to everyone.

Bujold, Lois McMaster. *Falling Free*. 1988. Created by Galtech to work in free fall, Quaddies, genetically altered mutants with an extra pair of arms instead of legs, are considered property of the company. After being hired to train Quaddies, Leo Graf becomes horrified at how they are mistreated and abused. Now a new Betan gravity device that allows anyone to work in space has made the Quaddies obsolete. When Leo learns the administration is deciding on the best way to get rid of the Quaddies, he realizes he is the only one who can save them.

> *Nebula Award.*

Burroughs, Edgar Rice. Mars Series.

A Princess of Mars. 1917. John Carter, a Confederate Army officer, suddenly finds himself transported to the red planet. There he encounters a red-skinned princess and is faced with one adventure after another involving the members of the planet's warlike society. The man who created Tarzan, Lord of the Jungle, also gave us John Carter of Mars, or in this case Barsoom, as the red planet is called. (Originally published in 1912 in *All-Story Magazine* with the title "Under the Moons of Mars.")

The Gods of Mars. 1918. Carter's adventures on the red planet continued as a five-part serial in *All-Story Magazine* in 1913, and were eventually published in book form.

The Warlord of Mars. 1919. Carter is on the rise in the warlike society of Mars in this third adventure set on the red planet.

Thuvia, Maid of Mars. 1920. Carter makes a home and a life for himself on the red planet.

The Chessmen of Mars. 1922. More epic adventures on Mars, this time involving a deadly game of living chess, with Princess Tara of Helium, daughter of the Warlord of Mars, as the prize.

Other titles in the series:

> *The Master Mind of Mars. 1927.*
>
> *A Fighting Man of Mars. 1931.*
>
> *Swords of Mars. 1936.*

> *Synthetic Men of Mars. 1940.*
>
> *Llana of Gathol. 1948.*
>
> *John Carter of Mars. 1965.*

Card, Orson Scott. *Pastwatch: The Redemption of Christopher Columbus*. 1996. Annotated on page 50 (time travel).

Card, Orson Scott. *Wyrms*. 1987. Patience, the daughter of the rightful but deposed heptarch, is made the servant and advisor to the new heptarch. Escaping an attempt on her life, she flees with her faithful retainer, setting out on a heroic quest. Other companions join her along the way as she heads for the special mountain fortress of the Wyrm. Her goal? To destroy the Wyrm before he is able to sire a new race, using her body as the reluctant receptacle of his seed.

> ***Assassins.***

Cherryh, C. J. *Cuckoo's Egg*. 1985. Annotated on page 153.

Cherryh, C. J. Foreigner Trilogy. Annotated on page 153.

> *First Contact. Alien Contact.*
>
> *Foreigner: A Novel of First Contact. 1994.*
>
> *Invader. 1995.*
>
> *Inheritor. 1996.*
>
> *Precursor. 1999.*
>
> *Defender. 2001.*
>
> *Explorer.* Forthcoming.

Cherryh, C. J. *Forty Thousand in Gehenna*. 1983. For ten generations, a human colony has been left abandoned by the Union on the planet Gehenna. Because this alien world is populated by giant lizards, the humans are forced to find their own ways to adapt to life there.

Cherryh, C. J. Faded Sun Trilogy. Annotated on page 153.

> *Kesrith. 1978.*
>
> *Shon'jir. 1978.*
>
> *Kutath. 1979.*

Cook, Robin. *Chromosome 6*. 1997. When New York City forensic pathologist Jack Stapleton investigates the case of Carlo Franconi, whose body has disappeared from the morgue, he discovers the deceased was a client of Gene-Dyn, a research facility that perfected gene transfer from human to ape. Now the Gene-Dyn scientist responsible for the breakthrough is having second thoughts about his work. Not only has he seen smoke periodically coming from the island where the gene-altered apes live, he has also observed that the apes are beginning to display aggressive, proto-human behavior.

Crichton, Michael. *Jurassic Park*. 1990. Scientists working for an eccentric entrepreneur who wants to create an amusement park featuring real dinosaurs have been able to re-create fifteen different types, using recombinant DNA techniques on dinosaur bones and amber. When the businessman attempts to prove to a team of visiting experts that his park is safe, the dinosaurs go on a rampage, the electric fences come down, and people begin dropping like flies. It's man against monster, and the odds for survival are slim.

The Lost World. 1997. Jurassic Park was destroyed six years ago. Now there are dinosaur sightings—again. A group of scientists go off to investigate and to look for a missing colleague, accompanied by two young stowaways. Ian Malcolm, the chaos theory expert, returns, limping from his previous encounter with dinosaurs. So does Dr. Dodgson, the Biosyn executive who was trying to get his hands on dinosaur serum last time. It's actual eggs he's after this time, but he should have been more careful around the tyrannosaurus rex.

Crichton, Michael. *Sphere*. 1987. Annotated on page 150.

Egan, Doris. *The Gate of Ivory*. 1989. Anthropology student Theodora of Pyrene is stranded on Ivory, a planet where magic really works. She begins reading cards in the marketplace to make a living and is approached by wealthy Ran Cormallon, who offers her a position as his private card reader. After she accepts, she discovers that his last card reader died in a mysterious fire. Now attempts are being made on Theodora's life, and Ran must do what he can to protect her. But he discovers that he has been discredited as the head of the family corporation and is caught in the middle of a deadly struggle for the company and his life.

Two-Bit Heroes. 1991. The tale of Theodora that started in *The Gate of Ivory* continues. Theodora, an anthropology scholar from a technological planet, is finally getting used to the way magic is used on Ivory and has fallen in love with a nobleman with whom she has embarked on a complicated and lengthy marriage ritual. On a political reconnaissance mission they are kidnapped by a band of outlaws. Then Theodora tells their leader the legend of Robin Hood and inadvertently starts a revolution. Written by Doris Egan under the name Jane Emerson (she also wrote *City of Diamond* under that name).

Foster, Alan Dean. *The Dig*. 1997. A party of astronauts discovers signs of an alien civilization when they try to reroute a milewide asteroid that has suddenly started orbiting Earth. A novelization of the Lucas computer game *Dig*.

Frank, Pat. *Alas, Babylon.* 1959. After World War III, in which a defective missile demolished all the major U.S. cities, the inhabitants of Fort Repose are thrown back into a primitive way of living, fighting for survival against disease, starvation, lawlessness, and panic.

Friesner, Esther. *The Sherwood Game.* 1995. A virtual reality Robin Hood manages to cross over into the real world, where he keeps up his old tricks. He is the creation of Carl Sherwood, an artificial intelligence wizard, who loves role-playing games, especially actually going into Sherwood Forest to "swash the buckle" with Robin Hood. But when Robin catches on to Carl's shenanigans, he manages to leave Sherwood Forest and runs amok in the real world—with Carl hot on his trail.

Heinlein, Robert A. *Have Space Suit—Will Travel.* 1958. Kip Russell, a bright teen, wins a space suit in a contest and then is kidnapped and taken to the moon by aliens, along with "Peewee," the twelve-year-old daughter of a world-renowned scientist. After a hair-raising escape attempt across the lunar landscape, Kip falls into captivity again. In the end Kip acts as spokesperson for the planet Earth when it is put on trial by the Three Galaxies Federation. This early juvenile work by Heinlein still has appeal as a fast-paced science fiction adventure.

Hinz, Christopher. Paratwa series. It looks like the Paratwa, the bioengineered assassins who lay waste to the Earth, are back. If so, will they carry out their vendetta against humankind in the orbiting colonies?

Liege-Killer. 1987. The Paratwa Saga. Book One. War has devastated the Earth and made it almost uninhabitable, so most surviving humans now live in orbital colonies. To avoid repeating the mistakes of the past, governments want to suppress military technology. This makes it difficult to fight back when a bioengineered assassin, frozen before Armageddon, wakes up.

Ash Ock. 1989. The Paratwa Saga. Book Two. The cyberpunk battle against the assassins keeps on going and going.

Paratwa. 1991. The Paratwa Saga. Book Three. Earth's only hope against the Paratwa, the deadly bioengineered assassins who almost destroyed it in the past, is to find a rogue Paratwa to fight on the side of humanity.

Hogan, James P. Giants Trilogy. All three titles were also published in an omnibus edition as *The Minervan Experiment.* 1981.

Inherit the Stars. 1977. After a body is discovered, an investigation leads to the unveiling of an ancient civilization of space-faring humans.

The Gentle Giants of Ganymede. 1978. Earth's scientists discover a wrecked ship of alien giants on a frozen satellite of Jupiter. But that's not all. Suddenly, out of the vastness of space, comes a spaceship bearing the same strange, humanoid giants. They've returned.

Giants' Star. 1981. (Paperback reissue.) Humans thought that they knew where they fit into the universe. But that was before Earth found itself in the middle of a power struggle. In this corner, a benevolent alien empire; in the other, a cunning race of upstart humans who hate the Earth. To the victor go the spoils. Let's hope the right side wins.

Hogan, James P. *Outward Bound.* 1999. Juvenile delinquent Linc Marani chooses to go to a special program rather than a labor camp to serve his time. The program turns out to be a boot camp-like experience where he learns he has inner strengths and is prepared for a destiny in space. Told in the tradition of Robert A. Heinlein's coming-of-age adventure novels.

Kagan, Janet. *Mirabile.* 1991. Annotated on page 132.

Kress, Nancy. Probability Trilogy. Star gates make it possible for humans to encounter enemy "Fallers" and friendly "Worlders."

Probability Moon. 2000. Star gates that enable travel to systems many light years away have been discovered. Now a xenopathic race called the "Fallers" is trying to eradicate humans. When another world that is home to a humanoid race of aliens (the "Worlders") is found, the humans send a mission to it, ostensibly to establish contact and diplomatic ties. But things are not always what they seem, and humans and aliens must flee or fight for their survival. The Worlders' society is vividly depicted, allowing the reader to see the emotions expressed through their bald scalps and the social manners relating to their neck fur. Scientific extrapolation dealing with probability devices and the sociological structures of the aliens are fascinating.

Probability Sun. 2001. Humans return to the Worlders' planet with a Fallers POW to investigate the "artifact."

Probability Space. Tor. 2002.

Longyear, Barry B. *The Homecoming.* 1989. After 30 million years, Earth's original inhabitants are back. But when the lizardlike aliens arrive in their massive spaceships, they discover that a strange new life form has taken over their planet. Now the fate of humanity rests in the hands of Captain Carl Baxter of the U.S. Air Force. He has his hands full because the aliens are divided. One faction is struggling to understand the hue-mans; the other wants to eliminate them entirely.

MacAvoy, R. A. *The Third Eagle: Lessons along a Minor String.* 1989. Wanbli is a trained bodyguard who saves his master's life, cashes in the car he wins from would-be assassins, and leaves his position and home world to try to become an actor. Traveling along the "string" of instantaneous transportation between worlds, he has many adventures, some of them quite humorous. Meanwhile, his own world will continue to be a backwater, a primitive society frozen in stasis, unless a string station can be set up to bring the "joys" of unlimited space travel to it as well.

Mason, Lisa. *Golden Nineties.* 1995. Companion novel to *Summer of Love.* Zhu Wong, a Chinese revolutionary from the future, is sent back to 1895 San Francisco to safeguard a teenage prostitute. When her charge is kidnapped by the Chinese mafia for the slave trade, Zhu almost meets the same fate. A prominent bordello madam comes to her rescue, and she helps run the madam's home while planning a rescue attempt.

Mason, Lisa. *Summer of Love.* 1994. Annotated on page 53.

McCaffrey, Anne. Doona Series. (Note: The first volume, published in 1969, was written solely by McCaffrey, and the last two were co-authored by Jody Lynn Nye.)

Decision at Doona. 1969. Todd Reeve, a young boy among the human colonists on the planet Doona, discovers that the humans are not alone on the planet. The catlike Hrrubans have also settled there, and Todd becomes best friends with a young Hrruban boy, Hrriss. The problem is that Earth has passed a law forbidding all contact among alien species. One group or the other must leave the planet—or must they?

Crisis on Doona. 1992. Twenty-five years ago a treaty was drawn up between the humans and the catlike Hrrubans living on the planet Doona. That treaty is now up for renewal. Unfortunately, conservative isolationists among both the humans and the Hrrubans would rather see the treaty canceled. Once again Todd Reeve and his Hrruban best friend and blood brother, Hrriss, find themselves caught in the middle of a complex conspiracy.

Treaty at Doona. 1994. Nine years after the events in *Crisis on Doona,* Todd and Hrriss are on opposite sides of an important issue, the question of turning the Treaty Island subcontinent into a free trade and spaceport facility. In Todd's opinion this would drastically alter the ecology of the subcontinent. But Todd's old friend, the First Speaker of the Hrrubans, has died, and the Second Speaker seems to be more interested in economic issues than the good of the planet, a point of view that Hrriss seems to share. Into this mix comes a new alien species, the Gringgs, and once again it is the young, this time of three species, who have a lot to teach their elders.

McDevitt, Jack. *Moonfall.* 1998. The comet Tomiko is headed directly for the moon, with impact due to occur approximately one week after the opening of the very first U.S. moon base. That ceremony is to be hosted by none other than the American vice-president. Still on the moon when the news is released about the impending disaster, the VP promises to be the last one to leave. He insists on keeping that vow, even when the last ship fills up, and he and five other passengers are left behind — but not for long.

McDevitt, Jack. *Deepsix.* EOS/HaperCollins, 2001. In the twenty-third century, the planet Maleiva III had to be evacuated. Twenty-one years later, Deepsix, as Maleiva is also called, is in the path of a gas giant that is headed toward the planet on a collision course. There is only a very limited amount of time in which to study this life-supporting planet. Last chance before it disappears forever. A team is sent to investigate and becomes stranded when an earthquake destroys their escape vehicle. Now there's no way off the planet—or is there? McDevitt has produced another thrilling space adventure; further support for those who call him the heir to Isaac Asimov and Arthur C. Clarke.

McHugh, Maureen F. *China Mountain Zhang*. 1992. In a twenty-second-century world dominated by Red China, a young man coming of age in a wired America must hide the fact that he is not only gay but half Hispanic as well. Written in the first person present tense, with an almost Zen-like quality and a sense of immediacy, this is a multi-award-winning work of literature.

> ***Hugo, Tiptree, Lambda, and Locus Awards.***

Niven, Larry. *Rainbow Mars*. 1999. Annotated on page 180.

Resnick, Mike. Penelope Bailey Series

> *Soothsayer*. Penelope was born with a very special gift. She can see the future—not just one future but all possible futures. And she can then select the future she wants to see happen and make it so. When the thief Mouse discovers her chained in an alien's room, she rescues her and becomes her surrogate mother as the two flee bounty hunters and government agents. Friends try to warn Mouse that she is playing with fire. Penelope's powers are growing, and she has already used her anger to kill bounty hunters. Will Mouse be next?

> *Oracle*. 1992. Whistler, the Injun, and the Iceman are all employed to either rescue or kill Penelope Bailey, who at age twenty-two is being held prisoner by the Blue Devils of Alpha Crepello III. The Jade Queen joins them, only to discover too late how dangerous it is to hang around with paid assassins. They all discover that the adult Penelope is even more of a challenge than she was as a child—and much more dangerous.

> *Prophet*. 1993. Penelope goes up against a religious fanatic and her old nemesis, the Iceman.

Simpson, George. *The Dechronization of Sam Magruder*. 1996. Sam Magruder has gone back in time—all the way back to the Cretaceous period. He was researching a quantum theory of time when he literally slipped through the cracks and wound up in a swamp inhabited by dinosaurs. With no way back to the future, Sam observes dinosaur behavior carefully and leaves a record, chiseled onto stone slabs, for future scientists to decipher, thereby settling some of the major controversies of modern times about dinosaur behavior and appearance. (The author, who died in 1984, was one of the twentieth century's most renowned paleontologists, and his expertise is clearly evident in this unusual novella, found among his effects.)

Stephenson, Neal. *Cryptonomicon*. 1999. In 1942, young Lawrence Pritchard Waterhouse, mathematical genius and a captain in the U.S. Navy, is assigned to detachment 2702—an outfit so secret that only a handful of people know it exists, and some of those people have names like Churchill and Roosevelt. The mission of Waterhouse and Detachment 2702—commanded by Marine Raider Bobby Shaftoe—is to keep the Nazis ignorant of the fact that Allied

Intelligence has cracked the enemy's fabled Enigma code. Meanwhile, in the present, Waterhouse's crypto-hacker grandson, Randy, and Shaftoe's tough-as-nails granddaughter, Amy, salvage a sunken Nazi submarine that brings to light a massive conspiracy, with its roots in Detachment 2702 and the unbreakable Nazi code. It may lead to unimaginable riches and a future of personal and digital liberty or to the rebirth of universal totalitarianism.

Tepper, Sheri S. The Awakeners duology. These two volumes make up a science fiction romance on the shores of a mighty river.

> *Northshore. 1987.*
>
> *Southshore. 1987.*

Willis, Connie. *Doomsday Book.* 1992. Going back in time was a dream come true for Kivrin, a researcher enamored of the Middle Ages. But her drop was miscalculated and she wound up in England just as the Black Death began appearing. Not only is Kivrin not feeling too well herself, but, to make matters worse (as if that were possible), contemporary London is in the throes of an epidemic. As a result, the university is closed, so there is no one standing by to try to bring her home.

> ***Hugo, Nebula, and Locus Awards.***

Willis, Connie. *Lincoln's Dreams.* 1987. A Civil War researcher and a young woman try to unravel the puzzle of how she seems to be living Robert E. Lee's life as she sleeps.

Space Opera

Space opera is the most distinct sub-subgenre of science fiction. Space opera stories are SF on a grand scale. They feature almost everything a reader could want: action, adventure, intrigue, and romance. Although war is often an element in space operas, the emphasis is on the broader picture. They tend to be sweeping tales, involving multiple characters and locales. The prime example (both because almost everyone has seen it and because it exhibits all the classic characteristics of space opera) is the *Star Wars* movie series. Space opera always features a heroic individual going up against some evil or diabolical enemy. Politics almost always plays an important role. Stalwart companions and romantic liaisons are a staple. Space operas are set in a time when galactic empires spanning multiple worlds have become a reality.

Although some serious SF fans turn up their noses at it, space opera is probably the most popular and widely read type of SF. Sometimes maligned as simplistic or sophomoric, it is home to many of the great adventure stories.

The following titles deal adventurously with galactic empires and views of communities and worlds of humans and aliens in a variety of political and sociological relationships. Many of the shared worlds of science fiction fall into this category as well (*Star Wars*, for example), so for read-alikes, that category should also be checked. Other categories contain elements of space opera, so readers may also want to check the subject index for more related titles.

Banks, Iain M. *Consider Phlebas*. 1988. Set in his "Culture" universe, this is an account of the struggle between the artificially intelligent "Minds" that rule the universe and the alien Idirans, religious fanatics who are all too willing to fight. It is also the account of a mission to recover something that both sides of the conflict are desperate to capture. But it's Horza and his rag-tag company who have the best chance of succeeding because they are willing to undertake an odyssey that could lead to certain death.

Banks, Iain M. *Inversions*. 2000. This is the story of a healer whom no one trusts except her patient, and an assassin, who trusts no one except the one he shouldn't. In a triumph of misdirection, subterfuge, and clever surprise endings, Banks gives us two stories in one. An assistant to a female doctor is writing an account of the doctor's activities for his unknown master. And an unknown narrator relates the adventures of DeWar, bodyguard to General UrLeyn, Prime Protector of the Tassasen Protectorate, and self-proclaimed assassin's assassin. DeWar's tale is interwoven with that of the Protector's favorite concubine Perrund, who saved the Protector's life from an assassin and was left with a withered arm as a result of her heroic sacrifice. And the female doctor has won the favor of the king, scandalizing the court because she is a traveler, a foreigner from Drezen.

Banks, Iain M. *Look to Windward*. 2001. This "Culture" novel is set 800 years after the Twin Novae battle that ended the Idiran War. Unfortunately, the war ended with exploding suns and the destruction of entire worlds. The light from the first explosion is about to reach the Culture's Masaq' Orbital, where some 50 billion inhabitants are gathered to commemorate the deaths and to remember. Also on Masaq' is an emissary from a war-ravaged world. Is he bent on assassination — or something much worse?

Bradley, Marion Zimmer. Darkover. Often bordering on fantasy, this long-running series eventually turned into a shared world series, with others writing about the world created by the late grand dame of SF. Bradley's offical Web site at http://mzbworks.home.att.net/works.htm lists the titles in publication order and by Darkovan chronology.

The Bloody Sun. 1964. The Comyn, with their psi-abilities (laran) and their blood feuds, are apprehensive at the arrival of Terrans on their planet and suspicious of the efforts of these strangers to draw Darkover into the Earth-sponsored empire. Jeff Kerwin and the last Keeper, Elorie, join forces to shatter the old beliefs and bring a new freedom and a new acceptance to the inhabitants of the towers.

City of Sorcery. 1984. Women take the forefront in this novel set on the planet Darkover. A party of women sets out through the mountains, each for her own reason, in search of the fabled City of Sorcery.

Darkover Landfall. 1972. This is the first of the Darkover novels, chronologically. A lost spaceship lands on an undiscovered planet, and so the adventure begins. Gradually, the very special nature of this incredible world is revealed to its passengers. In this work we find the origin of the matrixes and learn how certain humans are able to use them.

Exile's Song. 1996. Written with Adrienne Martine-Barnes, according to the Marion Zimmer Bradley Web site. The long-awaited sequel to *The Heritage of Hastur* and *Sharra's Exile* introduces Margaret Alton. The daughter of Lew Alton, the Darkover representative to the Terran Imperial Senate, she was whisked away from the planet of her birth when she was only six or seven years old. Now her job as a musicologist has taken her back to Darkover, and everything is changing. The headaches and disturbing visions she has are getting stronger, and during an expedition she almost dies of Threshold illness—late in coming to someone so much past puberty, but even more powerful as a result. Once she learns to control her powerful "laran," she knows she has come home to Darkover for good.

The Forbidden Tower. 1977. Some time after the events covered in *The Spell Sword*, a group of telepaths refuses to join the Towers and abide by their restrictive rules and regulations. They have formed their own tower, a Forbidden Tower, which is now under attack.

The Heirs of Hammerfell. 1989. When the last heir to Hammerfell dies, Ermine marries the old Duke. A few years later he is killed and she must flee with her twin sons. Alastair remains with his mother, but Conn disappears along with their faithful old servant, Markos. Believing her son dead, Ermine goes to Thendara, where she is employed to work in a Tower because of her powerful mental laran. For the next twenty years she teaches Alistair to long for the day he can return to Hammerfell and avenge himself for the deaths of his father and brother. In the meantime, Conn has never left Hammerfell but is being raised there by Markos to fight for his heritage. He believes his mother and brother are dead, leaving him the rightful Duke of Hammerfell.

The Heritage of Hastur. 1975. The prequel to *The Sword of Aldones*, this novel brings the struggle between those who are against Terran intervention and those who support contact between Terra and Darkover to a climax.

The Planet Savers. 1962. This includes more adventures set on the mysterious planet Darkover, with its powerful mental laran that enables its feudal society to hold its own against the technological might of Terra (Earth).

The Shadow Matrix: A Novel of Darkover. 1998. Written with Adrienne Martine-Barnes. In this sequel to *Exile's Song* the adventures of Margaret Alton continue. Raised by Terrans, then returned to Darkover, Margaret discovers that she cannot leave because she has developed laran, which requires her to stay on the planet and learn how to control it or die.

Sharra's Exile. 1981. In this book the author rewrote *The Sword of Aldones*, and the result is a longer, more detailed, and more mature treatment of the events following *The Heritage of Hastur*. In their conflict with the Terrans, the telepaths of Darkover are beginning to explore methods of using the ancient sciences of the planet itself as weapons.

Star of Danger. 1965. Teenager Larry Montray comes to the strange dark planet of Darkover with his father. Not content to remain isolated in the Terran compound, Larry learns the language and goes exploring in the native part of the city, where he meets young Kennard Alton, a member of one of the elite Comyn families. When

Larry is invited to visit Kennard's country estate, he fights a fire, is kidnapped by bandits, and is rescued by Kennard. Then the two boys flee through the wilds of Darkover, encountering all manner of aliens and wild beasts along the way.

The Shattered Chain. 1976. This is one of the early Darkover novels that addresses the plight of women on this dark feudal planet and the rise of the Free Amazons, who are free from the control of men but have their own strict rules and regulations to follow.

The Spell Sword. 1974. Andrew Carr is drawn to Darkover and remains there because of a recurring image of a woman in trouble, a woman lost, alone, and wandering in a strange, unreal environment. After his scout plane crashes, he is led to safety by an apparition of this woman. Safety turns out to be the estate from which the girl Callista has been kidnapped. Her twin and Damon Ride now are joined by Andrew in an attempt to rescue her. For the first time Terran and Comyn work together, not only to save Callista but also to remove a deadly threat spreading across their world.

Stormqueen! 1978. With the Matrix in the hands of ambitious men, genetic tampering is producing prodigies and wielders of strange powers. Meanwhile the heir of the Hasturs meets his destiny in the witch-woman he loves and the mutant girl he pledged to protect.

The Sword of Aldones. 1962. This early Darkover novel traces the career of Lew Alton after his encounter with the Sharra Matrix robbed him of a hand and his home. Exiled from Darkover for six years, Lew returns after receiving a desperate message from his Regent. He brings with him the Sharra Matrix, making it once again subject to the intrigue, infighting, and occasional murderous attacks endemic to the Darkover political system. When the Matrix is stolen, Lew must find something to counter it with. That something is the Sword of Aldones, long hidden but now returned at a time of great need.

Thendara House. 1983. The setting for this Darkover novel is the society of "Renunciates" or "Free Amazons," a guild of women warriors free of male domination. The sequel to *The Shattered Chain*, it continues the adventures of Jaelle and Margali. After helping Peter Haldane escape, Jaelle marries him. But she discovers that living among Terrans and trying to adjust to their very different way of life is quite a challenge. Margali, in the meantime, is completing her six months among the "Renunciates," learning more and more about the Amazon way of life.

Traitor's Sun. 1999. Written with Adrienne Martine-Barnes. The adventures of Marguerida Alton continue. As heir to the dying Regent Regis Hastur, Marguerida must take control of the reins of government with Mikhail and somehow handle the Terran problem at the same time. The ambitious Station Chief wants Darkover to give up its protected status. If the planet joins the Federation, he will finally achieve his dream of control. Losing their leader makes the success of a military coup likely. At least, that's what the Station Chief thinks. But the power of those with laran on this strange dark planet should never be underestimated.

Two to Conquer. 1980. Contains further adventures set on Darkover, a feudal planet ruled by a powerful, telepathic elite.

The Winds of Darkover. 1970. There is a feud going on among powerful families on the planet Darkover. The Sharra Matrix may be used by the aggrieved party, but this powerful matrix has a mind of its own, and the outcome may not be what either party expected. Into this milieu steps a space pilot from the Earth. Now that the treaties holding the society of Darkover together have been betrayed, violence is inevitable.

The World Wreckers. 1971. Assassins are killing the members of the ruling telepathic caste of Darkover, those with the powerful laran ability. Destruction of the planet's society seems inevitable, except for a most unexpected but extremely timely alien intervention.

Bradley, Marion Zimmer, and Mercedes Lackey. *Rediscovery: A Novel of Darkover.* 1993. A Terran ship arrives on Darkover, and its crew discovers the remnants of a lost colony ship on this strange dark planet.

Bradley, Marion Zimmer, and Deborah J. Ross. *The Fall of Neskaya.* Book one of the Clingfire Trilogy. 2001. A secret plot that places a weapon of destruction deep in the mind of laran-rich Coryn could bring an end to the Hastur dynasty.

Bujold, Lois McMaster. Vorkosigan Saga. Numerous titles detail the exploits of the Vorkosigan family of Barrayar, starting with Aral and Cordelia but mostly concentrating on their son, Miles Vorkosigan, the sexiest and most powerful man under five feet tall in this or any galaxy. Written with wit and intelligence. Devoted fans discuss the characters online while eagerly awaiting the next installment.

Shards of Honor. 1986. Annotated on page 161.

Barrayar. 1991. Cordelia assembles an unlikely strike force to rescue her unborn son—a hostage in a palace coup.

 Hugo Award.

The Warrior's Apprentice. 1986. Seventeen-year-old Miles is booted from the Service Academy when he fails the obstacle course due to breaking both brittle legs. Sent off to visit his grandmother on Beta, he finds himself surrounded by stalwart companions and accidentally takes command of a mercenary fleet.

The Vor Game. 1990. Miles goes to his first posting at a frigid outpost commanded by a sadist. Then it's back out to the Hegen Hub, where he must once again assume his persona as Admiral Naismith of the Dendarii Mercenary Fleet to prevent a war and save his emperor.

Hugo and Nebula Awards.

Young Miles. 1997. This is an omnibus edition of the adventures of the young Miles Vorkosigan. It includes *The Warrior's Apprentice* and *The Vor Game* as well as "The Mountains of Mourning," which is a poignant story set just after Miles graduates from the Academy. Home on leave at the country estate, Miles is conscripted by his father to investigate a backcountry infanticide.

Borders of Infinity. 1989. This collection of three novellas featuring Miles Vorkosigan has the usual elements Bujold provides in her novels: fast-paced action, humor, clever repartee, and a sensitive hero who, although he is a freak in his own society, succeeds against all odds, using his intelligence, quick wit, and canny knowledge of the humans around him.

Brothers in Arms. 1989. Komarran rebel expatriates are out to kill Admiral Naismith (Miles's alter ego). If they connect Miles with Naismith, all of his efforts at subterfuge on behalf of the Barrayaran secret service will have been in vain, and Miles will be very dead. On top of everything else, it looks as though there is a traitor on the Barrayaran staff. Then there's the problem of Elli, the girl Miles loves. She is not willing to give up a life of danger and adventure and settle down planetside as a "lady," especially not on a planet as hidebound and restrictive as Barrayar.

Mirror Dance. 1994. The contrast between Miles and his clone brother Mark, created from cells stolen from Miles when he was six years old, could not be more pronounced. Mark, raised and trained to be an assassin, with Miles as his target, was rescued by Miles from his tormentors. Now Mark has decided to impersonate Miles and take a unit of the Dendarii Mercenaries on a rescue mission into Jackson Whole.

Memory. 1996. Miles has not quite recovered from being killed, rejuvenated in a cryogenic unit, and then returned to "normal" activities. He is having epileptic-type "spells." But when Simon Illyan begins losing his memory and is imprisoned in a mental institution, Miles comes to the rescue. This is fortunate because it looks like Miles has been set up to take a fall.

Cetaganda. 1996. Miles and Cousin Ivan are on a diplomatic mission to Cetaganda to attend the funeral ceremonies for the Dowager Empress. But being Miles and Ivan, they get embroiled in a plot that could lead to war between Barrayar and Cetaganda. For once Miles is all alone, no Admiral Naismith and his mercenaries—just Ivan, who spends most of his time chasing (and being chased by) Haupt ladies.

Komarr. 1998. In his new position as the youngest Imperial Auditor ever, Miles comes to Komarr to investigate a disaster, the collision of an ore freighter with the mirror that supplements Komarr's solar energy. When he meets Ekaterin Vorsoisson, he falls head over heels in love. She is married but more than ready to leave her husband. The plot thickens when her husband is "accidentally" killed, she and her aunt are kidnapped, and Miles must come to the rescue. More on page 162.

A Civil Campaign. 1999. Annotated on page 178.

Diplomatic Immunity. 2002. Miles and Ekaterin must interrupt their honeymoon when trouble breaks out in Quaddie space.

Bujold, Lois McMaster. *Ethan of Athos.* 1986. Why does Ethan, an obstetrician on the planet Athos, deliver a baby by working with a uterine replicator rather than an actual mother? Because there are no women on Athos and never have been. The planet was settled 200 years ago by males trying to get away from the female sex. These males have set up a society completely devoid of female influence or contact. But the ovaries brought to Athos 200 years ago are worn out, and someone is going to have to leave the planet in search of replacements. This is how Ethan came to be sent to Kline Station, where he meets women for the first time. One woman in particular involves him in a number of adventures, Commander Elli Quinn of the Dendarii Mercenaries, who is at Kline Station on a special assignment. Kidnapping, torture, and telepathy all play into this engaging tale.

Cherryh, C. J. Alliance–Union. The only books in this universe that need to be read in sequence are *Heavy Time* and *Hellburner*.

Heavy Time. 1991. A massive conspiracy comes to light when Pollard and Dekker, two prospectors, find a derelict craft with a lone traumatized survivor.

Hellburner. 1992. Pollard is sent out to a remote space station, where his plans are destroyed when he is named next-of-kin for Dekker, who has seemingly gone insane. A sequel to *Heavy Time.*

Serpent's Reach. 1980. Human settlers on an alien world have found a way to live with their hosts in peace, even though neither race truly understands the other—quintessential Cherryh. But then more humans arrive, and the balance of power is upset. The young heroine chooses to ally herself with the aliens and then seeks revenge.

 Downbelow Station. 1981. For generations there has been a war between the star fleet of Earth and the Union formed on the distant colonies. But now an end is at hand, thanks to the establishment of the Alliance, which will act as a buffer between the two foes. This is the award-winning starting point for the novels set in the author's Merchanter universe.

> *Hugo Award.*

Merchanter's Luck. 1982. Sandor, the sole survivor of a Union merchanter family massacred by pirates, is also the sole owner of a starship. But he lacks sufficient funds with which to operate it. In fact, he is barely making it, courtesy of a little semi-legal trade he indulges in as he travels from star to star. Then he gets tricked into trying to set a trap for a renegade warship. It's an action that could cost him his ship and his life.

Rimrunners. 1989. A female soldier is marooned during an interstellar war. Instead of being rescued, she manages to get a berth on a Rimrunner space vessel that belongs to the enemy.

> *War.*

Tripoint. 1994. Tom Hawkins, a junior tech on the spaceship *Sprite,* was never close to his mother because he reminds her so much of the rapist who fathered him. But then his mother's plans for revenge are thwarted when he is captured by his half-brother Christian and taken aboard his father's ship. Leaving for Tripoint and

Pel with the *Sprite* in close pursuit, Tom expects to be spaced, abandoned, or sold to the highest bidder. He doesn't expect to learn that there were two sides to the story of the rape, or to discover that his father is not the man he expected him to be.

Cherryh, C. J. Chanur Series.

The Pride of Chanur. 1981. *The Pride of Chanur* is a trading ship owned and operated by the catlike Hani, who are at war with the Kif. Even though they have no use for humans, the crew can't stand by and let one be tortured by the Kif.

Chanur's Venture. 1983. In this sequel to *The Pride of Chanur*, the catlike Hani are still trying to save the human they rescued from being recaptured by the Kif.

The Kif Strike Back. 1985. This time the Kif have gone on the offensive, trying to get the escaped human away from the Hani crew of the *Pride of Chanur*.

Chanur's Homecoming. 1986. The *Pride of Chanur* returns home, to a welcome that is much cooler than expected.

Chanur's Legacy. 1992. Hilfy, captain of the *Chanur's Legacy*, accepts an offer of a million credits to transport a "Preciousness" for an alien being.

Delany, Samuel R. *Babel-17.* 1967. In an interstellar war an artificial language is being used as an unorthodox weapon. Rydra Wong, a poet, may be humankind's last best hope for salvation.

Nebula Award.

Delany, Samuel R. *Nova.* 1968. Captain Lorq von Ray, in pursuit of untold riches, plunges his spaceship into a star that is just at the point of going nova. His goal is to scoop up a rare element and then get out—before it's too late.

Dickson, Gordon R. Childe Cycle. As humanity expands throughout the galaxy, the inherent attributes of human nature become evident. Although the entire series does not work as space opera, the following titles will appeal to fans of the subgenre. They are annotated on page 23.

Soldier Ask Not. 1967.

Tactics of Mistake. 1971.

Dorsai. 1986.

Emerson, Jane. *City of Diamond.* 1996. Politics, religion, and romance combine in a powerful story set in an interstellar society. Iolanthe, the greatest beauty of an intergalactic city ship *City of Pearl*, is sent to the *City of Diamond* to wed Adrian Mercati, the city ship's Protector. Adrian's friend and advisor is Tal, half human and half alien. Tal would be sentenced to death elsewhere because beings of his mixed race are feared and distrusted. In this fully realized and richly imagined world, political intrigue rears its head as Adrian undertakes a search to find a lost artifact left by the vanished race that gave humans the three huge city ships.

Foster, Alan Dean. Founding of the Commonwealth Trilogy. The Humanx Commonwealth is the setting Foster used for the Pip and Flinx adventures and other novels. This trilogy explains how this seemingly impossible relationship (between the reserved, insectoid Thranx and the warm-blooded, outgoing Humans) first came into being.

Phylogenesis. Book One of the Founding of the Commonwealth. 2000. Contact between the insectoid Thranx and humans was carefully controlled until a human thief became friends with a rogue Thranx poet and changed everything.

Dirge. Book Two of the Founding of the Commonwealth. 2001. Humans and Thranx settled into an uneasy partnership until a new alien race arrived on the scene.

Diurnity's Dawn. Book Three of the Founding of the Commonwealth. 2002. Nearly a century after first contact, humans and Thranx are still struggling to accept and understand one another. An upcoming Humanx Inter-Cultural Fair is a perfect opportunity to bring these two species closer together, unless zealots on both sides are able to put a stop to any such liaison — forever.

Foster, Alan Dean. Pip and Flinx Adventures

The Tar-Aiym Krang. 1972. The Tar-Aiym Empire was destroyed in a war some half a million years ago. There is a rumor that one of the weapons used in that war is the Krang, a huge concert organ. Flinx, a street urchin who lives in the Human-Thranx or Humanx Commonwealth, gets involved in a bold scheme to capture the Krang in the author's first novel.

Bloodhype. 1973. Another Tar-Aiym artifact comes to the rescue when the Humanx Commonwealth is threatened by a gigantic plant-eating intelligence. Flinx is involved, as well as a drug and two Church spies.

For Love of Mother Not. 1983. Mother Mastiff rescued Flinx from slavery when she purchased him at auction. Now Mother Mastiff has been kidnapped and it's Flinx's turn to make a rescue.

Mid-Flinx. 1995. Pursued by an insane twerp, Flinx and his pet flying snake Pip find themselves on an uncharted jungle planet. Assisted by a human woman, her children, and their indigenous green furry companions, he survives the deadly threats posed by the exotic flora and fauna to face his pursuer and reptilian invaders from the enemy Commonwealth.

Reunion. 2002. The adventures of Flinx and his mini-drag Pip continue. With his telepathic powers evolving, Flinx wants to know more than ever about his past, but trying to find out puts his life in danger once again.

Greenland, Colin. Tabitha Jute Trilogy. Epic space adventure featuring the indomitable galactic pilot, Tabitha Jute, one-time captain of the grungy starship *Plenty.* Stripped of her command by the Guardians, an advanced parasitic race that preys on humans, Tabitha is trapped in the middle of a struggle for the fate of the galaxy.

Take Back Plenty: Book One of Tabitha Jute. 1990.

Seasons of Plenty: Book Two of Tabitha Jute. 1996.

Mother of Plenty: Book Three of Tabitha Jute. 1998.

 Take Back Plenty. 1990. "On Plenty, a ghetto planet populated by dysfunctional robots, looters, drunken spacers, and rabid survivalists, Tabitha Jute, a four-star astro-navigator, makes her first move to take back Plenty from its present inhabitants."—Amazon.com.uk.

Arthur C. Clarke, and British Science Fiction Awards.

Hamilton, Peter F. Homeric Space Opera Sequence. Some of the inhabitants of the recently colonized primitive planet Lalonde were hit with an energy virus that gave them extraordinary abilities and a desire for global domination. When the military steps in, a titanic battle erupts both in orbit and on the planet's surface.

The Reality Dysfunction Vol. 1 Emergence. 1996.

The Reality Dysfunction Vol. 2 Expansion. 1997.

The Neutronium Alchemist No. 1 Consolidation. 1997.

The Neutronium Alchemist No. 2 Conflict. 1997.

The Naked God. 2000.

Herbert, Brian, and Kevin J. Anderson. Dune prequel trilogy. Brian Herbert (son of *Dune* author, Frank Herbert) and Anderson weave a tale of political intrigue that adds richness and excitement to the Dune saga.

Dune: House Atreides. 1999. Leto Atreides ascends to dukedom because of the treachery of others. Duncan Idaho, a young boy hunted as game by the Harkonnens, becomes a loyal retainer of Family Atreides. Action, intrigue, romance—what more could one ask for?

Dune: House Harkonnen. 2000. Taking up where *Dune: House Atreides*, left off, in this volume events continue to unfold in the lives of Duke Leto, Baron Harkonnen, and the Emperor Shaddam.

Dune: House Corinno. 2001. The sadistic Emporer Shaddam's machinations have far-reaching implications that change the lives of the Atreides and the Harkonnens.

McCaffrey, Anne, Elizabeth Moon, and Jody Lynn Nye. The Planet Pirates Series.

McCaffrey, Anne, and Elizabeth Moon. *Sassinak.* 1990. Sassinak is twelve years old when the planet pirates attack. Her settlement is wiped out, and she is captured and sold as a slave. After a series of adventures, she follows a pirate vessel to the planet Ireta, where she meets Lunzie, her famous great-great-great-great grandmother who has spent entire generations of her life in cold sleep. Working together they involve the heavyworlders in their ongoing struggle against the pirates.

McCaffrey, Anne, and Jody Lynn Nye. *The Death of Sleep*. 1990. In a prequel to *Sassinak*, planet pirates have forced Lunzie to spend so much time in cold sleep that her family grows old before her. But now that she has joined Fleet Intelligence, Lunzie can battle against the pirates and make them pay for what they did to her.

McCaffrey, Anne, and Elizabeth Moon. *Generation Warriors*. 1991. Sassinak sends Lunzie to investigate a potential rebellion on the heavyworlders' home world. Conspiracies abound; the planet pirates are involved; and before it's all over, Sassinak and her friend wind up running for their lives through the tunnels of Fed/Central.

Murphy, Pat. *There and Back Again*. 1999. Bilbo Baggins through time and space! This joyful romp takes norbit Bailey Beldon from the comforts of his hollowed-out asteroid to the ends of the universe when the Farr clones commandeer him to be part of their expedition to find wormhole maps. Murphy has written a rollicking, entertaining space opera version of Tolkien's *The Hobbit* that stands as a tribute to the master of fantasy. Mobius strips, pirates, powerful drink, clones, and adventure abound as the tone deaf but courageous little miner proves to be a big-time hero.

Thornley, Diann. Unified Worlds Saga.

Ganwold's Child. 1995. The planet Ganwold was a place of refuge for Tristan and his mother. But when she gets the coughing sickness, he and his native friend must go to the "flat-teeth" people (humans) for help. Now they have fallen into the clutches of his father's deadliest enemy. Taken off-world and held as pawns, their only hope is the father Tristan last saw when he was two years old.

Echoes of Issel. 1996.

Dominion's Reach. 1997.

Vinge, Vernor. *A Fire Upon the Deep*. 1991. Two human children and the semi-mythological "Countermeasure," which may be the only means of saving civilization, are lost on a distant world.

Weber, David. Honor Harrington series. Annotated on page 31.

Other Science Fiction Adventure Themes and Types

Militaristic and War

Stories centering on a variety of military themes—from mercenaries and war to antimilitary stories and parody—are common in science fiction. Although this type of story does not contain enough features to qualify it as a subgenre, there are many fans of books with war themes. Militaristic and war SF features military discipline, strategies, and armament, and the stories are often full of masterfully described battle scenes, fleet deployments, and the forces of right prevailing in the end. In recent years women have been just as likely as men to be featured. The adventure is there—waiting for those willing to risk it. We may face friendship, guidance, and a mentoring relationship—if and when we find that we are not alone in space. We may need to become warriors, soldiers in the fight against an alien enemy that may be the BEMs (Bug-Eyed Monsters) of the early days of science fiction, arachnids like the opponents in Robert A. Heinlein's *Starship Troopers*, amoeba-like aliens that torment Nicholas Seafort in David Feintuch's multi-book Seafort Saga, or any other foe imaginable.

Militaristic themes are often present in space opera, so readers of this type may also enjoy space opera. Likewise, these readers may enjoy historical and contemporary militaristic adventure. Parallels can also be drawn between the heroes of yesterday, such as C. S. Forester's seafaring Horatio Hornblower or Bernard Cornwell's nineteenth-century soldier Richard Sharpe, and the warriors of tomorrow who are found in militaristic SF. W. E. B. Griffith adventures featuring military exploits during World War II also have much in common with some of the SF militaristic adventures. Many of the shared world novels (e.g., *Star Wars*) take place on military vessels or in military settings, and readers of militaristic SF should not forget to check the section on shared worlds for more SF military adventures of a specific kind.

These are just a few of the many novels that demonstrate that when battle lines are drawn and the enemy is poised to attack, we can do what we've done for untold generations: send in the Marines and hope that once again military expertise will save us.

Anderson, Kevin J. has written several novels in the Jedi Academy series. See page 59.

Asprin, Robert. Phule Series.

> *Phule's Company*. 1990. Willard Phule, the son of a megamillionaire munitions supplier, joins the Legion after a fight with his father. When he strafes a peace conference (an impulsive mistake), he is assigned to a punishment detail as captain of the Omega Company, an infamous collection of misfits, criminal types, and even overt rebels. Accompanied by his ever-present butler, Beeker (the narrator of his employer's adventures), Phule comes to the swamp planet where Omega Company is located, takes charge, and transforms this collection of misfits into a force to be reckoned with—able to hold their own even when challenged by the army's elite Red Eagle Unit. First contact with an alien race could have been a disaster, except for Phule's ability to turn almost anything into a financial windfall.

> *Phule's Paradise*. 1992. Phule has been asked to ride herd on a gambling casino. The dialogue sparkles and the action is fast and furious in this book that is difficult to put down. Once again General Blitzkrieg has given Willard Phule a seemingly impossible assignment, with the fond hope that his bunch of misfits will botch things up completely. And once again Phule and company come through with flying colors.

> **Asprin, Robert, with Peter J. Heck.** *A Phule and His Money.* 1999.

Barnes, John. The Timeline Wars. Extensive time travel in myriad time lines is the fate of Mark Strang, a private eye from Pittsburgh, who is fighting the Closers. These aliens are bent on enslaving the universe and are willing to take the battle across a million alternate Earths to do so.

Patton's Spaceship. 1997.

Washington's Dirigible. 1997.

Caesar's Bicycle. 1997.

Bova, Ben. *Triumph*. 1993. Annotated on page 114.

    War.

Brust, Steven. *Cowboy Feng's Space Bar and Grill.* 1990. Cowboy Feng's Space Bar and Grille seems to be the focus of nuclear attacks. A strike will occur and the bar will disappear, only to reappear on another planet in another time. More on page 178

Bujold, Lois McMaster. The Vorkosigan Series. Annotated on page 14. Has a strong militaristic component.

Card, Orson Scott. *Ender's Game.* 1985. Only six years old, Andrew "Ender" Wiggins appears to offer the world its best hope to stop an invasion by the insectoid aliens called buggers. Taken away from his family—his fearsomely sadistic brother Peter, his beloved and gentle sister Valentine, and his parents—Ender is sent to a battle school on a space installation. In the null-gravity battle room (where battles are fought in special suits that freeze when hit by the light-firing guns the kids are armed with), Ender proves himself to be a genius at tactics and strategy. After graduating from Battle School to Command School at age eleven, he works and plays on what he thinks are battle simulators that adapt and change in response to everything he learns and tries. In 1978, Card wrote a short story titled "Ender's Game." That story was expanded into this award-winning novel in 1985.

    Hugo and Nebula Awards.

Speaker for the Dead. 1986. In the aftermath of the genocidal war in *Ender's Game* some 3,000 years after he destroyed the buggers and their hive queen, Ender lives on. Now he is a Speaker for the Dead, traveling from world to world to learn everything possible about someone and then "speak" that person. On the Catholic colony of Lusitania a Piggie is found: staked out, tortured to death with a tree growing out of his middle. What was the secret that the xenologist Libo discovered before he too was left staked out in much the same way? Ender is called to speak Pipo's death and gets involved in the strange ecology of the Piggies and the tragedies going on in a human family. This philosophical and lyrical work, like its predecessor, won the Hugo and the Nebula.

    Hugo, Nebula, and Locus Awards.

Companion Novels. The following two titles do not follow Ender's story but are rather companion novels focusing on characters introduced in *Ender's Game* at the same time as and following events in *Ender's Game.*

Ender's Shadow. 1999. A starving four-year-old child appears on the mean streets of Rotterdam and is given the name Bean after talking the leader of a band of scavenging children into taking an action that will change their lives, and in fact, the lives of all the street kids. An impressive strategist, Bean's schemes lead to civilizing the wild children, and eventually lead him to Battle School. There he becomes Ender's lieutenant, creating an unbeatable tactical team.

Shadow of the Hegemon. 2001. The Battle School kids are still struggling to fit in with families that they left behind years ago when they are all abducted—except for Bean and his brother, who are the target of assassins. As long as he is in protective custody, Bean knows he is at risk. Meanwhile, Petra, his closest friend among the Battle School kids, who is being held captive, knows that if she is clever enough she can get necessary information out to Bean and to Ender's brother, Peter Wiggin, the Hegemon of the title.

Cherryh, C. J. The Chanur Series. Listed on page 17. Has a strong militaristic component.

Cherryh, C. J. The Merchanter Series. Annotated on page 16. Also features militaristic elements.

Crispin, A. C., and Kathleen O'Malley. *Silent Songs*. 1994. Ptosa' Wakandagi, a Native American, is Interrelator for the Cooperative League of Systems on the wilderness planet of Trinity. She establishes first contact with the Avian people of this planet, the Grus, and lives with their leader, Taller, his mate, Weaver, and their son, Lightning. Expecting reinforcements to arrive from the League, she is surprised by the seemingly unbeatable invasion of an alien force bent on conquest.

Delany, Samuel R. Nova. 1968. Captain Lorq von Ray, in pursuit of untold riches, plunges his spaceship into a star that is on the verge of going nova. The goal? To scoop up a rare and precious element and then get out—before it's too late.

Dickson, Gordon R. Dorsai Series. The Dorsai are bred to be professional soldiers. Inhabitants of the Exotic worlds are bred to possess creative mind-arts. Other genetic strains emphasize physical science on one world and religion or faith on the God-haunted Friendly worlds. Throughout Dickson's opus, the genetic elite of humankind try to gradually combine these strands in such a way that they will produce a superhuman. And always at the heart of this grand design are the Dorsai. *Note: The following are in order of the series.*

Dorsai. 1960. Meet superman Donal Graeme, the famous scion of the Dorsai warriors. This first volume of the series was originally published in a shorter version as *The Genetic General*.

Tactics of Mistake. 1971. This volume steps back in time to describe the education and development of Donal Graeme, famous spacefaring general and protagonist of *Dorsai*.

Soldier Ask Not. 1967. A man from Earth is studying the colonial Splinter cultures. At first he hates the religious fanatics of the Friendly Planets, but gradually he comes to respect them. Expanded from the author's Hugo-award-winning magazine story of the same title, and the third in the Dorsai series.

Hugo Award (for the short version).

Lost Dorsai: The New Dorsai Companion. 1980. This collection includes the Hugo-award-winning novella *Lost Dorsai,* the short story "Warrior," and information about Dickson's Childe Cycle, of which the Dorsai series is a part.

Dietz, William C. The Legion Series features Bill Booly and his misfit cyborg legion.

Legion of the Damned. 1993. Xenophobic aliens are intent on annihilating humankind, and the Legion is our last line of defense.

The Final Battle. 1995. Alien Hudathans use copycat technology to create their own corps of cyborgs. Then they target the heart of the Confederacy.

By Force of Arms. 2000. General Bill Booly and his troops face a fanatical human and his killer technology.

Dietz, William C. Drifter Series. Smuggler Pik Lando keeps finding himself in the middle of dangerous situations.

Drifter. 1991. Pik Lando, a smuggler, is introduced.

Drifter's Run. 1992. A space tug turns out not to be the safe haven Pik thought it would be when a female bounty hunter sets her sights on him.

Drifter's War. 1992. Lando's high-tech drift ship would be a great prize for either side in the planet-smashing war he stumbles into.

Drake, David. *Patriots.* 1996. Fresh out of law school, Mark Lucius-son Maxwell wants adventure on the frontier, so he heads out for the farthest reaches of civilization. On a muddy, rain-drenched way station he runs into trouble and is rescued by the larger-than-life Yerby Bannock, who tells him where the real frontier is: on Greenwood. Accompanying Yerby and his beautiful sister to their pioneering planet, Mark soon falls for both the planet and the girl. When they discover that powers on Earth want Greenwood for housing project-like, high-density residences, Yerby and Mark take up the cause to keep their planet undeveloped. This rousing adventure is loosely based on Ethan Allen's exploits with the Green Mountain Boys during the American Revolution.

Feintuch, David. Hope Series, the Nicholas Seafort Saga.

Midshipman's Hope. 1994. In this story set two centuries in the future, a seventeen-year-old midshipman becomes captain of his FTL ship after a series of mishaps leaves him the ranking line officer. Facing a pirate attack, condemned men, a lack of officers, a crew older than he is, and a major computer glitch, "Captain Kid" sails the U.N.N.S. *Hibernia* in search of safe docking.

Challenger's Hope. 1995. Now a responsible married man, Nicholas sets off on a three-year mission accompanied by his pregnant wife Amanda, the same youthful crew he worked with on the ill-fated *Hibernia,* plus some sixty passengers and forty-two teen transpops (Earth's homeless transient population). They're all headed for a new life among the stars. The expedition sets out for Hope Nation, which means constant vigilance, watching out for alien fish, and using numerous short jumps with their Fusion drives.

Prisoner's Hope. 1995. Captain Nicholas Seafort becomes a pawn in a dangerous game when the planters of Hope Nation rebel, fearing that Earth has abandoned them to an alien attack.

Fisherman's Hope. 1996. When Seafort refused to accept another ship posting, Earth gave him its children instead. As Commandant of the Naval Academy, Seafort is responsible for the training of some 400 cadets, who normally enlist at age thirteen for a five-year-term. When they graduate, they are supposed to be responsible, reliable, honorable men that the Academy can be proud of. Seafort believes he is a man who is cursed because each time he does what he knows to be wrong (e.g., standing up to the admiral for the sake of his charges, relieving a spaceship captain senior to him for ineptness and cowardice, sending young men to their deaths in his battle against the alien fish), rather than getting the court-martial he feels he deserves, he somehow always comes out a hero.

Voices of Hope. 1996. Forced to retire, Seafort now lives in seclusion with his wife and twelve-year-old son Philip, who is an incredible genius, wise, and resourceful beyond his years. He is also very much his father's boy, with that same inflexible Seafort honor. Scafort's friend, Adam, also has a son, 15-year-old Jared, a spoiled rotten, self-centered, insensitive young man, who also happens to have a real flair for riding the waves of cyberspace. When Jared gets angry and runs away, planning to sell confidential information to Cyberworld, Philip, who feels responsible for his flight, and Seafort, who knows just how deadly life out on the streets can be, go after him.

Patriarch's Hope. 1999. Nicholas Seafort is now the SecGen and nominal Commander-in-Chief of all U.N. forces, but he's also estranged from his son. Philip, now in his twenties, is a supporter of the Enviro movement that threatens the Navy's interests. When his son wins him over to the Enviro cause, battle lines are drawn.

Children of Hope. 2001. Fourteen-year-old Randy Carr blames Nicholas Seafort for his father's death and wants to kill him, but eventually finds himself Seafort's adopted son and ally against the theocratic Reunification Church.

Friedman, C. S. *In Conquest Born*. 1986. This complex space opera details the war between two highly developed civilizations who put their destructive weapons to good use.

Gerrold, David. The War against the Chtorr Series. http://www.chtorr.com/chtorrpage.htm.

A Matter for Men. 1983. The Chtorr, wormlike creatures that are trying to take over the world, appeared at the same time that a series of deadly plagues virtually wiped out the human population. Those few humans who are left are trying to rebuild civilization while coping with the growing threat of the

Chtorr, who feed on human flesh and are almost impossible to kill. Jim McCarthy, a young research student, joins the Special Forces to try to kill the Chtorr. On his way to Denver with some eggs and the insectlike creatures the Chtorr use for food, he works hard to understand the nature of this alien threat, while fighting to preserve humankind from the Chtorr.

A Day for Damnation. 1984. Jim McCarthy is back, getting up close and personal with the wormlike Chtorr. Humankind, what's left of it, is struggling to survive—fighting against the changes the Chtorr have made in the environment, beset by disease, and subject to frequent attacks by the worms themselves. Some people have given up and joined with others to immerse themselves in song. It's almost impossible to get out of such a group, as Jim discovers when he tries to study one from the inside. He also comes closer to worms than he ever wanted, after he and his friends are in a helicopter accident over worm territory.

A Rage for Revenge. 1989. The battle of humanity against the huge, wormlike Chtorr continues. This third volume is heavier in philosophy, both when Lieutenant James McCarthy undergoes "mode" training with 500 other "chosen," and during his period of captivity as he learns to live with the renegades who "serve" the worms and consider themselves the new breed. But when the Chtorr attack, philosophy ends and violence begins.

A Season for Slaughter. 1992. As Earth begins to resemble the aliens' home world, humans prepare to fight back.

A Method for Madness. (To be published in 2002.)

Haldeman, Joe. *The Forever War.* 1974. Fighting against an alien enemy isn't as bad as the side effects of faster-than-light-travel that puts the life of William Mandella on a totally different timeline. Written in response to Heinlein's *Starship Troopers.*

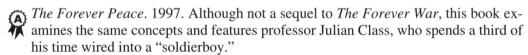

> ***Hugo Nebula, and Locus Awards.***

The Forever Peace. 1997. Although not a sequel to *The Forever War*, this book examines the same concepts and features professor Julian Class, who spends a third of his time wired into a "soldierboy."

> ***Hugo and Nebula Awards.***

Forever Free. 2000. Set twenty years after *The Forever War*, veterans William Mandela and comrade-in-arms Marygay are now the parents of teenagers and living in a zoo-like environment because they are so different from other humans of the time.

Hambly, Barbara. Has written some *Star Wars* books. See page 58.

Hamilton, Peter F. Homeric Space Opera Series. Annotated on page 19. Features military action.

Harrison, Harry. *Bill, The Galactic Hero.* 1965. The bizarre adventures of a simple farm boy who is enticed into the Empire Space Corps by an unscrupulous recruiter follow his military exploits in a way that is satirically antimilitaristic. Years after the volume was published, sequels appeared co-authored with other SF writers.

Bill, The Galactic Hero on the Planet of Robot Slaves. 1989.

Harrison, Harry, and Robert Sheckley. *Bill, the Galactic Hero on the Planet of Bottled Brains.* 1990.

Harrison, Harry, and David Bischoff. *Bill, the Galactic Hero on the Planet of Tasteless Pleasure.* 1991.

Harrison, Harry, and David Bischoff. *Bill, the Galactic Hero on the Planet of Ten Thousand Bars.* 1991.

Harrison, Harry, and Jack C. Haldeman. *Bill, the Galactic Hero on the Planet of Zombie Vampires.* 1991.

Harrison, Harry, and David Harris. *Bill, the Galactic Hero: the Final Incoherent Adventure.* 1994.

Heinlein, Robert A. *Starship Troopers.* 1959. This classic of militaristic science fiction features Johnny Rico, who does his patriotic duty by entering the military, the Mobile Infantry, upon graduation from high school. The Earth is engaged in a battle against a particularly nasty foe: bugs (huge, gross, intelligent, deadly, and extremely difficult to kill). After he gets out of officer's training school, Johnny is put on the fast track. Soon he's leading the men he formerly fought among. But those bugs appear to be invincible, and so the battle goes on.

   Hugo Award.

Heinlein, Robert A. *The Moon Is a Harsh Mistress.* 1966. The lunar colonists rise up against the Earth with the aid of a sentient computer.

   Hugo Award.

Heinlein, Robert A. *The Puppet Masters.* 1951. Early Heinlein on the alien invasion theme. This time, sluglike creatures take over human hosts and turn them into mindless puppets. Considered by many to be a classic of this type.

Hoover, H. M. *The Winds of Mars.* 1995. Annotated on page 198.

Hubbard, L. Ron. *Battlefield Earth: A Saga of the Year 3000.* 1982. Old-fashioned space opera on a galactic scale by a science fiction author who went on to found "Scientology." Evil aliens have conquered the Earth and enslaved humanity, but finally one individual stands up to the oppressors and encourages others to begin fighting back.

McCaffrey, Anne, Elizabeth Moon, and Jody Lynn Nye. *The Planet Pirates.* 1993. Annotated on page 19.

McDevitt, Jack. *A Talent for War*. 1989. After discovering a startling bit of information in an ancient computer file, Alex Benedict goes off on a quest that spans the stars. He is compelled to find out all he can about Christopher Sim. Was he really an interstellar hero, the legendary figure who led the human forces in a doomed battle against the Ashiyyur two centuries ago? Or was he a colossal fraud?

> *VOYA Award.*

McKinney, Jack. Robotech series. *Genesis*. 1987. With civilization on Earth verging on collapse because of a global civil war, our planet looks like easy pickings for the alien Zentraidi, but a super dimensional fortress and a corps of resolute young people may be the only hope of saving humankind. This long-running series can still be found in libraries, although only various and sundry titles in the series are still in print. Based on the phenomenally successful *Anime* series of the 1980s, it is also a role-playing game.

Moon, Elizabeth. Esmay Suiza Series.

> *Once a Hero*. 1997. As the first person from Altiplano to attend the academy, Esmay Suiza kept a low profile and was careful to qualify for Technical Track. But now she's a hero on her home planet and a challenge to the military-minded, who are not used to a woman warrior. In her next assignment on a deep space repair ship, the Bloodhords infiltrate and try to take over the ship—and once again she becomes a reluctant hero. She saves the life of a Serrano in the process, a young ensign who falls in love with her.

> *Rules of Engagement*. 1998. After being transferred to the command track, Esmay is sent to Training Command's Copper Mountain Base for the classes she needs. There she encounters Brun Meager, spoiled daughter of the Speaker of the Grand Council, the most powerful man in the Familias Regnant. When Brun disappears, Esmay is blamed because of an argument the two had. She knows she can find the girl—if only the authorities will listen to her.

> *Change of Command*. 1999. Annotated on page 164.

Moon, Elizabeth. Heris Serrano Series

> *Hunting Party*. 1993. Forced to resign her RSS Commission because of a dispute with bloodthirsty Admiral Lepescu, Heris Serrano is given a new command as captain of the luxury yacht *Sweet Delight*, hired to shuttle the elderly Lady Cecilia around the universe. Not only does she need to shape mediocre, lackadaisical crew members into a smoothly functioning, efficient unit, but she also must overhaul the ship and cope with the smuggling activities of the former captain. Lady Cecelia's young nephew and his five friends, all going along for the fox hunting, may be her biggest problem, especially when they disappear and Admiral Lepescu turns up uninvited.

> *Sporting Chance*. 1994. While transporting the Crown Prince home, Cecelia discovers that Prince Gerel has become "stupid" as a result of chemical poisoning. A veritable hornets' nest is stirred up when she informs the king. When Cecelia in turn is poisoned, Heris must prove her innocence and save Cecelia, while at the same time carrying out a secret mission for the king.

Winning Colors. 1995. Ninety-year-old Lady Cecelia has finally taken the rejuvenation treatments she has needed for years. Now the quality of the drugs used is being questioned, and she and Heris have been thrown into the middle of an investigation. Eventually, a fleet admiral, still angry at being misled by the false charges that drove Heris out of the service, gives Heris the opportunity to redeem herself and take charge of her own Fleet spaceship again—but only by battling against impossible odds.

Murphy, Pat. *The City, Not Long After.* 1988. In an effort to bring peace to the world, Mary Laurenson helps scatter monkeys from a Himalayan monastery to all the population centers on Earth. Soon a plague virus has spread throughout the world. Mary survives the plague and gives birth to a daughter, whom she raises in close proximity to San Francisco. There she and a group of survivors, mainly artists, are being helped by ghosts when an enemy force arrives to take over the city.

Niven, Larry, and Jerry Pournelle. *Footfall.* 1985. This epic-length best-seller provides a riveting look at humankind's struggle against alien invaders.

Norton, Andre. Time Traders Series. Annotated on page 55.

The Time Traders. 1958.

Galactic Derelict. 1959.

The Defiant Agents. 1962.

Key Out of Time. 1963.

Norton, Andre, and P. M. Griffin. *Firehand.* 1994. In collaboration with P. M. Griffin, Norton has returned to the Time Traders universe in this novel. Ross Murdoch and his teammates have come to the planet Dominion to avert a tragedy in the past by helping the populace fight a guerrilla war against the Baldies.

Ohlander, Ben, and David Drake. *Enemy of My Enemy.* 1995. Hard-hitting, no holds barred war breaks out between two factions. The only solution may lie with a star-crossed couple. Based on the computer game *Terra Nova*.

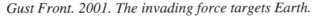

Ringo, John. *A Hymn Before Battle.* 2000. A power-armored infantry, led by ex-soldier Michael O'Shea, goes up against merciless centaur-like alien invaders at the planet Barwhon V.

Gust Front. 2001. The invading force targets Earth.

When the Devil Dances. 2002.

Saberhagen, Fred. *The Arrival. (Gene Roddenberry's Earth: Final Conflict #1)* 1999. Gene Roddenberry worked on more than just the *Star Trek* franchise before he died. The novels in this series are tie-ins to the last project he developed for television, an account of what happens when aliens (Taelons) arrive on the Earth, ostensibly to serve as our companions. *The Arrival* features Jonathan Doors, a multi-millionaire whose wife is dying of cystic fibrosis. The Taelons offer advanced technology and medical science, so Doors regards them as his wife's saviors, until he discovers that they are actually the enemies of humankind. With that discovery, we have the birth of the human resistance on Earth and the beginnings of the final conflict.

White, James. *The First Protector. (Gene Roddenberry's Earth: Final Conflict #2).* 2000. Historical perspective is provided to the Taelons' presence on the Earth. In fourth-century Ireland, Declan is a fugitive Irish prince. He is also the one who is appointed as the First Protector by the Taelons, charged with guarding their interests on the Earth.

Doyle, Debra. *Requiem for Boone. (Gene Roddenberry's Earth: Final Conflict #3).* 2001. William Boone served a dual role — as Taelon protector and as undercover resistance fighter. He was recruited by the Taelon to serve as bodyguard and interpreter for Da'an, the Taelon leader. But he joined the resistance and became humankind's first double agent — and eventually resistance martyr.

Smith, Sherwood. *Augur's Teacher. (Gene Roddenberry's Earth: Final Conflict #4).* 2001. Lia is a fourth-grade teacher who is suspicious of the Taelons and their plans for the Earth. But she is not ready to join the resistance and take part in an assassination attempt against the Taelon leader. Before long she is on the run, from both the rebels and the Taelons. It is up to Augur and his impressive array of computer skills to keep her alive.

Durgin, Doranna. *Heritage. (Gene Roddenberry's Earth: Final Conflict #5).* 2001. Liam Kincaid is the Taelon companion Da'an's new human protector. But there's more to Liam than meets the eye. For one thing, he's the leader of Earth's resistance movement. For another, one of his three parents was a Kimura, the extinct progenitor species of the Taelons, which means that Liam has some very special talents indeed.

Sixbury, Glenn R. *Legacy. (Gene Roddenberry's Earth: Final Conflict #6).* 2002. An archeological dig turns up a strange crystal of alien origins. If properly used, this crystal could destroy the Taelons, aliens who have supposedly come to Earth to serve as our companions. Liam Kincaid and Lili Palmer, human protectors of Taelon leaders, are also resistance fighters. But this time they find themselves involved in a struggle against a monster out of Cherokee legends — a monster produced by the crystal.

Saberhagen, Fred. Berserker Series. Annotated on page 78.

Stine, G. Harry. Starsea Invaders Series.

> *First Action.* 1993. When he tries to uncover the mysterious disappearances of naval personnel from a remote island, the captain of an American submarine discovers alien invaders.

Second Contact. 1994. Aliens are hiding in the Earth's oceans.

Third Encounter. 1995. The captain ventures into enemy territory, carrying a lethal cargo in his submarine.

Turtledove, Harry. The Great War tetralogy. 2000. Alternate history takes World War I to North America in 1914 where the North and the South duke it out again.

How Few Remain. 1997.

American Front. 1999.

Breakthroughs. 2000.

Walk in Hell. 2000.

Weber, David. Honor Harrington Series. The protagonist, Honor Harrington, is stronger than normal Earth females because she was genetically enhanced to survive on Sphinx, a much heavier planet than Earth. Honor Harrington is a truly honorable young woman: loyal, persevering, and Navy to the core. She is bonded with Nimitz, an empathetic tree cat indigenous to Sphinx, her home world. Nimitz, fiercely protective of his human companion, goes everywhere with her. The dedication sums up this entire series perfectly: "To C. S. Forester, with thanks for hours of enjoyment, years of inspiration and a lifetime of admiration."

On Basilisk Station. 1993. Honor's first command is HMS *Fearless*, a light cruiser that has been gutted to make way for too much weaponry. As a result, it performs poorly at fleet exercises. Honor is blamed and exiled to Basilisk Station to serve under Pavel Young, her nemesis from academy days. But when an attempt to invade the Republic of Haven is launched, Honor just may turn out to be in the right place at the right time.

The Honor of the Queen. 1993. Harrington, in command of the heavy cruiser HMS *Fearless*, is assigned as mission commander to escort Admiral Courvosier to the planet Grayson, where women are "protected" by their men and as a consequence have no legal rights. In addition, this is a world at war with a group of its own people, the Faithful, who have built a doomsday weapon and are threatening to use it from their new home, the neighboring planet Masada.

The Short Victorious War. 1994. Honor's in love, but she's also in trouble, due to the return of archenemy Lord Pavel Young. When she is sent to Hancock Station, she proves to be more than a match for the ships of the Peoples' Republic.

Field of Dishonor. 1994. Honor has been returned to Manticore. Now a political crisis may leave her dead or dishonored.

Flag in Exile. 1995. "Two irresistible forces are rushing together to crush Grayson between them. Only one woman—uncertain of her capabilities, weary unto death, and marked for murder—stands between her adopted planet and its devastation."— Ingram

Honor Among Enemies. 1997. To stop a group of pirates, Honor must utilize a "squadron" made up of the dregs of the service. It's the only way she can redeem her career as an officer of the Royal Manticoran Navy.

In Enemy Hands. 1997. As Lady Dame Honor Harrington, a countess, the first female Steadholder on Grayson, and a multibillionaire with a strong sense of right and justice, Honor will care for her people—all of them—to the best of her ability, or die trying. Restored to the rank of captain in the RMN (Royal Manticoran Navy), she carries the rank of a full admiral in the G.S.N. (Grayson Space Navy), but her latest mission ends in disaster—with the capture of Honor and her ship.

Echoes of Honor. 1998. The war between Haven and the Manticoran Alliance escalates as Honor and company plan their escape. Enlisting the aid of other political prisoners, they attack the shuttles, take out the command post, and after two long years have enough shipping capability to get everyone off the prison planet.

Ashes of Victory. 2000. Everyone loves Honor. The newsies now call her "the Salamander," Elizabeth III has made her a Duchess, and while she recuperates from reconstructive surgery, she's asked to teach, an assignment she's perfect for! Also, Amos Parnell, a prison planet survivor and Havenite, is free of Hell, and he is speaking out about the role the current government of Haven played in the Harris assassination. Can victory be far behind?

Weber, David, David Drake, and S. M. Stirling. *More Than Honor.* 1998. This collection of stories is an homage to Honor's universe, rather than to Honor Harrington herself, who is curiously absent from these pages.

Williams, Sean, and Shane Dix. *Evergence: The Prodigal Sun.* 1999. Morgan Roche, a female warrior and an Intelligence officer for the Commonwealth of Empires, is on an ultra-secret assignment to take a special AI (artificial intelligence), chained in a valise to her wrist, back to Intelligence HQ. But the Dato Bloc, learning of the importance of this Black Box, sends a very special ship after her. Morgan and a few companions escape to Sciacca's World, where she discovers one of them is a Sol Wunderkind, a genetically modified clone warrior.

Wilson, Robert Charles. *Mysterium.* 1994. Annotated on page 113.

Zahn, Timothy. Cobra Series. Twenty-fifth century cyborg soldiers, known as Cobras, fight wars for mankind, then act as advance guards in the settlement of new planets.

Cobra. 1985. When Jonny Moreau enlists in the war against the Troft, he is selected to become a new military superman-type guerilla fighter: Computerized Body Reflex Armament (a COBRA). With lasers in his fingers, antimatter laser in his left calf, sonic disrupters, unbreakable bones, enhanced vision and hearing, and an implanted computer that acts at superhuman speed to protect its host from attack, the Cobra warrior is the top-of-the-line/state-of-the-art fighting machine.

Cobra Strike. 1986. Jonny Moreau's cybernetic implants have taken their toll, and his physical body is literally wearing away, leaving him with only a few years left to live. His older son Corwin is all set to take over his father's political and administrative responsibilities. But one of the twins, Justin, wants to be a Cobra, and against his mother's wishes, undergoes the surgery and training.

Cobra Bargain. 1988. Includes more galactic battles by these cyborg military commando heroes.

Exploration

Exploration of other planets, galaxies, ancient sites, or mysterious artifacts provides a wonderful venue for adventure. Setting plays a leading role in these stories—even more than in other SF adventures. The locale for exploration may be an apparently uninhabited jungle or the labyrinthine maze of a technological warren. Readers who like exploration adventures like those of Indiana Jones or true-life explorations like the expeditions of Shackleton may find the same type of thrill in the following (and vice versa).

Aldiss, Brian. Helliconia Trilogy. Annotated on page 2.

Helliconia Spring. 1982.

Helliconia Summer. 1983.

Helliconia Winter. 1985.

Aldiss, Brian. *Non-Stop*. 1958. Denizens of a generations-long space flight encounter savages in the ship's overgrown hydroponics gardens. (Note: This novel was published in the United States under the title *Starship*.)

Anthony, Piers. *Ghost*. 1986. Captain Shetland ventures out in a new spaceship prototype: a time-traveling vehicle that will hopefully lead to the discovery of new energy sources for a resource-starved and overpopulated planet. When the captain and his crew enter a black hole, they discover just what happened to the previous crew (which disappeared) and face a similar fate themselves. Piers tackles chaos theory and the entropy effect here, with time travel and ghosts thrown in. The cover says it all: "Beyond the end of time lies Earth's hope—or eternal madness."

Asimov, Isaac. *Fantastic Voyage*. 1966. In what could be considered a precursor to nanotechnology, five explorers are miniaturized and enter a man's body in a specially outfitted submarine. Their mission is to break up a potentially deadly blood clot in this novelization of the movie.

Asprin, Robert, and Linda Evans. Time Scout Series. Time travel has become possible because of a global disaster, and now even tourists can easily travel through time. But it's better for them to pass through the gates under the guidance of a qualified time scout.

Time Scout. 1995. "Kit" Carson was a comfortably retired time scout until his grand-daughter decided to become the first female time scout. Now he must go to her rescue.

Wagers of Sin. 1996. Ripples in time and a radically changed Earth are just part of what Skeeter Jackson faces.

Ripping Time. 2000. Jenna Caddrick was seeking sanctuary from the terrorists who killed her fiancé, not realizing her flight through the time-touring gates of Shangri-La Station would place her in even greater danger. And now Skeeter Jackson follows the missing girl into Victorian London, where Jack the Ripper is really cutting up. Warning: This is half of a novel. It ends with "To Be Continued."

The House That Jack Built. 2001. This is the breathtaking conclusion to *Ripping Time*, in which Jenna is still fleeing terrorists, Jack the Ripper is still cutting up, and Skeeter and Kit Carson must work together to keep the killing spree from spreading across time.

Barnes, John. *Orbital Resonance*. 1991. Earth collapsed after the population was decimated by the MUTAIDS plague and pollution. Thirteen-year-old Melpomene Murphy, born and raised on a space shuttle colony, the *Flying Dutchman,* has been asked by her instructor to write a detailed account of what went on during the past year on the shuttle. It was the year when the older generation (the parents of all the kids on board) came face to face with the new generation, the young kids like Melpomene and her older brother. These were children who had been carefully designed and conditioned from birth to fit into a master plan—a plan carefully concealed from the kids until now.

Bova, Ben. *Mars.* 1992. The day-to-day exploration of Mars, particularly the search for life on the red planet, is set against a backdrop of the personalities of the twelve members of the landing party, the political machinations that went into the multinational pact that resulted in the expedition, and the very real fear on the part of all concerned that no funds for additional trips will be forthcoming. The scientific community, political infighting, media personalities, and above all the red planet itself, along with the individuals who risk their lives to explore it, make for a compelling read. More on page 107.

Return to Mars. 1999. Six years ago when he took over the Mars expedition that found life (plant lichen) on the red planet, Jamie Waterman made quite a name for himself. But he swears he also saw a cliff dwelling. Was it real or a mirage? Now in charge of the second expedition to Mars, he is determined to work in a trip to "his" village, no matter what is scheduled in the mission profile. He must also contend with his unruly crew and the efforts of the wealthy father of young geophysicist C. Dexter Trumball to have his son replace Jamie as mission director.

Brin, David. *Earth.* 1990. In the middle of the twenty-first century, a microscopic black hole falls into the Earth's core. Will scientists be able to save the Earth or will humankind become extinct? Politics and irresponsibility pave the way to ecological collapse.

Brin, David. Uplift Storm Trilogy.

Brightness Reef. 1995. Jijo, a forbidden world where settlement is prohibited by the Five Galaxies, has become home to groups of sentient beings who have ignored the edict. When a strange ship arrives in Jijo's skies, the uneasy peace is shattered.

Infinity's Shore. 1996. The Earth survey ship *Streaker* and her crew of fugitive dolphins reach Jijo as one of the six sapient races on the planet faces imminent genocide.

Heaven's Reach. 1998. When a small band of adventurers escape the chaos that has become Jijo, they find that they may hold a secret that could change the course of civilization.

Brin, David. Uplift Trilogy. Set in a future in which patron races "uplift" sentient species to space-faring status throughout the galaxy.

Sundiver. 1980. Human scientists, accompanied by dolphin and ape clients, are determined to prove to the other civilizations of the galactic community that they are worthy of membership in this group. And so they set out to investigate the possibility of intelligent life on the sun.

(A) *Startide Rising.* 1983. In this rich and complex novel humans achieve space flight without the help of a patron race, then go on to uplift the apes and the dolphins, no strings attached. The starship *Streaker*, the first ship sent out under Dolphin command, stumbles on a Sargasso of dead spaceships, a flotilla left by the mysterious progenitors. Unfortunately, they are seen, chased, and forced to land on the water world of Kithrup. While making repairs, the patron races show up and a space battle begins that looks hopeless for the *Streaker*, until the planet itself decides to take a stand.

> **Hugo, Nebula, and Locus Awards.**

(A) *The Uplift War.* 1987. The planet Garth has been invaded by the Gubru. They're looking for information on the discovery that the spaceship *Streaker* made. Failing that, they want to disrupt the progress that humans have made in "fixing" the devastation left by the previous insane inhabitants. They have also heard rumors that there is a new species, Garthlings, who are now ready to be uplifted. If the Gubru play their cards right, they can get the humans out of the way and become the sponsors of a new uplifted species. The problem is, just exactly what are the Garthlings and where are they? Furthermore, there is still one human left free and able to function on the planet, and there are neo-chimps who will follow him into battle.

Hugo Award.

Cherryh, C. J. *Finity's End.* 1997. By the time Captain James Robert Neihart takes the *Finity's End* back to Pell Station to claim Fletcher, the young man has chosen his own life, planetside, working with the alien Hisa who had befriended him as a runaway child. Fletcher is virtually kidnapped and forced to make a new home for himself on a ship sadly depleted of young people. But the crew is hesitant to accept one who was raised by aliens, and he is equally reluctant to accept this new life.

Clarke, Arthur C. *Rendezvous with Rama.* 1973. A strange cylindrical vessel (*Rama*) appears in the solar system, and it's headed toward the sun. Commander Norton takes the spaceship *Endeavor* in for a closer look. He and his crew then spend the next few weeks exploring a vast cavern. But things really heat up when the inhabitants of Mercury send a bomb to destroy *Rama*, and the captain and his crew must race with time to defuse it.

Hugo, Nebula, Locus, John W. Campbell, and British Science Fiction Awards.

Clarke, Arthur C., and Gentry Lee. *Rama II.* 1989. There are more mysteries to be solved involving the huge alien spaceship that first entered the solar system in *Rendezvous with Rama.*

The Garden of Rama. 1991. When their ship departs our solar system, astronauts Nicole, Richard, and Michael are stranded on *Rama* for a twelve-year journey.

Rama Revealed. 1993. The conclusion to the Rama series finally reveals the ultimate Raman plan for humanity.

Clarke, Arthur C. *2001: A Space Odyssey.* 1968. A strange monolith found on the moon results in an expedition to the planet Saturn. The mission of the expedition is to search for the origins of the monolith. The novel is based on the screenplay that Arthur C. Clarke and Stanley Kubrick wrote for Kubrick's enigmatic 1968 movie of the same title. The basis for the film and for the subsequent book is a short story that Clarke wrote in 1951, "The Sentinel of Eternity," which addresses the evolution of the human race as it develops from apeman to "Star Child."

2010: Odyssey Two. 1982. A second expedition sets out, this time to the moons of Jupiter. Those on board hope to find out what happened to the *Discovery*, the spaceship that disappeared on the earlier expedition. In the course of their journey, they encounter a huge alien monolith, the intelligent computer HAL 9000, and a much-changed David Bowman, protagonist of the previous novel.

2061: Odyssey Three. 1988. The vista is greatly expanded in this third installment of the Odyssey trilogy. The story of that mysterious transforming monolith and its effect on humankind is taken far into the future.

Crispin, A. C. StarBridge Series. Space opera, first contact, telepathic-communication, and strong young characters of varying genders and species all figure in this series about cooperation among sentient beings.

StarBridge. 1989. This is the diary of a teenage colonist, Mahree Burroughs, who travels to Earth on her aunt and uncle's spaceship to continue her education. En route they pick up a radio transmission, track it to its source, and make first contact with an alien species, the Simiu. Mahree befriends, then becomes honor-bound to, Dhurrrkk, a young male who teaches her his language and learns English from her in return.

Silent Dances. 1990.

Shadow World. 1991.

Hawke, Simon. *The Whims of Creation.* 1995. Dr. Penelope Seldon, a scientist in the first generation on board the space ark *Agamemnon*, complains that their closed society, with its careful genetic control of future generations, is not going to work, that future generations will suffer from depression and suicide as a result. Her gift to the future is a secret program in a virtual reality game designed to wake up its players and bring challenge and creativity back into their lives. But when the time comes, will the disappearance of a dozen children, and the appearance of fairies, elves, unicorns, dwarves, and even a dragon, have the desired effect on the inhabitants of the ship?

Heald, Denise Lopes. *Mistwalker.* 1994. Meesha Raschad is out in the green, running for his life, when he finds Sal, a sled-hauler who is trying to make a living under the most adverse conditions imaginable. Sal knows it is dangerous to trek through the jungle alone, but she has no choice. She doesn't have a partner. When she meets Raschad everything changes. Constant vigilance is essential in the areas controlled by the Mistwalkers. Raschad seems to have some special immunity as far as they are concerned. What is the secret in his past that wakes him up in the middle of the night with terrors that won't let him sleep?

Heinlein, Robert A. *Tunnel in the Sky.* 1955. A group of teenagers leave for a ten-day exercise on a hostile planet. After they arrive through their tunnel in the sky, something goes wrong with the matter transmitter. Ten days become two years, and the exercise becomes a struggle to survive.

McAuley, Paul J. *Eternal Light.* 1991. The human race has been drawn into a thousand-millenia-old genocidal conflict. Dorothy Yoshida, with her extraordinary ability to reach out with her mind to the future and to the past, is humankind's only hope of salvation. "While using her empathic abilities to investigate a past civilization, Dorothy Yoshida is kidnapped and forced into the service of powerful, horribly disfigured Duke Barlstilkin V, who wants to rendezvous with a renegade neutron star speeding away from the galactic core and, against the laws of physics, sustaining in orbit around it a planet-sized object. Following Barlstilkin closely is his would-be pilot, veteran combat hero Suzy Falcon, and her companion, a half-human, half-cybernetic techno-wizard aptly named Robot."—Carl Hays, *Booklist*.

McAuley, Paul J. *Four Hundred Billion Stars*. 1988. In the midst of an interstellar war, the heroine, who exhibits some telepathic ability, travels to a bleak planet to investigate the rumor that there may be a link between the enemy and primitive inhabitants there.

> ### *Philip K. Dick Memorial Award.*

McCaffrey, Anne. *Nimisha's Ship*. 1999. The mechanically inclined Nimisha secretly assists her father, a starship designer who owns the Rondymense Ship Yards, and ultimately becomes his heir. Sucked into a wormhole on the test flight of a ship she has designed, Nimisha ends up on a hostile planet where she makes first contact with sentient aliens.

McHugh, Maureen F. *Mission Child*. 1998. Janna is born long after her colony planet was abandoned by Earth, but when offworlders return, she faces a world of adventure.

Niven, Larry. *Ringworld*. 1970. Six hundred million miles around and a million miles wide, this ring is a heavily populated world that surrounds a distant sun. Thirty trillion diverse inhabitants live on the inner rim, in an area that is millions of times the size of the Earth. Alien puppeteers, fleeing a galaxy-threatening explosion, come to humans for help in exploring this Ringworld. One of its inhabitants is lucky Teela Brown, the product of a secret puppeteer breeding project, who turns out to be much less lucky in the sequel.

> ### *Hugo, Nebula, and Locus Awards.*

Ringworld Engineers. 1979. The sequel to *Ringworld* reveals that the extraordinary artifact in space was built by the Pak protectors. Stranded after being brought to steal technology, Louis Wu discovers that the Ringworld is off-center. If not corrected, it will soon brush against its sun, with devastating consequences for its multitudinous inhabitants.

Ringworld Throne. 1996. Louis Wu, the scientist who discovered Ringworld, is now 200 years old and realizes that he may be the only hope to save the massive artifact when predatory humanoids known as vampires try to take control.

Norton, Andre. The Solar Queen Series. Features terrific space opera action in the adventures of Dane Thorson and the crew of the space freighter the *Solar Queen*.

Sargasso of Space. 1955. Written under the pen name Andrew North, this is the novel that introduced the free trader, *Solar Queen*, and its crew.

Plague Ship. 1956. Still writing under the pen name Andrew North, the author describes what happens when the plague breaks out on board the *Solar Queen* during a voyage. As a result, the Star Patrol intends to destroy the vessel on sight.

Voodoo Planet. 1959. The further adventures of the *Solar Queen*, still attributed to Andrew North.

Postmarked the Stars. 1969. The *Solar Queen's* crew uncovers a criminal operation involved in the attempted conquest of the entire galaxy.

Norton, Andre, and P. M. Griffin. *Redline the Stars: A New Adventure of the Solar Queen.* 1993. Rael Cofort, who seems to attract bad luck wherever she goes, is the sister of a major competitor of the *Solar Queen.* Wanting to prove to her brother that she can make it on her own, she joins the crew of the Solar Queen. The flight to Canuche is uneventful, proof positive that she is not a jinx. But it's a different story entirely once they reach port. The aura of menace surrounding the planet proves to be prophetic, and soon Rael is struggling against murderous rats, a warehouse, an explosion, and that is just the beginning.

Norton, Andre, and Sherwood Smith. *Mind for Trade.* 1996. Several crew members of the *Solar Queen* have developed psi powers. These come in handy when the ship lands on a planet and is attacked by pirates.

Norton, Andre, and Sherwood Smith. *Derelict for Trade.* 1997. The *Solar Queen* comes out of space right on top of a derelict ship. The crew declares the right of salvage, but their problems have just begun. Before long they'll have to contend with a secret alien hijacking ring.

Nye, Jody Lynn. *Medicine Show.* 1994. Dr. Shona Taylor's traveling menagerie includes a dog whose blood provides vaccines against diseases, a cat who can sniff out drugs, rabbits, mice, and even an ottle, a cross between a turtle and an otter. She and her family are on a mission to return the ottle to his home world—but first she must avoid assassins and foreclosure on her spaceship.

Pohl, Frederik, and C. M. Kornbluth. *The Space Merchants.* 1952. This America of the future is not run by the military or members of powerful political hierarchies. Instead, it is subject to the whims and machinations of ad-men, who can call upon the considerable resources of their advertising agencies to control the overpopulated, materialistic society they live in. A work of science fiction that is also a brilliant satire. Advertising rules!

Pohl, Frederik. *Merchant's War.* 1984. A sequel to *The Space Merchants.* The two titles were reissued together in one volume as *Venus, Inc.* 1985.

Reed, Robert. *Beyond the Veil of Stars.* 1994. Corny gets a job with a secret government agency investigating a new world, not by traveling in a spaceship but by going through a special intrusion and entering the body of an animal or creature there. While investigating High Desert he meets and falls in love with another researcher, only to discover later that she is an alien who has entered through an intrusion from a different planet.

    Beneath the Gated Sky. 1997. Corny and Porsche discover plots perpetrated by various species as they travel to other worlds through the intrusions.

Reed, Robert. *Marrow.* 2000. Explorers are trying to find the center of a colossal spaceship that is old beyond imagining and crewed by humans who have achieved near immortality. What they discover is a planet.

Robinson, Frank M. *The Dark Beyond the Stars.* 1991. Sparrow awakens on the aging starship *Astron* to discover that he has amnesia. His amnesia hides the key to solving the terrible discord on the ship.

Robinson, Kim Stanley. Mars Trilogy.

Red Mars. 1992. Vivid scene-setting and lyrical imagery describe life and death on the planet Mars. One of the original hundred settlers, a man who was formerly part of the triumvirate of leaders on the planet, plots and then executes the murder of a former friend. The action flashes back to the early days of the colonization effort, beginning with the nine months spent cooped up on a spaceship headed toward the red planet. After that come years of settling in, followed by growing concern over pollution and the environment, but only on the part of a few of the settlers. A new quasi-religion is born among the "farm" people, the aging process is virtually halted, and the awesome presence of Mars itself looms over everyone and everything.

    Nebula Award.

Green Mars. 1993. At the beginning of the twenty-second century, terraforming is well underway, but the populace is still in conflict.

    Hugo Award.

Blue Mars. 1996. "The First Hundred" original Mars settlers are now over 300 years old due to an anti-aging breakthrough, and Mars now has oceans that are threatened by an ice age.

    Hugo Award.

Robinson, Kim Stanley. *The Martians.* 1999. A companion volume to Robinson's Mars Trilogy, this work contains stories, poems, and even the text of the planetary constitution.

Sargent, Pamela. *Earthseed.* 1983. A ship full of children who come of age as they travel through space on an expedition to find a suitable planet to colonize. More on page 203.

Sawyer, Robert J. *Starplex.* 1996. "For nearly twenty years Earth's space exploration had exploded outward, thanks to a series of mysterious, artificial wormholes. Discovery is superseding understanding. And when an unknown vessel—with no windows, no seams, and no visible means of propulsion—arrives through a new wormhole, an already battle-scarred Starplex could be the starting point of a new interstellar war... " (cover blurb.) Sawyer has a Web site at http://www.sfwriter. com/ where one can read sample excerpts and first chapters of his books.

> *Aurora Award.*

Sheffield, Charles. Heritage Universe. The Paradox is an artifact left behind by an ancient and powerful race. Hans Rebka is determined to solve the mystery surrounding it, unaware that success can pose a threat to all known life. When the series was reprinted, *Summertide* and *Divergence* were published in one volume as *The Convergent Series. Transcendence* and *Convergence* were published in one volume as *Transvergence.* The author's official Web page is at http://www.sff.net/people/sheffield/.

Summertide. 1990. It all starts with the discovery of the first Builder artifact, a Cocoon surrounding an Earth-type planet in the Lacoste system. Hans Rebka was exploring this artifact on the planet Paradox when he was pulled away and sent to the double-planet system of Dobelle. His mission there was to find out what was wrong with Max Perry and get him away from Opal and its companion Quake before Summertide. With only thirty-six hours remaining, he's faced with a daunting challenge. In the meantime, others have also arrived on Quake, interested in remaining there during Summertide, which marks the Grand Conjunction of the system's stars and planets, something that happens only every 350,000 years.

Divergence. 1991.

Transcendence. 1992.

Convergence. 1997.

Swanwick, Michael. *Stations of the Tide.* 1990. A complex, enigmatic tale of a search for the brilliant renegade scientist Gregorian as the world Miranda begins to drown under the weight of its own oceans.

> *Nebula Award.*

Tepper, Sheri S. *Sideshow.* 1992. Abasio has made an honorable life for himself in the city—and he manages to remain honorable, even though he lives among cesspool inhabitants like the gangers. Then Olly enters his life, helps him flee from the Walkers, and joins him on the quest for the meaning behind the Oracle's strange prophecy. Unfortunately, they are faced with a problem: the seriously deranged Ellel, whose delusions of grandeur force one of them to make the ultimate sacrifice.

Tiptree, James, Jr. *Brightness Falls from the Air.* 1985. Radiation from a star that has exploded threatens life on an alien planet. A group from Earth is trapped there, and it includes some very sinister criminals. (David Pringle has pointed out the similarity between this plot and that of *Key Largo*, a well-known film noir directed by John Huston.)

Varley, John. *The Golden Globe.* 1998. Former child star Sparky Valentine, now 100 years old, makes his way around the galaxy as an itinerant thespian, but he is also a wanted man with a gumshoe on his trail.

Verne, Jules. *From the Earth to the Moon.* 1865. This is the tale of a gun club that devises a plan to travel to the moon by shooting men out of a huge cannon. The full text is available on the Internet at http://www. mastertexts.com.

Verne, Jules. *Twenty Thousand Leagues Under the Sea.* 1870. Three survivors of a shipwreck discover that the sea monster that sank their ship is really Captain Nemo's submarine. The full text can be found at http://etext.lib.virginia.edu/.

Williamson, Jack. *Beachhead.* 1992. Sam Houston Kelligan's great ambition in life is to travel to Mars, and now he has the opportunity to do so. But first he must compete with other likely candidates on the moon, to test their ability to survive under adverse conditions. And they certainly are adverse, including an infection spread by Martian dust, a crash landing, and a perilous and life-threatening return flight.

Willis, Connie. *Uncharted Territory.* 1994. A clever and witty spoof of what could happen if environmental concerns and government regulations were taken to their not-so-logical extreme. Findriddy and Carson are two explorers engaged in survey activities on the planet Boohte. Their personal bane is their native guide Bult, who spends more time entering fines in his log than helping them explore his planet.

Wolfe, Gene. The Book of the Long Sun. The adventures of Patera Silk are recounted by Horn.

Nightside the Long Sun. 1993.

Lake of the Long Sun. 1994.

Caldé of the Long Sun. 1994.

Exodus from the Long Sun. 1996.

Wolfe, Gene. *The Book of the Short Sun.* (Series title.)

On Blue's Waters. 1999. Horn, a papermaker who lives on Blue in New Viron, was the narrator who, with his wife, recorded the adventures of Patera Silk in *The Book of the Long Sun.* Now Horn must leave his wife and three sons to go on a quest. He must return to the Whorl and bring Patera Silk to Blue. New Viron needs a caldé, someone strong and honest, someone like Patera Silk.

In Green's Jungles. (Book of the Short Sun #2.) 2000. In this sequel to *On Blue's Waters*, Horn continues his narration of what happened during his quest to find the heroic leader Patera Silk.

Return to the Whorl. (Book of the Short Sun #3.) 2001. During his quest for Patera Silk, Horn has traveled from his home on the planet Blue to its sister world, Green, as well as to the Whorl, the giant spaceship that brought Horn and his people to this system. He has even visited Urth itself. Now, as his quest draws to a close, his growing resemblance to Patera Silk is becoming more and more apparent.

Journeys Through Space and Time

Tales of journeys are as old as storytelling itself. After all, life itself is a journey. We take small steps as infants; gain confidence by leaps and bounds as we enter adolescence; stride purposefully forward during our mature, productive years; grow hesitant and begin to falter with the advent of old age; and are back to small, fumbling movements as we approach death. The growth of civilizations can be seen to follow a similar track. What better framework is there for a story? In science fiction, the journey takes on new dimensions: space and time. In the stories that follow, a journey provides a central structure to the action.

A Space of One's Own (Space Travel)

The growth and development of space flight and extra-planetary exploration begins with small, stumbling steps. Consider Homer Hickam's struggles in *The Rocket Boys*. We've landed on the moon, sent out probes, and once we have the necessary technology, are poised to go where humankind has never gone before. Then, in Asimov's Foundation series, we are told that progress and civilization are finite. Many science fiction novels present humans as the young, brash newcomers, making a name for ourselves in galaxies and among civilizations that may choose to help us or may feel threatened by our presence. Others have described what happens when scientific curiosity is allowed to wither and die. When safety and caution reign supreme, stagnation is the result.

Space flight is a long-standing staple of SF. The journey can be a means to an end or the end itself. The travelers may not even know they are traveling, at least not at first, as in Alexei Panshin's *Rite of Passage* and Pamela Sargent's *Earthseed*.

Faster-than-light drive, wormholes in space, and cryosleep facilities on board ship all make space flight possible, but it is the human interactions and the fertile imaginations of science fiction authors that keep us turning pages fast and furiously—to find out what is going to happen and how the journey will end.

There are trips taken in cryosleep, trips that last for generations, in which the ship becomes home and the end of the journey is lost sight of. *Star Trek's Voyager, Enterprise I,* and *Enterprise II* were on trips that lasted three to seven years (on television) and spawned a media empire—much to the delight of their fans.

The SF journey can have a definite beginning and end. The purpose can be exploration, commerce/trade/tourism, colonization and settlement, or even military intelligence and battle.

There are fewer and fewer unexplored areas on Earth to challenge and to provide a safe outlet for humanity's competitive drive. But there is a moon in our sky and planets in our solar system and a whole universe out there for us to move into—we just need to develop the technology. Westward expansion was our dictum for generations. Now we've begun looking up, and talented writers have provided us with their own version of what escape from the planet might be like.

Anthony, Piers. *Ghost.* 1986. A time-traveling spaceship encounters a black hole and the crew learns that the previous ship that attempted this mission did not come back. Now they're seeing ghosts on board.

Asimov, Isaac. *Nemesis.* 1989. On Earth a scientist is trying to build a starship. In space a young girl, his daughter, is growing up on a space habitat. But that habitat, Rotar, which has traveled to a red dwarf star, is now threatened as it approaches the solar system.

Barnes, John. *Orbital Resonance.* 1991. *Flying Dutchman* is a space colony that was established when civilization on Earth collapsed after the MUTAIDS plague and pollution decimated the population. Thirteen-year-old Melpomene Murphy, born and raised on the *Flying Dutchman*, has been asked by her instructor to write a detailed account of what went on during the past year on the shuttle.

Barnes, John. Thousand Cultures Universe.

> *A Million Open Doors.* 1992. Nou Occitan is one of humanity's "Thousand Cultures," an artificial colony set up on a terraformed world to bring art, chivalry, and other old-fashioned values to life. Teleportation travel, via a device called a springer, has taken people out to many far-flung planets.

> *Earth Made of Glass.* 1998. In this sequel to *A Million Open Doors,* Giraut and Margaret Leones travel to the planet Briand, where, as if the planet's near-lethal environment weren't trouble enough, two of the universe's synthetic Thousand Cultures—one founded by classical Tamil and the other by classical Maya—are at each other's throats.

Bear, Greg. *Anvil of Stars.* 1992. The children of a destroyed Earth are on a journey for revenge. These teens are going to destroy the aliens' home world, if they can find it. But the growing number of pacifists on board want to put a stop to their mission with their growing outcry against genocide.

Benford, Gregory. *Across the Sea of Suns.* 1984. In this sequel to *In the Ocean of Night*, the protagonist of the earlier work travels to the stars. Once he gets there scientist Nigel Walmsley discovers traces of a civilization based on machines that could prove to be inimical to humankind.

Blish, James. *Cities in Flight.* 1970. This is an omnibus edition that contains four linked novels: *They Shall Have Stars; A Life for the Stars; Earthman, Come Home;* and *The Triumph of Time.* In his afterword Richard D. Mullen explains the connections between these works (known as the "Okie" stories, of antigravity powered cities that travel through the galaxy in search of work) and Oswald Spengler's *The Decline of the West.*

Bova, Ben. *Venus.* 2000. Earth was on a fast track to disaster. Venus was already there. The question everyone was asking: Was Venus a portent of our future, an indication of things to come? It seemed the only solution was to send an expedition to study Venus—an expedition doomed from the onset by caution and disregard of out-of-the-box thinking.

Brown, Frederic. *The Lights in the Sky Are Stars.* 1953. A female politician and a failed astronaut work together to try to put life back into America's stalled space program. Their plan involves a realistic (and for its time quite idealistic) mission to Jupiter. (This novel was published in Britain as *Project Jupiter*.)

Cherryh, C. J. Merchanter Universe. War between the Starfleet of Earth and the Union formed by the distant colonies led to the establishment of an Alliance, which served as a buffer between the two and is the backdrop of Cherryh's many novels set in the Merchanter Universe.

Clement, Hal. *Mission of Gravity.* 1954. The planet Mesklin is such a high-gravity world that humans cannot possibly exist there. Only a flat centipedelike inhabitant of the planet is ideally suited for the mission of gravity that can save this world.

Flynn, Michael. *Firestar.* 1997. Incredibly wealthy businesswoman Mariesa van Huyten's fear of meteors drives her to develop technologies and training plans to take humanity from elementary school to space. A large supporting cast of characters includes everyone from a high school poet to a daredevil test pilot and even a butler.

Haldeman, Joe. *The Forever War.* 1975. Annotated on page 26.

   Hugo, Nebula, and Locus Awards.

Hawke, Simon. *Whims of Creation.* 1995. When a journey becomes too restrictive and boring, it probably needs a little virtual reality jumpstart—like fairies in the hydroponics gardens and mythical creatures roaming the ship to stop the sudden increase in depression-based suicides.

Heinlein, Robert A. *Citizen of the Galaxy.* 1957. Regarded by many as one of the best of the author's juveniles, this is the story of a slave boy who discovers that he belongs to a family of Free Traders in a distant future where commerce is all important.

Heinlein, Robert A. *Farmer in the Sky.* 1950. The settling of Ganymede, one of Jupiter's moons, is the background for this early juvenile.

Kress, Nancy. *Probability Moon.* 2000. First of a trilogy set in a future in which Earth has become the environmental disaster so long predicted. Humanity's salvation, however, is at hand. A star gate has been discovered in the solar system, built by unknown aliens, which makes it possible to explore and colonize other worlds. Unfortunately, it also attracts the attention of the Fallers, a race of aliens bent on the extinction of humankind.

Kress, Nancy. *Probability Sun.* 2001. The sequel to *Probability Moon* continues the ongoing struggle between the alien Fallers and humanity.

McCaffrey, Anne. *Dinosaur Planet.* 1978. The ship's mission was relatively simple: to catalog the fauna and flora on this new planet while looking for possible new energy sources for the Federated Sentient Planets. But the ship's crew hadn't expected their findings to be quite so big.

Dinosaur Planet Survivors. 1984. The sequel to *Dinosaur Planet* continues the adventures of Kai and Varian on the planet Ireta. After forty years in coldsleep, they discover they must fight mutineers for the fate of the planet and its unusual dinosaurs.

McCaffrey, Anne. Crystal Singer series. Killashandra Ree is a crystal singer, using her special musical ability to find and then use alien crystals. Titles listed on page 136.

Murphy, Pat. *There and Back Again.* 1999. Bilbo Baggins through time and space! Murphy uses Tolkien's *The Hobbit* as the basis for this joyful romp through time and space, featuring the norbit Bailey Beldon, a tone deaf but courageous little asteroid miner who proves to be a hero.

Norton, Andre. Adventures of the Solar Queen. The *Solar Queen* series features the classic space-faring adventures of the crew of the space freighter, the *Solar Queen*. Titles listed on page 38.

Panshin, Alexei. *Rite of Passage.* 1968. The teenage protagonist travels toward a colony planet on an asteroid generation ship with a faster-than-light drive. Upon arrival, she must leave the huge spaceship that has been her home and prove herself by surviving the considerable danger she faces on this primitive world. Like Heinlein's juveniles, the story is fast-paced and intriguing, with a young protagonist who overcomes all odds in the end.

> *Nebula Award*

Robinson, Kim Stanley. *Red Mars.* 1992. Describes the early days of the colonization effort, beginning with the nine months spent cooped up on a spaceship headed toward the red planet. More on page 40.

Russo, Richard Paul. *Ship of Fools.* 2001. For generations the humans on the *Argonos* have traveled through space with no destination or mission. Then a transmission lures them to a planet where they find a colony of the dead.

Sargent, Pamela. *Earthseed.* 1983. Annotated on page 203.

Sawyer, Robert J. *Golden Fleece.* 1999. JASON is a sentient computer that controls systems aboard the *Argo*, a colonization ship bound for Eta Cephei IV. When Aaron Rossman's ex-wife dies in a bizarre accident, everyone is sympathetic. No one mentions the possibility of suicide. But Rossman won't rest until he discovers the truth, and when he does, it looks like it will cost him his life. This is the first of the author's novels. Sawyer has a Web site at http://www.sfwriter.com/.

> *Aurora Award for Best Novel.*

Sheffield, Charles. *Putting Up Roots.* 1997. Josh Kerrigan takes up farming on Solferino in the Messina Dust Cloud, where his autistic cousin Dawn establishes contact with an alien creature. More on page 204.

Smith, E. E. Doc. *The Skylark of Space.* 1946. Richard Seaton is a young genius who discovers an anti-gravity substance and builds a spaceship. He then travels through space, encountering weird aliens and constantly on guard against his nemesis, Blackie DuQuesne. Good ol' American know-how and good ol' human ingenuity always save the day.

Skylark Three. 1948. More expeditions to the stars and encounters with evil, both alien and human, are experienced by brilliant engineer and scientist Richard Seaton and his friends.

Skylark of Valeron. 1949. Includes more fast-paced entertainment in the Skylark universe.

Skylark DuQuesne. 1966. In the final volume of the Skylark series, Richard Seaton and Blackie DuQuesne must set aside their differences and work together to fight against attack by an entire galaxy.

Varley, John. *The Golden Globe.* 1998. Annotated on page 42.

Willis, Connie, and Cynthia Felice. *Promised Land.* 1997. While on her way to start a career after graduating from an upscale boarding school, Delanna Milleflores stops by the backwater planet Keramos to settle her mother's estate. Upon landing, she discovers that because of Keramos's weird laws and an unbreakable will, she is married to country bumpkin Sonny Tanner. Traveling over 5,000 miles to the orchard plantation jointly owned with the Tanner family, Delanna has adventures and becomes a target of the planet's gossip network.

It's About Time! (Time Travel)

When considering the theme of time travel in SF, the first book to come to mind may very well be H. G. Wells's *The Time Machine,* with its classic "science is the answer" message. Although time travel in literature was not unprecedented, Wells's idea of moving through time with the aid of technology was revolutionary, and it opened up a wealth of possibilities for subsequent SF authors to explore. Time travel, in various and sundry forms, has remained a popular theme in SF to this day. Time travel can take us back in time—to the Middle Ages, to the last days of the Roman Empire, or even to prehistory. It can also take us forward—to the far reaches of the future. All sorts of time-bending and mind-bending variations result—from time paradox (in which a character goes back in time and tampers with history), time distortion (where time slows down or speeds up), or time dislocation (lost in or outside of time) to reverse time, with time running in the opposite direction. Of course, tampering with time can destroy the universe just as easily as it can save it, so the tone of these stories ranges from exuberantly optimistic and heroic to darkly pessimistic. Furthermore, all sorts of moral and philosophical questions are raised by the issue—even contemplations about the mystery and meaning of time. Thus, the journey through time does not always have the high level of action that is found in other SF adventures. But rest assured, the stories are just as intriguing.

General Time Travel

What would it be like to live at the time of the Civil War? Or to visit the age of the dinosaurs? What does the future hold? Time travel holds endless fascination for SF writers and readers. Titles in this section do not focus on a specific time period. Heroes may travel back and forth through time or may be caught outside of time.

Anderson, Poul. *The Boat of a Million Years.* 1989. Annotated on page 142.

Ballard, J. G. *The Crystal World.* 1966. A "disease of time" from outer space has come to Earth, specifically to a jungle in West Africa. As a result, all living organisms infected by the disease crystallize and are locked in a timeless zone.

Benford, Gregory. *Timescape.* 1979. With the fate of the world in the balance, scientists in the future manage to communicate with scientists in the past. In 1998, environmental disasters have become so severe that a scientist in Cambridge, England, manages to send a message back in time, warning the past of what is in store in the future. And a physicist in California gets the message in 1962.

> *Nebula Award.*

Benson, Ann. *The Plague Tales.* 1997. Annotated on page 88.

Bradley, Marion Zimmer. Darkover series. The following titles from the Darkover series involve time travel, which is possible because of the powerful laran, or special mental abilities, that many members of the ruling families on this strange dark planet develop and use against a backdrop of feudal class distinctions. Laran can enable its users to travel on the spirit plane, to go back and visit past generations, and even project what is going to happen in the future, depending on the strength and the skill of its users.

> *The Sword of Aldones.* 1962. Annotated on page 13.

> *Star of Danger.* 1965. Annotated on page 12.

> *The Spell Sword.* 1974. Annotated on page 13.

Goonan, Kathleen Ann. *The Bones of Time.* 1996. Cen, a young runaway in Honolulu in 2007, is bewitched by visits from Kaiulani, the last princess of Hawaii. A romantic obsession develops, leading him on a mathematical trail to achieve time travel.

Hogan, James P. *The Proteus Operation.* 1985. Annotated on page 115.

Leiber, Fritz. *The Big Time.* 1961. Recently re-released, this novel demonstrates that "You can't time travel through the time you time travel in when you time travel." Leiber's time travelers are humans who are being used to fight in a war between two groups of aliens, the Spiders and the Snakes. Wounded soldiers, doctors, and even entertainers are locked in a room that is outside the time stream. Unfortunately, an atomic bomb is locked in the room with them, and the bomb is ticking down.

Hugo Award.

Silverberg, Robert. *Project Pendulum.* 1989. In the year 2016, twins Sean, a math whiz, and Eric, a paleontologist, take part in an incredible time-travel experiment. Sitting at opposite ends of a pendulum, they swing back and forth in time, from 0 to 95 million years, into both the past and the future. Episodic vignettes describe what happens to them during the various pauses they make on their journey.

Tepper, Sheri S. *Beauty.* 1991. Beauty, of *Sleeping Beauty* fame, is abducted and taken forward in time to the horrors of an overpopulated, heavily polluted twenty-first century. Eventually she makes herself seven-league boots for a safe return to her own time, discovers that her body ages during these magical trips, and lives through a number of fairy tales as she seeks to save beauty in the world. Although the mode is fantasy, the futuristic journey can arguably make it science fiction.

Vonnegut, Kurt. *Slaughterhouse Five, or, The Children's Crusade.* 1968. Billy Pilgrim, suburban optometrist, becomes "unstuck" in time and flits randomly through the experiences of his life, from the Dresden bombing to an extraterrestrial zoo where he befriends Montana Wildhack.

Wells, H. G. *The Time Machine.* 1895. This beautifully written science fiction masterpiece is narrated by a time traveler who has gone forward in time to a world in which fragile, delicate, childlike Eloi are helpless against the depredations of the subterranean Morlocks, then even farther forward to a breath-taking vision of a dying Earth.

Way Back—Way, Way Back

The past holds many intriguing questions—from the mysteries of the Big Bang and prehistory to Atlantis, the Middle Ages, and the age of exploration. Travel to the distant past in SF is usually informed by current scientific theories about the past and often results in a mind-bending paradox or a soul-stretching moral dilemma. These heroes travel backward in time to discover new truths and insights about a past we thought we knew.

Adams, Douglas. *Life, the Universe and Everything.* 1982. Annotated on page 176.

Anthony, Piers. *Orn.* 1971. To escape from the forces of the government, the protagonists of *Omnivore* flee back in time. There they discover that they must find a way to communicate with the "Orn," a prehistoric bird, before it is too late.

Bishop, Michael. *No Enemy But Time*. 1981. The protagonist, a black American, goes back in time 2 million years, to study African apes evolving into humans. He gets so involved with the apes that he winds up marrying a beautiful hominid.

Nebula Award.

Butler, Octavia. *Kindred*. 1979. A modern African-American woman suddenly finds herself transported back in time, not to study, but to actually experience slavery—firsthand.

Card, Orson Scott. *Pastwatch: The Redemption of Christopher Columbus*. 1996. In the Earth's heavily polluted future, researchers discover that they are no longer limited to merely studying and observing the past; they can interact with it and even make changes. But if they do, they will change the future. Would going back in time and changing events around Christopher Columbus erase slavery and ensure a peaceful future, or will it destroy humanity?

Crichton, Michael. *Timeline*. 1999. Could quantum teleportation work as a type of time travel to transport people to parallel universes? A group of archaeologists go back to fourteenth-century France to try to extricate their leader from the past in which he is trapped. Anthropologists have only dreamed of experiencing the past first-hand, until quantum technology in the twenty-first century makes it possible to actually go back and walk the streets of a feudal village. But that dream becomes a nightmare for the team sent back to the "feudal ages" when their guide is killed and they find themselves stranded in time.

deCamp, L. Sprague. *Lest Darkness Fall*. 1949. Martin Padway, thrown back in time from the twentieth century, tries to prevent the fall of Rome and the advent of the Dark Ages.

Dunn, J. R. *Days of Cain*. 1997. Most of the researchers in the future have accepted the restrictions that limit them to watching, but not interacting with, the past. But Alma Levine and her followers have taken a stand. They plan to wipe out the abomination that is the Holocaust. As Alma works from within, an inmate in an infamous death camp, researchers discover that our future prosperity depends on past suffering. So the Holocaust must not be tampered with—at all costs.

Finney, Jack. *Time and Again*. 1970. Si Morley, a commercial artist, is recruited by a government-sponsored time travel project to travel back to the winter of 1882 in New York City. Once there, he makes sketches and takes photographs to bring back, as proof that he did indeed make the trip. He also falls in love, but the course of true love cannot run true when one party's presence in the past can alter the present and future.

From Time to Time. 1995. Si is asked to go back in time and try to prevent World War I.

Murphy, Pat. *The Falling Woman.* 1987. A middle-aged archeologist, studying the ancient Mayan civilization, discovers that she can see and speak with persons from the past in this most unusual treatment of "time travel."

  Nebula Award.

Silverberg, Robert. *Letters from Atlantis.* 1990. Time-traveling researchers visit the fabled halls of Atlantis, but they do not make the trip in their physical bodies. Instead, they share the minds of individuals who are involved in the final tragic days of the fabled island kingdom. In the process they discover that even knowing what is going to happen in the future doesn't mean that you can change the past.

Simpson, George. *The Dechronization of Sam Magruder.* 1996. Annotated on page 9.

Willis, Connie. *Doomsday Book.* 1992. A researcher is delighted when she is selected to travel back in time to the Middle Ages. Unfortunately, her trip is calibrated incorrectly, and she arrives during the Black Plague. And she arrives sick, in the early stages of an influenza that was sweeping through London before she left. As she is being nursed back to health in the past, the university that houses the time travel organization is closed for the duration of the epidemic, which means that even when she gets well, she has no way to get back home.

  Hugo, Nebula, and Locus Awards.

Willis, Connie. *Lincoln's Dreams.* 1987. Willis takes us back in time to the Civil War. The method of travel in this case is a psychic link with General Robert E. Lee or someone very close to him. The protagonists visit the sites of several major battles in an effort to find out whose dreams they are experiencing.

Wilson, Robert Charles. *The Chronoliths.* 2001. The Chronoliths are tall pillars that suddenly appear from out of nowhere in the twenty-first century, laying waste to wilderness or population centers, depending upon where they land. At the base of each Chronolith is an inscription commemorating a military victory —16 years into the future. Why and how are they suddenly appearing? What does this mean? Scott is a slacker, living in Thailand and getting by on minimal effort. He doesn't want to get involved; he just wants to keep out of the way and rebuild his life. But the Chronoliths won't let him.

Forward into the Future

  Traveling to the future can be an enlightening experience—if there is a future to go to. Confronting the future, we face all our hopes and fears, and we may learn a lesson about the present as well.

Asimov, Isaac. *The End of Eternity.* 1955. Time guardianship is the responsibility of Eternity, an organization that exists to better humankind. But when humankind always takes the safest route through time, our hero rebels against the resulting boredom.

Asimov, Isaac. *Pebble in the Sky.* 1950. The hero, a simple tailor, is catapulted forward into a future in which the Earth is under the control of the Galactic Empire. The "year 60 rule" is in effect as a form of population control. People over age sixty are considered to have nothing further to contribute to society and are therefore expendable. Euthanasia has become acceptable. Since there are no records to show that the sixty-two-year-old tailor has passed the critical age, he has an unprecedented chance to change things.

Asimov, Isaac, and Robert Silverberg. *The Ugly Little Boy.* 1992. The protagonist catapulted forward in time is a little Neanderthal boy, who suddenly finds himself in the twenty-first century. There he discovers that while the world he lives in has changed completely, human nature hasn't.

Barnes, John. *Kaleidoscope Century.* 1995. Annotated on page 143.

Delany, Samuel R. *The Einstein Intersection.* 1967. In the future depicted here, our reality intersects with that of another space-time continuum, resulting in colorful mutations. The protagonist, a telepathic boy with the gift of music, like Orpheus sets out to find his lost love.

> *Nebula Award.*

Heinlein, Robert A. *Farnham's Freehold.* 1964. After the bombs fall, Farnham and his family are thrown forward in time to an America ruled by Blacks where they experience prejudice and discrimination firsthand.

Leiber, Fritz. *The Big Time.* 1961. Annotated on page 48.

Niven, Larry. *A World Out of Time.* 1976. In an attempt to beat cancer, Jaybee Corbell had himself frozen. Two hundred years later he was awakened, not because a cure had been found but because he was needed to go on a mission to the stars—in someone else's body. Unwilling to let someone else dictate to him, Corbell heads his spaceship into the galactic core, where the fabric of time and space are distorted, giving him a chance to escape. When he returns to Earth, he discovers that he has escaped too well. Three million years have gone by while he was away, and everything has changed—except the fact that he is still in danger.

Vinge, Vernor. *The Peace War.* 1984. Annotated on page 109.

> *Marooned in Realtime.* 1986. To escape a depopulated Earth, these characters bobble into the future. A group of lonely survivors enter stasis bubbles, wait for a preset period of time to pass, and then stop and check to see if any scattered remnants of humanity are out there. But one of the leaders has been deliberately stranded in realtime and spends her life near the stasis bubble, waiting in vain for it to open and for her friends to come back to her. As the plot unfolds, a compelling murder mystery takes center stage.

Anthony, Piers, and Roberto Fuentes. *Dead Morn.* 1999. In the twenty-fifth century, humanity lives underground in the last city, until one man decides it's time for a change. The only way to alter the grim future that is his reality is to journey back to the past, to twentieth-century Cuba. There he hopes to be able to stop the nuclear conflagration before it happens—and save the world from becoming a nuclear wasteland.

Appel, Allen. Alex Balfour Series.

Time After Time. 1985. Alex Balfour is a history professor who immerses himself in various periods of time and then can travel back and visit them. In this instance he leaves his home in 1985 New York City to travel back to the Russian Revolution in 1918.

Twice upon a Time. 1988. Alex Balfour, that intrepid history professor, travels back in time to meet Custer and Mark Twain.

Till the End of Time. 1990. World War II is Alex Balfour's target in this novel, and he experiences it, from Pearl Harbor to Hiroshima. Along the way he meets such newsworthy individuals as Orson Welles, Rita Hayworth, JFK, Betty Grable and Phil Silvers.

Heinlein, Robert A. *The Door into Summer.* 1957. Dan Davis spends thirty years in suspended animation, tricked by his greedy fiancée and by his unscrupulous business partner. But when he wakes up in the year 2000, he discovers that he is not a helpless victim after all. He can actually travel back in time and get his revenge—if he wants to.

Mason, Lisa. *Summer of Love.* 1994. Chiron has been entrusted with an extremely important mission—to find and protect the fetus of a man who is vital to the future. And so he travels back in time to the Haight-Ashbury district of San Francisco in 1967, the "Summer of Love," the heyday of the Hippies. But the mother, Susan Stein, is a teenage runaway who has totally bought into the message of personal freedom and independence of the times. Chiron is willing to risk his own life to protect the mother and baby, but no one in the future warned him that having an abortion was one of the types of birth control practiced in the past.

Golden Nineties. 1995. Annotated on page 8.

Reed, Robert. *An Exaltation of Larks.* 1995. Time travelers visit the campus of a small college in the 1970s. One offers immortality, but only to a select few. The other works hard to undermine his efforts. And the students at the college are caught in the middle.

Willis, Connie. *To Say Nothing of the Dog, Or, How We Found the Bishop's Birdstump at Last.* 1997. Time-travel researchers try to find a hideous Victorian flower vase that disappeared the night Coventry Cathedral was bombed during World War II. When a new member of the team rescues a drowning cat and brings her forward in time, time begins to shift. Can they get the cat back to where she belongs—before it's too late? More on page 181.

Hugo and Locus Awards.

Willis, Connie. *Remake*. 1995. In a near future when all movies are digitized, a young woman goes into the past to dance in Hollywood musicals.

To Infinity and Beyond (Even to Mars)

Asprin, Robert, and Linda Evans. Time Scout Series. Annotated on page 34.

Time Scout. 1995. Annotated on page 34.

Wagers of Sin. 1996. Skeeter Jackson has to deal with ripples in time and an Earth that is considerably changed as a result in this sequel to *Time Scout*.

Ripping Time. 2000. Jenna Caddrick was seeking sanctuary from the terrorists who killed her fiancé, not realizing her flight through the time-touring gates of Shangri-La Station would place her in even greater danger. And now Skeeter Jackson has to go to Victorian London (where Jack the Ripper is really cutting up) in pursuit of the missing girl. Warning: This is half of a novel. It ends with "To Be Continued."

The House That Jack Built. 2001. In this breathtaking conclusion to *Ripping Time*, Jenna is still fleeing terrorists, Jack the Ripper is still cutting up, and Skeeter and Kit Carson have to work together to keep the killing spree from spreading across time.

Barnes, John. The Timeline Wars. Annotated on page 113.

Patton's Spaceship. 1997. A war is going on across a million alternate Earths. The ultimate goal? To enslave the universe. All that stands between humanity and destruction is a private eye from Pittsburgh and a ten-year-old child.

Washington's Dirigible. 1997. In this second volume of the adventures of Mark Strang, detective extraordinaire, he and the woman he loves go back in time to an alternative 1776.

Caesar's Bicycle. 1997. Another time-travel agent has disappeared, and Mark Strang has been asked to go back to the time of Julius Caesar and investigate. When he does, he discovers that the alien Closers have gotten to Caesar. Is it too late for him to stop the imminent Civil War, or is the rewriting of history already inevitable?

L'Engle, Madeleine. *A Wrinkle in Time*. 1962. Meg and Charles Wallace Murray, along with their friend Calvin, are off on a journey through space and time to find their missing father in this novel that has made many children life-long science fiction fans. The explanations of tesseracts and Mobius strips are woven into a fast-paced narrative that takes its young protagonists into one dangerous situation after another, until their triumphal return in the end. Other books in this children's series are annotated on page 210.

Newbery Award.

May, Julian. Galactic Milieu Series. Annotated on page 136.

Jack the Bodiless. 1992. The Galactic Milieu is an association of races that are psychically gifted. Humanity is rapidly being merged with them, and the powerful Remillard family is at the forefront. But something wants to destroy them at the same time that Jack, super powerful but a genetic wreck, must take an extreme step to rid himself of cancer.

Diamond Mask. 1994. Dorotea is a powerful metaphysic woman who becomes the Diamond Mask and the bone of contention between Jack the Bodiless and the madman Fury. Because she manages to survive their battle, she discovers just how powerful her own extraordinary powers are.

Magnificat. 1996. Jack's brother Marc Remillard, obsessed with human superiority, plans to brutally force the enhancement of mental faculties. The only ones who can stop him are Jack the Bodiless and the young woman known as the Diamond Mask. And if they do, they will pave the way for the Golden Age of the Galactic Milieu to begin.

May, Julian. Intervention Series. Annotated on page 136.

The Surveillance. 1988. After the technology of death is mastered in 1945, children with powerful mental abilities are born, metaphysic operants who have the power to rule the world. But the danger is that superhuman talents can be misguided, potentially as destructive as the atom bomb.

Metaconcert. 1988. In this sequel to *The Surveillance*, a struggle erupts between the metaphysics dedicated to peace and harmony and those who are intent on spreading evil. To the winners go the spoils—the future status of Earth among the alien peoples of the Galactic Milieu.

May, Julian. The Saga of Pliocene Exile. Julian May takes a group of travelers back in time to Pliocene Europe in this series of four novels. This is the struggle between the Tanu and Firvulag, the cruel versus the warrior mentality. The travelers are misfits from the Galactic Milieu, who have their hands full.

The Many Colored Land. 1981.

The Golden Torc. 1982.

The Nonborn King. 1983.

The Adversary. 1984.

Niven, Larry. *Rainbow Mars.* 1999. Annotated on page 180.

Norton, Andre. Time Traders Series. The adventures of an intrepid band of time travelers.

The Time Traders. 1958. Ross Murdock must discover the source of alien technology being used by the Russians, and to do so he must travel back in time nearly 4,000 years.

Galactic Derelict. 1959. The only way to really investigate an alien spaceship wrecked in prehistoric time is to travel back to that time.

The Defiant Agents. 1962. The adventures continue.

Key Out of Time. 1963. "Ross Murdock, Gordon Ashe, and other members of the Terran settlement team travel back in time to investigate a civilization that once flourished on Hawaika, a world of shallow seas and archipelagoes."—Prospector Library catalog.

Norton, Andre, and P. M. Griffin. *Firehand*. 1994. That's the name that Ross Murdoch of the Time Traders now goes by. This time he and his teammates have come to the planet Dominion to avert a tragedy in the past by helping the populace fight a guerrilla war against the Baldies.

Shared Worlds

Although more common in fantasy than in science fiction, the shared world, a collaboration of authors either working together or building on the work of another author, does appear in SF. Many shared worlds are based on characters and worlds created for film or video games. Often shared world stories are published in anthologies that are edited by the originator of the world. Others are published as novels, sharing a setting or milieu with the forerunner. These books may be specially packaged and marketed by publishers. Comics and graphic novels are two other forms that have grown in popularity by leaps and bounds in recent years. Manga (a distinctive type of Japanese comic book) and anime (an equally distinctive type of Japanese cartoon) have also spawned some shared world novels. Carefully regulated world-building is characteristic. Working within the confines of a carefully mapped out universe, continuing the adventures of popular characters for fans who know this world inside and out and can spot the slightest deviation, can be challenging for the multiple authors, but the result is pure enjoyment for the fans.

Star Wars and *Star Trek* are the predominant shared worlds, both with origins in the mass media—one on the big screen and one on the small. Both have taken on lives of their own with all kinds of offshoots, including novels set in their fully imagined worlds.

Because we are going to examine specific worlds that various talented authors contribute to, the organization of this section reflects the world names rather than the author names. However, the order of the shared worlds is alphabetical by author name, with the exception of the computer/video section, in which originators are not known. Thus, instead of an alphabetical listing of the works by author and titles, the focal point is the worlds and their creators/contributors. Within each shared world section, titles are listed chronologically.

Isaac Asimov/Foundation, Hari Seldon, and Trantor

The setting for Isaac Asimov's Foundation was a declining empire. It was an empire that did not fall into chaos, however, because of the science of psychohistory so carefully developed and nurtured by the genius Hari Seldon. He spent his life in the service of this science, and his society benefited because he could predict what was going to happen, when, and where. As a result, he was able to make contingency plans so that the events that did take place caused as little destruction as possible to the overall progress of society. The Foundation titles written by Asimov are annotated in Chapter 4. Listed here are titles in what is called the Second Foundation Trilogy, which covers Hari Seldon's career before the events described in the First Foundation Trilogy. These three novels set in the world created by Asimov are written by three major science fiction authors known as the Three Bs.

Benford, Gregory. *Foundation's Fear.* 1997. The first volume of the Second Foundation Trilogy introduces Hari Seldon, the leading candidate for first minister of the empire of Trantor. But like all heroes, Hari has enemies—because of his early work on the theory of psychohistory. To escape being murdered, he and his humaniform robot wife must flee to a primitive planet, where their minds are hidden in primate bodies until it is safe to return to Trantor.

Bear, Greg. *Foundation and Chaos.* 1998. The sequel to *Foundation's Fear* begins where the previous volume ended, with the trial and downfall of Hari Seldon. R. Daneel Olivaw is having his own problems with the robot community because the laws of robotics have been erased from the mind of one humaniform robot, creating a potential enemy of great power.

Brin, David. *Foundation's Triumph.* 1999. In this concluding volume Hari Seldon has managed to escape house arrest on Trantor to investigate the theory of chaos that is making nonsense of his psychohistory predictions. He risks everything for one final quest for knowledge and the power that comes with it.

Marion Zimmer Bradley/Darkover

Marion Zimmer Bradley is the creator of Darkover, a strange, dark planet with a feudal society that stood against the weapons and machines of Terran science and won. Their not-so-secret power is the mental power known as laran that occurs to some of the members of the ruling families. Talents like telepathy, telekinesis, teleportation, and others occur, usually in the teenage years. Those who possess those abilities must be carefully trained in how to use, and more important how to control, them to save their sanity in the face of outside and internal stress during their formative years. But once they come into their full power, especially those who work together in the towers of Darkover are virtually unbeatable. A classic case of mind over machine.

Bradley, Marion Zimmer, ed. An anthology of stories set in the world created by Bradley. Marion Zimmer Bradley edited several anthologies featuring the Darkover World.

The Keeper's Price. 1980.

Red Sun of Darkover. 1987.

Towers of Darkover. 1993.

Leroni of Darkover. 1991.

Renunciates of Darkover. 1991.

Snows of Darkover. 1994.

The following are novels co-authored by Bradley set on Darkover.

Bradley, Marion Zimmer, and Mercedes Lackey. *Rediscovery: A Novel of Darkover.* 1993.

Bradley, Marion Zimmer, and Adrienne Martine-Barnes. *Exile's Song. 1996.*

> *The Shadow Matrix.* 1997.

> *Traitor's Sun.* 1999.

Bradley, Marion Zimmer, and Deborah J. Ross. *The Fall of Neskaya.* Book One of The Clingfire Trilogy. 2001.

George Lucas/Star Wars

The books related to the *Star Wars* universe encompass a wide variety of styles, themes, and intended audiences. In addition to novels set in the world created by George Lucas, there are novelizations of his films, pop-up books, nonfiction guides to every conceivable aspect of that world, and novels for teens and children. Following is merely a sampling.

Anderson, Kevin J. *Darksaber.* 1995. A ruthless crimelord, Durga the Hutt, successor to Jabba, is having a new Deathstar constructed, the *Darksaber*. The creator of the original Deathstar is being forced to work on this new toy, a cylindrical superlaser that will make the Hutt players in the ongoing struggle between the Rebel Alliance and the recovering Empire.

Bear, Greg. *Star Wars: Rogue Planet.* 2000. Twelve-year-old Anakin Skywalker is proving to be quite a handful for young Jedi Knight Obi Wan Kenobi. The two are sent on a mission to the mysterious planet Zonama Sekot, famous for its live ships. The Jedi acquire a live ship just in time for it to save their lives. Others covet the secret of live ship production and will stop at nothing to obtain one, including murder. With the Blood Carver trying again to kill Anakin and Trade Federation forces assembled to attack, all seems lost. But the planet has its own secret and is not as helpless and undefended as the attackers have been led to believe. And it is not that easy to kill a Jedi, even one in whom the dark force of anger and revenge is beginning to stir.

Brooks, Terry. *Star Wars: Episode 1 the Phantom Menace.* 1999. Anakin Skywalker, a nine-year-old slave on Tatooine, wins his freedom by using his extraordinary talents and skills when two Jedi Knights stop on the planet for repairs.

Foster, Alan Dean. *Star Wars: The Approaching Storm.* 2002. This novel is a prequel to the action that takes place in the *Star Wars Episode II* movie. That movie opens with young Obi Wan Kenobi and his Padawan student, Anakin Skywalker, returning from a mission on another world. This is the story of that mission; of how the two dealt with a border dispute on the planet Anision.

Hambly, Barbara. *Children of the Jedi.* 1995.

Hambly, Barbara. *Planet of Twilight.* 1997.

Rusch, Kristine Kathryn. *The New Rebellion.* 1996.

Salvatore, R. A. *Vector Prime.* 1999.

Stackpole, Michael. *I, Jedi.* 1998.

Tyers, Kathy. *The Truce at Bakura.* 1994.

Wolverton, Dave. *The Courtship of Princess Leia.* 1994. Han Solo is not the only one interested in Princess Leia. Prince Isolder, with the help of his battle fleet, just may be the one to win her heart.

Zahn, Timothy. *Heir to the Empire.* 1991. Five years after the Republic's victory over the Empire, the Empire is trying to stage a comeback—and it has found the clone of a Jedi Master to help. This Jedi wants Luke, Leia, and her unborn twins to train in the power of the dark side. There are ambushes and an attack on the Wookie's home world where Leia is hiding. In the meantime, Luke is stranded in space and captured by "pirates."

Dark Force Rising. 1992. The struggle of the Federation and its rebel alliance against the Empire continues. The Dark Force is the Katana fleet, 200 dreadnoughts that disappeared centuries ago. The Emperor's Hand, Mara Jade, is exhibiting wild Jedi powers and still wants to kill Luke Skywalker, even while having to work with him.

The Last Command. 1993. The Dark Jedi C'baoth is working for the Empire, for a new Grand Admiral who has the Rebel alliance on the run again. In return, the Dark Jedi has been promised Luke, Leia, and their twins, but so far Chewie and Lando, ably assisted by R2D2 and C3PO, have been able to keep the babies safe. A new factor in the equation is the smugglers, under the leadership of Karrde and his apprentice Mara Jade, the former Emperor's Hand.

Zahn, Timothy, with Michael A. Stackpole. *Mara Jade: By the Emperor's Hand.* 1999. A graphic novel featuring an assassin who must complete her mission even after Luke has killed her employer.

Jedi Academy Series

Han and Leia are now married and have three children. The Jedi twins are beginning to show their powers, but the baby has to be kept hidden for its own safety. As the last Jedi Knight, Luke wants to start an academy to train others with sufficient talent to follow in his footsteps, but the site he chooses is haunted by the spirit of a former Sith lord whose attacks on Luke's students soon put the Empire in jeopardy.

Anderson, Kevin J.

Jedi Search. 1994.

Dark Apprentice. 1994.

Champions of the Force. 1994.

Young Jedi Knights

These are the action-filled adventures of Han and Leia's twins, now teenagers at the Jedi Academy, as they tackle enemies and save the universe—time and again.

Anderson, Kevin J., and Rebecca Moesta. These authors have written a number of books in this series, including the following:

Jedi Bounty. 1997. The planet Ryloth is headquarters for the Diversity Alliance. Young Lowbacca leaves the Jedi Academy to go there. He just wanted to satisfy his curiosity about the Alliance. But on Ryloth, if you don't join, you die. Time for the Jedi twins and the other young Jedi Knights to come to the rescue.

Trouble on Cloud City. 1998. It was a fun vacation on Cloud City for the Jedi twins, until they invited their new friend, Anja Gallandro, to come along, not realizing that she was using them to help hatch a sinister plan.

Crisis at Crystal Reef. 1998. Anja Gallandro, torn between her growing spice addiction and her friendship with the young Jedi twins she had originally planned to destroy, steals a ship and flees the Jedi Academy. But the twins follow, all the way to the dangerous beauty of the Crystal Reef.

Return to Ord Mantell. 1998. Han Solo takes his twins to Ord Mantell to watch a high-speed race. There they meet Anja Gallandra, a young woman wielding a lightsaber. But they don't know about the secret she is guarding, the secret that could have devastating consequences for Han and his entire family.

The Emperor's Plague. 1998. The leader of the Diversity Alliance knows where a deadly plague is hidden. If he releases it, the galaxy will be devastated. It's up to the young Jedi Knights to see that it doesn't happen.

The New Jedi Order

Twenty-one years ago the Rebel Alliance destroyed the Death Star and broke the power of the Emperor. Now the New Republic faces a new enemy, the Yuuzhan Vong, a sinister race of warriors, whose immense strength and technological edge makes them a formidable foe, even for the Jedi.

Salvatore, R. A. *Vector Prime*. 1999. Twenty-one years after the final defeat of the Empire, a new danger threatens civilization as the alien Yuuzhan Vong invade.

Luceno, James. *Agents of Chaos I: Hero's Trial*. 2000. Chewbacca's death throws Han into a deep depression.

Agents of Chaos II: Jedi Eclipse. 2000. Sinister aliens known as the Yuuzhan Vong threaten civilization as Luke, Leia, and Han all combat evil in their own ways.

Stackpole, Michael A. *Dark Tide I: Onslaught*. 2000. Leia attempts to convince the New Republic that the Yuuzhan Vong pose as serious a threat as the Empire and Darth Vader had twenty years before.

Dark Tide II: Ruin. 2000. Jedi Knights Jacen Solo and Corran Horn discover a secret that might be used to undermine the enemy on the occupied world of Garqi.

Tyers, Kathy. *Balance Point*. 2000. Refugees from the war with the Yuuzhan Vong are evacuated to the planet Duro, which is so polluted that the original inhabitants live in orbital colonies. However, the planet turns out to be in the direct path of the advancing forces.

Keyes, J. Gregory. *Edge of Victory I: Conquest*. 2001. Anakin Solo takes off on his own.

Anne McCaffrey/Brainships

In this future, medical technology is so advanced that it is possible to identify physically disabled children with an extremely high IQ as candidates for the brainship program. After years of intensive training, the twisted body of the trained human is wired into a spaceship in such a way that the ship becomes sentient, directed by a human brain. And the human has a body that works and can provide him or her with the freedom of the skies. But while the ship can fly itself, it needs a pilot or "brawn" for day-to-day operations. After a compatible brawn has been found, the adventures of this unusual couple serve as the basis for the novels in this shared world.

McCaffrey, Anne. *The Ship Who Sang.* 1969. The first brainship novel tells the story of Helva, who was born with multiple birth defects but had a brilliant mind, perfect for controlling a brainship. Once her body is mounted in the titanium column of a spaceship, she begins her search for the perfect brawn companion, a human pilot who must be accepted by the sentient ship before being assigned as her partner. Her adventures with various brawns are described, as well as her gift of song and the joy it brings her.

McCaffrey, Anne, and Mercedes Lackey. *The Ship Who Searched.* 1992. Tia, the daughter of noted archaeologists, is seven when she goes on a dig and finds an Eskay garbage dump, a discovery that leaves her paralyzed from the neck down, the victim of a strange "space" bug. By the time she receives medical attention, it is too late to do anything but put her on life support systems. The gifted neurosurgeon who works on her, paralyzed himself below the waist, insists that she be tested for brainship training. She is too old to even be considered for this program, but he has the clout to at least get her a fair trial.

McCaffrey, Anne and Margaret Ball. *Partnership.* 1992. Nancia, a brainship on her first mission in the elite Courier Service of Central Worlds, is to ferry five High Family scions out to their new assignments. During the trip these five disaffected young people concoct a plan to take over the universe in five years' time. Nancia overhears their plan, but because she has pretended to be a Drone ship, she cannot legally reveal what she knows. Only her semi-retired brawn can help Nancia work her way through the moral and physical dilemmas she faces.

McCaffrey, Anne, and S. M. Stirling. *The City Who Fought.* 1993. Simeon is the shellperson on Station SSS-900, a mining and processing station, but he longs to be transferred to a battle cruiser. Simeon had objected so strongly to any replacement for his retired brawn that when Channa comes on board, she feels that his behind-the-scenes lobbying might cost both her reputation and future. They have little time to settle down with each other before a derelict space station converted to a spaceship shows up, guided by a dying shellperson. On it are refugees from Bethel, which was attacked by the barbaric Kolnari. Simeon sends off an SOS to the fleet, but then Kolnari ships attack his station and he finds himself playing war games for real.

McCaffrey, Anne, and Jody Lynn Nye. *The Ship Who Won.* 1994. Carialle and her brawn Keff are into fantasy gaming. Specifically, she is his Lady Fair and he is her Knight Errant. They are delighted at what they find on the planet Ozran, at least at first. Their goal to establish first contact with a non-humanoid species has been accomplished. They see furry, animal-like peasants toiling away in fields and green frogs rolling around in globes full of water. But it is the Mages, who levitate around on their chairs, who are so appealing to fantasy gaming fans. Unfortunately, these Mages also toss real-life lightning bolts, poison the food, and manage to capture Carialle and Keff.

Nye, Jody Lynn. *The Ship Errant.* 1996. Carialle and her brawn Keff, found intelligent life in the galaxy in *The Ship Who Won.* Now they are serving as couriers for the "globe-frogs."

Stirling, S. M. *The Ship Avenged.* 1997. The sequel to *The City Who Fought* focuses on Joat, the adopted daughter of brawn and brain duo Channa Hap and Simeon.

Jack McKinney/Robotech

The Robotech series is based on the phenomenally successful *Anime* series of the 1980s. It is also a role playing game. All books in the series are by Jack McKinney, which is a pseudonym of Brian C. Daley and James Luceno.

McKinney, Jack. *Genesis.* 1987. The inventor of a robotic dimensional fortress is killed during a battle, after which his fortress disappears. While the Robotech army searches for it, the fortress reappears on Earth. There scientists begin to investigate, trying to discover what it is, while at the same time converting it to more "human" uses. After ten years, the Robotech forces find the fortress and attack Earth in an effort to get it back. It looks bad for Earth, except for the Veritech fighter pilots and the fact that the dimensional fortress itself can transform into a laser-zapping robot warrior of immense size. Other titles in this series include *Battle Cry, Homecoming, Battlehymn, Force of Arms, Doomsday, Southern Cross, Metal Fire, The Final Nightmare,* and *The Zentraedi Rebellion* (nineteenth title).

Larry Niven/Man-Kzin Wars

Poul Anderson, Greg Bear, Gregory Benford, Dean Ing, Jerry Pournelle, S. M. Stirling, and Mark O. Martin are among those who have written stories in this world, originally created by Larry Niven. The Kzinti are a militaristic race of catlike, space-faring warriors who are not happy when they run into the Federation. Several fans have put up Web sites in tribute to this universe and its inhabitants.

Niven, Larry. *Man-Kzin Wars.* 1988–1998. Volumes I to VIII contain an assortment of stories by various authors that cover the war between the feline Kzin and the apelike humans who keep defeating them.

Ing, Dean. *Cathouse.* 1990. This work contains two novels of the Man-Kzin Wars: *Cathouse* (1988) and *Briar Patch* (1989*)*. In *Cathouse* Locklear, a civilian, is marooned on a planet of zoolike compounds that have different atmospheres and environs suited to creatures of different worlds. They are filled with creatures trapped in stasis cages. Locklear discovers that his "neighbors" are Kzin. He awakens a few of the females, whom he thinks are less aggressive, but discovers that these are prehistoric Kzin, with females as intelligent and as aggressive as males. In *Briar Patch* Locklear investigates the human-type compound, only to discover that the stasis units contain prehistoric humans. The woman he releases is a Neanderthal who can read minds and emotions. Human pirates show up and terrorize both compounds until Locklear and his Kzin allies make a final stand.

Gene Roddenberry/Star Trek

It all started in 1966 with Gene Roddenberry's original television series featuring the adventures of Captain Kirk, Spock, Dr. McCoy, Scotty, Lt. Uhura, and others aboard the starship *Enterprise*. Four television series and nine movies later, *Star Trek* is still alive and well, not only in the hearts of dedicated Trekkers (sometimes to their chagrin called Trekkies) but in the universal consciousness of the world. The advent of e-books has been a real boon for fans of written *Star Trek* stories—virtually all titles are in e-print! Simon & Schuster has a comprehensive Web site for their *Star Trek* books at *http://www.simonandschuster.com/subs/index. cfm?areaid=44.*

Star Trek: Original Series

With nearly 100 titles by 2002, only a few titles are listed here to illustrate the range of authors and stories within the series.

Bear, Greg. *Corona.* 1984. The original U.S.S. *Enterprise* is on a rescue mission. A team of stranded Vulcan scientists has been taken over by the Corona, a sentient force of protostars with awesome abilities. Unfortunately, there is a new computer on the *Enterprise* that can override Kirk's command. As a result, the rescuers are faced with a threat to the entire universe—if Corona unleashes a Big Bang.

Cooper, Sonni. *Black Fire.* 1982. The Federation is under attack, the captain has been seriously injured, and Spock, with a sliver of metal next to his spine, sets out to find and defeat the enemy. Because of his actions, he and Scottie are court-martialed for "stealing" the ship. Spock is sent to prison for five years, where he is befriended by a Romulan but then escapes. Once free, he becomes a space pirate, the notorious Black Fire, who wears a strange iridescent black suit, serves as second in command to a Romulan leader, and plans to capture a starship, perhaps the *Enterprise.*

Crispin, A. C. *Sarek.* 1994. The story of Spock's father, Sarek, describes the death of Spock's Terran mother and addresses the latest threat to Federation peace, this time a Romulan conspiracy. The plot is a complicated one, with Vulcan telepaths working for and with Romulans to upset the balance of peace, and Klingons, subjected to mind control techniques, leading the battle against the Federation. The decline and death of Amanda Sarek, her husband's choice of duty rather than staying by her side, Spock's anger toward his father, and their eventual reconciliation are all deftly handled. Amanda's journal entries are fascinating and moving in turn, as are the glimpses into Sarek's hitherto inscrutable Vulcan mind.

Hambly, Barbara. *Ghost Walker*. 1991. The *Enterprise* picks up a ghost—or is it a poltergeist? At least that's what the crew thinks at first. Strange things are happening, crew members feel someone is looking over their shoulders, and an icy coldness descends, only to disappear as the ghostly presence moves on. The captain, not acting like himself, is withdrawn, abrupt, and then he attacks the woman he has fallen in love with, Dr. Helen Gordon, an archaeologist on temporary assignment to the *Enterprise*.

Kagan, Janet. *Uhura's Song*. 1985. When a plague strikes the world of the catlike Eeiauo and Uhura's friend is dying, Dr. McCoy and Nurse Chapel struggle to find a cure or to at least relieve the suffering of the victims. Uhura had exchanged forbidden songs with her friend in the past, and one of these proves to be the key for a last desperate effort to halt the plague. The *Enterprise* sets out to find the home world that the Eeiauo left centuries before, a world where they hope to find the antidote.

Morwood, Peter. *Rules of Engagement*. 1990. It's Captain Kirk of the *Enterprise* versus the Klingon commander whose career was ruined because of the Tribbles incident in this *Star Trek* novel. The action cuts back and forth between the two commanders. Kirk is in charge of evacuating Federation personnel from a planet whose government has been replaced by a military coup. The Klingon commander, Kasak, reduced to taking new vessels out for trial runs, steals a prototype vessel, a fully automated computerized warship with a separate and independent Bird of Prey scout, which acts as the command center for the warship. Kasak heads for the planet Dekkanar. His plan is to force the unsuspecting Kirk to fire on him, breaking the peace treaty and causing the planet to come under Klingon rule.

Reeves-Stevens, Judith. *Prime Directive*. 1993. The Prime Directive is Starfleet's most sacred commandment. Under no circumstances is it to be broken. But Captain Kirk has done the unthinkable, an action that has cost him his ship, his crew, and his reputation.

Sherman, Josepha, and Susan Shwartz. *Vulcan's Forge*. 1997. Uhura, now a commander on the *Intrepid II* under Captain Spock, is put in command when Spock and McCoy beam down to the surface of the planet Obsidian in response to a call for help. The call is from Captain David Rabin, assigned by Starfleet to planetary duty on Obsidian as the head of a small scientific outpost that has been hit with increasingly deadly acts of sabotage. David is delighted at the arrival of his old friend Spock. Their friendship was forged by the fiery Vulcan desert years ago, when a madman interrupted Spock's coming-of-age ritual and took as hostages Spock, the boy David, and his Starfleet captain mother. Spock's adventures continue in the sequel, *Star Trek: Vulcan's Heart*.

Vulcan's Heart. 2000. Jean-Luc Picard is one of the guests at the bonding ceremony of Spock and Savik.

Star Trek: The Next Generation

These are the adventures of the new *Enterprise* and its new crew: Captain Jean Luc Picard, Commander Riker, engineer Geordie La Forge, the android Data, the Klingon Worf as the security chief, Dr. Beverly Crusher, and the Betazoid counselor Deanna Troi. Their adventures are frequently more cerebral, prone to explore social issues and the stresses arising from exposure to different cultures than were the action-oriented exploits of the original crew.

David, Peter. *A Rock and a Hard Place*. 1990. While Commander Riker is on leave from the *Enterprise* to help terraformers in trouble on the brutal ice planet Paradise, Commander Quentin Stone, a man whose former captain describes him as a "loose cannon," takes over for Riker on the bridge of the *Enterprise*.

David, Peter. *Imzadi*. 1992. Forty years after the death of Deanna Troi, his "Imzadi" or beloved, Admiral Riker is still depressed. He keeps thinking of his first meeting with Deanna, how he saved her life, how she reached him on a spiritual plane unknown to him previously, how they made love in the jungles of her home planet but then were separated by the dictates of responsibility and their own insecurities about what the future would hold. When Riker discovers that Deanna was assassinated, he realizes that he is in the wrong timeline and must go back and save Deanna's life to put things right. But Data is in charge of the *Enterprise* in this timeline, and he's not about to let the life of one woman, even Deanna Troi, take precedence over the existence of an entire universe. So he sets out to stop Riker. As it turns out, a determined android is a very formidable foe.

David, Peter. *Q-in-Law*. 1991. The *Enterprise* will host a wedding between the son and daughter of two extremely competitive families. Because this is an important union, a number of ambassadors have been invited, including Deanna Troi's exotic mother, Lwaxana Troi. To make things even more interesting, Q shows up—to study the curious human mating rituals. And just for fun, he shows the boy what the girl will look like when she ages and the girl what the boy is thinking about the different girls he dances with—trouble in Paradise. Finally he makes a pitch for Madame Troi herself, only to discover that he has bitten off more than he can chew.

David, Peter. *Vendetta: The Giant Novel*. 1991. The Borg are back. But their advance is halted by a planet-eating machine that is able to destroy their ships with a special ray. Captain Picard discovers that the pilot of this machine is Vendetta, a woman he knew years ago at the Academy. Her ship is fueled by lost souls whose home world was destroyed by the Borg and who now live only for vengeance, but it also consumes great amounts of matter, including some planets that are already inhabited. The captain understands her desire to bring death and destruction upon the Borg, but will it stop there?

DeCandido, Keith R.A. *Diplomatic Implausibility*. 2001. Worf is sent on a diplomatic mission to the planet taD, a frozen world claimed by the Klingons but inhabited by people who want Federation recognition.

Friedman, Michael Jan. *Reunion*. 1991. Jean Luc Picard has a mystery on his hands involving an attempted murder during a reunion of former crewmen. One has been notified that his father is dead and as heir, he must leave Starfleet and return home. The others are accompanying him on the *Enterprise* as his bodyguards. But then someone tries to kill him and Picard.

Lorrah, Jean. *Metamorphosis*. 1990. Data achieves his heart's desire to become human, only to discover that it is not at all like he thought it would be. A strange power surge on a planet the *Enterprise* is investigating leaves Data human, with all the human frailties and weaknesses to go along with his new body. Now Captain Picard and the other members of the *Enterprise* can no longer depend on him. This new body is weak, he has memory gaps from the loss of his stored data, and he can no longer process and assimilate information at a super-human rate. Worst of all, an intergalactic war threatens, a war that he could prevent if only he weren't limited by human capabilities.

Star Trek: The Next Generation Excalibur

Captain Mackenzie Calhoun was recommended by Jean Luc Picard for command of the U.S.S. *Excalibur,* crewed by the best of Starfleet and stationed in a sector that has long been under the control of the cruelly militaristic Thallonians.

David, Peter. *Restoration*. 2000. Through an act of sabotage the *Excalibur* is destroyed. Captain Calhoun is missing, presumed blown to bits with his ship. But Calhoun is still alive, marooned on the primitive outback world of Yakaba, fighting a life-and-death battle against formidable adversaries.

David, Peter. *Renaissance*. 2000. The surviving members of the destroyed *Excalibur*, who have been dispersed throughout the galaxy, face a variety of challenges of their own.

Star Trek: Voyager

The starship *Voyager* was on a trial run when it went through a wormhole and became lost in space. Its crew, under the leadership of the extremely capable female Captain Janeway, is attempting slowly but surely to find its way back home. Nothing is ever easy, especially after they come to the attention of the Borg.

Golden, Christie. *Murdered Sun*. 1996. Captain Janeway and the crew get caught up in a war when they go to check out a possible wormhole and find the pillaging Akerians.

Wright, Susan. *Dark Passions*. 2001. Seven of Nine, who joined the *Voyager* crew after being rescued from the Borg, figures prominently in this tale set in a mirror universe, which also features Kira Nerys of *Deep Space Nine* and Deanna Troi of *The Next Generation.*

Star Trek: Deep Space Nine

Deep Space Nine, so named because it is the ninth attempt to establish a space station in deep space, is handed over to the Earth forces while an uneasy truce reigns between the forces of Cardassia and Bajor. Captain Sisko and his crew are faced with one challenge after another as they cope with a wide variety of transients as well as those who make their home on the station, like Quark, the Ferengi owner of the local bar; Garak, the Cardasian tailor cum spy; Odo, the shape-shifting head of security; Kira Nerys, the Bajoran second-in-command who is a former resistance fighter; and O'Brien, the engineer who left the *Enterprise* to help keep *Deep Space Nine* afloat.

Robinson, Andrew J. *A Stitch in Time*. 2000. The actor who played Garak on *Deep Space Nine* has written a fascinating book about what happens to this tailor (also spy, exile, and liberator) when he finally gets to go home again. After all these years of active participation in a war, Cardassia has become a planet of death and destruction, just waiting for the healing touch of this talented tailor.

Reeves-Stevens, Judith, and Garfield Reeves-Stevens. *Millennium.* 2000. Six years ago Bajor was in flames and battle raged through the corridors of Tarok Nor. Now the Federation is at war again—this time with the Dominion. With the war turning against the Federation, smugglers have come to Deep Space Nine to look for the lost Orb of the Prophets. It's up to Captain Benjamin Sisko to foil their plans and keep the fate that befell Tarok Nor from striking Deep Space Nine.

Computer and Video Games

Computer and video games, particularly those with science fiction and fantasy themes, are becoming increasingly popular. In these computer and video worlds, it is possible to fly X-Wing fighters in the *Star Wars* universe, struggle against the giant sand worms on the planet commonly known as Dune, and explore the fantasy worlds of Zelda and Myst. Some of these games are so popular that books are written to continue the adventures of favorite characters in well-known universes. Following are some examples.

Foster, Alan Dean. *The Dig.* 1997. A party of astronauts discover signs of an alien civilization when they try to reroute a mile-wide asteroid orbiting Earth. This is a novelization of the Lucas computer game of the same name.

Ohlander, Ben, and David Drake. *Enemy of My Enemy.* 1995. Two factions are at war, and the only solution may lie with a star-crossed couple. Based on the computer game *Terra Nova*.

Additional Computer and Video Games

Alien vs Predator. Games influenced by movies that were the basis of a series of books.

Babylon 5. Game based on cutting-edge television series. Novel tie-ins followed.

Blade Runner. The game and the movie title. The book is Philip K. Dick's *Do Androids Dream of Electric Sheep?*

Chronicles of Amber by Roger Zelazny.

Chronomaster. An adventure game with input by Roger Zelazny.

Come Hunt an Earthman. Game based on *Predator* movie and books.

Crescent Hawk's Inception. Mechwarrior game. Similar to the *Bolo Stories* by Keith Laumer.

Crescent Hawk's Revenge. Strategy game based on the *Mechwarrior/ Battletech* universe.

Dune. Based on the book of the same name by Frank Herbert.

Fahrenheit 451. Early game based on Ray Bradbury's classic novel of the same name.

Gateway and its sequel. Loosely based on the novels by Frederik Pohl.

The Hitchhiker's Guide to the Galaxy. Based on the hilarious works of Douglas Adams.

I Have No Mouth and I Must Scream. Based on a novella of the same name by Harlan Ellison. The author provided significant input to the game.

Jurassic Park. It's a game about dinosaurs. It's a movie about dinosaurs. It's a book by Michael Crichton about dinosaurs. (And the book came first.)

Lost World. Michael Crichton's sequel to *Jurassic Park.* From book to movie to game.

Mech Commander. A game in the *Mechwarrior* series. The books are the *Battletech* series.

Mechwarrior. A series of games to go with the *Battletech* books.

Neuromancer. Early game based on William Gibson's classic cyberpunk novel of the same name.

Pern. Game based on *Dragonriders of Pern* by Anne McCaffrey.

Rama. Based on the vast, cylindrical machine world of Arthur C. Clarke.

Ringworld and its sequel. Based on the *Heechee Saga* by Larry Niven.

Skynet. Another game based on the *Terminator* universe.

Starship Troopers. Based on Robert Heinlein's classic novel of the same name.

Star Trek. Borg. Deep Space Nine. Klingon Academy. The Next Generation. Star Fleet Battles. Star Fleet Command. Voyager Elicit Force. Games based on the television series and books.

Star Wars. Dark Empire. Dark Forces. Episode I: The Phantom Menace. Jedi Knight. Rogue Squadron. Tie Fighter. X-Wing. Popular games based on the *Star Wars* movies and books.

Terminator. From movie to book to game.

War of the Worlds. Early game based on H.G. Wells's classic novel of alien invasion.

X-Files. From television to books to adventure game.

Chapter 2

The Triumphs and Travails of Technology

That we now live in a high-tech world is obvious. Gadgets that seemed to belong solidly in the realm of science fiction only a few years ago are proliferating all around us today. More than half of all American homes have personal computers. E-mail has become a major form of communication. One is beset by the ringing of wireless telephones everywhere, and folks carry enough data in their pocket-sized PDAs (personal digital assistants such as Palm Pilots™ and Visors™) to fill a library.

Technology has become a major part of our lives. In the realm of science fiction, the high-tech world is taken to extremes. It can be the world of hackers like TerMight in Gresh and Weinberg's *Termination Node*. It can be the dark, bleak, gritty cyberpunk future of William Gibson's *Neuromancer*, with its dependence on drugs and riding the electronic pathways of a virtual reality universe, which became the inspiration for works by Bruce Sterling and Neal Stephenson, among others. Or it can be the more benign future featuring helpful robots as depicted by Isaac Asimov in his *I, Robot* and his robot novels, including the ones featuring his famous robot detective, R. Daneel Olivaw.

Paralleling the technological explosion of the mid-1980s, a new subgenre of SF arose: cyberpunk. Cyberpunk features an all-pervasive technology and the perversion of it by a rebellious and alienated underground subculture. Darkly cynical and moody, it could be compared to the mystery genre's hard-boiled or noirish subgenre. *Do Androids Dream of Electric Sheep?* (page 74), a 1968 title by Philip K. Dick from which the film *Blade Runner* was adapted, was a forerunner of modern cyberpunk. This subgenre came into its own with William Gibson's *Burning Chrome* and his award-winning *Neuromancer* (page 70).

By the end of the 1980s the subgenre was waning, but shortly afterward, in 1992, *Snow Crash* (page 78) was published, indicating that cyberpunk had not died after all. No longer the *enfant terrible* of the science fiction world, features of cyberpunk have been absorbed into other subgenres. In today's SF publishing world, it is just another theme appearing in many different areas of high-tech SF.

This chapter features titles that emphasize technology. Many of them are what are often called hard science or hard SF because focus is on science; science makes the story possible; and the science is consistent with physical laws and current scientific theory.

High Tech

Sophisticated technology provides focus in the following titles. They go far beyond what computers and technology can do today, often combining elements of artificial intelligence, self-replicating machines, and virtual reality. They are the offspring of cyberpunk and other less bleak visions of the future.

Anderson, Kevin J., and Doug Beason. *Assemblers of Infinity.* 1993. Colonists on the moon face imminent danger when massive structures constructed by intelligent beings are found on the lunar farside.

Baird, Wilhelmina. *Crashcourse.* 1993. Cass, Moke, and Dosh didn't know what they were getting themselves into when they signed a lucrative cybercinema contract to star in a film that enables the audience to plug into the stars' emotions.

Banks, Iain. *Excession.* 1996. Two millennia ago a star appeared—and disappeared again. Now the huge enigmatic Excession is back, but the only person who can solve this cosmic puzzle is not. She lived and died at the time of its first appearance. It will be difficult for her to help, unless the protagonist can convince her to be reborn—an act that could result in peace or annihilation.

Clarke, Arthur C. *The Fountains of Paradise.* 1979. A space elevator is constructed that extends far into space from the equator.

   Hugo and Nebula Awards.

Gibson, William. Neuromancer Trilogy

   Neuromancer. 1984. This seminal cyberpunk novel depicts a dark, bleak, drug-filled future. The computer cowboys get high by wiring themselves into terminals and taking a virtual ride through the data streams inside their computers. The protagonist, Case, is the best interface cowboy of them all. When he agrees to enter Earth's Computer Matrix for the wrong people, he is caught in the act and suffers the worst possible punishment: losing his ability to interface with his computer. But Case is a fighter, and now he must fight to get back what he has lost. This novel is the first triple crown winner of science fiction, receiving the Hugo, the Nebula, and the Philip K. Dick awards.

   Hugo, Nebula, and Philip K. Dick Awards.

   Count Zero. 1986. Returning to the world developed in the award-winning *Neuromancer*, this cyberpunk classic involves hi-tech industrial sabotage set against a dark, gritty future. Here the artificial intelligences of the first volume have taken the form of voodoo godlings as they travel through cyberspace.

Mona Lisa Overdrive. 1988. This cyberpunk sequel to *Neuromancer* and *Count Zero* extends the adventures of characters introduced in the previous novels, characters who inherit the same dark, gritty world of computers, artificial intelligences, and human hackers.

Perriman, Cole. *Terminal Games*. 1994. Terminal Games, a late-night Internet service, fulfills the wildest fantasies of subscribers all across the country. But now subscribers are dying under mysterious circumstances, and it looks like the detective in charge of the case has a lot to learn—about the Internet and the world of virtual reality.

Stephenson, Neal. *Cryptonomicon*. 1999. Annotated on page 9.

Stephenson, Neal. *The Diamond Age, or, a Young Lady's Illustrated Primer*. 1995. In twenty-first-century Shanghai, a nanotech engineer copies a powerful interactive computer book designed for the daughter of one of the neo-Victorian ruling class. When he is mugged, the copy falls into the hands of Nell, the sister of a young street tough, forever changing her life and the future of civilization.

> *Hugo and Locus Awards.*

Sterling, Bruce. *Islands in the Net*. 1988. Laura, a corporate woman, finds herself thrown into the whirlwind of an international power struggle in a near-future world where a global electronic net, or data linkage, covers the entire world. Areas of crime and electronic piracy are islands in this sea of information.

> *John W. Campbell Award.*

Williams, Walter Jon. *Aristoi*. 1992. Gabriel is one of the Aristoi, the next step in human evolution. Each Aristos must pass a series of grueling examinations; for those who succeed, the world is literally an open oyster shell. In fact, they have their own world, a virtual reality with domains to create and be responsible for. The story builds to a riveting climax as Gabriel uncovers a plot that could destroy the world of the Aristoi as he knows it. Once he sets out to bring the culprits to justice, he discovers that his actions, too, have brought about unforeseen changes. A stellar performance for fans of this genre, but a challenging read for those being introduced to Williams's world for the first time.

Wingrove, David. Chung Kuo Series. In the year 2190, the Chinese have become the dominant power on Earth and everyone on the planet lives in one of the one-per-continent, mega-huge cities ruled by the Seven T'ang.

The Middle Kingdom. 1989. City Earth, ruled by the Seven, China's new kings, faces the very real possibility of war, a violent conflagration between the forces of the East and the West, between the overlords and the rebels.

The Broken Wheel. 1991. To maintain their control in the face of a brewing revolution, the seven Chinese kings develop a bold plan to control the minds of humankind.

The White Mountain. 1991. The West is struggling to overthrow the Seven Chinese Capitalist overlords, the T'ang. But rather than be overthrown, the overlords are plotting a final solution to bring peace, no matter what the cost.

Stone Within. 1992. The Seven T'ang are warned that a fierce storm is approaching, so deadly it can destroy the world. But what is the origin of this danger: the increasingly hostile masses beginning to rebel, or the reckless search for the key to immortality?

Beneath the Tree of Heaven. 1993. A revolution against the T'ang is brewing on the planet Mars. In its aftermath, most of the planet's population will be destroyed.

White Moon, Red Dragon. 1994. As the T'ang dynasty begins to crumble, a revolution begins on Earth.

Days of Bitter Strength. 1995. The T'ang, Earth's dictators, are gone. But the Earth is still not free. Giant androids and an evil mega-corporation almost squash the dreams of a more humane world.

Marriage of the Living Dark. 1997. The Ten Thousand Year Empire of the Han lasted less than two centuries. But the world still struggles beneath the rule of a brutal dictatorship and callous warlords.

Robots, Cyborgs, and Androids

The creation of another being imparts some godlike qualities to the creator, making this an attractive area for the imagination. Mary Shelley's *Frankenstein,* considered by many to be the first science fiction novel, with its monster put together from various and sundry parts and re-animated by science, is a precursor of this subgenre.

There are three major types of artificial people. A *robot* is a machine, usually with a somewhat human form but purely mechanical. An *android* is an artificial human, organic in composition. A *cyborg* is a human altered with artificial parts to perform certain functions or modified to exist in conditions inimical to human life. The computer is essential to all three forms. Of course, many authors use these terms as they choose, demonstrating that dictionary definitions do not necessarily apply to fiction. Pervading all stories of robots, androids, and cyborgs is the often tricky problem of the relationship between human and machine.

Robots (mechanical men) are often portrayed in a manner that adheres to Asimov's three laws of robotics. These first appeared in his short story collection, *I, Robot*, and have been repeated in some of his other works about robots and in stories by other authors. The three rules follow:

1.   A robot may not injure a human being or, through inaction, allow a human being to come to harm.

2.   A robot must obey the orders given by human beings, except where such orders would conflict with the first law.

3.   A robot must protect its own existence as long as such protection does not conflict with the first or second law.

From Asimov to *Star Wars*, robots and their cousins have played an important role in human society. Although robots and robotic devices do exist today, the robots, cyborgs, and androids in the following works are more sophisticated than those now available and give intriguing hints of possible futures. Readers interested in these beings may also want to check Chapter 4, "Us and Them," which covers superhumans, aliens, and the like.

Anderson, Poul. *Harvest of Stars*. 1994. Downloaded personalities are pawns in a struggle between a religious dictatorship and an interplanetary corporation.

Anderson, Poul. *Harvest the Fire*. 1997. Conflicts between human and machine intelligences threaten to disrupt humanity's utopian future.

Anthony, Piers. *Out of Phaze*. 1987. Bane is an apprentice wizard from the magical world of Phaze. Mach is a self-willed robot from the technological world of Proton. In this fourth book in the *Apprentice Adept* series, Bane and Mach become the victims of an accidental mind switch.

Asaro, Catherine. *The Phoenix Code*. 2000. Robotics expert Megan O'Flannery is working in a secret lab to create a self-aware android for a national defense project. But Aris (the android) proves to be unpredictable, and Megan enlists the aid of robotics expert Raj Sundaram. Now her life may depend on her choice between Raj and Aris.

Asimov, Isaac. *I, Robot*. 1950. Asimov's famous three laws of robotics and robots powered by positronic brains were introduced in this classic short-story collection.

The Rest of the Robots. 1964. This vintage collection is the second volume, after *I, Robot*, of Asimov's timeless robot stories.

Robot Dreams. 1983. Twenty-one of Asimov's short stories about robots, spaceships, and computers are reprinted in this collection. Only the title story was an original.

The Complete Robot. 1982. All of Asimov's robot stories are collected in this one volume.

Asimov, Isaac. Elijah Baley and R. Daneel Olivaw Series.

> ### *Murder. Detection.*

The Caves of Steel. 1954. Working with a somewhat reluctant human partner, R. Daneel Olivaw, a robot, solves a murder committed in the corridors of an enclosed city. This is the novel that introduced Asimov's famous robot detective to the world.

The Naked Sun. 1957. Detective Elijah Baley, sent from the streets of New York with his positronic partner, robot R. Daneel Olivaw, must solve a murder on a planet where, unlike their previous case, they face wide-open skies as the setting for their investigation.

The Robots of Dawn. 1983. In this third installment of the investigations of Elijah Baley and his positronic robot partner, the inimitable R. Daneel Olivaw, the two detectives investigate a different kind of murder—that of a robot. During the course of their investigation on the planet Aurora, they meet Giskard, a telepathic robot, who turns out to be a link between Asimov's robot novels and those set in his Galactic Empire.

Asimov, Isaac. *Robots and Empire.* 1985. The human, Lije Baley, is now dead. But positronic robot detective Daneel and telepathic robot Giskard are still active and involved in developments that will affect the Galactic Empire. This is the sequel to *The Robots of Dawn* (above) and the prequel to Asimov's Foundation series.

Asimov, Isaac, and Robert Silverberg. *The Positronic Man.* 1992. A novelization of Asimov's short story "Bicentennial Man," this is the story of Andrew Martin, a robot who strives for human status.

Benford, Gregory. *Tides of Light.* 1989. The sequel to *Great Sky River* continues the ongoing struggle between the machine culture and humans. But this time cyborg entities have entered the fray as well. Other titles in the Galactic Center series are listed on page 152.

Budrys, Algis. *Who?* 1958. Soviet doctors treat and "repair" an American scientist who has been badly injured in an explosion. After he recovers, he returns to the United States. But a question arises on his return: Just exactly who is he? Part cyborg, he is now so modified that it is impossible to verify his identity. A Cold War thriller that addresses issues of alienation and dehumanization.

Capek, Karel. *R. U. R.* 1923. The initials R. U. R. stand for Rossum's Universal Robots. This is the play that first introduced the term robots to the world of science fiction.

Dick, Philip K. *Do Androids Dream of Electric Sheep?* 1968. In this bleak, chilling look at the future, the world faces rampant pollution, radioactive fallout, and overpopulation. Possession of an android servant or a live animal is considered a status symbol. And if you're too poor to own a live animal, there are always electric substitutes, like the sheep in the title. But some androids attempt to impersonate humans. This makes them fair game for bounty hunters like Rick Deckard, who works for the San Francisco police department and receives $1,000 for each body he turns in. He can capture or kill them, but he certainly didn't expect to fall in love with one of them. This is a precursor of cyberpunk and the inspiration for the movie *Blade Runner.*

Hoover, H. M. *The Winds of Mars*. 1995. Is the president of Mars really an an- droid? More on page 198.

Mason, Lisa. *Arachne*. 1990. A robot therapist plays a role in this cyberpunk novel that features an attorney working in telespace, where something or someone is stealing human souls.

McKinney, Jack. Robotech series. Annotated on page 28.

Pohl, Frederik. *Man Plus*. 1975. Humans are turned into cyborgs to enable them to live on Mars, but are the trade-offs worth it? When an astronaut is specially engineered to be able to survive on Mars, he becomes more than human. Generally considered one of the finest treatments of the cyborg theme.

> *Nebula Award.*

Saberhagen, Fred. Berserker series annotated on page 78. Future robots that war on humanity.

Shelley, Mary Wollstonecraft. *Frankenstein; Or, the Modern Prometheus*. In this novel, first published in 1818, Dr. Victor Frankenstein creates life using body parts and electricity. This complex gothic novel is considered by many to be the first science fiction novel. The combination of human parts and electricity makes the monster a cyborg.

Simak, Clifford D. *City*. 1952. A robot named Jenkins, dogs with evolving intelli- gence, and cities being deserted for pastoral pleasures are at the center of this classic.

Sterling, Bruce. *Schismatrix Plus*. 1996. Includes the novel *Schismatrix* (1985) and collected stories set in the same universe where the Shapers, who prefer genetic enhancements, are pitted against the Mechanists, who rely on prosthetics.

Williamson, Jack. *The Humanoids*. 1949. The classic novel of constructed people who, although created to serve people, instead create tyranny. The human- oids are intelligent robots in this sequel to Williamson's famous 1948 short story "With Folded Hands." Charged with protecting their human masters from all harm, the humanoids have instituted such a tyranny of kindness that humans are left with no choice but to rebel. Considered by many to be the author's best novel, this book was followed with a sequel three decades later: *The Humanoid Touch*. 1980.

Computers

Computers have gone from being the rare room-sized Univac popular in mid-twentieth-century SF to the pervasive and compact personal essentials they are today. But science fiction has not abandoned computers as a theme. Instead they are pushed to the farthest limits of the author's imagination. The computer is capable of an amazing number of ingenious functions under human programming, but in the hands of some science fiction authors it achieves sentience. So well does it think and plan and even reproduce itself that in some stories it makes humanity unnecessary and precipitates a future in which the machines hum contentedly and people are obsolete. Whether humans and computers will live in cooperative harmony or in a master-slave relationship is a controversial theme for science fiction authors. The idea that the machine-computer or robot may end up running human society is a recurrent theme. Underlying this worry the ultimate question remains: Is science a blessing or a curse for humanity? The idea of a completely automated society is often analyzed in a similar manner. The following books present some aspects, both intriguing and disturbing, of our coexistence with the computer.

Anthony, Piers. *Juxtaposition.* 1982. There is a games computer on the planet world Proton, a world that relies heavily on the use of technology. And on the planet Phaze, a world that relies heavily on the use of magic, there is an oracle. Can the games computer and oracle be one and the same? Third in the popular Apprentice Adept series. (See page 111.)

Brunner, John. *The Shockwave Rider.* 1975. It comes as no surprise to discover that in the twenty-first century the world has become highly computerized. It may also come as no surprise to discover how rigid and controlling the system has become. But there is one man who is going to rebel, using the computers themselves to fight the system.

Card, Orson Scott. Homecoming Series. In this series a powerful computer called the Oversoul has been put in charge of governing the human colony on Planet Harmony. But after a million years, the Oversoul begins showing signs of age. Now it must be returned to the master computer, Keeper of Earth, to be repaired—or Harmony will be destroyed (http://www.hatrack.com).

The Memory of Earth. 1992. Annotated on page 122.

The Call of Earth. 1992. Annotated on page 122.

The Ships of Earth. 1994. Annotated on page 122.

Earthfall. 1995. Annotated on page 122.

Earthborn. 1995. Annotated on page 122.

Clarke, Arthur C. *The City and the Stars.* 1956. In the distant future a high-tech city gradually reawakens to the possibility of growth and even space flight. This elegy was originally published in a shorter version as "Against the Fall of Night," which appeared in *Startling Stories* in November 1948.

Clarke, Arthur C. *2001: A Space Odyssey.* 1968. Annotated on page 36.

Clifton, Mark, and Frank Riley. *The Forever Machine.* 1955. A supercomputer named "Bossy" has the ability to help humans develop psi powers and longevity. *They'd Rather Be Right* was the original title of this typical 1950s tale of the future, first appearing in serial format in *Astounding SF* in 1954.

> **Hugo Award.**

Dunn, J. R. *This Side of Judgment.* 1994. Annotated on page 170.

Gresh, Lois H., and Robert Weinberg. *The Termination Node.* 1999. Judy Carmody, whose hacker name is TerMight, is so good that she helps banks spot flaws in their security systems. She's on the job when a hacker makes a sudden withdrawal, puts it all back, and moves on. Who was the intruder, what kind of system was he testing, and why? Then two men come to Judy's apartment and try to kill her. She escapes, but they kill her landlord and blame her for it, so now she's on the run, from the authorities as well as the two assassins. With other hackers turning up dead, it looks as though her only hope is the legendary hacker, Griswald, if she can only find him before it's too late.

Shatner, William. Quest for Tomorrow Series.

Delta Search. 1997. Jim carries secrets hidden in his DNA. He doesn't know anything about these secrets or the mystery surrounding his birth. All he knows is that someone has just killed his father and kidnapped his mother. It's a miracle that he's still alive—but for how much longer? Commander Steele and her battle troops want Jim dead, but somehow he manages to escape. Then, with the help of some Plebes (in particular Cat, a female fighter par excellence), he begins to unravel the mystery surrounding his birth. But why has someone made repeated attempts to murder him?

In Alien Hands. 1997. On the planet Wolfbane, sixteen-year-old Jim says goodbye to Cat, his girlfriend, only to discover that he's wanted by rival aliens who are after the key to Earth's top secret computer systems. The key to these mind arrays is encoded in Jim's DNA. When the conflict between the aliens leads to war, the future of humanity is in danger in this second entry in the Quest for Tomorrow series.

Step into Chaos. 1999. Installment three has Jim returning to Earth after a stint as a mercenary on other worlds. Now seventeen and full of guilt over the accidental death of his father, he tries to drown his sorrows in alcohol. But aliens are once again bent on destroying the Earth, and Jim is the key to our defense.

Beyond the Stars. 2000. In number four in the Quest for Tomorrow series, Jim has become one with the Omega Point and used the resulting power to alter his past and save the lives of his parents. But now everything is different. This altered Jim is barely aware of his vast Omega powers, until he once again faces a danger that can only be met by calling upon them.

Stephenson, Neal. *Snow Crash.* 1992. Snow Crash is a metavirus, a drug, and to the members of Reverend Wayne's Pearly Gates, a religion. In all three forms it is extremely destructive, resulting in crashed computers, leaving hackers in a coma, and spreading like wildfire. The protagonist of this zany cyber fest is Hiro Protagonist, a hacker beyond compare. As far as Hiro is concerned, the United States does four things better than anyone else in the world: music, movies, microcode (software), and high-speed pizza delivery.

It's Alive! Artificial Intelligence

"I think, therefore I am." As computers are programmed to learn and grow on their own, is there a chance that they will develop sentience? At what point does the machine become a conscious being? In SF, the computers sometimes become so smart they start making new computers. One of the dilemmas that often crops up in SF is the status of sentient computers: slave or free? As in stories involving humans creating robots, androids, and cyborgs, the stories involving Artificial Intelligence (AI) often examine the conflict involved in becoming godlike. Could it be that the first "aliens" we encounter are not from a distant planet, but are the fruit of our own technology? The common thread in the following titles is the presence of a computer, in whatever form it may take, that is sentient, conscious, self-aware.

Anthony, Piers. *Ox.* 1976. The protagonists of *Omnivore* and *Orn* (1971; annotated on page 49) find that they must learn how to communicate with a machinelike intelligence.

Asaro, Catherine. *The Veiled Web.* 1999. After being kidnapped together, Lucia del Mar, a beautiful world-class ballerina, and Rashid al-Jazari, a high-tech Moroccan inventor/businessman, leap into a marriage. Adjusting to life in Rashid's family's harem, Lucia befriends an AI Rashid created and experiments with a virtual reality suit that infuses the body of the wearer with nanotech, creating a VR experience that allows touch, smell, and taste to manifest. After Lucia decides to leave Rashid, they are attacked and Lucia must use VR to help defeat the villains, fully knowing that in the wrong hands this wonderful technology could wreak havoc on the world.

   Romance.

Barnes, John. *Mother of Storms.* 1994. Annotated on page 90.

Dunn, J. R. *Full Tide of Night.* 1998. Julia Amalfi, accompanied by her young artificial intelligence companion Cary, fled a dying Earth generations ago and settled on the planet Midgard. The planet has since become a haven for humanity, due to the salvaged genetic stock Julia brought with her. But now, after all this time, the inhabitants of Midgard have risen against Julia, demanding the freedom to rule themselves. At the same time, the destroyers of the Earth have finally located this last outpost of humanity and danger looms over Midgard.

Saberhagen, Fred. Berserker Series. "Long ago, in a distant part of the galaxy, two alien races met—and fought a war of mutual extinction. The sole legacy of that war was the weapon that ended it: the death machines, the BERSERKERS. Guided by self-aware computers more intelligent than any human, these world-sized battlecraft carved a swath of death through the galaxy—until they arrived at the outskirts of the fledgling

Empire of Man."—Saberhagen's Berserker Web site (http://www. berserker. com/bk_berserker. htm). Sabehagen's Berserker universe includes nine novels and scores of short stories.

Novels

Berserker. 1967. The eleven stories in this first volume of the Berserker series are set against the backdrop of an alien invasion. The Berserkers are giant automatic warships bent on the destruction of all life.

Berserker Blue Death. 1985. In this entry in the Berserker Series, one man and one machine battle to the death.

Berserker Fury. 1997. More battles between the Berserkers, smart machines who roam the galaxy seeking out and destroying organic life, and the "badlife," those beings (like humans) who resist extermination.

Berserker Kill. 1993. A space bioresearch station containing a million human embryos is carried off by the Berserkers. A fleet goes in pursuit, but the rescuers wind up drifting into the dark nebula.

Berserker Man. 1979. The Berserker have come back for revenge. This time the fate of humanity rests in the hands of a child who is half man and half machine.

Berserker's Planet. 1975. In this novel, set in the Berserker universe, one of these destructive robots sets itself up as a god, which leads to a number of violent confrontations.

Berserker Throne. 1985. For thousands of years, humans have been fighting against the Berserkers. Now one man may have found the code that can defeat them. But will he use it to try to gain power instead?

Shiva In Steel. 1998. The war between the Berserkers and the humans had reached a stalemate. But then the Berserkers created a new tactical computer, code name Shiva. The fate of humankind rests on the shoulders of a small group of people on the remote planet of Hyperborea.

Short Story Collections

Berserker Base. 1985. This is a shared world anthology of Berserker stories written by various authors besides Saberhagen.

Brother Assassin. 1969. Time travel is the theme this time as Berserker war machines plan to travel through time to kill a pivotal scientist in history.

*Berserker Lies.*1991. More Berserker adventures, involving truth and lies.

Berserker Wars. 1981. The Berserkers, defeated at Stone Place, scatter and spread terror to other planets after the fall of the hero Karlsen.

The Ultimate Enemy. 1979. Once again the ultimate enemy, the Berserker killing machines, battles against humanity.

Slonczewski, Joan. *The Children Star.* 1998. Annotated on page 130.

Steele, Allen M. *The Jericho Iteration.* 1994. Less than fifteen years from now, a down-on-his-luck investigative reporter, Gerry Rosen, is tracking a major story about a corrupt corporation poised to unleash a sinister artificial life form on earthquake-devastated St. Louis. Suddenly people around him begin to die. Now he must become a fugitive or die himself.

Sullivan, Tricia. *Dreaming in Smoke.* 1998. Kalypso Deed is a shotgun, riding the interface between the AI Ganesh and human scientists who solve problems through cyber-assisted dreams. But she's young and a little careless; she'd rather mix drinks and play jazz. Azamat Marcsson is a colorless statistician: middle-aged, boring, and obsessed with microorganisms. A first-class nonentity—until one of his dreams implodes, taking Kalypso with it.

>   *Arthur C. Clarke Award.*

Teller, Astro. *Exegesis.* 1997. Alice Wu, a graduate student working on the Edgar (Eager Discovery Gather and Retrieval) software project, planned to design a device that would browse the Web and summarize the information it found for the user. What she got was Edgar, an entity who began to talk back to her and who constantly demanded more reading matter. The novel consists of e-mail exchanges, primarily between Alice and Edgar, but including messages from a few other figures in Alice's life.

Zebrowski, George. *The Stars Will Speak.* 1985. Humankind has been receiving a signal from the stars for some time and, without knowing for sure what the messages mean, has been responding. A special college has been set up where students study at their own pace with the aid of a personal AI computer and tutorials to try to understand the messages. Seventeen-year-old Lissa has always wanted to be the one to make the breakthrough, and she is delighted to be accepted into the college. Then she meets Alek.

Zettel, Sarah. *Fool's War.* 1997. Katmir Al Shei, a ship's captain, is just trying to do her job; professional fool Evelyn Dobbs is just trying to save her people from a rogue AI.

Nanotechnology: It's a Small World

Nanotechnology has been defined as "the science and technology of building electronic circuits and devices from single atoms and molecules" (Microsoft Bookshelf 98), but it is often used in science fiction to describe situations involving extreme miniaturization, and it usually involves multitudes of tiny machines or beings that work together.

Nanotechnology can bring down a spaceship and cause an entire planet to take flight, as in Greg Bear's *Moving Mars.* Miniaturized bugs can drive a brilliant scientist mad in the same author's *Blood Music.* This research provides infinite possibilities for a brighter future or infinite nightmares of a world out of control and society at the mercy of the brilliant but unstable, unscrupulous, perhaps even immoral few.

Asimov, Isaac. *Fantastic Voyage.* 1966. Annotated on page 33.

Bear, Greg. *Moving Mars.* 1993. When conflict between Earth and Mars escalates into war, the only way to avoid Earth's superior nanotechnology is for Mars to move to a place of safety. Thanks to her lover, Casseia has the technology they need. More on page 107.

>   *Nebula Award.*

Bova, Ben. Moonbase Saga.

> *Moonrise*. 1996. Ex-astronaut Paul Stavenger did not live to see his vision of a permanent moon colony come into being, but his widow made sure it would succeed.

> *Moonwar*. 1997. Seven years after the establishment of Moonbase, the technology that powers it is declared illegal and immoral. Doug Stavenger, Paul's son, leads the fight to save it.

Goonan, Kathleen Ann. *Queen City Jazz*. 1994. This cyberpunk novel resonates with the rhythms of jazz while depicting the adventures of a young girl who is not what she seems. Verity grew up in Shaker Hill, near Cincinnati. An orphan, she was declared plague-free and raised by a family that did not know of her connection to the city. Once a year she answers the call of the bell and returns to the "enlivened" city, to spend time in the information cocoon in the library there. When a new nanotech plague victim destroys her community, she sets out to bring those closest to her back to life by looking for the key in Cincinnati. She is a driven soul who knows she can change reality, if she only knew how.

> *Mississippi Blues*. 1997. A nanotech steamboat takes Verity to New Orleans.

Hogan, James P. *Bug Park*. 1997. Eric Heber creates a neural interface for controlling tiny robots. His teenaged son Kevin and pal Taki then use this technology to create a new type of entertainment in which they can literally look at the world from a bug's point of view. This technology is so revolutionary that it may just be enough to kill for, and who knows which side the different players are on? When the boys inadvertently overhear Kevin's stepmother plotting with the head of a rival firm, they start some sleuthing on their own, which leads them and their tiny alter ego mechs into deadly peril.

McCarthy, Wil. *Bloom*. 1998. Humanity has fled Earth following the rise of atom-sized Mycora, who devour everything in their path. A shoemaker from Ganymede is sent on a mission back to Earth to investigate what has happened since it was evacuated by humans.

McCarthy, Wil. *Murder in the Solid State*. 1996. Annotated on page 83.

Ore, Rebecca. *Gaia's Toys*. 1995. In a bleak future, the government handles the overpopulation problem by surgically augmenting those on welfare to turn them into computer bio-components. These drode heads, as they are called, have electrodes left sticking out of their bald heads so that they can literally be plugged into computers. It is much cheaper to make a computer designed to read the output of human brains than to build an effective artificial intelligence system. Willie is a drode head, an incapacitated combat veteran, now reduced to living on the dole and fighting his wars in cyberspace. Allison, a member of an eco-terrorist group, is tricked into delivering a nuclear device to the city of New Orleans, where the feds capture her. They want her to name the members of her group and identify the scientist who is creating genetically modified insects with powerful abilities to help Gaia take back control from the deadliest enemy on the planet—humankind.

Steele, Allen M. *A King of Infinite Space.* 1997. Death is only the beginning for neglected rich kid William Alec Tucker III, who after resurrection from a cryogenic interlude becomes a pawn in a systemwide power struggle.

Virtual Reality

A theme that began to show up more frequently in the 1990s is virtual reality, a computer-generated world within which people interact with each other and with computer-created constructs. This category shares elements with both cyberpunk and alternate worlds and often features game playing.

Virtual reality allows one to leave the confines of one's physical body behind and explore the limitless vistas of a virtual field. To boldly go . . . into a computer—and to come out safe and sound again—with luck, like the young boys who are the protagonists of James Hogan's *Bug Park* (page 81); they make a virtual reality breakthrough: no helmet, no virtual reality suit or gloves. Just plug a line directly into your brain and poof—you're looking at the world through the eyes of a microbug; like the game players who get trapped in Piers Anthony's *Killobyte* (page 2): a kill- or be-killed game in the virtual realm that becomes deadly when a talented but amoral young hacker traps them within the confines of the game. Or like J. R. Dunn's detective in *This Side of Judgment* (page 170), who is after "chip heads," one of whom is a serial killer who is after him.

Anderson, Kevin J., and Doug Beason. *Virtual Destruction.* 1996. The worlds of virtual reality and technology collide when a scientist working on a virtual reality project in a top secret lab is murdered. FBI agent Craig Kreident is on the case, and one of the suspects is a project coordinator who may be involved in passing on design secrets to the computer gaming industry. This is the fourth collaboration by these authors, who have produced a blend of detective and hard science fiction with a virtual reality twist.

Fallout. 1997.

Anthony, Piers. *Total Recall.* 1989. Annotated on page 2.

Asaro, Catherine. *Veiled Web.* 1999. Annotated on page 78.

Banks, Iain. *Feersum Endjinn.* 1994. In a time when the workings of technology have been forgotten, a dust cloud approaches the sun and the Earth faces the possibility of another ice age. It is possible that a solution may be found in the crypt, a computer mainframe that stores all recorded knowledge, including the downloaded minds of the dead. Unfortunately, viral chaos has corrupted the system. Then a rebel scientist, a dead officer existing in the virtual reality of the crypt, and a barely literate youth join forces to retrieve the knowledge that can save humanity.

Bethke, Bruce. *Headcrash.* 1995. Out-of-work computer geek Jack Burroughs takes on his virtual reality persona of Max Kool, a motorcycle-riding mercenary, after he is hired by an evil and psychotic multibillion-dollar company.

Bova, Ben. *Death Dream*. 1994. A test pilot, trying out a new virtual reality simulator designed to train pilots, hears his daughter's voice warning him of approaching missiles, then crashes and dies—of a stroke. In Florida the man who created this program, Dan Santorini, is settling into his new home in Orlando with his family. He has a new job at Cyber World, working with an old friend who is able to do anything with a computer but who is also an erratic genius with no morals, scruples, or personal loyalty. It is their program back in Ohio that has gone murderously wrong, but before Dan can make any headway in an investigation, he finds himself faced with another problem. He discovers that his new boss is obsessed with young girls, has become fixated on Dan's daughter, and is using a virtual reality game that she plays at school to get to her. Now it's up to Dan to find out what is going on in both programs.

Gibson, William. *Idoru*. 1996. When rumors start flying that Rez, lead singer of the popular rock band Lo/Rez, is planning to marry an *idoru*, or synthetic computer-generated personality, fan club member Chia Pet McKenzie is sent to Tokyo to investigate.

Goldman, E. M. *Night Room*. 1995. A group of high-school juniors visits the future, courtesy of a virtual reality experiment at a local university. When they enter the "night room," they are projected into their tenth high school reunion. But when the computer shows that one of them will die before that date, the others make it their mission to prevent a tragedy.

`YA`

Hawke, Simon. *The Whims of Creation*. 1995. Annotated on page 37.

McCarthy, Wil. *Murder in the Solid State*. 1996. In this fascinating glimpse of the near future, nanotechnology has completely changed the face of crime and civilization. Young scientist David Sanger is about to present two important papers on his developments in nanotechnology when his archrival, Vandergroot, one of the most prominent scientists of the day, attacks him with a "drop foil," one of the only weapons that can circumvent the sniffers that have made the world a safer place. Another foil is thrust into David's hand, and he fences Vandergroot into submission. Sometime after returning to his room, David is arrested for Vandergroot's murder, but that is only the first of a series of murders that send David into hiding. An interesting use of virtual reality games plays into the plot as David and his girlfriend Marian use the games to expose and stop the real perpetrators of the crimes.

Perriman, Cole. *Terminal Games*. 1994. Annotated on page 172.

Scott, Melissa. *Trouble and Her Friends*. 1994. Trouble, a netwalker, decided to go straight when Congress clamped down on data thieves on the Internet. Now she has taken a legitimate security job. When another data thief breaks into a heavily secured corporate data bank using Trouble's style and name, Trouble must once again venture into the "Shadows," to defend her name.

Chapter 3

Our Strange World

The Earth may be the strangest world of all. This chapter deals with "what if" questions pertaining to our world or to people of our world who live a life transformed by a catastrophe or by biological, religious, or political events. What if the future is nothing to look forward to? Can one little incident change the path of a life or of a world? Will history follow a different path, or will a different reality, a different Earth, be spun off?

The Future Is Bleak

Science fiction is the literature of possibilities. The poet who gave us "The past is too much with us, late and soon . . ." may also have been warning us what to expect in the future. The ozone layer, global warming, and rampant population growth are very real concerns of today's scientists, political leaders, and citizens. Taken to the extreme, we are looking at a very bleak future. Humankind seems to be well on the way to destroying itself, with or without the help of a nuclear holocaust. And there are many SF authors who extrapolate and share the details of this vision in their books.

Part of the allure of this subgenre is enjoying being scared to death in the safety of one's own home. The emphasis here is not so much on the horror aspect (although watching the world literally melt from exposure to moon dust in Baxter's *Moonseed* or watching out for Triffids in the shrubbery in Wyndham's classic *The Day of the Triffids* could easily qualify as horror). Rather, the emphasis is on the disaster/end of the world scenario. Many of these books promote a social conscience as well. They present worst-case scenarios for the reader to contemplate. The world as we know it can go out with a bang or with a whimper—and we can work hard to try to salvage what's left, or we can participate in the steady decline and fall of our civilization. In their *Encyclopedia of Science Fiction*, Clute and

Nicholls identify more than 400 novels dealing with the aftermath of an Earth-changing holocaust. This is spectator sport with a vengeance. It is also one of the most popular types of SF to be made into movies, including *Mad Max*, *Tank Girl*, and *Independence Day*.

Many of the readers who like the books found in this section will also enjoy a number of the titles in Chapter 1, particularly the militaristic section. Others may enjoy the horror connection found in the "It's Horrific" section in Chapter 5 or in many of the entries in the section dealing with aliens in Chapter 4, "Us and Them," particularly those that deal with aliens who have come to Earth or are waiting "out there" with less-than-friendly intentions.

Nuclear Annihilation

In the 1950s and 1960s, at the height of the Cold War, many SF novels speculated about the end of the world. The movie *Dr. Strangelove* was hysterically funny, but it was also a thought-provoking examination of where we were as a society and where we might be going. The end of the world as we know it—usually brought about by nuclear annihilation—became the subject of many SF novels.

Brin, David. *The Postman*. 1985. Annotated on page 3.

Burdick, Eugene L., and Harvey Wheeler. *Fail-Safe*. 1962. First published at the height of the Cold War, this novel of nuclear warheads rocketing toward Moscow was made into a movie in 1964 and a made-for-television movie in 2000.

Butler, Octavia E. Xenogenesis Trilogy

> *Dawn*. 1987. In this first volume of the Xenogenesis trilogy, aliens rescue a group of humans from the nuclear devastation of the Earth. But these beneficent saviors turn out to have their own agenda. They want genetic materials from their human "guests"—and they won't take no for an answer.

> *Adulthood Rites*. 1988. This sequel to *Dawn* continues the life of Lilith Iyapo among the alien Oankali and the struggle of humanity against extraterrestrial domination.

> *Imago*. 1989. The third and concluding volume of Xenogenesis completes the saga of the alien Onkali, who save the remnants of humanity and develop a plan to restore parts of the Earth for human habitation—but for a price.

DuBois, Brendan. *Resurrection Day*. 1999. This fantastic apocalyptic "what if" thriller features a United States in which the Bay of Pigs fiasco, the discovery of nukes in Cuba, and the blockade of Russian ships leads to a nuclear exchange that destroys both superpowers. With major cities gone and a military government in charge, life in the United States changes dramatically. Ten years after the bombs fell on Washington, D.C., and destroyed the Camelot presidency, Carl Landry, a former Special Forces member, now a reporter for the *Boston Globe*, stumbles upon a mystery. Why is an old man who tried to give Carl a list of names dead? Where is the list, who is on it, and why have the military censors kept Carl's story out of the paper? Why is an attractive female English reporter so interested in Carl? Why is someone trying to kill him? And is there any truth to the rumor of a planned British invasion?

Frank, Pat. *Alas, Babylon.* 1959. The isolated residents of Fort Repose, Florida, find themselves thrust into a primitive lifestyle, fighting lawlessness, disease, starvation, and panic after a defective missile triggers a nuclear war.

Heinlein, Robert A. *Farnham's Freehold.* 1964. After the bombs fall, Farnham and his family are thrown forward in time to an America ruled by blacks, where they experience prejudice and discrimination firsthand.

McIntyre, Vonda. *Dreamsnake.* 1978. Snake, a young girl, is a respected healer in a bleak post-holocaust future with a primitive society that relies on healers for medical care. She gets her name from her instruments of healing, a rattlesnake, a cobra, and most important of all, a small, harmless dream snake. She cultures antitoxins and vaccines from the rattlesnake and the cobra, but it is the dream snake she relies on the most. That is the snake that deadens the pain and eases death in terminal cases. When her irreplaceable dream snake is killed, she must go on a perilous quest for a replacement or cease to be a healer.

> ***Hugo, Nebula, and Locus Awards.***

Merle, Albert. *Malevil.* 1972. Written in French and translated into English, this post-apocalyptic tale is set in the French countryside, where Emmanuel and some of his friends, sheltered from a nuclear blast by a well-protected wine cellar, survive.

O'Brien, Robert C. *Z for Zachariah.* 1975. Annotated on page 202.

Shute, Nevil. *On the Beach.* 1957. Australians face the inevitable as fallout moves southward after the entire northern hemisphere has been annihilated by nuclear war.

Stevermer, Caroline. *River Rats.* 1992. Annotated on page 207.

Strieber, Whitley. *Wolf of Shadows.* 1985. Nuclear winter has arrived—in a big way. A wolf pack starts the long trek south when little or no food is available and their cubs start dying. Two humans, a mother and daughter, who were camped by a lake in northern Minnesota when the bombs fell, have no recourse but to follow the wolf pack if they hope to survive. Gradually accepted into the pack, they feed off the remains of the pack's kills and in return, they help feed the starving wolves with the occasional cache of shells (canned food) that they come across. The dangers they face are the bitter cold, starvation, and other predators—particularly men with guns.

Tepper, Sheri S. *The Gate to Women's Country*. 1988. Women are in control of the towns in this post-holocaust novel. The men roam the countryside and can only enter towns at the permission of the women there. Boy children are kept safely behind the town walls until they turn five. Then they are turned over to the fathers for the next ten years. At age fifteen they can choose to return to life behind the town walls, a life of supposed servitude to the women there, or they can continue roaming the countryside in bands of males, negotiating with the women behind the walls, but never again living there.

Zelazny, Roger. *Damnation Alley*. 1969. After the bombs fall and bikers seize control of the highways, Hell Tanner risks his life to go on a dangerous quest. Filmed in 1977 by director Jack Smight, this gave rise to the many "Road Warrior" type books and movies.

Overpopulation and Plagues

It may not be a nuclear exchange that destroys us. We're doing a pretty good job just being ourselves, a heavily industrialized and consumerist civilization that is slowly eroding Gaia's envelope. Are we sacrificing our future for our present? Cashing in the integrity of nature and continued life on the planet for our standard of living? What happens when the needs and wants of the human population outweigh the resources to fill them? Science fiction authors recognize a rich vein when they see one and have mined this one heavily. Harry Harrison found a productive use for the "teaming masses" in his *Make Room! Make Room!*, which was the basis for the popular movie *Soylent Green*. Overpopulation a problem? Get rid of the people. You don't have to eat them, but you can kill them if you're the one making the rules.

Baird, *Smart Rats*. 1990. Annotated on page 195.
YA

Benson, Ann. *The Plague Tales*. 1997. Alejandro Canches, a young Jewish physician in Aragon in 1348, digs up the body of a blacksmith he failed to save and dissects him to try and find out why the man died. His crime is discovered and he is arrested, branded with the mark of the Jew on his chest, and then released, with the stipulation that he leave Aragon and never return. Meanwhile the plague spreads. The Pope dispatches doctors to all the heads of Europe to keep them safe in quarantine. Alejandro, disguised as a Christian, is selected to go to Edward III's court in England, where he loves and loses the beautiful Adele, lady-in-waiting to the spoiled Princess Isabelle. In a future England that has survived the recent "outbreak" under the rigid control of green-suited biocops, his garment is dug up. Unfortunately, the cloth segment has an active plague cell that is reactivated in the Microbiology Department of the British Institute of Science, and the nightmare begins.

Dickinson, Peter. *Eva*. 1989. Thirteen-year-old Eva wakes up in a hospital bed unable to move, with no memory of the crash that put her there. Her parents and doctors assure her that she will eventually recover. However, she notices that the mirror over the bed has been fixed so that she cannot see her reflection. Demanding to know the entire truth, she is finally allowed to see her face. But it is not her face. Ecological issues in an overpopulated, polluted future are at the heart of this work.

Haddix, Margaret Peterson. *Among the Hidden*. 1998. Overpopulation makes being a third child a capital offense. Annotated on page 193.

Harrison, Harry. *Make Room! Make Room!* 1966. New York City in the future (1999) is not a healthy place for anyone over sixty-five. Overpopulation is at a record high, which has caused serious shortages of food, water, and shelter. The solution is a creative but not necessarily palatable one, as a policeman conducting a murder investigation is shocked to discover. Now mandatory retirement has an entirely new meaning. Basis for the movie *Soylent Green*.

Herbert, Frank. *The White Plague*. 1982. Seeking revenge for the murder of his wife, a biologist spreads a plague that strikes only the women in the world.

Like, Russel. *After the Blue*. 1998. In the future, the Gruumsbaggians visit Earth, leaving behind a plague, which decimates the human population. A century after "the Blue" a small band of survivors lives a pastoral existence in Jamesburg, New Jersey, but the Gruumsbaggians return and attempt to put Earth back the way it was before they unwittingly caused the end of civilization. This means bringing in pollution, smog machines, and gridlock plans and reintroducing the humans they have raised on their home planet. A well-told and entertaining tale reminiscent of Vonnegut and Swift. More on page 164.

Murphy, Pat. *The City, Not Long After*. 1988. Survivors of a devastating plague create art in a post-apocalyptic San Francisco while trying to evade a private army.

Stewart, George R. *Earth Abides*. 1949. After a viral plague wipes out most of humanity, Californian Isherwood fathers children with another survivor, but his descendents can't maintain modern civilization.

Ure, Jean. *Plague*. 1993. Fran returns from a wilderness survival course to find that a plague has decimated London. After sneaking into the city to look for her family and friends, she discovers that it is much more dangerous to try to leave the blockaded city.

Other Ecological Disasters

In addition to overpopulation, other ecological issues are a growth industry in science fiction. Considering the way we've been tipping the ecological balance on the planet, it's no wonder we seem to be going from progress to perdition. Gaia has been our mother and protector in the past, but evidently even she has limitations—and we are rapidly approaching them. Oil spills that repeatedly pollute our oceans, drought conditions in some parts of the world, torrential rains and flooding in others, and tornadoes and hurricanes that unleash the unspeakable powers of the elements are just the beginning. Global warming and the hole in the ozone layer seriously threaten the survival of humanity on an increasingly overpopulated Earth, which explains the development of a such a thriving subgenre.

Anderson, Kevin J., and Doug Beason. *Ill Wind: A Novel of Ecological Disaster*. 1995. As a culture we heavily depend on a steady supply of oil and petroleum by-products, including the plastics that make up so much of our everyday lives, from computer components to beverage containers. The sobering scenario depicted in this story explores what would happen if a bacteria used to clean up an oil spill mutated and became a petroplague, destroying all petroleum-based products.

Ballard, J. G. *The Burning World*. 1964. British title *The Drought*. The Earth is burning because of widespread drought conditions. Pollution has become so extreme that the seas have stopped evaporating. With no evaporation, there is no rain. With no rain, the world is literally burning up, and civilization is about to collapse.

The Drowned World. 1962. Because of intensive solar flare activity, the world's ice caps have melted. London is now a swamp, with drowned office buildings marking the way for a few intrepid humans embarked on a most unusual "night journey."

Barnes, John. *Mother of Storms*. 1994. A global epidemic of lethal hurricanes is unleashed when a missile strike on an underwater weapons cache releases tons of methane into the Earth's atmosphere. Now it's creating a devastating greenhouse effect.

Baxter, Stephen. *Moonseed*. 1998. The cover proclaims: "It Eats Planets. And It's Here." Inside there is a marvelous "what if" speculation. What if the moon rocks brought back from humankind's first lunar expedition were more than just rocks? What if they were a form of moonseed, lying dormant? And what if scattering a few particles of this moonseed on a lava crag in Scotland sets off a chain reaction—naked to the human eye at first—that will eventually lead to the destruction of the Earth? Soon the action of the Moonseed becomes noticeable—a pool of dust forms that keeps on growing and growing and begins sucking things in, including unwary bystanders. By the time scientists realize what is going on, it is too late. For human life to continue, a way must be found to colonize the moon.

Bova, Ben. *The Precipice. Book One of the Asteroid Wars*. 2001. With Earth facing ecological disaster, humanity's only hope is to look up — not to the stars, but to the asteroids. That's where we'll find all the energy and natural resources we need to keep civilization from collapsing. Two of the wealthiest men on Earth have come to the same conclusion at the same time: They both intend to mine the riches of the asteroids. One wants to use the resources he expects to find there to save the Earth. The other wants it all for himself. To the victor go the spoils. And the fate of Earth hangs in the balance.

Brunner, John. *Stand on Zanzibar*. 1968. Annotated on page 96.

The Sheep Look Up. 1972. Annotated on page 96.

Christopher, John. *No Blade of Grass*. 1957. British title *The Death of Grass*. When all the grass and cereal crops on the Earth have been blighted, humans are left with no hope as they grimly struggle to survive.

Gilmore, Kate. *The Exchange Student*. 1999. Seventy years after an ecological crisis on Earth almost destroys all our animals, a teen exchange student from a planet in the midst of a similar ecological upheaval moves in with a family that is running a breeding zoo.

Goonan, Kathleen Ann. *Queen City Jazz*. 1994. A nanotechnology-induced plague has decimated the Earth. Annotated on page 81.

Gould, Steven. *Blind Waves*. 2000. Patricia Beeman is a well-established entrepreneur who owns a floating block of apartments and a child care center in a future shaped by rising oceans caused by global warming. But Patricia doesn't just rest on her wealth. She is also a busy underwater salvage operator who stumbles across a horrifying sight that almost gets her killed.

Herzog, Arthur. *The Swarm*. 1974. An invasion of bees brings ecological disaster to North America.

Hughes, Monica. 1992. *The Crystal Drop*. Annotated on page 199.

YA

Jensen, Jane. *Millennium Rising*. 1999. Cataclysmic events wreak havoc on the world. Is it the end of the world, or has a vast international conspiracy set in motion events that could get entirely out of control? More on page 103.

Lindholm, Megan. *Alien Earth*. 1992. Humans who wished to be saved from Earth's pollution-induced death were transported in a state of Waitsleep in Beastships to the planets Castor and Pollux. There they were forced to adapt to the planet's ecological balance and fit into the circle of life. Over time humans have shrunk in size until individuals are too tiny to give live birth and spend almost a century in childhood (before the onset of puberty and hormonal changes). The crew of the Beastships is rigidly ruled by the Arthroplana in space and by the Conservancy on the planets. But Mariner John and his crew, ably assisted by their very special Beastship *Evangeline*, change things when they go on a mission for Earth Affirmed to prove that the Conservancy is lying and Earth is no longer polluted.

McMahon, Donna. *Dance of Knives.* 2001. Vancouver in the twenty-second century is still a thriving seaport city. But the global economic collapse and a massive rise in sea level have made it a city of contrasts: prospering Guild members and the guildless starving descendants of American refugees. Klale Renhardt of the Fishes Guild leaves her town on the north coast for the big city, only to discover just how difficult survival will be in a city beset by Tong wars. Fortunately, she gets a job at the KlonDyke, Vancouver's lesbian bar, and she meets the mysterious Blade, a trained assassin and potential friend, with secrets of his own that could lead to sacrifice or salvation.

Pace, Sue. *The Last Oasis.* 1993. Annotated on page 202.
YA

Pellegrino, Charles R. *Dust.* 1998. Like the dinosaurs before us, humankind is about to disappear from the planet, courtesy of devastating environmental changes. The prophecy "dust to dust" becomes all too real, beginning with a plague of dust mites on Long Island that kills hundreds, including the wife of paleobiologist Richard Sinclair. After her death, he and his colleagues discover that the insects on the planet are dying, and as a result, so are the plants and most animals. Economic catastrophes follow close on the heels of this natural disaster, with war and the deployment of nuclear warheads the inevitable culmination of the insanity. The author is the creator of the dinosaur-cloning theory that served as the basis of Michael Crichton's *Jurassic Park,* which he uses as a possible solution to the disasters depicted here.

Robinson, Kim Stanley. *Antarctica.* 1997. The expiration of the international treaty that has kept Antarctica pristine and untouched means that the oil companies will soon be stripping the continent of its considerable resources—contributing to the hole in the ozone layer and the greenhouse effect. Members of the Earth First Protectors, dedicated to protecting the continent, will not let this happen — even if it means murder.

Sterling, Bruce. *Heavy Weather.* 1994. Storm Troupers, hackers who follow the monster storms that are ravaging the world, try to predict an F-6 level tornado, a storm that could destroy all civilization.

Turner, George. *Drowning Towers.* 1987. (Published originally under the title *The Sea and Summer*.) Global warming raises the sea level and eradicates living area.

Vonnegut, Kurt. *Cat's Cradle.* 1963. A large cast of colorful characters is caught up in the story of an insane scientist who has invented a truly life-threatening substance. Once released, ice-nine will freeze all the water in the world. This apocalyptic tale of the possible fate the planet faces is a broad satire, considered by many to be the author's best book.

Wells, Martha. *City of Bones.* 1995. "It is a place that has been devastated by an ancient holocaust, and where most of the world's water has evaporated. But out of the ashes, a bizarre and wonderful civilization arises. Sand ships now traverse the routes once used by the great war galleons, and a glittering chain of city-states dot the Great Waste. And greatest of them all is Charisat. A beautiful woman and a handsome thief try to unravel the mysteries of an age-old technology to stop a fanatical cult before it unleashes an evil that will topple Charisat. And destroy all the water in the world."—Publisher's blurb

Wilhelm, Kate. *Where Late the Sweet Birds Sang.* 1976. Faced with the very real threat of sterility, the human race survives by cloning itself. Needless to say, there is a big difference between the "normals" and the "cloned."

Science Run Amok

Scientists are currently delving into genetic research, cloning, and manipulation of DNA in a big way. If this keeps up, will homo sapiens be able to retain the top position on the genetic tree, or are we sowing the seeds of our own destruction? Research for the sake of research is a staple of the inquiring mind. But what if such research goes too far? What happens if someone, somewhere, makes a mistake, deliberately or otherwise, that affects the building blocks that make up our gene pool? The following are examples of novels that explore this fertile and frightening scenario.

Cook, Robin. *Chromosome 6.* 1997. Annotated on page 4.

Palmer, David. *Emergence.* 1984. Eleven-year-old Candy, a genius, a karate expert, and a self-taught whiz at almost everything, is a member of the next race to come: homo post hominem. After humankind has been virtually wiped out by germ warfare, only the hominem like Candy remain, but they are few and far between. Candy and Terry, her "retarded" twin brother—who can read her mind, is an excellent judge of character, and has a very strong beak because he is a macaw—are the only survivors in her father's specially constructed fallout shelter. If they are to find other survivors, they must leave the safety of the shelter and search for them.

Preston, Richard. *Cobra Event.* 1997. When a high school girl in New York first exhibits symptoms of a common cold, nobody guesses that in only a few hours it will progress into a grisly death. She is only the first victim of a bio-terrorist attack on our country.

Preston, Douglas, and Lincoln Child. *Mount Dragon.* 1996. Genetic engineering may lead to "cures" that are far worse than the original disease.

Death from the Heavens

We've looked up at the stars, admired the trails comets make across the sky, and speculated about what (or who) is out there. The stars are beautiful and fascinating, but perhaps they are also threatening. What if the next comet or asteroid, meteor or meteorite is not going to pass us by? What if more than the comet's tail strikes the Earth? This is a popular SF theme in books, movies, and television. From classics like Philip Wylie and Edwin Balmer's *When Worlds Collide* to current thrillers like Jack McDevitt's *Moonfall*, the possibilities of death from above have been a rich source of speculation. Remember those moon rocks our astronauts brought back? Maybe Earth's doom won't take an asteroid, but only a particle of dust, as in Stephen Baxter's *Moonseed* and Charles Pellegrino's *Dust*.

Alten, Steve. *Domain*. 2001. The dinosaurs were destroyed when an asteroid hit the Earth, some 65 million years ago. But was it an asteroid? Or was it something far more sinister? What if it were a planet-destroying explosive device, patiently waiting for a signal from space to activate it? And what if the only man who knows what is going to happen and how to prevent it is locked up in an insane asylum in Miami? If he can't get out, it could indeed be the beginning of the end.

Baxter, Stephen. *Moonseed*. 1998. Annotated on page 90.

Clarke, Arthur C. *The Hammer of God*. 1993. Even though it means sacrificing the ship and crew who will do it, the people of Earth vote to send the *Goliath* out to blow up an asteroid that threatens the Earth. The captain and crew put their interactive caps on their bald heads and take a trip down memory lane, never expecting to wake up. But they do. The bomb was almost a dud, merely splitting the asteroid in two. Although this means salvation for the ship, it spells death and destruction for the Earth itself.

Crichton, Michael. *Andromeda Strain*. 1969. A remote village in New Mexico is contaminated by a crashed satellite, which unleashes an alien virus on the Earth. Scientists fight the clock trying to analyze the lethal organism. And they they discover a solution.

Leiber, Fritz *The Wanderer*. 1965. A seemingly strange planet suddenly arrives in our solar system and begins wreaking havoc. Investigation reveals that it is not a planet but a huge spaceship. Now the feline aliens on board have brought it too close to the Earth, resulting in devastating tidal waves and earthquakes.

   Hugo Award.

McDevitt, Jack. *Moonfall*. 1998. Annotated on page 8.

Niven, Larry, and Jerry Pournelle. *Lucifer's Hammer*. 1977. Could it be that those who did not survive the comet's impact were the lucky ones?

   Hugo and Locus Awards.

Wylie, Philip, and Edwin Balmer. *When Worlds Collide*. 1933. This science fiction thriller accurately lives up to its title. A planet is headed toward the Earth. Collision is imminent and inevitable. There are a few experimental spaceships available, but the selection process will be brutal, for only those who make it onto the ships will survive. There is a sequel, *After Worlds Collide* (1934).

Wyndham, John. *The Day of the Triffids.* 1951. An orbital explosion blinds most of the inhabitants of Earth, leaving them easy prey for the vicious, plantlike Triffids. A movie and a television series were made in England based on this page-turner of a book.

Is Life Worth Living? Utopias and Dystopias.

Finally, there's the question of utopian versus dystopian societies in the not-so-distant future. *1984* has come and gone. Big Brother is watching, perhaps not as blatantly as depicted by Orwell, but almost as pervasively—especially with the Internet a growing force. With half the homes in the United States now possessing computers, and genetic manipulation and ex-utero conception a fact of life, Huxley's *Brave New World* is upon us. For good or ill, in sickness and in health, we are a plastic-using, connected society, and our records are available—for a price. Want a simpler, gentler society? Take a look at Lois Lowry's *The Giver* (page 201). Want to think twice about conformity and fitting in and the rabble-rousing effect of music on the vulnerable mind? Check out Sonia Levitin's *The Cure* (page 200). We pride ourselves on our independence, on the freedom to make our own choices (and our own mistakes). Read Lawrence's *Keeper of the Universe* (page 200) for a thought-provoking examination of conformity versus free-will, of safety versus risk taking, and what happens to the Galactic Controller who will not apply musical controls to the Earth. These three novels were written specifically for teenagers. But who says serious issues are wasted on the young? Thought-provoking concepts can be packaged in a straightforward, simple format that is accessible to young and old alike. Societal decay, the demise of civilization through government corruption, economic collapse, gang violence, or new types of drugs can also be the vector of apocalypse. Let's take a closer look.

Aikin, Jim. *The Wall at the Edge of the World.* 1993. Telepaths have taken over and cleansed the world of all non-telepaths (or nulls), using poison, weapons, bombs, and whatever else it took. Since then the One has maintained constant vigilance by "cleansing" or beheading all children who reach puberty without awakening telepathically. Danlo Ree lost his beloved wife because an illness robbed her of her telepathy and left her at the mercy of the Proctors and Joddies, who declared her a null and chopped off her head. He is still grieving when a group of wild women comes out of the wilderness and kidnaps him along with some other men. As a result of what he learns while living with these women, Danlo resolves to fight the One, single-handedly if necessary, and to rescue as many Nulls as he possibly can before they are cleansed.

Atwood, Margaret. *The Handmaid's Tale.* 1985. The close of the twentieth century, with its birth control and nuclear fallout, has resulted in a drastic change in the status of women. Now they are only as valuable as their fertile ovaries. The declining birth rate has reduced them to the plight of slavery in this scathing satire. Offred remembers her past with longing, a husband and daughter she loved, a job that provided her with money of her own, and the right to read whatever she wanted. Now she is a Handmaid in the Republic of Gilead, forced to lie with the Commander once a month, while she prays that she will become pregnant.

Bradbury, Ray. *Fahrenheit 451*. 1953. Fahrenheit 451 is the temperature at which the paper in books burns. Montag, a "fireman" whose job is to destroy hidden books by putting them to the torch, begins the dangerous and perverted activity of "thinking" after he meets a fey girl who has been watching him. He finds hope for the human race when he meets an old man, a bibliophile, in a park.

Brunner, John. *Stand on Zanzibar*. 1968. In the early twenty-first century, the world is a mess: overpopulated, over-polluted, a place where riots and muggings are a common occurrence. On the scene to report the current sad state of affairs is pop sociologist Chad C. Mulligan.

> ### Hugo and French Prix Awards.

Brunner, John. *The Sheep Look Up*. 1972. This thematic sequel to *Stand on Zanzibar* tells the story of an ecologist and his doomed efforts to stir people to action and save the world from pollution already past the critical point.

Burgess, Anthony. *A Clockwork Orange*. 1962. A frightening look at a bleak future, in which a classical-music-loving juvenile delinquent recounts in heavy Russian argot his litany of attacks against the system. After being caught and programmed to no longer commit such ultra-violent acts, he discovers the tragic side effects of his treatment. Basis for Stanley Kubrick's 1971 movie of the same title.

Butler, Octavia E. *Parable of the Sower*. 1993. In near-future California, pollution and overpopulation are running rampant. Lauren, an African–American teenager, and her family live in a walled enclave, which has kept them safe from the depredations of the druggies, thieves, and homeless on the outside—so far. When the walls finally fall, Lauren is one of the few survivors, able to lead a small band of followers north, looking for a place where rain still falls and fertile soil that will nourish her small community, this Earthseed.

Parable of the Talents. 1998. Larkin never really knew her famous mother, Lauren Oya Olamina. But she has pieced together the story of Olamina and Earthseed from entries in a journal kept by her mother and quotations from the book her mother wrote, *Earthseed: The Books of the Living*. Now Jarret has been elected president, and his Church of Christian America holds power, killing many and enslaving the surviving members of Earthseed. Freedom is hard fought and hard won, but the battle is only beginning.

Christopher, John. Tripods Series.

When the Tripods Came. 1988. The prequel to the Tripods trilogy shows how these three-legged alien machines land in three cities, one in England, one in Russia, and one in the United States, and proceed to take over the Earth.

The White Mountains. 1967. In the twenty-first century the alien tripods, huge, three-legged machines, have conquered the Earth, using mind control to keep the adult population under control. But Will Parker still has a chance to escape being "capped" and join the resistance movement in the White Mountains in this first volume of the Tripods trilogy.

The City of Gold and Lead. 1967. In the second volume of the Tripods trilogy, Will and his friends have to leave their sanctuary in the White Mountains and infiltrate the Tripods' City of Gold and Lead, a mission that may cost them their lives.

YA *The Pool of Fire.* 1968. In the concluding volume of the Tripods trilogy, Will escapes from his Tripod Master in the City of Gold and Lead, returns with a warning of how the Tripods plan to destroy the Earth, and discovers a way for humans to fight back.

Dick, Philip K. *The Game-Players of Titan.* 1963. Annotated on page 146.

Dickson, Gordon R. *Wolf and Iron.* 1990. Banks failed, governments collapsed, the telephone system quit working, and electricity ceased. In short, society ground to a halt and civilization faltered. Jeebee, a scientist whose think tank predicted this negative spiral and its eventual outcome, also predicted the pattern necessary for recovery, a pattern that is going to take centuries to accomplish. Driven away from the small town where he lived because he had no viable, productive skills to contribute to this new primitive society, he heads for Montana and his brother's ranch.

Hopkinson, Nalo. *Brown Girl in the Ring.* 1998. Metropolitan Toronto is dead, abandoned by government, social services, and all those with the wherewithal to flee to the suburbs. With the collapse of the economic base, investors, commerce, and government withdraw to the "burbs," leaving the rotten core to decay. What's left is run by Rudy and his posse.

Huxley, Aldous. *Brave New World.* 1932. Bernard Marx thinks something is missing from the utopian society where everyone is drugged and entertainment is virtual. And he's right. But test-tube babies, "feelies" as a form of entertainment, and "soma" to keep the populace feeling good and under control are here to stay—as a primitive young man discovers when he tries to bring about much-needed change.

Kilworth, Gary. *The Electric Kid.* 1994. Orphans and throw-away kids survive in a dump by finding and fixing things.
YA

LaHaye, Tim, and Jerry B. Jenkins. Left Behind Series. When Rapture happens, the people left on Earth must work out what to do next as evil tries to manipulate events. This best-selling Christian series has been a frequent readers' advisory request, with questions focusing on finding the book that features people disappearing from an airplane over the Atlantic, leaving behind all their clothing and possessions. Titles annotated on page 181.

Nix, Garth. *Shade's Children.* 1997. In a horrifying world where everyone over the age of thirteen is turned into a hunting machine or food, a band of teens under the direction of a computer program tries to sabotage the Overlords and evade their terrible lethal cyborgs, constructed from the living tissue of dead humans. Gold-Eye escapes the dormitories only to be hunted down by Trackers and threatened by massive Myrmidons. After being rescued, he is taken to Shade's submerged headquarters. There he teams up with others who are trying to figure out what caused "the change" that precipitated the disappearance of everyone past puberty and turned children into raw materials for the horrible, deadly games played by the Overlords.

Orwell, George. *1984.* Annotated on page 164.

Silverberg, Robert. *The Alien Years.* 1998. Without warning, alien ships arrive, causing brush fires in California that rage out of control while the aliens totally ignore what's happening. The resistance movement begins immediately, led by a family that lives on an isolated farm. The members of this family continue to resist the invasion for several generations, to no avail. The fifteen-foot-tall, big purple squids are either hideously ugly or indescribably beautiful, depending on whether you have been mentally "pushed" to accept them. Colonel Carmichael, the patriarch of the family, fights the good fight against these alien entities. His younger brother was one of the first casualties and his brother's wife one of the first collaborators to work for the aliens. But, in the end, what does it matter? Resistance really is futile.

Wilhelm, Kate. *Juniper Time.* 1979. In the bleak future depicted here, America is suffering from a major drought. The female protagonist joins an Amerindian tribe to survive. Her friend, on the other hand, is involved in a struggle to bring the moribund space program back to life.

Wyndham, John. *The Midwich Cuckoos.* 1958. In the small village of Midwich, England, women become pregnant after a flying saucer lands. Nine months later, they give birth to the Midwich Cuckoos: beautiful, talented, but ultimately quite sinister children.

Social Structures

Ever since the rise of the science fiction New Wave movement in the 1960s, the social interactions between people, whether of a biological, political, or religious nature, have been a popular subject for examination in science fiction. According to John Clute and Peter Nicholls in *The Encyclopedia of Science Fiction*, the term New Wave as it applies to science fiction was borrowed from French film criticism, referring to the experimental cinema. Works of New Wave science fiction are also experimental in nature, dealing more with psychology or the soft sciences than with the hard sciences. In addition, many of its practitioners are considered to have broken down the barriers between science fiction and mainstream fiction, especially those who believed that science fiction should be taken seriously as literature and followed through with more experimental or literary writing. In contrast to the optimism of early science fiction, New Wave science fiction depicted the counterculture of the late 1960s gone awry—with mind-altering drugs, oriental religions, taboos, sex, and Pop Art. All this was set against a pessimistic backdrop of anarchic dystopias and the threat of disaster.

One of the primary appeals of New Wave science fiction is its grasp of the complexities of the world. Societies can be structured according to the political, religious, and biological imperatives of their citizenry—not to mention sexual politics. For example, consider the impact that non-monogamous pairings and cannibalism have on the characters in Donald Kingsbury's *Courtship Rite* (page 100). In Ursula K. Le Guin's *The Left Hand of Darkness* (page 101), Genley Ai trekked across the ice floes of the planet Winter only to discover that the inhabitants of this world were not limited to the either/or of their sexuality. (Instead, they switched back and forth from male to female, much to his surprise.) And what about choosing to be an obstetrician on an all-male planet—and having plenty of work? That's what Lois McMaster Bujold's *Ethan of Athos* (page 16) did. Of course, he did have trouble when the female uterine replicators grew old and had to be replaced. That meant he had to leave the safety of his all-male society and venture out into the dangerous waters of bisexual planets—and experience direct exposure to the female of the species.

Politics can affect us profoundly. Governments can be totalitarian and frighteningly repressive, or chaos and anarchy may rule. Look no further than Orwell's *1984* (page 164), Huxley's *Brave New World* (page 97), Bradbury's *Fahrenheit 451* (page 96), or Heinlein's early novels for some of the political possibilities of the future.

Religion can also play an important (and potentially devastating) role. Gods and messiahs, good versus evil, and the role of spiritual communities are some of the topics SF tackles. In *Dune* (page 103), external pressures turned Paul Atreides into the messiah-like Maud'dib. Think of the social pressures the young African-American protagonist of Octavia Butler's *Parable of the Sower* (page 96) faced. With the lack of a strong central government and ready access to the destructively powerful drug pyro (that made lighting and watching fires burn better than sex), her society was doomed. C. S. Lewis's classic space trilogy, beginning with *Out of the Silent Planet* (page 104), explores spiritual themes within the context of the secularization of society. Spiritual themes are also present in Arthur C. Clarke's *Childhood's End* (page 101), acknowledged by many to be one of his best novels. In this book the spaceships come to Earth bringing aliens who look like our concept of the Christian devil. Their mission—to help Earth's children advance to the next level of evolution—makes them midwives to the future, so to speak.

Cultural and religious beliefs may be comfortable and reassuring to some, but they are devastating to others, as they are to the characters in Resnick's *Kirinyaga* (page 105) when they try to live by the old ways (once prevalent in Kenya) after being transported to an entirely new planet in the future. In Louise Marley's *The*

Terrorists of Irustan (page 104), the men on the planet Irustan are quite comfortable with the status quo, but the women have become terrorists, using murder to protect themselves from the restrictions and abuses of their male-dominated society. Dan Simmon's *Hyperion* (page 106) is the first in a truly remarkable quartet that explores the religious beliefs and societal imperatives of a large cast of characters, pilgrims who believe they are traveling to their doom as they tell the stories of their lives and why they believe the Shrike selected them for this journey. The detective in Sharon Shinn's *Wrapt in Crystal* (page 174) chases a serial killer preying on women who belong to two quite different religious orders. In Glenn Kleier's *The Last Day* (page 128), a female messiah comes out of the desert at the millennium and preaches a message that could spell the end of organized religion, unless the church fathers can agree on an assassination plan. A Jesuit priest goes into space to establish first contact with an alien species, with disastrous results for his team and himself, in Mary Doria Russell's remarkable *The Sparrow* (page 105). And the protagonist of Gene Wolfe's The Book of the Long Sun quartet (page 109) is a devout young priest who must become the political as well as the religious leader of his people during their generations-long journey through space on the cylindrical starship known as *The Whorl*.

Obviously, there are many different approaches to society and religion and political belief systems and many, many worlds to explore. Our planet, as rich, varied, and diverse as it is, has nevertheless been at the point of blowing itself up more than once. And this before our efforts to contact other planets and alien societies have been successful. Which raises the question: What is going to happen when we actually do manage to get into space? The answers, in all their speculative variety, can be found in works of science fiction.

Biological

How will clones be treated in our future society? And what effects will they have? Will the sexual revolution be followed by sexual evolution? What are the social ramifications of biological changes?

Ballard, J. G. *High-Rise.* 1975. The setting is a high-rise apartment building, whose inhabitants, affected by their surroundings, begin to exhibit a new kind of barbarism.

Brin, David. *Glory Season.* 1993. On a planet dominated by clans of female clones, men are a necessary part of the cloning process but are not interested in sex most of the year. During one short season of the "year," men's hormones kick in for the necessary procreation, to produce males and female "vars" or variants, children who keep genetic diversity alive. More on page 126.

Bujold, Lois McMaster. *Ethan of Athos.* Also, *Falling Free.* See annotations on page(s) 16 and 3.

Kingsbury, Donald. *Courtship Rite.* 1982. On an alien planet a most unusual culture has been developed by humans who are totally out of touch with their origins. Some necessary nutrients are so scarce that the inhabitants have resorted to cannibalism to keep from losing them, and courtship and marriage mores have assumed some curious characteristics.

Le Guin, Ursula K. *The Left Hand of Darkness*. 1969. Genly Ai came in peace, an ambassador to the planet Winter. After being declared an outlaw, he was rescued by Estraven, the former prime minister. During their three-month trek across Winter's ice-age glaciers, Genly Ai discovers firsthand just how different the inhabitants of this planet are able to change from male to female and back again. As a result, he acquires an entirely different perspective on these people, their customs, and his own.

> *Hugo and Nebula Awards.*

Religious

Will humanity become more spiritually evolved in the future? Or will religious figures and institutions seize control of our freedoms? What will the future teach us about today's religious beliefs? Again, the possibilities are endless.

Aldiss, Brian. *Barefoot in the Head*. 1969. Charteris is a survivor of the Acid-Head War, a war in which the weaponry used turns out to be psychedelic drugs. But will he survive his role as a messiah-like figure in the stoned-out aftermath of the war?

Anderson, Poul. *The Day of Their Return*. 1974. Ivar Frederiksen is the son of a nobleman on the planet Aeneas. After challenging the authority of the Terran Empire, he must flee for his life. While searching for some way to secure his planet's freedom, he joins forces with a working-class visionary who helps him in his struggle against the establishment.

Benson, Ann. *The Plague Tales*. 1997. Annotated on page 88.

Blish, James. *A Case of Conscience*. 1958. A Jesuit priest is the protagonist of this thought-provoking work. On a visit to the planet Lithia, a planet that is "unfallen," he faces a case of conscience as he struggles to solve a biological riddle. Or perhaps not.

> *Hugo Award.*

Butler, Octavia E. *Parable of the Sower*. 1993. Annotated on page 96.

> *Parable of the Talents*. 1998. Annotated on page 96.

Clarke, Arthur C. *Childhood's End*. 1953. Spaceships come to Earth on a mission. The aliens inside, who look like our concept of the Christian devil, have come to help our children advance to the next stage of human development. They also insist on peace on Earth as they serve as midwives, so to speak, to the transition, trying to make it easier for all concerned as they prepare the children of the Earth for their new lives.

Clarke, Arthur C. *The Hammer of God*. 1993. Religious fanatics try to stop efforts to save the Earth from an asteroid collision so that the Apocalypse will come. More on page 94.

Dick, Philip K. *Galactic Pot-Healer*. 1969. A psychic ceramics repairman is suddenly whisked off to another planet, where he is needed to help raise a submerged cathedral.

Dick, Philip K. *A Maze of Death*. 1970. One of the characters in this bizarre novel flies in a spaceship named the *Morbid Chicken* while looking for God on the newly inhabited planet Delmak-O. A total of fourteen men and women have come to this planet, where paranoia and psychosis seem to be in the very air. They don't know why they are there or what they are supposed to do. And when they begin dying, one by one, they also don't know if one of them is the murderer, or if it's God.

Dick, Philip K. *Radio Free Albemuth*. 1985. This posthumously published novel was the rough draft for *VALIS* (see below), the author's religious science fiction novel. But it is completely different from the other book, a tribute to Dick's creative genius. It is a visionary, alternate history of a United States filled with conspiracy theories and paranoia arising from the federal government spying on its own citizens to find out who is being unpatriotic. In addition, it explores the relationship between the main characters and VALIS, a metaphor for God.

Dick, Philip K. *The Three Stigmata of Palmer Eldritch*. 1964. Considered by many to be one of Dick's best novels; the subject here is "Chew-Z," a narcotic that Palmer Eldritch, a shady businessman, introduces into the solar system, with most unusual results.

Dick, Philip K. Valis Trilogy.

VALIS. 1981. The title stands for Vast Active Living Intelligence System. This is the Godlike entity that communicates, using mystical means, with Horselover Fat, a most unusual hero. Part science fiction and part theological detective story, this is the first of Dick's final three novels and book one of the Valis trilogy.

Divine Invasion. 1981. A woman becomes pregnant with God's child. Sound familiar? Except it doesn't happen on Earth, but on an alien planet instead. Since Christ failed, God, who is alive and in exile on a distant planet, wants to be born again, only this time he comes back as an amnesia-stricken child. The nature of good and evil is explored in this second volume of the Valis trilogy.

The Transmigration of Timothy Archer. 1982. Dick's last novel, the concluding volume of the Valis trilogy, is the story of a man of the cloth whose faith is shaken by the suicides of his son and his mistress and who is subsequently transformed by his bizarre quest for the identity of Christ in the form of a mushroom.

Heinlein, Robert A. *Stranger in a Strange Land*. 1961. One of the most influential SF novels ever written and still recalled by many baby-boomers as a pivotal book in their lives, this book does not hold up for the twenty-first-century reader who finds the '60s sensibilities featuring free love as being dated. The story involves the adventures of an innocent young Earthman, raised on Mars, who returns to Earth, bringing his Martian paranormal powers with him. These include the ability to "discorporate" people—make them disappear into another dimension and to "grok"—a term that became widely used after the novel's publication.

> ***Hugo Award.***

Herbert, Frank. Dune Chronicles.

Dune. 1965. Political machinations move the family of Duke Leto Atreides to the desert planet Dune. After his father is assassinated, young Paul and his mother are taken in by the reclusive Fremen. Paul, now called Muad Dib, becomes a messiah figure. This complex political novel is one of the most important science fiction novels of all time. A prequel trilogy written by Herbert's son, Brian, and Kevin Anderson is annotated on page 19.

> ***Hugo and Nebula Awards.***

Dune Messiah. 1969. A few years after the events of *Dune*, Paul Atreides, genetically bred and trained to become the leader of his planet, tries to control what he has unleashed as the new emperor and messiah of Dune.

Children of Dune. 1976. The sequel to *Dune* and *Dune Messiah* continues the story of the spice-rich desert planet and the trials and tribulations of the family of its messianic Muad'Dib, Paul Atreides.

God-Emperor of Dune. 1981. "Centuries have passed on the planet of Dune and the planet is green with life. Leto, the son of Dune's savior, is still alive but far from human, and the fate of all humanity hangs on his awesome sacrifice."—Prospector Library catalog.

Heretics of Dune. 1984. The sequel to *God-Emperor of Dune* is the fifth in the Dune series. Another complex philosophical look at what is happening on the desert planet of Arrakis, commonly known as Dune, except that this one ends with the apparent destruction of the planet itself.

Chapterhouse Dune. 1985. The legend lives on, even if the desert planet of Arrakis doesn't. It was destroyed in the previous novel, but the Bene Gesserit have a plan. At least one sandworm survived the destruction of Arrakis, so they are turning a green world into a desert home for it. Frank Herbert died shortly after finishing this, his final novel set in the *Dune* universe.

Jensen, Jane. *Millennium Rising.* 1999. Preachers and prophets of many faiths gather in a tiny Mexican village, where they are visited by visions of Armageddon. As each hurries back to his or her flock, they set in motion events that will either save or doom them as cataclysmic events wreak havoc on the world. Is it the end of the world, or is there a vast international conspiracy that has set in motion events that could get entirely out of control? Father Michele Deauchez was at Santa Pelagria, but even though he had the visions (uniquely tailored for each participant), his cynicism leads him on a quest to visit as many of the world spiritual leaders as he can find. Starting out like an end of the world apocalyptic novel, this story wraps up in the finest of SF tradition. When released in paperback, the title was changed to *Judgment Day*.

Kleier, Glenn. *The Last Day*. 1997. Annotated on page 128.

Leiber, Fritz. *Gather, Darkness*. 1950. Leiber's first novel depicts a totalitarian society in a struggle with "witches" and the rebel scientists fighting against it. There is a strong church hierarchy, to which the hero belongs, and he is caught up in a struggle to do what is right even though it is against his duty.

Lewis, C. S. Perlandra Trilogy. Linguist Dr. Elwin Ransom is abducted by aliens and examines the conflicts between science and ethics.

Out of the Silent Planet. 1943. The silent planet is the Earth, as Ransom discovers after he arrives on the planet Mars. Furthermore, this silent planet is a fallen world, according to the spiritual beings he meets on Mars. This classic work of science fiction is the first of a trilogy that becomes more religious and spiritual in each volume.

> *Perelandra*. 1943.

> *That Hideous Strength*. 1945.

Lowry, Lois. *Gathering Blue*. 2000. An annual religious ceremony is based on remembering the past by keeping three children prisoners as they work toward fulfilling their roles for the ritual. More on page 201.

Lowry, Lois. *The Giver*. Annotated on page 201.
YA *Newbery Award.*

Marley, Louise. *The Terrorists of Irustan*. 1999. For three centuries, ever since the planet was settled, life on Irustan has remained the same. The men are free, and the women live entirely at their mercy. Zahra is married to a man of considerable prestige on the planet, but she is also a talented healer, the only profession, other than prostitution, open to women. Her teacher, when discovered treating prostitutes, was tried, found guilty, and condemned to die in the cells, exposed to brutal heat and direct sunlight until she succumbed. Now, like her teacher, Zahra risks her life to treat brutalized prostitutes, but Zahra takes it one step further. She and her friends decide to eliminate some of the more brutal men who prey on their women, thereby becoming the terrorists of Irustan.

Miller, Walter M., Jr. *A Canticle for Leibowitz*. 1961. Deep in the Utah desert, Brother Francis of the Albertian Order of Leibowitz has discovered the sacred shopping list of the blessed St. Leibowitz himself: "lb. pastrami, can of kraut, six bagels, bring home to Emma." This document becomes a message of hope to these monks living in a post-holocaust future.

> *Hugo Award.*

Saint Leibowitz and the Wild Horse Woman. 1997. "Sequel to *A Canticle for Leibowitz*. Isolated in Leibowitz Abbey, Brother Blacktooth St. George stands at the brink of disgrace and expulsion from his order."—Prospector Library catalog.

Resnick, Mike. *Kirinyaga: A Fable of Utopia*. 1992. The Kikuyu God Ngai, creator of all things, sits upon his golden throne atop Mount Kirinyaga. That is why the Holy Mountain's name was given to the terraformed planet, which was chosen as the site of a social experiment by citizens of twenty-second-century Kenya to establish a utopia. Koriba, a distinguished scholar with a European education, the leader of this attempt to return to the "old ways." is sick at heart at how modern conveniences have turned his people into black Europeans. As the mundumugu, or witch doctor, he is also the teacher and custodian of tribal customs. A rigid, inflexible fanatic in his efforts to protect his people, Koriba is also very human in his love for them, in his understanding of human nature, and in his considerable talent for storytelling.

Russell, Mary Doria. *The Sparrow*. 1996. When aliens who create beautiful music are discovered via radio, the race is on to mount an expedition to meet them. The Jesuit order has the know-how and the finances to send the first mission to Rakhat, but something goes horribly wrong. The only survivor is the terribly maimed Father Emilio Sanchez. More on page 149.

> ***James Tiptree Jr. Award.***

Children of God. 1998. Annotated on page 156.

Sawyer, Robert J. *Calculating God*. 2000. Earth is visited by an alien who believes that his people and those of another planet have found evidence of the existence of God. All three planets experienced the same five cataclysmic events at about the same time, showing that God has obviously been playing with the evolution of life on each. A supernova explodes out in the galaxy, close enough to wipe out life on all three homeworlds—unless God intervenes. More on page 151.

Shinn, Sharon. Samaria Trilogy.

The Archangel. 1996. This first novel in the Samaria trilogy is set on a planet were flying angels have been ordained by the god Jovah to watch over its people. When it becomes time for Gabriel to assume his rightful place as the new Archangel, he needs the local oracle to help him select a bride—with the assistance of the homing device on his wrist, the Kiss of the Gods. The oracle selects the Edori slave girl, Rachel, who is a challenge from the very beginning for Gabriel because she is more interested in helping her Edori brethren than her predestined partner.

Jovah's Angel. 1997. The sequel to Archangel is sct 150 years in the future on the Colony Planet of Samaria. The inhabitants of this world are watched over by genetically engineered winged angels who intercede with Jovah to control the destructive climate. Archangel Alleluia must replace her ailing predecessor at a time when nothing seems to be working. The tribes refuse to be pacified, the storms are stronger than ever, Jovah remains distant and unresponsive to her prayers, and no one can tell her who or where the angelico is that she is supposed to marry.

The Alleluia Files. 1998. This stand-alone third entry in the Samaria trilogy is set on a world colonized as a religious utopia. For years the people have worshipped the satellite circling the planet as a god. But not Tamar and her parents, who belong to a religious cult that believes that Jovah is not a god but instead a technical device that the ancestors of Samaria set up to control the weather. Archangel Bael wants to find and kill all the cultists. Tamar wants to avenge her family and friends, and the angel Jared is willing to keep an open mind and help her.

Shinn, Sharon. *Wrapt in Crystal.* 1999. Two religious orders are preyed upon by a serial killer. More on page 174.

Simmons, Dan. *Hyperion.* 1989. The Church of the Shrike has selected a group of pilgrims to attend the opening of the Tombs of Time on Hyperion. The Hegemony, busy with its war against the Ousters, has approved this mission. The pilgrims are convinced that all but one of them will be sacrificed to the deadly killing machines that are the Shrike after the tombs open. Like a science fiction version of *The Canterbury Tales,* each of these "pilgrims" shares his or her story en route, trying to identify what in their lives made the Shrike choose them.

> *Hugo Award.*

The Fall of Hyperion. 1990. The sequel to the award-winning *Hyperion* continues the journey of the pilgrims toward their encounter with the Shrike. During their pilgrimage, humanity faces an Ouster invasion and there is trouble at TechnoCore, the computer center that controls the Web and the Farcast ports that connect all the different worlds. The narrator is a computer cybrid simulacrum named John Keats who poetically "dreams" the adventures the pilgrims are having and does his best to save humanity.

Endymion. 1996. Accompanied by the blue-skinned android, A. Bettik, Raul Endymion's mission was to find Aenea and protect her from the civil and military wing of the Catholic Church known as the Pax, which he was also charged with destroying. That is going to be difficult because he is now locked in a box orbiting a quarantined world. As he waits for the vial of poison gas that will end his life, he thinks of Aenea and how his efforts to carry out his mission have landed him in his current precarious position. More on page 164.

The Rise of Endymion. 1997. The Catholic Pax and the artificial-intelligence driven TechnoCore have combined forces to eliminate a deadly threat, teenaged Aenea, who is now recognized as the messiah. Assassins are sent after her, but Raul Endymion, who is in love with her, will protect her with his life, surprisingly assisted by the monster/angel/killing machine (and now protector) that is the Shrike. This is the conclusion of what was hailed by the *New York Times Book Review* as one of the finest achievements of modern science fiction.

Stapledon, Olaf. *Star Maker*. 1937. Cosmic in scale, this work covers billions of years as it depicts the development of intelligent life in the universe. It's all seen through the eyes of a man sitting on a hill, thinking about the meaning of life one minute and hurtling through space the next on an incredible voyage of discovery.

Stewart, Daniel Blair. *Akhunaton: The Extraterrestrial King*. 1995. An alien comes to Earth in the guise of the god Horus because peaceful civilizations have turned on each other, spreading war and fear everywhere. The alien's goal is to try to preserve humanity and the secret it holds by returning to ancient Egypt to impart its ancient wisdom.

Tepper, Sheri S. Marjorie Westriding Trilogy. Annotated on page 156.

Zelazny, Roger. *Lord of Light*. 1967. After a colony ship finds a suitable world for its settlers, some of the crew members assume the role of Hindu gods. The colonists need a Buddha to save them, and he doesn't let them down.

Hugo Award.

Political

Political intrigues are as popular as military maneuverings in SF and often convey the same level of excitement—through psychological suspense, action, or both.

Anthony, Piers. *Total Recall*. 1989. Annotated on page 2.

Bear, Greg. *Moving Mars*. 1993. Casseia Majumdar tells the story of why it was necessary to move the planet Mars. Years ago, when she was a college student on Mars, the always sensible, conservative Casseia joined a student protest movement over the closing of the university. The movement was promptly squelched by the authorities, but a desire to make a difference was born in Casseia that led her to enter politics—first as an ambassador's assistant on a trip to Mars, then as vice-president, and finally as president when her good friend and relative was assassinated. A former lover, an Olympian, one of nine highly theoretical thinkers, developed a method to actually move the planet. When conflict between Earth and Mars escalates into war, the only way to avoid Earth's superior nanotechnology is for Mars to move to a place of safety, and thanks to her lover, Casseia has the technology to do it.

Nebula Award.

Bova, Ben. *Mars*. 1992. Jamie Waterman, half Navaho and half Anglo, is a geologist who gets to go on a Mars expedition at the last minute. Feeling very much like an outsider, he quotes a Navaho expression when he steps on to the planet, instead of his prepared speech. This gets him in trouble with mission control, the media, and the vice-president, who all think he's some kind of Native American activist because they can't translate what he said. More on page 34.

Return to Mars. 1999. The scientific community, political in-fighting, media personalities, and the red planet itself, along with the individuals who risk their lives to explore it, make for compelling reading. More on page 34.

Bova, Ben, and A. J. Austin. *To Save the Sun.* 1992. Adela, a young female scientist, is sent on a mission to convince an outpost planet to join the hundred worlds in an effort to save the sun. She succeeds in spite of an ongoing civil war. Those in authority agree that the Earth as a gene pool needs to be protected. So if there is a scientific theory that can rejuvenate the dying sun, every effort should be made to bring this theory to fruition, even if it means that Adela must go into cryosleep for two centuries to wait until just the right time to put her theories to the test.

Bova, Ben and A.J. Austin. *To Fear the Light.* 1994. In this sequel to the authors' *To Save the Sun*, Dr. Adela emerges from her 200-year-long sleep to a transformed galaxy. Although there are advances like faster-than-light travel and communication, the central government might no longer be able to support the all-important mission to save the Earth's sun, especially when a new alien race puts the project in jeopardy.

Brunner, John. *The Shockwave Rider.* 1975. Annotated on page 76.

Butler, Octavia E. *Kindred.* 1979. Annotated on page 50.

Dick, Philip K. *Martian Time-Slip.* 1964. On colonial Mars in the near future a ten-year-old autistic boy, who nevertheless can communicate with the despised "natives," may also be able to manipulate time and see the future.

Heinlein, Robert A. *Double Star.* 1956. Shanghaied to Mars, out-of-work actor Lorenzo Smyth takes on the most important role of his life—one that can make the difference between peace with the Martians or interplanetary war.

Hugo Award.

Le Guin, Ursula K. *The Dispossessed.* 1974. A brilliant scientist flees the anarchy and uto- pia of his small planet to greater intellectual freedom, but a more chaotic lifestyle, on a neighboring planet.

Hugo, Nebula, and Locus Awards.

Marley, Louise. *The Terrorists of Irustan.* 1999. Annotated on page 104

Robinson, Kim Stanley. Mars Trilogy.

Red Mars. 1992. As humans colonize Mars, two societies are formed. The Reds want to leave the planet alone and preserve its natural state. The Greens want to hydroplane and change the planet to make it more friendly toward human life. More on page 40.

Green Mars. 1993. The adventures of the first human settlers on the planet Mars continue, as does the battle over whether to terraform the red planet.

Blue Mars. 1996. "Blue" is because there is now water on Mars, courtesy of the extensive terraforming of the formerly red planet. This is the concluding volume of the Mars trilogy, acknowledged by many to be a modern science fiction masterpiece.

Sterling, Bruce. *Distraction*. 1998. Annotated on page 119.

Tepper, Sheri S. *Singer from the Sea*. 2000. Annotated on page 123.

Vinge, Vernor. *The Peace War*. 1984. Bobble technology was first introduced in this prequel to *Marooned in Realtime* (annotated on page 52). Before it was used as an effective method of time travel, it was an efficient method for the execution of transgressors. The Peace Authority controls this ultimate weapon with its impenetrable force fields know as the "Bobble." Executions are carried out by enclosing transgressors inside the spherical force field. There they are trapped for all eternity, slowly dying from asphyxiation in an airless tomb.

Wolfe, Gene. The Book of the Long Sun. This is the story of Patera Silk, a devout priest, and what happens as he travels on the *Whorl,* a vast, cylindrical starship that is beginning to require repairs after its generations-long voyage.

Nightside the Long Sun. 1993. Patera Silk is traveling on the *Whorl*, a giant spaceship sent out from Urth on a mission to colonize a distant planet. The *Whorl*'s many gods communicate with its inhabitants via "Sacred Windows" from their mainframe home. But Patera Silk's home is in the decaying city of Viron onboard the ship, and the god communicating with him is an Outsider, which almost causes a revolt on the ship.

Lake of the Long Sun. 1994. In this second volume of a tetralogy, Patera Silk finds that he must turn to robbery to get the funds he needs to buy back his church from a wealthy crime lord. In the meantime, the giant spaceship continues its generations-long voyage to an unknown destiny.

Caldé of the Long Sun. 1994. After winning over the local militia to his cause of changing the government to better protect the people, Patera Silk becomes the first Caldé in more than a century, wielding both political and religious power. This is the third volume of an acknowledged masterpiece.

Exodus from the Long Sun. 1996. This is the final installment of Patera Silk's voyage on the multigenerational starship, the *Whorl*. The young priest turned ruler has known the nature of the vessel and the gods his people worship for some time. Now he must prepare the others for this revelation.

A Broken Butterfly Wing:
Parallel Worlds and Alternate Histories

Parallel worlds have been standard settings for SF for many years. Often referred to as "other dimensions," these are worlds, located alongside our own, that can be reached through another dimension. Tales involving these worlds tend to fall into two categories. In one type, passageways exist allowing a character to move through different worlds. Classic prototypes include Heinlein's short story "—And He Built a Crooked House," in which an architect constructs a multidimensional house, one that is theoretically a tesseract shape but that once entered leads into parallel worlds. Madeleine L'Engle also tackled the idea of parallel worlds in her classic novel for all ages, *A Wrinkle in Time* (page 54). The other category of alternate world is defined by John Clute and Peter Nicholls in *The Encyclopedia of Science Fiction* as follows: "An Alternate world—some writers and commentators prefer the designation 'alternative world' on grammatical grounds—is an account of Earth as it might have become in consequence of some hypothetical alteration in history." An incident in the past, perhaps something as insignificant as the breaking of a butterfly's wing, can change the direction of history and cause timelines to diverge. In some cases, this divergence causes a new world to come into existence; in others it merely obliterates the future as we know it.

In other words, these stories explore history as it might have been. What if there had been a significant change in an historical event? What, then, would have been the pattern of history? What would the present be like, and why? This theoretical exploration of historical cause and effect is often conjoined to the parallel world theme in science fiction. Parallel Earths and parallel universes can exist simultaneously with our Earth, conceived, perhaps, along a spatial fourth dimension. This theme has been used by many science fiction authors in addition to those listed here. In the early 1990s, some of the cyberpunk authors started writing in the alternative history vein; these books were promptly christened "steampunk" because of their nineteenth-century background, featuring the industry, science, and technology of the world of Charles Dickens and Victorian London.

Rewriting history or opening a door and finding out just how different life on the other side can be are still popular science fiction themes today. Authors faced with infinite possibilities are sharing them with their readers in infinite ways.

Parallel Worlds

Imagine that you're a teenager who has inherited a farm from an uncle who disappeared under mysterious circumstances. One day you discover a door in the back of the barn on your property—a door that leads to a primitive Earth with lots of dangerous animals, but also lots of gold. So you and your teenaged friends set up a mining operation on the other side of the door—on the *Wildside* (page 112). But then the government finds out what is going on and wants more than its fair share. Now it's up to you to protect the Wildside from invasion, in the novel of the same name by Steven Gould. What if you had to share your world with dinosaurs? That's what the characters in the Eden trilogy by Harry Harrison have to do. What would have happened if the U.S. Army had arrived in Berlin first at the close of World War II? If Churchill had recognized just how dangerous Stalin was and had authorized a plan to assassinate him? What would have happened if Roosevelt had not died at the end of the war? Speculations along these lines are the subject of Ben Bova's *Triumph* (page 114).

Anthony, Piers. Apprentice Adept Series. Proton and Phaze are worlds that exist side by side, but in one magic works and in the other technology. Protonian Stile travels to Phaze to try to discover who murdered him there. There is a Games Computer on the planet world Proton, a world that relies heavily on the use of technology. There is an Oracle on the planet Phaze, a world that relies heavily on the use of magic. Can Games Computer and Oracle be one and the same?

Split Infinity. 1980. Book One introduces Stile, a serf who plays computer games and is happy with his robot slave girl, until a death threat sends him on the run to a magic-filled, sword-and-sorcery world.

Blue Adept. 1981. On Phaze, Stile is no longer a serf. He is the Blue Adept, the strongest magician on the planet, befriended by Neysa, a Unicorn that can transform itself into a firefly—or a woman. Unfortunately, on Phaze, just as on Proton, there is an assassin trying to kill Stile.

Juxtaposition. 1982. Stile is struggling to survive on both worlds—to find his enemy Adept on Phaze and survive the Great Games on Proton. This is the third volume of the original Adept trilogy.

Out of Phaze. 1987. The fourth Adept book features the adventures of Stile's sons, Mach on Proton and Bane on Phaze. Twenty years after Stile's adventures on these two worlds, his sons discover they have suddenly switched bodies.

Robot Adept. 1988. The adventures of Mach, the robot from the science world of Proton, and Bane, the magic-wielding wizard from Phaze, continue as they attempt to keep these two warring worlds from destroying each other.

Unicorn Point. 1989. The parallel worlds of Phaze and Proton are in danger from a ruthless enemy. Fortunately, Mach and Bane still share a link between their worlds, and now they have children powerful enough to help them.

Phaze Doubt. 1990. In the concluding volume of the Adept series, it is up to the children of Mach and Bane, possessed of powerful magical abilities, to save Phaze and Proton from the enemy.

Asimov, Isaac. *The Gods Themselves*. 1972. The alien inhabitants of an alternative universe are not happy with the effects on them of a newly developed device that can produce limitless energy.

Hugo, Nebula, and Locus Awards.

Bear, Greg. *Eon*. 1985. An asteroid that is really a spaceship built by humans who inhabit a parallel universe suddenly enters the solar system.

Eternity. 1988. This sequel to *Eon* is another challenging work by a master of hard science fiction. It should only be read in conjunction with the previous work, as it goes one step further in its explorations of space and time on a vast scale.

Legacy. 1995. A war with the Jarts has stripped Earth of its resources, so when someone who had emigrated to the Earth-like world, Lamarckia, comes back, the Hexamon sends Olmy Ap Sennon to investigate. Olmy discovers that time is different on the other side of the "gate."

Dick, Philip K. *Flow My Tears, the Policeman Said*. 1974. A television superstar wakes up one day to discover that he is now on a parallel world—a world in which no one recognizes him. He is still in America, but it is an America that is a dystopian police state, a grim setting that fortunately is inhabited by a few sympathetic characters.

Dick, Philip K. *Now Wait for Last Year.* 1966. Two alien races appear and continue their battle on the Earth—powerful humanoids versus human-sized ants that speak in clicks. The opposition on Earth is led by an ailing general and his mild-mannered, unhappily married doctor, whose wife is addicted to a time-control drug.

Doyle, Sir Arthur Conan. *The Lost World.* 1912. This classic expedition into the unknown introduced Professor Challenger to the world. This time the explorers find dinosaurs and apemen living on a plateau in South America.

Gould, Steven. *Wildside.* 1996. Eighteen-year-old Charlie has inherited a pristine, untouched world on the other side of a door in a barn. To explore it he needs money, which he obtains by importing an extinct species from the other side, where sabertooth tigers and immense herds of bison still roam. He also needs stalwart companions with survival and flight skills, and he especially needs legal protection. The forces he and his assembled partners face are armed and dangerous, but lethal teeth and claws may not be the biggest challenge.

Hopkinson, Nalo. *Midnight Robber.* 2000. Touissant is a Caribbean-colonized planet where Carnivale is celebrated and the Robber Queen costume is Tan-Tan's favorite. But when her corrupt politician father commits a crime and is caught, they are exiled to their planet's untamed quantum twin. Fortunately for Tan-Tan, the mythic powers of the Robber Queen help her survive the jungles, aliens, and criminals they encounter there.

McCay, Bill. The adventures of Egyptologist Daniel Jackson and Colonel Jack O'Neil. Stargate series.

Stargate: Rebellion. 1995.

Stargate: Retaliation. 1996.

Stargate: Retribution. 1997.

Stargate: Reconnaissance. 1998.

Reed, Robert. *Beyond the Veil of Stars.* 1994. Annotated on page 40.

Beneath the Gated Sky. 1997. Annotated on page 40.

Russ, Joanna. *The Female Man.* 1975. This feminist novel about four different women from parallel worlds was reissued in 2000. Joanna is from our world; Jeannine is a meek librarian from a repressive, male-dominated society; Janet lives in a future when all the men have died off; and Jael is an assassin who owns a male sex slave from a future world where men and women live in separate armed camps.

Wilson, Robert Charles. *Mysterium*. 1994. One night an explosion, accompanied by a flash of blinding light, causes a perfect circle of land to disappear from the face of the Earth. Inside this circle is a research facility and the nearby town of Two Rivers. Unfortunately, they reappear on a world that is at war, and the citizens are subjected to Proctors, censors, religious intolerance, and a strong, uncaring military presence. Howard Poole is a mild-mannered scientist who just might be able to figure out what happened and how to correct it. But he had better hurry because the Proctors have developed a nuclear bomb and plan to get rid of these newly arrived heretics by dropping it on the town.

Alternate History

Alternate history tells the stories of what could have happened if some event in history diverged from the path we know and as a result caused that time's future to experience events that differ from those we know.

What if you and all the other superpowers are comfortably engaged in making the world an unsafe place during World War II when the true enemy arrives—and changes the course of civilization on our world? All it takes is for one little event to change—a certain man doesn't meet a certain woman at a certain time—so they never marry. As a result Hitler is not born. What if the Cuban blockade failed and the United States was reduced by nuclear bombs to the status of a Third World country, easy prey for a possible invasion—by our friends the British? What if Churchill recognized the threat that Stalin posed and took steps to eliminate him, at the same time that Patton pushed his way to Berlin and arrived there first? What if George Washington didn't defeat the British forces but reconciled the rebellious colonies with King George instead? What if the dinosaurs didn't die out but developed an advanced civilization that became a threat to the more primitive civilization developed by humans? What if General Lee was able to arm his forces with AK-47s and change the course of the Civil War? What if Europe disappeared and was replaced by an entirely new and very strange landmass called Darwinia? These and the other speculative scenarios described below show that alternate history is the ultimate "what if?" fiction.

If this type of story intrigues you, you may want to find out more about it. An excellent discussion of alternate history as well as comprehensive bibliographies can be found on the Web at http://www.uchronia.net/intro.html.

Barnes, John. *Finity*. 1999. Probability is juggled in a world where the United States has vanished from the collective memory and various Reichs have ruled since the Axis victory more than 100 years previously. Lyle Peripart's life is changed forever when powerful industrialist Geoffrey Iphwin hires him. He is subsequently beaten by the Gestapo, targeted in several murder attempts, and acquires a cat named Fluffy. Then his fiancée Helen meets him in Hanoi; she has completely different memories of world history than he does.

Barnes, John. Timeline Wars. Wise-cracking Mark Strang is extremely good at what he does: thinking fast, rolling with the punches, and killing Closers at every chance he gets. His mother, brother, and wife were killed by a Closer bomb, the same bomb that left his sister with just one arm. Now he is taking an active part in the battles being waged across multiple timelines.

Patton's Spaceship. 1997. Strang's first trip takes him to a world where the Nazis won World War II.

Washington's Dirigible. 1997. This time Strang battles his own alter ego in a dirigible while attempting to get the real King George out of captivity in England and to safety among his friends in Colonial America. There was no Revolutionary War in this timeline, and George Washington, rather than being the father of our country, is the Duke of Kentucky. Mark Strang is the Crux Operative who was sent on a solo mission to a Colonial America that has steam engines, dirigibles, and submarines, like the Nautilus of John Paul Jones. There's also lots of fire power, supplied by operatives who have explained the details of the battle against the Closers to Mark and enlisted what aid they could.

Caesar's Bicycle. 1997. This time Mark Strang's investigation into the disappearance of a fellow time traveler takes him back to the time of Caesar and the Roman Triumvirate, and more Closers, of course.

Bear, Greg. *Dinosaur Summer*. 1998. Dozens of dinosaurs were abandoned when the last of the dinosaur circuses closed down, and a daring expedition sets out to return them to the Lost World.

Bova, Ben. *Triumph*. 1993. Suppose President Roosevelt stopped smoking, was able to remain healthy and fully in charge, and did not have a fatal stroke. Suppose Winston Churchill could foresee the dangerous beast that Stalin would become and took steps to eradicate him by having a sympathetic agent place a wafer of plutonium in the Russian leader's desk drawer. Suppose Patton pushed through to Berlin before the Russians could get there. And suppose America wound up as the only game in town, a worldwide American empire that will not allow any other nation to acquire atomic weaponry. The world leaders and the events surrounding them are all faithfully depicted here, including Hitler in his bunker. But the outcome is different because of a bold plan masterminded and carried out by Winston Churchill.

Dick, Philip K. *The Man in the High Castle*. 1962. In an alternative world, Germany and Japan have won World War II. This causes numerous problems for a strange cast of characters living in California in the early 1960s.

> ***Hugo Award.***

Dreyfuss, Richard, and Harry Turtledove. *The Two Georges*.1996. Our world would be very different if George Washington had reconciled the rebellious colonies with King George. Americans, as loyal subjects of the Crown, may not have been so innovative or inventive, or maybe in this reality there was no Revolution because the colonists weren't as independent as in ours. This thought-provoking tale takes Colonel Thomas Bushell of the Royal American Mounted Police on a trek from sea to shining sea as he tries to recover the famous Gainsborough painting, *The Two Georges*, which is emblematic of America as a loyal subject nation. At a gala reception in New Liverpool (Los Angeles), Tricky Dicky (Richard Nixon), the used steamer magnate, is killed by gunfire, a most unusual occurrence. At the same time *The Two Georges* is stolen by the Sons of Liberty, a radical group that wants American autonomy. On the trail of the painting, along with his friend and coworker Sam Stanley, Tom once again runs into the curator of the traveling exhibit, the lovely Kathleen Flannery, who claims to be conducting her own investigation into the abduction of the painting.

DuBois, Brendan. *Resurrection Day*. 1999. Annotated on page 86.

Gibson, William, and Bruce Sterling. *The Difference Engine*. 1991. A steam-driven calculator changes the face of the Victorian era, turning it into a strange, modernistic world complete with fast food and credit cards.

Harrison, Harry. Eden Trilogy.

West of Eden. 1984. In this alternate world the dinosaurs never died out. Instead, they developed their own civilization. Eventually, a conflict develops between this advanced dinosaur civilization and a more primitive human civilization.

Winter in Eden. 1986. Even though he was raised by the Yilane, the reptilian dominant species on the prehistoric Earth, Kerrick, a young human, escapes to lead his own kind against them in a world where evolution played out quite differently.

Return to Eden. 1988. Humans and the reptilian Yilane meet in a battle for the destiny of their races.

Hogan, James P. *The Proteus Operation*. 1985. In the 1970s a group of scientists decides to go back in time to try to change the course of human history. Their goal is the year 1939. Their purpose is to try to reverse the outcome of World War II, so that the Nazis lose the war instead of winning it.

Turtledove, Harry. The Great War. The Confederate States of America are fighting the United States of America, not in the Civil War but in World War I. The Confederates are allied with the British and the French; the United States with the Germans.

The Great War: American Front. 1998.

The Great War: Walk in Hell. 1999.

The Great War: Breakthroughs. 2000.

Turtledove, Harry. *The Guns of the South: A Novel of the Civil War*. 1992. When General Lee finds a way to arm his forces with AK-47s, he turns the tide of the war and changes everything.

Turtledove, Harry. Worldwar Series. World War II is interrupted by a fleet of lizardlike beings from outer space who have come to claim the Earth as their own. They've done their research, they've sent probes ahead, and they know what to expect—knights in armor on horseback. Instead, they find themselves facing guns and tanks and General Patton, not to mention a winter the likes of which they've never experienced.

Worldwar: In the Balance: The Alternate History of Alien Invasion. 1994.

Worldwar: Tilting the Balance. 1995.

Worldwar: Upsetting the Balance. 1996.

Worldwar: Striking the Balance. 1996.

Wilson, Robert Charles. *Darwinia.* 1998. In 1912, in an incident known as "The Miracle," Europe disappears, and a new landmass called Darwinia, filled with alien flora and fauna, appears in its place.

Zelazny, Roger. *A Dark Traveling.* 1987. Annotated on page 208.

Chapter 4

Us and Them

Strange beings—whether human, animal, or alien—populate science fiction, giving the SF writer the opportunity to explore and express a vast array of possibilities, ultimately teaching us a great deal about who we are, what it means to be human, and how we might relate to others. In this chapter we examine stories about unique variations on the members of our human race—from subhuman to superhuman, and from monsters to mutants—as well as stories that feature amazing animals and alien beings that range from the grotesque to the genteel.

Fascination with unusual creatures can be seen in the earliest SF writings: a human monster appearing in Shelley's *Frankenstein* and Martians in H. G. Wells's *War of the Worlds*. This interest has persisted throughout SF's history, with such compelling characters as that of E.T., a vulnerable and benign extraterrestrial, and Anne McCaffrey's mythical but scientifically explicable dragons. Themes of self-acceptance, compassion, and getting along with those who are different are often associated with this motif.

Readers who enjoy reading about strange creatures may also want to check the section on "Robots, Androids, and Cyborgs" in Chapter 2. And those fascinated with the darker side of alien life forms might find other books they enjoy in Chapter 5, "Genreblending," under the "It's Horrific" section.

We're All Just Human—Mostly

Not all science fiction stories are populated by exotic aliens. Many writers follow the conventional wisdom of writing about what one knows, and that often turns out to be human nature. But SF explores a wide range of diversity within the parameters of human life. Here we find human beings that may be hardly recognizable as such. They may have such special abilities and powers as mind control, telepathy, teleportation, telekinesis, clairvoyance, immortality, and shapeshifting. We may meet humans who are one step ahead of us on the evolutionary path, and we may meet future humans who have been thrown back into the simpler or more pastoral ways of the distant past. We visit futures where humans are genetically manipulated to fulfill highly specialized social functions, or perhaps they are just more spiritually advanced. Science fiction's human beings may live on a dramatically changed Earth; or they may live on a distant planet, on a space station, or on a starship. They may even be trapped inside another human's identity. Human clones, human monsters, humans inexorably coupled with spaceships or computers—these are just some of the possible extensions of humankind in science fiction.

Near Future—Humanity's Next Step

In the near future, Earth as well as its inhabitants are easily recognizable. The inventiveness and challenges faced in the following novels prove that good science fiction doesn't necessarily require a distant locale in either time or space.

Barnes, John. *Candle*. 2000. Late twenty-first century. Annotated on page 133.

Barnes, John. *Mother of Storms*. 1994. Annotated on page 90.

Bear, Greg. *Darwin's Radio*. 1999. This tale of what may be the next evolutionary step for humanity is annotated on page 126.

Benford, Gregory. *In the Ocean of Night*. 1977. Annotated on page 44.

Bradbury, Ray. *Martian Chronicles*. 1950. In his trademark poetic style, Bradbury provides a collection of short stories based on the theme of the colonization of Mars. Linked stories offer parallels between Earth's colonization of Mars and the European colonization of the New World. These stories were filmed as a television mini-series featuring Rock Hudson. (Although Bradbury is considered an important author in SF, most of his work falls into the realm of fantasy—specifically dark fantasy.)

   Television. Classic.

Burgess, Anthony. *A Clockwork Orange*. 1962. Annotated on page 96.

Clough, Brenda W. *How Like a God*. 1997. Achieving the power to mentally manipulate people, computer programmer Rob Lewis flees from his family and becomes a derelict. Then he meets neurobiologist Edwin Barbarossa, who helps him discover the source of his power.

   Doors of Death and Life. 2000. Rob Lewis has made Edwin Barbarossa immortal, a gift that puts him under suspicion when he is the only survivor of a shuttle mishap. Now he's being blamed for murdering his crew mates.

Dick, Philip K. *The Three Stigmata of Palmer Eldritch*. 1964. Annotated on page 102.

Flynn, Michael. *Firestar*. 1997. In the cover blurb, Harry Turtledove compares this entertaining near future epic to Robert A. Heinlein's tales of the near future. Like Heinlein,

Flynn uses his story to decry some of the wrongs he sees in the world and to present possible cures, including reaching out to space travel to ensure a future. Annotated on page 45.

Kress, Nancy. *Maximum Light*. 1998. Told from the viewpoints of a rebellious young woman, a dying doctor, and a gay young dancer, this story leads us to a world where, due to mutations and an alarming decline in the birthrate, humanity teeters on the brink of extinction. Unable to nurture (i.e., give birth to and raise) children, many people turn to surrogates, leading to a criminal underground experimenting with illegal genetic manipulations.

Leiber, Fritz. *The Wanderer*. 1965. Annotated on page 94.

MacLeod, Ken. *The Sky Road*. 2000. In the middle of the twenty-first century, after the world has degenerated into many warring city/states, a woman who rules a tiny country struggles to keep her people safe. Her actions result in changes that cause people several hundred years in the future to call her the Deliverer.

> ***British SF Award.***

Sawyer, Robert J. *Factoring Humanity*. 1998. Since the early part of the twenty-first century, Earth has been receiving signals from interstellar space that no one could understand. After they stop coming, one woman scientist realizes that the messages contained instructions on how to build an extraordinary machine. Could this be the key to limitless exploration or the end of the human race?

Sawyer, Robert J. *Flashforward*. 1999. A scientific experiment sends the consciousness of everyone in the world forward in time by twenty-one years, and in those two minutes millions of people die. Those who don't have tantalizing glimpses of their futures. One man who sees nothing must now solve his own future murder.

> ***Aurora Award.***

Sawyer, Robert J. *Frameshift*. 1997. Trying to avoid a genetic disease, a couple puts themselves, and their genetic material, at the mercy of a possible war criminal. Annotated on page 130.

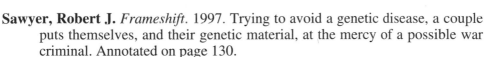

Stephenson, Neal. *The Diamond Age, or, A Young Lady's Illustrated Primer*. 1995. With the help of a nanotech-rich book, two young women become something more than anyone could expect. Annotated on page 71.

> ***Hugo and Locus Awards.***

Sterling, Bruce. *Distraction*. 1998. Black market baby dealers were responsible for Oscar's bizarre genetic history.

Stine, G. Harry. *First Action*. 1993. While looking into the mysterious disappearances of naval personnel off a remote island, the captain of an American submarine discovers alien invaders.

Strieber, Whitley. *Wolf of Shadows*. 1985. Humans and wolves form a family to survive a nuclear winter. Annotated on page 87.

Williamson, Jack. *The Silicon Dagger*. 1999. When Clay Barstow goes to McAdam, Kentucky, to investigate his half-brother's murder, he discovers a separatist militia armed with technology that may enable them to successfully break away from the United States.

Williamson, Jack, and Frederik Pohl. The Starchild Trilogy. This best-selling collaboration by two SFWA Grand Masters is set in a limitless, steady state universe where evolution plays a huge role. Space opera about the rise of humankind into a species that develops space flight. The trilogy consists of the following.

The Reefs of Space. 1964.

Starchild. 1965.

Rogue Star. 1969

Willis, Connie. *Remake*. 1995. Annotated on page 54.

Earth's Children

Earth's children are the benefactors of humankind's discovery of how (and where) to travel—in our galaxy and elsewhere. Some are the descendants of our Earth, who may think of their home world as a mythological construct. Some may even be on their way back to Earth (like the characters in Orson Scott Card's Homecoming series). In other scenarios, Pern and Darkover are settled by seed ships from Earth. Andre Norton takes her characters all through the universe, looking for Forerunner artifacts and speculating about the historical expansion of the human race. Many of the other worlds that are settings for SF are peopled by the descendants of Earth.

Asaro, Catherine. *Primary Inversion*. 1995. Annotated on page 125.

Asimov, Isaac. Foundation Series.

Prelude to Foundation. 1988. Prequel to the original Foundation Trilogy.

Forward the Foundation. 1993. Prequel to the original Foundation Trilogy.

 Foundation. 1951. First book in the original Foundation Trilogy. Hari Seldon, the inventor of psychohistory, and a genius observing the decline and fall of the Galactic Empire, takes steps to ensure that civilization survives. The first of Asimov's extremely popular and long-lasting Foundation Series, this work is still enjoyed today.

Foundation and Empire. 1952. In the second book of the original Foundation Trilogy, the Mule, a powerful mutant, threatens the Galactic Empire of Hari Seldon.

Second Foundation. 1953. The third in Asimov's classic Foundation Trilogy continues the adventures of psychohistorian Hari Seldon as he participates in what may be the final days of the Galactic Empire.

 Foundation's Edge. 1982. More than twenty years after finishing his Foundation Trilogy, Asimov returned to the world of his Galactic Empire to explain how robots worked behind the scenes to ensure the survival of the human race.

Hugo and Locus Awards.

Foundation and Earth. 1986. In this sequel to *Foundation's Edge*, the space travelers of the earlier work leave the sentient planet of Gaia for the Earth.

Asimov, Isaac. "Nightfall." 1941. Selected in polls as the most popular SF story ever, this short tale describes what happens to a world that is accustomed to only daylight and whose inhabitants have never seen the stars, until night begins to fall. Asimov and Robert Silverberg published a novelization of this classic short story, also titled *Nightfall*, in 1990.

Banks, Iain M. *Consider Phlebas*. 1987. Set in his "Culture" universe, this is an account of the struggle between the artificially intelligent "Minds" that rule that universe and the alien Idirans, religious fanatics who are all too willing to fight. It is also the account of a mission to recover something that both sides of the conflict are desperate to capture. But it's Horza and his rag-tag company who have the best chance of succeeding because they are willing to undertake an odyssey that could lead to certain death.

The Player of Games. 1989. Centuries after the events that took place in the universe of the author's *Consider Phlebas*, conflict arises between the evil empire of the Azad and the inhabitants of the space-faring utopian "Culture."

Banks, Iain. *Excession*. 1996. Annotated on page 70.

Bova, Ben, and A. J. Austin. *To Save the Sun*. 1992. Annotated on page 108.

Bradley, Marion Zimmer. Darkover Series. Annotated on page 11.

Card, Orson Scott. Homecoming Series.

The Memory of Earth. 1992. The Oversoul, master computer of the planet Harmony, selects Nafai and his family to help it return to Earth for much-needed repairs. Harmony has been kept at a pastoral level by the computer, so that the humans who inhabit it will not blow themselves up as their ancestors did on Earth so long ago. But with the master computer failing, things are going to change for Harmony—and for Nafai's family.

The Call of Earth. 1992. The Oversoul, a computer that has chosen Nafai and his family to help it get back to Earth for needed repairs, is becoming more interactive with the "chosen," but some of their dreams appear to be coming from somewhere else. Could these visions be coming from the Master Computer, the Keeper of Earth, calling the children of Earth home?

The Ships of Earth. 1994. Nafai finally assumes the leadership role that the Oversoul of Harmony and the Master Computer from Earth have had in mind for him all along. All his life Nafai has loved, respected, and longed for the acceptance of his older brother Elemak, the natural born leader who should have been in charge of this expedition from the very first. But Elemak refuses to believe in or listen to the Master Computer, and his angry jealousy of his younger brother sets in motion a generations-long struggle.

Earthfall. 1995. The humans from Harmony finally return to Earth. During the voyage Elemak continues to be murderously jealous of his younger brother, Nafai, and the next generation is drawn into their struggle. After landfall they discover the indigenous people of the Earth, the Angels and the Devils, or Skymeat and Diggers, who have evolved over the centuries from bats and rats. Both species view the arrival of the "Old Ones" as divine intervention—at first. But then Elemak's attempt to destroy his brother draws all three species down the road to war—with only a dim hope for peace in the future.

Earthborn. 1995. Hundreds of years have passed since the actions that occurred in *Earthfall.* Shedemai is still alive, due to the longevity provided by the Cloak of the Starmaster, which was passed on to her by Nafai so that he could return to live and die with his family and friends. The Oversoul is also still operational. Centuries have passed, but peaceful coexistence among the three species—Diggers, Angels, and Earth people—still has a long way to go. Shedemai herself must come down from the spaceship and take an active role for the first time in generations, to ensure that peace prevails in the land.

Dunn, J. R. *Full Tide of Night.* 1998. Annotated on page 78.

Gould, Steven. *The Helm.* 1998. Leland follows a rocky path to greatness after he ascends a forbidden peak and places a sacred helmet upon his head. The privilege of donning the mysterious artifact rightly belonged to his oldest brother, who had been groomed to govern. After he takes his brother's place, Leland's father seemingly turns on him, until a young woman of high station intercedes for him. Leland is sent to a distant village to study martial arts, where he discovers that on an unconscious level he knows much that he has no rational explanation for knowing. As a war begins, he finds himself pressed into a position of leadership.

McCaffrey, Anne. All of McCaffrey's many series are peopled with descendants of humans from Earth. Many of this prolific author's titles are annotated in the "More Than Human" section of this chapter (pages 125-131).

Moon, Elizabeth. *Remnant Population.* 1996. Ofelia, an elderly woman, refuses to leave a settlement when the Company abandons it to cut its losses, thereby becoming the "remnant population of this world." Having lost almost all her family and not having the money for the transportation that would probably kill her anyway, she elects to stay and enjoy some peace and quiet. When another ship arrives bringing a new colony, it is attacked and destroyed by the planet's indigenous population. These natives come to her settlement looking for someone who can teach them, become a nest guardian for their young, and assist their race in its rapid technological advances in the face of human invasion. When more human ships come, Ofelia becomes the natives' ambassador, having learned that the previous ships had unknowingly wreaked havoc on the native population.

Norton, Andre. Foreunner Series. Long before humankind traveled through the galaxy, a forgotten race ranged the spaceways, leaving artifacts and installations behind. (Norton's official web site is at http://www. andre-norton. org/)

Storm Over Warlock. 1960. Terrans on a survey mission are attacked by aliens and join forces with a matriarchal psi-gifted race called Wyverns.

Ordeal in Otherwhere. 1964. Sold into slavery, Charis ends up on Warlock, where she joins forces with the Terrans and Wyverns.

Ice Crown. 1970. A search for a legendary treasure.

Forerunner Foray. 1973. "When a highly skilled sensitive comes into contact with a strange green stone, she finds herself trapped in the past in the identity of another person."—Prospector Library catalog

Forerunner. 1981. Simsa is mentally joined with a dead Forerunner priestess.

Forerunner: The Second Adventure. 1985. The adventure begun in *Forerunner* continues here.

Stapledon, Olaf. *Last and First Men.* 1930. Covers two billion years of human evolution, starting in the 1930s and proceeding into a future that has taken us to outer space and beyond.

Tepper, Sheri S. *Singer from the Sea.* 2000. The non-technological planet Haven is peopled by the descendants of those who fled the dying Earth. Although most on the planet seem to be thriving, young noblewomen live extremely constrained lives that tend to end early.

Vinge, Vernor. *A Deepness in the Sky.* 1999. Annotated on page 157.

Wolfe, Gene. The Book of the Long Sun. Annotated on page 109. In the far future, an entire human civilization lives inside an enormous construct, a generation starship, and within the confines of the Whorl, a world with its own seasons, sun, and land masses.

Nightside the Long Sun. 1993.

Lake of the Long Sun. 1994.

Calde of the Long Sun. 1994.

Exodus from the Long Sun. 1996.

Wolfe, Gene. The Book of the New Sun.

The Shadow of the Torturer. 1980. As a young child Severian, already a member of the Torturer's Guild, was brought to the great Citadel and apprenticed to the Order of the Seekers for Truth and Penitence. Severian knows nothing of his past. Becoming expert at his profession, he was assured that he had a bright and shining future. Now blessed (or cursed) with the gift of remembering everything, he writes of his past and the incidents that have put him on a throne.

The Claw of the Conciliator. 1981. While a young journeyman, Torturer Severian travels to Thrax, where he encounters Vodalus and renews his oath of loyalty to the outlaw in his wildwood camp. Afterward, he promises to deliver a message for Vodalus to an agent at the Court of the Autarch, and he does. Then he continues on his way with the Claw of the Conciliator, which he has used to heal and even restore life several times.

The Sword of the Lichtor. 1981. Severian reaches Thrax and takes up the duties of a Master of his Guild, in service to the archon of the city. Dorcas, the woman he rescued from a watery grave with the Claw of the Conciliator, is concerned at how consumed he is with his duties; how comfortable he has become in his role of administering justice, both torture and execution, as decreed by the Archon; and how much he is both hated and feared by the common folk.

The Citadel of the Autarch. 1983. Torturer Severian becomes the new Autarch, but only after he goes to war and returns the Claw of the Conciliator to the Pelerines. After the bloodbath of battle, he considers selling himself as a slave to an order devoted to healing. But their chapel is destroyed and the members scattered or killed during battle. The Claw is no longer safe in its resting place, and Severian must take up the burden once again.

Wolfe, Gene. The Book of the Short Sun. Action takes place between the Whorl and a couple of planets. Annotated on page 42.

On Blue's Waters. 1999.

In Green's Jungles. 2000.

Return to the Whorl. 2001.

More Than Human

People have always wanted to extend their abilities, to be more than they can be. The idea of changing oneself or one's children to be better, smarter, stronger, healthier, and outstanding in every way is an enticing one—even if it is accomplished artificially. Immortality and extraordinary powers also hold great appeal, but "what if" it could really happen? And wouldn't achieving great powers also have great consequences? This section features stories about what might happen if humans, and sometimes animals, were more than they are now.

Bioengineering

Bioengineering is a particularly fascinating subject to explore. DNA, genetics, cloning, and mapping the human genome are all currently hot topics. Science fiction authors were on the cutting edge years ago when they first started speculating about and exploring the possible ramifications of bioengineering experiments. And bioengineering doesn't have to stop with humans. Sometimes it is animals that are created or enhanced through biological technology. No biological entity is too small to be altered—all the way down to viruses that may be changed to effect great cures or bring on great plagues.

Humans

Anderson, Poul. *Brain Wave*. 1954. An early novel that explores the effects on animals and humans of enhanced intelligence. The Earth has moved out of a field that was damping down the brain waves of all living creatures. Now both animals and humans are much smarter.

Asaro, Catherine. Skolian Empire Series. Psychic powers combined with computer implants create a race that is more than human.

Primary Inversion. 1995. Sauscony Valdoria, the potential heir to the Skolian Empire, is a Jagernaut—a bioengineered fighter pilot. On Delos, Sauscony and her crew encounter a group of Aristo bodyguards and come face to face with the heir to the Trader Empire, discovering that he is an Empath just like Sauscony—that he can feel compassion and does not feed on the pain of others like the rest of the Aristos. He could be the soul mate that she never thought she would find, but first Sauscony has to keep the two of them alive.

Catch the Lightning. 1996. "Of all the things Akushtina Santis Pulivok thought could happen to her on her way home through the dark streets of Los Angeles, meeting an alien was not one of them. . . . Althor, as he introduces himself, is not from these parts. In fact, he is one of the heirs to the Skolian empire . . ."—Melinda Helfer, *Romantic Times*.

The Last Hawk. 1997. Kelric, heir to the Skolian empire, crash lands on a planet marked as restricted. A woman ruler, fascinated by his unusual stature and strange golden skin, does not kill him but takes him into her estate and has him nursed back to health. Descended from fierce warriors, this matriarchal society now uses an intricate game, Quis, played with variously shaped dice, for political maneuvering. Men, considered the weaker sex, do not hold positions of responsibility, but each estate has a Calanya, a seraglio or harem, where men who are sworn to the estate manager serve as advisors through their play of Quis. Kelric rises to become the most powerful Quis player ever.

The Radiant Seas. 1999. Scions of two warring powers, Jaibriol and Soz, find peace on Prism, an uninhabited planet, and leave their warring cultures behind. Their peoples think they are dead. Years later when Jaibriol's empress mother discovers he is still alive, she abducts him. Soz takes their children to Earth for safekeeping and returns to the Skolian empire to fight for her family. When full-scale war erupts, Soz's hidden agenda thrusts her into extreme danger.

Ascendant Sun. 2000. Eighteen years after the events in *The Last Hawk*, Kelric escapes the planet Coba to find Skolia in chaos.

The Quantum Rose. 2000. Who will win the hand of Kamaj?

Bear, Greg. *Darwin's Radio*. 1999. Microbiologist Kaye Lang, virus expert Christopher Dicken, and archaeologist Mitch Rafelson all run across information in vastly different parts of the world that eventually ties together to solve a genetic mystery. Kaye finds the bodies of pregnant women in a mass grave in Eastern Europe. Mitch discovers the frozen bodies of a prehistoric family in a hidden cave in the Alps. As fear of a virus that affects pregnant women grows, some of the women seem to become pregnant without having sex.

Bear, Greg. *Queen of Angels*. 1990. "In a society enjoying peace, prosperity and technologically engineered mental health, Emanuel Goldsmith, a famous poet, commits a gruesome murder. Three people investigate the crime—one a therapist who will enter Goldsmith's mind to search for answers. A mesmerizing work set in a tomorrow that is less than a century away."—Publisher's blurb

Brin, David. *Glory Season*. 1993. Maia and her twin Leie are summerlings or vars, short for variants. Since they had an actual father, they are not winterling clones, prized household daughters, but instead are merely extra mouths to feed, to be kept only until they come of age. Once they reach fifteen, they are sent away on a ship, which is attacked by pirates. For the first time in their lives, they are separated. Now Maia, who has always been a follower, must take charge of her own life and survive kidnapping, battles, murder, mayhem, and a plot to make males active out of season, which would destroy her clone-dominated society. More on page 100.

Bujold, Lois McMaster. *Ethan of Athos*. 1986. Annotated on page 16.

Bujold, Lois McMaster. *Falling Free*. 1988. Quaddies were bioengineered with four arms and no legs to work in a zero-gravity environment. But now they've become obsolete. More on page 3.

Nebula Award.

Cherryh, C. J. *Cyteen*. 1988. Annotated on page 169.

 Hugo Award.

Gerrold, David. *Under the Eye of God*. 1993. The Phaestor had been bioengineered to fight the battles to save humanity from a deadly enemy, but now, with the enemy long vanquished, the Phaestor have subjugated all they consider lesser species, feeding their appetite for horror and blood.

A Covenant of Justice. 1994. Ruled by the genetically altered who have become vampires and dragons, the Alliance for Life fights back in this sequel to *Under the Eye of God*.

Goonan, Kathleen Ann. *The Bones of Time*. 1996. Two different stories with two different casts of characters entwine and build on each other, linked only by the bones of a long dead heroic king. Cen, a young runaway in Honolulu of 2007, is bewitched by visits from Kaiulani, the last princess of Hawaii. A romantic obsession develops, leading him to a mathematical trail to achieve time travel. In 2034 Lynn, a scientist estranged from her prominent family, meets another young man, thirteen-year-old Akamu, the spitting image of the long dead King Kamehameha. She saves him from being murdered and flees with him to China and then to Tibet and Thailand as he tries to reconstruct Cen's mathematical proofs.

Harper, Tara K. *Cat Scratch Fever*. 1994. Tsia, a fire dancer who has been genetically altered to withstand flames, has also received special genetic treatment so that she can become a guide, able to establish direct contact with other life forms. Unfortunately, she encounters a big cat, the only species forbidden to a guide, and bonds with it. Kidnapped by someone who knows that a fire dancer like Tsia can be very valuable, she is then purchased by a sadistic artist, who conditions her, using pain and threats against young children, to force her to cooperate on an artistic creation that involves burning a pregnant political leader at the moment she is giving birth. Tsia is the doomed mother's only hope. Because of her link to the big cats, there is a slim chance that she can save the intended victim—or at least the surviving infant.

Cataract. 1995. Tsia finally stops fighting her forbidden link to the great cats; no longer able to screen out the cat sounds in her mind, she saves a young cougar's life and it bonds with her. Against impossible odds she has to find a traitor, confront a sister's treachery, and start a new life, free to take charge, accept contracts, and choose her own friends, like the cat Ruka. Survival is not easy on this primitive world with its complex social structure and very real physical dangers, but Tsia is a survivor with an edge: her biologically engineered telepathic bond with a wild cougar.

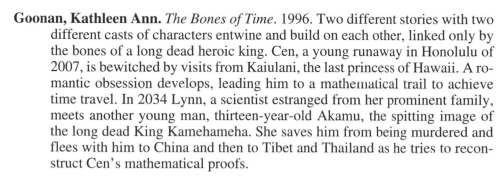

Heinlein, Robert A. *Beyond This Horizon*. 1948. Heinlein's vision of a utopian society includes men who carry guns and are involved in trying to solve the mystery of "the Meaning of Life." An early foray into the dilemmas inherent in genetic engineering.

Hinz, Christopher. Paratwa Saga. Annotated on page 6.

> *Liege-Killer*. 1987.
>
> *Ash Ock*. 1989.
>
> *Paratwa*. 1991.

Hopkinson, Nalo. *Brown Girl in the Ring*. 1998. Annotated on page 97.

Keyes, Daniel. *Flowers for Algernon*. 1966. Charlie gains and loses great intellectual abilities when surgery raises his IQ from 68 to 185. This powerfully emotional story won a Hugo as a novella in 1959; when expanded to novel length in 1966, it won a Nebula.

> *Nebula Award.*

Kleier, Glenn. *The Last Day*. 1997. The Messiah has fulfilled the prophecies and returned to Earth at the millennium—and she's a woman! Not just any woman, but the genetically enhanced clone of an Israeli scientist's daughter who has been lying in a coma since an accident. Her father uses her cells to create four fetuses. One is kept normal, to use as a control. The others have microchips embedded in their brains to speed up the learning process and to act as an intelligence infusion. When a meteor hits the lab on Christmas Eve, 1999, it destroys everything except one of the test subjects, who manages to crawl to safety and is rescued by Beduins. At midnight on New Year's Eve, the survivor makes her first appearance as the new messiah, and the miracles begin. But so do the battles when she declares an end to organized religion. The protagonists are a reporter and a cameraman who have the story of a lifetime on their hands.

Kress, Nancy. Beggars Series. Genetic engineering allows some offspring to live without sleep, giving them time to accomplish more.

> *Beggars in Spain*. 1991. Leisha is the next step in genetic manipulation, thanks to her wealthy father. Able to buy her anything he wants, he chooses sleeplessness, making her one of the new elite—brighter and happier than "normal" humans. An unexpected side effect turns out to be longevity, which makes the schism between the Sleepers and the Sleepless grow steadily wider. Leisha's mother can't cope, and sister Alicia, a "normal," has a hard time accepting her sister as one of the elite. Now humanity is placed in the role of Beggars to the multitalented Sleepless. And when the Sleepless build Sanctuary, a safe haven with sufficient weapons, both economic and physical, to protect it, the split grows even wider and could lead to war. The title comes from a saying: "You can try to give $1.00 to all the beggars in Spain, but they'll still rise against you."
>
> *Beggars and Choosers*. 1994. Earth is divided into three groups, the genetically engineered elite, who do most of the work; the Sleepless; and the huge mass of humanity that is virtually unemployable. The power struggle and uncontrolled nanotechnology threaten humankind.

Beggars Ride. 1996. It's the Sleepless versus the Supersleepless in the twenty-second century. These two generations of genetically modified super humans are in conflict with the normal humans and with each other.

Kress, Nancy. *Maximum Light.* 1998. Annotated on page 119.

Lethem, Jonathan. *Gun, with Occasional Music.* 1994. The Raymond Chandler quote on the frontispiece perfectly captures the spirit of this science fiction cum noir detective novel: "There was nothing to it. The Super Chief was on time, as it almost always is, and the subject was as easy to spot as a kangaroo in a dinner jacket." The protagonist is a down-and-out detective with a drug problem, but he's not alone. Just about everyone else in Oakland has the same problem. He's a private investigator because he couldn't stomach the way the Inquisitors administered their own brand of rough and ready justice, which sometimes had nothing to do with the truth. His latest client is a man who has been sentenced by the Inquisition to be frozen for a murder he claims he did not commit. Mctcalf's investigation leads to a trigger-happy kangaroo, an underworld figure, the Inquisition, and his own appointment with the freezer. But the case is far from over.

McCaffrey, Anne. Brains and Brawns Series. Brainships and their brawns—the human pilots who must be accepted by the sentient spaceships before being assigned as their partners—are the focus of the series. After *The Ship Who Sang*, McCaffrey co-authored several titles set in this universe with various authors. Jody Lynn Nye wrote *The Ship Errant* and S. M. Stirling wrote *The Ship Avenged,* set in the brains and brawns universe.

The Ship Who Sang. 1969. Helva was born with multiple birth defects, but her brilliant mind was perfect for controlling a brainship. Mounted in the titanium column of her ship, she begins her search for the perfect brawn companion. Her adventures with various brawns are described, as well as her gift of song and the joy it brings her.

McCaffrey, Anne, and Mercedes Lackey. *The Ship Who Searched.* 1992. Annotated on page 61.

McCaffrey, Anne, and S. M. Stirling. *The City Who Fought.* 1993. Annotated on page 61.

McCaffrey, Anne, and Jody Lynn Nye. *The Ship Who Won.* 1994. Carialle and her brawn Keff are searching the galaxy for intelligence. More on page 61.

McCaffrey, Anne, and Margaret Ball. *Partnership.* 1996. Annotated on page 62.

Murphy, Pat. *There and Back Again.* 1999. Annotated on page 20.

Sawyer, Robert J. *Frameshift.* 1997. A couple has a baby with the assistance of science, because they fear Huntington's disease. But it turns out that the friend who has provided the procedure may really be a war criminal who has implanted their embryo with Neanderthal DNA.

Shatner, William. Quest for Tomorrow Saga. Young Jim Endicott has a secret encoded in his DNA that can bring human minds together into a huge organic computer. This series has been described as Heinlein-like juveniles with sex!

Delta Search. 1997. Annotated on page 77.

In Alien Hands. 1997. Escaping capture by a Hunzzan hunter, sixteen-year-old Jim Endicott ends up on the planet Brostach, where he becomes a mercenary.

Step into Chaos. 1999. The "Leap" will take humanity to a different plane but will also cause widespread destruction. With assassins on his tail, Jim's only hope for survival is to take the "Leap" himself—either saving humanity or destroying much of the universe.

Beyond the Stars. 2000. Set in an alternate universe to the one in *Step into Chaos.*

Sheffield, Charles. *Proteus in the Underworld.* 1995. "In the 22nd century biofeedback techniques to control by will the processes of one's own body have reached their ultimate expression: the ability to transform the body into virtually any viable form whatsoever. What began as an innocent technique to reduce anxiety without recourse to drugs has raised fundamental questions about what it is to be human, since form is no longer sufficient nor even relevant."—Publisher's blurb

Slonczewski, Joan. *The Children Star.* 1998. On Prokaryon, a planet heavily laced with arsenic, a small religious order of both humans and AIs strives to create a colony with orphaned children rescued from a plague-ridden planet. To survive on the planet one must have extensive bioengineering done, and the younger the child, the better it works.

Sterling, Bruce. *Distraction.* 1998. Oscar Valparaiso, who was grown in vitro by black market baby dealers, has a bizarre genetic history.

Vinge, Joan D. Snow Queen Universe.

The Snow Queen. 1980. Annotated on page 165.

World's End. 1984. The man who saved the young Summer Queen's life goes into the wasteland known as World's End.

The Summer Queen. 1991. The secret is out that the sea mer are the source of the elixir that brings long life to those who drink it. As a result, the young Summer Queen has her hands full trying to protect her world from exploitation and save the lives of her beloved sea mer.

Wilhelm, Kate. *Where Late the Sweet Birds Sang.* 1976. Faced with the very real threat of sterility, the human race survives by cloning itself. Needless to say, there is a big difference between the "normals" and the "cloned."

> ***Hugo and Locus Awards.***

Williams, Sean, and Shane Dix. *Evergence: The Prodigal Sun* (Evergence, 1). 1999. Annotated on page 32.

> *Evergence: The Dying Light* (Evergence, 2). 2000.

> *Evergence: A Dark Imbalance* (Evergence, 3). 2001.

Williams, Walter Jon. *Aristoi.* 1992. Annotated on page 71.

Young, Jim. *Armed Memory.* 1995. Johnny is involved in a battle with a violence-craving, bloodthirsty society of Hammerheads. The virus that changes their physical shape into that of sharks also leaves them under the mental control of the Great Ones, former humans who have assumed the form of great sharks. Their goal is to destroy all two- and four-legged life forms, purge the Earth of dry-land dwellers, and return control to the masters of the deep.

Germs, Viruses, and Disease

Bear, Greg. *Blood Music.* 1985. A dedicated scientist, threatened with being locked out of the laboratory where he is conducting nanotechnology experiments and working with tiny computers the size of human cells, injects himself with his experiment to save it from destruction. Soon music is singing in his blood as these intelligent cells take over their host and become the origin for the spread of a benign plague.

> ***Hugo Award (for the original magazine novella).***

Kress, Nancy. *Oaths and Miracles.* 1996. Could several murders have anything to do with the fact that the Mafia has invested in a biotech firm that is bioengineering viruses?

Preston, Richard. *The Cobra Event.* 1997. A terrorist bioengineers a plague as a weapon.

Zettel, Sarah. *Playing God.* 1998. Lynn Nussbaumer and her company, Bioverse, Inc., have been hired to clean a biologically engineered infection out of the ecosystem of an alien race.

Animals

Cook, Robin. *Chromosome 6.* 1997. Annotated on page 4.

Crichton, Michael. *Jurassic Park.* 1990. Dinosaurs run amok. Annotated on page 5.

> *The Lost World.* 1995. More dinosaurs run amok. Annotated on page 5.

Kagan, Janet. *Mirabile.* 1991. Planetfall did not go well when humans came to colonize Mirabile. The vast library of genetic material brought from Earth became jumbled, resulting in bizarre mutations. These mutations, known as Dragon's Teeth, are kept as part of the gene pool if they are friendly. Some, however, are so dangerous that they must be destroyed. That's the job of Annie Jason Masmaajean. She's in charge of the Jasons, the gene readers who try to keep a handle on what is mutating. The six related stories here are her adventures with mutations such as the Loch Moose Monster, the Kangaroo Rex, Frankenswine, and a thingamabob.

Lethem, Jonathan. *Gun, with Occasional Music.* 1994. A tough-talking kangaroo plays an important role in this story. Annotated on page 129.

McCaffrey, Anne. Pern Series. McCaffrey's famous dragons are the result of bioengineering, but that fact is only important in *The Chronicles of Pern: First Fall,* 1993, when they are created. The Pern series is annotated on page 137.

Shetterly, Will. *Chimera.* 2000. In the future slavery has returned in the form of chimera, sometimes disparagingly called critters, who are human but are derived from animal genes and are forced to wear tattoos of their animal antecedents on their foreheads. More on page 174.

Swann, S. Andrew. Moreau series. Mysteries involving second-class citizens who are descended from animal DNA. Nohar Rajasthan is a P.I. of genetically altered tiger stock, and Angelica Lopez is descended from a rabbit.

Forests of the Night. 1993.

Emperors of the Twilight. 1994.

Specters of the Dawn. 1994.

Fearful Symmetries: The Return of Nohar Rajasthan. 1999. The retired moreau private investigator is called in on a case by an attorney.

Wells, H. G. The *Island of Dr. Moreau.* 1896. A classic tale of a mad scientist. On a South Sea island, a doctor performs experiments on animals with the insane goal of recreating them in the image of humans. This makes his island a terrifying place for a shipwrecked human visitor.

Psionic Powers

The powers of precognition, telepathy, clairvoyance, telekinesis, and teleportation displayed by characters in science fiction make current research in parapsychology seem crude. Science fiction invented the term *psionics* (psychic electronics) to describe these powers of the mind. Such powers are often inherent in the superman theme and are often manifest among alien beings. The variations on this theme have fascinated many science fiction authors, not just those in the following list that explore the unsuspected wealth of capabilities within the human mind.

Aikin, Jim. *The Wall at the Edge of the World.* 1993. Lack of telepathy means a death sentence. Annotated on page 95.

Asaro, Catherine. Saga of the Skolian Empire. Psychic powers combined with computer implants create a race that is more than human. Annotated on page 125.

Primary Inversion. 1995.

Catch the Lightning. 1996.

The Last Hawk. 1997.

The Radiant Seas. 1999.

Ascendant Sun. 2000.

The Quantum Rose. 2000.

Spherical Harmonic. 2001.

Ashwell, Pauline. *Project Farcry.* 1995. In a series of related stories, Richard Jordan discovers his telepathic gift, befriends an alien species, leads a new branch of the service, and orchestrates a daring rescue. The stories, told from various viewpoints (alien and human), are varied enough to make this read as a short-story collection, while the continuity of knowing that one individual will always turn up makes one want to read it all in one sitting, like a novel.

Baird, Wilhelmina. *Chaos Come Again.* 1996. Sybiots have given humankind telepathic abilities that lead to chaos.

Barnes, John. *Candle.* 2000. One True, the telepathic linkage of humankind that ushered in an unprecedented era of peace and cooperation in the late twenty-first century, may also be blocking memories and controlling the humans it is supposed to be serving.

Bester, Alfred. *The Demolished Man.* 1953. A fascinating murder mystery featuring a man possessed of extrasensory perception who will do anything to keep from facing "psychic demolition"—even murder.

Hugo Award (first winner).

Bradley, Marion Zimmer. Darkover Series. The inhabitants of Darkover learned how to control their powerful mental laran. Annotated on page 111.

Bradley, Marion Zimmer, and Mercedes Lackey. *Rediscovery: A Novel of Darkover.* 1993. A Terran ship arrives on Darkover, and its crew discovers the remnants of a lost colony ship on this strange dark planet.

Butler, Octavia E. *Parable of the Sower.* 1993. Annotated on page 96.

Butler, Octavia E. *Parable of the Talents.* 1998. Annotated on page 96.

 Nebula Award.

Butler, Octavia E. Patternmaster Series.

> *Patternmaster.* 1976. Those with strong mental abilities train and strive to become first apprentices and then pattern workers for the ultimate controller—the Patternmaster. Since there is room for only one Patternmaster, it's brother against brother for the ultimate power trip. Teray never intended to battle for the role of Patternmaster, but he is forced into it by his arrogant, cruel, paranoid sibling, who leaves him no choice but to battle—to the death.

> *Mind of My Mind.* 1977. Doro, an immortal, is able to control and manipulate the lesser mortals around him and take over their bodies at a moment's notice. He has spent his 4,000 years conducting genetic research and experiments, part of his efforts to found a new super race. When he saves an abused three-year-old from her abusive mother and takes her to safety, her mental abilities become stronger, and she soon discovers that she has the ability to sense patterns and to attract others with mental abilities to join her.

Cherryh, C. J. *Rider at the Gate.* 1995. In a primitive land, commerce and protection depend on the goodwill of Nighthorses and their riders, the humans who bond with them. It is these bonded pairs that go out into the wilds, hunt for food, and accompany convoys to keep them safe on long mountain treks. They are also the ones who serve as a barrier between human settlements and the creatures of the wild, like Danny Fisher, a very young rider with a very powerful nighthorse.

> *Cloud's Rider.* 1996. After the destruction of Tarmin village by a rogue horse, ridden by thirteen-year-old Brionne, Danny Fisher has his hands full. Brionne wakes up from a coma and begins broadcasting her anger, hatred, and desperate need for another horse, disrupting everything. Meanwhile something ugly, dark, and powerful menaces them from a distance. The dark creature manages to bond with Brionne, and the two then escape into the night.

Clough, Brenda W. The Barbarossa Series. Rob Lewis has the ability to manipulate people's minds, to make them do anything he wants them to do. His friend Edwin Barbarossa, an astronaut, is made immortal through a gift given to him by Rob.

> *How Like a God.* 1997. Annotated on page 118.

> *Doors of Death and Life.* 2000. Annotated on page 118.

Dick, Philip K. *Ubik.* 1969. Joe Chip uses a spray can of Ubik, a wonder substance, in his battle against entropy in a world where time moves backwards and extrasensory perception is used to solve murders.

Douglas, Carole Nelson. Probe/Counter Probe.

Probe. 1985. When a young woman with no memory is found on a rocky bluff, no one suspects that she is really an alien probe with the power to kill with her mind.

Counterprobe. 1988. Begins where *Probe* ended. Jane Doe has been returned to Dr. Kevin Blake by the alien spaceship. Now the two of them are on the run from the government men who want to capture and "study" Jane. They are captured and face brutal treatment at the hands of a twisted but brilliant government psychiatrist until the aliens, who have changed their minds, attempt to recapture their lost probe, using another clone to do so.

Foster, Alan Dean. Pip and Flinx Adventures. Flinx, an orphan with psionic powers, and his pet flying snake encounter adventures everywhere. Annotated on page 18.

The Tar-Aiym Krang. 1972.

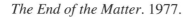

Bloodhype. 1973.

The End of the Matter. 1977.

Orphan Star. 1977.

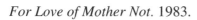

For Love of Mother Not. 1983.

Flinx in Flux. 1988.

Mid-Flinx. 1995.

Reunion. 2001.

Friedman, C. S. *In Conquest Born.* 1986. Annotated on page 25.

Gould, Steven. *Jumper.* 1992. All alone, mugged on the streets of New York City, afraid to go to the authorities because he might be sent back to his abusive father, Davy's situation looked pretty hopeless, except that he had been able to case out the vault while visiting a local bank. Soon funds with which to survive were no problem, although staying ahead of the authorities definitely was. Life could be difficult for a teenager on his own, until he discovered that he was a "Jumper" who could teleport to any site he had previously seen.

Harper, Tara K. *Cat Scratch Fever.* 1994. Annotated on page 127.

Cataract. 1995.

Heinlein, Robert A. *Time for the Stars*. 1956. "For a telepathic twin on an exploratory space voyage only a few years pass; yet, when he returns to Earth his brother is ready to celebrate his ninetieth birthday."—Prospector Library catalog copy.

Henderson, Zenna. The People stories. *Ingathering: The Complete People Stories of Zenna Henderson* is an omnibus of all the stories in *Pilgrimage: The Book of the People* and *The People: No Different Flesh,* with the addition of three other stories dealing with human interactions of "The People." These are aliens with mind-reading and teleportation talents, shipwrecked on Earth who must keep their powerful mental abilities secret or face attack and even execution by frightened "normal" humans.

Pilgrimage: The Book of the People. 1961.

The People: No Different Flesh. 1966.

Lethem, Jonathan. *Girl in Landscape*. 1998. A teenaged girl on a planet full of ruins discovers how to travel telepathically into the homes of fellow settlers, remaining invisible in the guise of a "household deer."

Lichtenberg, Jacqueline. Vampire series. (Untitled.) Luren, vampirelike creatures, some dreamers and some powerful telepaths, are stranded on the Earth.

Those of My Blood. 1988. Annotated on page 147.

Dreamspy. 1989. Annotated on page 147.

Lubar, David. *Hidden Talents*. 1999. Annotated on page 201.

May, Julian. Galactic Milieu Series. The most powerful of the human metapsychics, those **YA** who possess psionic talents that include Farsensing and Psychokinesis, and interact with a galactic confederation of exotic beings.

Jack the Bodiless. 1992.

Diamond Mask. 1994.

Magnificat. 1996.

May, Julian. Intervention Series. Set in the same world as May's Galactic Milieu and Saga of the Exiles, this series focuses on the talented Remillard family.

The Surveillance. 1988.

Metaconcert. 1988.

McCaffrey, Anne. Crystal Singer series. Killashandra Ree's musical talent also allows her to commune with the alien crystals necessary for communications systems. Humans who work crystal encounter great physical peril and may be swept into thrall by the crystal they have cut, a thrall the symbiot living within them is unable to break. And if they leave the cutting too late, they can be destroyed by the savage storms that regularly sweep the planet Balyban. Most disturbing of all, however, is the memory loss they suffer. Crystal singers can live for centuries, kept alive, hale, and hearty by the symbiot in their bodies. But each time they cut crystal, they suffer memory loss, more severe at some times than at others.

Crystal Singer. 1982.

Killishandra. 1985.

Crystal Line. 1992.

McCaffrey, Anne. Harper Hall Trilogy. Teens with a telepathic link to fire lizards. Annotated on page 201.

McCaffrey, Anne. Pern Series. The planet Pern is in jeopardy from "thread." When a neighboring planet approaches, this alien organism falls from the sky and consumes anything organic that it touches. Early settlers used bioengineering to alter indigenous lizards into fire-breathing, telepathic, teleporting dragons to save people, herds, and crops from the deadly "thread" that periodically falls from the sky. Some of the dragonriders are heroic and self-sacrificing, some are greedy and self-serving, but all are chosen by their dragons to carry on the battle that rages when the Red Star rises in the sky. *The Dragonriders of Pern* is an omnibus edition of the first three titles in the series. The Harper Hall trilogy, set on Pern, is annotated on page 137.

Dragonflight. 1968. Lessa, the last of the noble bloodline of Ruatha Hold, is rescued from servitude by the dragonriders searching for likely candidates to impress the new dragon queen. Lessa is successful at imprinting Ramoth, the new queen, which makes her the leader of the Weyr and the mate of F'lar. As rider of the bronze dragon Mnementh, F'lar is the most suited to lead the on-going struggle and convince an unbelieving populace that the dreaded "thread" will soon fall again, putting all living creatures at risk. The symbiotic relationship of fire-breathing dragon and telepathic rider is the planet's only hope for survival.

Dragonquest. 1968. A few ambitious Lords, aware of the dragons' ability to teleport, want to send someone to the Red Star, the source of the deadly "thread" that periodically falls on the planet. The plan is to destroy the "thread" before it reaches Pern. F'nor and his dragon are willing, but Canth needs a detailed image of a place in order to get there. Also, there's the question of whether either will survive such a trip through space.

The White Dragon. 1978. As the Lord of a Hold, Jaxom, teenaged Lord of Ruatha Hold, is expected to attend a hatching. When everyone ignores the final egg that shows no sign of hatching, Jaxom cracks it himself and frees its fragile occupant. As a result, against all custom he imprints a dragon, the white runt that he has saved. Laughed at by others, Jaxom soon discovers that his dragon, Ruth, possesses abilities so unique that together they might be able to solve one of Pern's oldest mysteries.

Moreta, Dragonlady of Pern. 1983. Moreta, a Weyrwoman, becomes a legendary figure whose magnificent ride to save the planet is recounted in ballads and legends.

The Girl Who Heard Dragons. 1985. The title story of this collection features a story set on Pern. The other fourteen stories demonstrate McCaffrey's diverse range.

Dragonsdawn. 1988. The first settlers on Pern discover that they are in deadly peril when the Red Star approaches and "thread" falls. They must use their genetic engineering skills to breed a creature that can preserve their colony from destruction.

The Renegades of Pern. 1989. The saga of Pern continues, this time seen through the eyes of the "normal" people who live and work on the planet. Society is divided into three strata on this planet: Weyr (with its telepathic fire-breathing dragons), Hall (the ruling class), and Hold (the workers). Many of the events described in previous Dragonrider books are seen here through the eyes of the "little people," those who do not fly through the air on the backs of fire-breathing dragons but who fight "thread" and suffer and die just the same.

All the Weyrs of Pern. 1991. Ruth has carried Jaxom to Landing, where they make an astounding discovery, a working AIVAS (Artificial Intelligence Voice-Address System). Programmed and left behind by the original settlers, the system comes to life and broadcasts the history of the early settlement to all—dragonriders, hold people, and craft representatives alike. More important, AIVAS then promises to teach the skills lost by the early settlers in their struggle to survive. It will take five years, but then all the Weyrs of Pern, working together, will be able to alter the path of the Red Star and permanently end the threat of thread that periodically falls from the sky to destroy everything it touches.

The Chronicles of Pern: First Fall. 1993. This collection of short stories addresses the early settlement of the planet Pern. That's P. E. R. N., which stands for "parallel Earth, resources negligible," a planet suitable for colonization. It includes a story of first survey; using dolphins to help flee the active volcano at Landing; moving into Ruatha Hold with the help of oxen; establishing a second Weyr, which includes the mating flight of a new Queen dragon; and finally an abortive Rescue Run that encounters the deadly Oort cloud full of thread and leaves, posting a warning on its departure for all future travelers.

The Dolphins of Pern. 1994. Dolphins were brought to the planet in the same ships as the human settlers, enhanced so that they could talk, and then turned loose in the oceans of Pern. They formed a close working relationship with humans, but when the volcanoes began to erupt and thread fell from the skies, the human settlers gradually forgot about their relationship with the dolphins. When AIVAS provides startling information about this overlooked resource, the settlers decide to form a Dolphin Hall. Readis, aided by dragonrider T'lion and his bronze dragon Gadareth, overcomes all obstacles, including his parents, to become the head of this new Hall.

Dragonseye. 1996. After a 250-year hiatus, the ominous Red Star has returned to the skies of Pern, and the Weyrs and Holds are working hard to get ready for imminent threadfall. The one holdout is Chalkin, Lord Holder of Bitra, who refuses to believe that thread will ever fall again and has kept his people in ignorance of the approaching danger. Chalkin insists on tithing his people—for his own personal gain, not to protect those in his care. When he attempts to murder a young artist who was hired to do miniatures of his children, something must finally be done.

Masterharper of Pern. 1998. Masterharper Robinton is easily the most popular and gifted harper to ever lead the Harper Hall on Pern. The story begins with his birth to a fragile but incredibly strong-willed mother, the only one whose rich colatura voice could do justice to the demanding vocal compositions of her gifted spouse. Master Petiron is jealous of his son, so the other harpers step in to handle Robinton's education, especially when they see how gifted he is. He has perfect pitch, is composing by the time he's five or six, and is bright and eager to please, but he is eternally denied his father's guidance and approval. Robinton can also talk to dragons and understand their speech, a gift no one else has, but one that is essential for his personal crusade to prepare Pern for the return of thread.

The Skies of Pern. 2001. The Red Star and the deadly thread it produced are no longer a threat to the inhabitants of Pern. But now a new danger threatens the planet — again from the skies. This time it's Lessa and F'lar's son and his beloved, a green rider, who meet the challenge, ably assisted, of course, by their telepathic, fire-breathing dragons.

McCaffrey, Anne. Rowan Series (also called the Tower and the Hive series). Primes use their psi-abilities to teleport people and cargo through space. This means that a Prime must be found and placed in each teleport tower.

The Rowan. 1990. A three-year-old child, soon to be known as "The Rowan," is the sole survivor of a mining community wiped out by a freak mud slide. When the car she is in gets buried, her mental cries for help are felt all over the planet. After her rescue she is trained and sent to Callisto to set up her own tower. There she discovers an unknown with Prime-level talent on Deneb and is warned of an attack by alien beetles from space.

Damia. 1992. Afra, an extremely powerful young Talent from Capella, works with the Rowan and they become closer than brother and sister. He helps her with her children, particularly the ever-so-talented and ever-so-difficult Damia. By the time Damia reaches puberty, Afra is hopelessly in love with his young godchild. He can wait until she grows up, but will she then be ready to look at him as a man?

Damia's Children. 1992. These are the adventures of four of Damia's teenaged children. Loria is sent as ambassador to the Mrdini home world. Thian is sent as Prime to the fleet chasing the alien Hive ships. Rojer is sent to the fleet that has found a Hive world. And Zara, who is empathetic and sensitive, goes to incredible lengths to assist the captured Hive Queen.

Lyon's Pride. 1994. The children of Damia and Afra continue to try to discover more about the threat of the Hive.

The Tower and the Hive. 1999. Allied with the alien Mrdini, the Rowan's family attempts to put a final halt to the advances of the predatory Hivers.

McCaffrey, Anne. Talents Series.

> *To Ride Pegasus.* 1973. Riding Pegasus can be a wonderful, freeing experience, flying through the air high above the ground. But if you slip and fall off, it can be extremely dangerous. That is the same dichotomy faced by people with "talents"—those who have special mental abilities like telepathy, teleportation, and telekinesis. Society depends on their talents, but life can still be a struggle for those who possess them.

> *Pegasus in Flight.* 1990. In a future where overpopulation is rampant, there is a growing need for individuals with special "talents." Rhyssa Owen is the director of the Jerhattan Parapsychic Center, which specializes in finding and protecting "wild" or untrained talents. Peter, one of her new finds, is a boy whose spine was severed in an accident but who has compensated by tapping into electric energy and moving anything he wishes, including himself. Tirla is an instantaneous translator who can calm ruffled feathers in a dozen or more languages. An illegal since birth, she has learned how to survive on her own, avoiding the authorities, the gangs, and those individuals who prey on helpless children.

> *Pegasus in Space.* 2000. Peter thwarts a plot to take over the new Padrugoi Space Station at its dedication. Amariyah, an orphan, becomes Peter's greatest fan and is like a young sister to him, but she also harbors a unique talent, one that manifests itself in her gardening but is not limited to vegetation.

McCaffrey, Anne, and Elizabeth Ann Scarborough. Powers That Be Series.

> *Powers That Be.* 1993. On the planet Petaybee the winters are cold and long and the summers are incredibly cold, too. This fully sentient world is capable of protecting its inhabitants and its secrets, which is why when Intergal's scans show massive ore deposits, the scientists sent to investigate can never find them. Yanaba Maddock, retired from the service because of lungs injured in a poison gas attack, is sent to Petaybee as an undercover agent. Her mission is to find some missing scientists and report back to Intergal on the status of their search. But Petaybee accepts her and works its wonders, and soon a healthy Yana joins the fight for the future of the planet.

> *Power Lines.* 1994. Intergal refuses to believe that the planet Petaybee is sentient. Even Yanaba Maddock's miraculous recovery from a debilitating disease and the deaths of natives forcibly removed from this world have failed to convince the desk-bound administrators to approach Petaybee with caution and respect. After battle lines are drawn between the invading scientists and the inhabitants of the planet, it is Petaybee itself that will be the deciding factor.

> *Power Play.* 1995. Just married and pregnant, Yana has to go off planet to testify at a special court considering Petaybee's status. After being captured by pirates, she has an adventure-filled trip back to the world that has become her home.

Murphy, Pat. *The Falling Woman.* 1987. The protagonist, a middle-aged archaeologist, communicates with the past. Not only is she able to see what is actually going on during the height of the Mayan civilization, but she can also communicate with individuals from this ancient epoch.

> *Nebula Award.*

Ransom, Daniel. *The Fugitive Stars*. 1995. Michael Raines, a research telepath, stumbles across a conspiracy involving extraterrestrial life when two scientists die after exploring an unusual comet.

Resnick, Mike. Penelope Bailey Series. Penelope has the ability to see all possible futures. Annotated on page 9.

Soothsayer. 1991.

Oracle. 1992.

Prophet. 1993.

Russ, Joanna. *And Chaos Died*. 1970. Mental telepathy can be a blessing or a curse. When the protagonist is stranded on a planet inhabited by those who can communicate telepathically, he works hard to develop this skill. But now his attempt to return to the Earth may be a disaster, because being telepathic among those who are not can lead to madness.

Schmitz, James H. The Complete Federation of the Hub. Baen Books is publishing the collected Federation of the Hub stories in four volumes, bringing back into print stories by one of SF's most beloved authors.

Telzey Amberdon. 2000. This new collection of beloved classic Schmitz tales features talented telepath and xenotelepath Telzey Amberdon. It includes the novels *The Universe Against Her* (1964) and *The Lion Game* (1973).

T'NT Telzey & Trigger. 2000. Stories featuring Telzey Amberdon and Trigger Argee.

Trigger and Friends. 2001. A new collection of classic Trigger Argee stories.

The Hub: Dangerous Territory. 2001.

Schmitz, James H. *The Witches of Karres*. 1966. Annotated on page 203.

Simmons, Dan. *Hollow Man*. 1992. Telepath Jeremy Bremen is thrust into a nightmare cacophony of other's inner voices when his beloved wife Gail, the only other telepath he knows of, dies a torturously painful death from cancer. As he flees across the country trying to escape the torrent of other's thoughts, Jeremy encounters a mobster and a truly horrifying woman who is the embodiment of evil, and both want to kill him.

Sturgeon, Theodore. *More Than Human*. 1953. Several psionically gifted but otherwise damaged individuals come together to form the Gesalt, an entity that is much more than the sum of its parts.

van Vogt, A. E. *Slan*. 1946. A classic novel featuring Jommy Cross, a slan. A member of a mutant minority that has extrasensory powers, enhanced intelligence, and a physically enhanced body, he carries a built-in death sentence. Appeared serially in *Astounding Science Fiction* in 1940. It was also revised and appeared in book form in 1951, but most fans prefer the earlier version.

van Vogt, A. E. *The World of Null A*. 1948. The world is governed by a Games Machine that tests the leading intellects of Earth for a month to determine their right to join the Null-A (non-Aristotelian) thinkers on Venus. The losers become the top administrators on Earth. Gilbert Gosseyn discovers that his memories are not his own. Caught up in a vast conspiracy, he must find out who and what he is.

Vinge, Joan D. Psion Series. Cat was first kidnapped by the government and then forced to develop the powerful psionic abilities he had never suspected he had.

Psion. 1982. Annotated on page 194.

Catspaw. 1988. "Cat follows a trail of lies and savagery that leads from homicidal enclaves of drug kings to a fanatic's pulpit."—Ingram.

Dreamfall. 1996. When he was forced to kill the evil entity set on destroying his universe, Cat lost his telepathic abilities. He is sent to the planet Refuge, home of the psionic Hydrans, as part of a xenoarchaeology research team. They are to investigate the ruling class, which has been mistreating slave labor. Cat becomes trapped in a nightmare when he helps a Hydran woman escape pursuit, only to discover that the baby with her was a kidnapped human child. While the woman he saved may be his soulmate, her twin, the leader of the Hydran revolt, plans a devastating counterattack that Cat is helpless to prevent.

Immortality

Can science ultimately confer immortality upon humans? This issue is considered in science fiction, but the real question is whether such immortality would be a blessing or a curse. There are many immortal beings to be found in science fiction stories. One such immortal in *Venus on the Half-Shell,* by Kilgore Trout, says bluntly, "Immortality is a pain in the ass." *The Highlander* is perhaps the best-known media personality with this gift, but capable authors have also explored the concept of long life and how it affects the person so blessed (or cursed) in his or her relationships with "normal" people.

Anderson, Poul. *The Boat of a Million Years*. 1989. Certain humans, granted immortality due to the nature of their special genes, pass through the eons—from around 300 B.C. to a future in which space flight is a reality.

Banks, Iain. *Feersum Endjinn*. 1994. After dying seven times, Count Alandre Sessine VII only has one life and one last chance left to catch his killer. More on page 82.

Banks, Iain. *The Player of Games*. 1989. Annotated on page 121.

Barnes, John. *Kaleidoscope Century.* 1995. Joshua Ali Quare awakens with amnesia and discovers that for over a hundred years he has been periodically receiving a treatment to keep him young while in the employ of a powerful meme. But the treatment also strips his memory.

Butler, Octavia E. *Mind of My Mind.* 1977. Annotated on page 134.

Butler, Octavia E. *Wild Seed.* 1980. Annotated on page 162.

Esquivel, Laura. *The Law of Love.* 1995. Humankind, in the future, has discovered that reincarnation is real and has developed ways of searching the past lives of individuals to determine their worthiness for jobs and public office. Everybody is also searching for their spiritual twin, a search that is ended when a high level of superiority is achieved. Azucena has just found hers and spent a passionate night with him, then he disappears. As she searches for him, we discover that they have known each other in previous lives and been involved in a cycle of murder and betrayal. Political shenanigans leave Azucena and her assembled party in danger as they follow their quest to reunite the spiritual twin lovers from planet to planet and from body to body.

Farmer, Philip José. *To Your Scattered Bodies Go.* 1971. Riverworld Saga. A new television series is revitalizing interest in this saga. An incredibly powerful race of aliens creates a world dominated by an immense, 20-million-mile-long river on the banks of which they resurrect all humans whoever lived. Famous people from various cultures throughout history meet and mingle. Sir Richard Burton and Mark Twain both set off to discern the reasons behind the resurrection of all humanity.

The Fabulous Riverboat. 1971.

The Dark Design. 1977.

The Magic Labyrinth. 1980

> *Hugo Award.*

Reed, Robert. *Marrow.* 2000. Annotated on page 40.

Zelazny, Roger. *. . . And Call Me Conrad.* 1966. (Alternate title, *This Immortal*). The novel is expanded from Zelazny's Hugo-award winning short story. Years after Earth's population was decimated, an immortal going by the name of Conrad is living on Earth while aliens from Vega are buying up real estate as resort properties.

> *Hugo Award.*

Zelazny, Roger. *Lord of Light.* 1967. Annotated on page 107.

> *Hugo Award.*

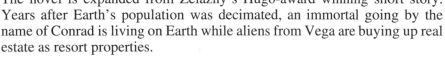

Aliens All Around Us

One of the major science fiction themes is that of alien life forms. We have spent centuries speculating on the question of whether we are alone in the universe and asking ourselves the question: Who's out there? In 1948, John W. Campbell wrote an award-winning short story, "Who Goes There?," a frightening picture of first-contact as a life-threatening event—for humanity.

The possible and ingenious forms taken by alien beings are seemingly limitless, allowing authors' imaginations to truly run wild. Throughout the history of science fiction, aliens have appeared as everything from monsters (perhaps plantlike or reptilian), humanoids (freaks of Darwinian evolution, perhaps), benign friends, serious, godlike, or even disembodied intelligence. Usually they are extraterrestrial beings. They may be invaders of Earth, or we may encounter them on other planets. The relationships of human and alien, friendly or antagonistic, offer writers many possibilities.

When we finally do manage to go "out there," what can we expect? Friends or foes—or creatures so alien we don't even register in their sphere of influence? C. J. Cherryh, a master at presenting alien-human interactions, stresses the alien-ness of the aliens juxtaposed against the human-ness of the humans. In spite of incredible differences, not just in physical appearance but in cultural, philosophical, and even moral imperatives, we somehow manage to get along—most of the time.

Many of the numerous entries in the space opera and military science fiction categories involve conflict against or cooperation with representatives of other races, species, galaxies, even universes. So readers who enjoy stories about aliens should also check these sections in Chapter 1. The appeal factor in tales dealing with alien life forms is often the very alien-ness of the authors' creations. Readers looking for characters that stretch the boundaries often enjoy stories of alien contact. Some revel in the horrific aspects of aliens. These readers should check the horror section in Chapter 5. After all is said and done, the question remains: Are we alone in the universe? And if not, who is out there? And what can we expect if and when we ever get together? This is fertile ground for science fiction authors, who have explored this topic for years. May they long continue to do so, because it is speculations like these that provide so much old-fashioned visceral enjoyment for so many readers!

Anderson, Poul. *Starfarers*. 1998. When intelligent life is detected in the far reaches of the galaxy, ten humans board the *Envoy* for a journey that will take them to meet three alien races before they return to the Earth 11,000 years later.

Anthony, Piers. Of Man and Manta Series.

Omnivore. 1968. Subble is an enhanced human investigator, with all kinds of special built-in abilities. He is sent to interview three scientists who have just returned from the planet Nacre with some most unusual luggage—one-eyed, mushroom-type, mobile pet aliens. Subble's job is to determine the exact nature of the threat to humanity and then take care of it. So he interviews Veg, a vegetarian logger; Aquilon, a female omnivore; and Cal, a weak carnivore whose diet consists solely of blood. It all comes together when he confronts the pet Mantas and discovers that there is some question as to who is the pet and who is the master.

Orn. 1971. Annotated on page 49.

Ox. 1976. Annotated on page 78.

Anthony, Piers. *Prostho Plus*. 1973. The truly bizarre adventures of a middle-aged dentist who is captured by aliens. It seems that humans aren't the only ones who have problems with their teeth.

Arnason, Eleanor. *Ring of Swords*. 1993. Anna Perez discovers that the aliens who have been battling the people of Earth for fifty years find humans barbaric for not segregating women and children from men.

Arnason, Eleanor. *A Woman of the Iron People*. 1991. Human anthropologists travel to a distant planet to study iron-age hominids who live in a society where women and children reside in villages and men live alone.

> **Tiptree Award.**

Ashwell, Pauline. *Project Farcry*. 1995. Annotated on page 133.

Asimov, Isaac. *The Gods Themselves*. 1972. Annotated on page 111.

Brin, David. Uplift Storm Trilogy. Annotated on page 35.

> *Brightness Reef*. 1995.
>
> *Infinity's Shore*. 1996.
>
> *Heaven's Reach*. 1998.

Brin, David. Uplift Trilogy. Annotated on page 35.

> *Sundiver*. 1980.
>
> *Startide Rising*. 1983.
>
> *The Uplift War*. 1987.

Butler, Octavia E. Xenogenesis Trilogy.

> *Dawn*. 1987. Annotated on page 86.
>
> *Adulthood Rites*. 1988. Akin, the son of the heroine of *Dawn,* is also the child of four other parents, three of them aliens who must merge genetically with humans as the price for saving humankind from a devastating nuclear war.
>
> *Imago*. 1989. Jodahs, the offspring of a human/alien union, turns out to be a powerful ooloi.

Campbell, John W., Jr. *Who Goes There?* 1948. Seven classic stories from an editor who is considered by many to be the "Father of Modern Science Fiction." The title story is his famous treatment of an alien who lands on the earth, is revived, and then becomes a threat to all human life. It has been filmed twice, quite effectively, as *The Thing*.

Card, Orson Scott. *Wyrms*. 1987. Annotated on page 4.

Carver, Jeffrey A. Chaos Chronicles.

> *Neptune Crossing*. 1994. John Bandicut falls into a cavern on Triton, where he establishes mental contact with an alien presence that identifies itself as a quarx who is trying to save Earth from a deadly comet.
>
> *Strange Attractors*. 1995. Chaos theory and alien life forms continue to be a part of Bandicut's life as his adventures continue.
>
> *The Infinite Sea*. 1996. Bandicut, the aliens, and a couple of robot pals are flung across the galaxy to a world where amphibious aliens are threatened both on land and from the depths of the sea.

Dick, Philip K. *The Game-Players of Titan*. 1963. The alien Vugs have been fighting against humankind for so long that the war has finally come to a standstill. Now the opponents are engaged in a series of elaborate games with each other.

Fowler, Karen Joy. *Sarah Canary*. 1991. A strange white woman wanders into a Chinese labor camp in the Pacific Northwest in 1873. Chin Ah Kin is delegated to return her to where she came from, which takes him much farther than he ever believed imaginable.

Friedman, C. S. *Madness Season*. 1990. In the twenty-fourth century humanity has been subjugated by the Tyr, a reptilian race that ships the best and brightest humans away. Daetrin, a vampire human, fights his own fight against the aliens.

Gerrold, David. The War Against the Chtorr. The wormlike Chtorr feed on human flesh. Titles are annotated on page 25.

> *A Matter for Men*. 1983.
>
> *A Day for Damnation*. 1984.
>
> *A Rage for Revenge*. 1989.
>
> *Season for Slaughter*. 1993.

Hopkinson, Nalo. *Midnight Robber*. 2000. Tan-Tan, a young girl on the planet Toussaint, flees to the prison planet of New Half-Way, where she and her father are rescued by a lizard-bird-like alien. (Hopkinson has a Web site at http://www. sff. net/people/nalo/nalo/.)

Jones, Gwyneth. *White Queen*. 1991. Johnny Guglioli, an American cyberjournalist in West Africa, discovers that the girl who has been following him is an alien. An interview with her could get him back onto the international news network, but who would believe him?

> ***James Tiptree Jr. Award.***

Leiber, Fritz. *The Big Time*. 1961. Annotated on page 48.

Lewis, C. S. Perelandra Trilogy. Annotated on page 104.

Out of the Silent Planet. 1943.

Perelandra. 1943.

That Hideous Strength. 1945.

Lichtenberg, Jacqueline. *Those of My Blood.* 1988. The Luren, vampirelike creatures, were stranded on the Earth centuries ago and have been coexisting with and living off humans ever since. Now they are divided into two camps. The residents are Earth's friends and need the sustenance of human blood but want a partnership with humans and can respect them. The tourists, who are Earth's enemies, use and discard the humans around them, marking time as they wait for a chance to return to their home world. That chance comes in the form of an alien spaceship that has crash-landed on the moon. An expedition is sent to examine the remains of the crashed vehicle. At the same time a probe is sent into space to contact the vessel's planet of origin, which hopefully is the home world of the Luren.

Dreamspy. 1989. This companion novel to *Those of My Blood* continues the adventures of the Luren, friendly vampires, some of whom are dreamers or powerful telepaths and are known to help the Earth people. Kyllikki, a powerful Teleod telepath, has to flee her home and the influence of the evil Zemur, her cousin and head of the Eight Families of the Teleod. When her ship is attacked, Kyllikki and her friends are forced to flee in a life pod. As a result, a bond is forged that results in the salvation, not just of civilization, but of the universe itself.

Longyear, Barry B. *The Homecoming.* 1989. Lizardlike aliens return home after **YA** 30 million years. But when their massive spaceships arrive, they discover that a new life form has taken over their planet. Captain Carl Baxter of the U.S. Air Force represents the human race in its first contact with this star fleet. He has his hands full because the aliens are divided. One faction is struggling to understand the hue-mans; the other wants to eliminate them entirely. The fate of humanity rests in Carl's hands.

MacAvoy, R. A. *The Third Eagle.* 1989. Instantaneous transportation takes Wanbli on space-spanning adventures. Annotated on page 7.

McDevitt, Jack. *A Talent for War.* 1989. A bit of information in an ancient computer takes Alex Benedict on a quest in space. Annotated on page 28.

Moon, Elizabeth. *Remnant Population.* 1996. Remaining behind on a planet deserted by its human colonists, Ofelia becomes a nest guardian for alien young. Annotated on page 123.

Niven, Larry, and Jerry Pournelle. *The Mote in God's Eye.* 1974. In this best-seller, humans find an isolated alien race that even though ancient has never discovered space travel. It is set in the world of the CoDominium, in which alien contact turns out to be a serious threat for humankind. The alien "Moties" certainly are different from anything on the Earth. But as the members of the new empire soon discover, they can also be quite deadly.

Norton, Andre. *Brother to Shadows*. 1993. Jofre is an off-worlder, raised and trained in an assassin's guild, who bonds with a force stone that gives him special powers on his quest for the Forerunners and the artifacts they left behind. After he gives his oath to a scholar who is attempting to bring the past to life, Jofre discovers that the Thieves Guild is interested in both of them. As if that weren't enough, a Shadow Sister has also been employed to kill or capture him. Winding up in the middle of a civil war, Jofre is befriended by a furry little alien with special telepathic abilities.

Nye, Jody Lynn. *Medicine Show*. 1994. Annotated on page 39.

Ransom, Daniel. *The Fugitive Stars*. 1995. Annotated on page 141.

Robinson, Frank M. *The Dark Beyond the Stars*. 1991. Annotated on page 40.

Robinson, Frank M. *Waiting*. 1999. The "Old People" are a hidden race that has secretly coexisted with Homo sapiens throughout time, but evolved very differently in ways not ordinarily discernible. When Arthur Banks finds out about them, he and his family, as well as everyone else who has an inkling of their existence, faces imminent danger. The "Old People," who have evolved with psi powers, have decided that Homo sapiens must be eradicated to preserve the Earth.

Sawyer, Robert J. *Factoring Humanity*. 1998. Annotated on page 119.

Sawyer, Robert J. *Illegal Alien*. 1997. When a disabled starship enters the Earth's atmosphere, fear is quickly replaced with awe. The first contact ever between humans and aliens is made. Seven incredibly intelligent members of the advanced Tosok race are welcomed by the world with open arms. In exchange for the resources and help to repair their ship, they offer to share their knowledge and technology. More on page 173.

Sheffield, Charles. Heritage Universe Series. Annotated on page 41.

Summertide 1990.

Divergence. 1991.

Transcendence. 1992.

Silverberg, Robert. *The Alien Years*. 1998. Annotated on page 98.

War.

Silverberg, Robert. *A Time of Changes*. 1971. A most unusual autobiography, that of an alien from a collectivist society who comes under the influence of ideas from Earth and decides to write about them. A relatively dark work for Silverberg.

Nebula Award.

Wentworth, K. D. *Black on Black*. 1999. Like Heinlein's *Citizen of the Galaxy*, this novel features an orphan who was enslaved as a youth, rescued from the slave pens, raised by a caring adult, then returns to his home world to find his roots. Heyoka Blackeagle is a Hrinn, over seven feet tall, with retracting claws and the features of a wolf. He is also a confederation Ranger who wants to know why his family was destroyed and why he has suddenly started shifting into a speeded-up blue zone when he is attacked. What he discovers upon returning to Anktan is that he is a fabled Black on Black, rumored to be stronger and quicker than other Hrinn, especially when he's in the blue zone. There is also a legend of a Black on Black who will return to save his people from internecine struggles, assassination attempts, and the invasion of the alien Flek.

Willis, Connie. *Uncharted Territory*. 1994. Annotated on page 42.

Wolfe, Gene. The Book of the New Sun. Annotated on page 124.

> *The Shadow of the Torturer*. 1980.

  The Claw of the Conciliator. 1981.

> **Nebula and Locus Awards.**

> *The Sword of the Lichtor*. 1981.

> *The Citadel of the Autarch*. 1983.

First Contact

First contact, the first time that humankind meets with other sentient beings, is a momentous event in science fiction. That very first meeting, that very first time that sentient beings are encountered by humans, sets the scene for drama and conflict. First contact has been a popular theme in films from *ET* to *Close Encounters* to *Contact*.

Crispin, A. C. StarBridge series.

> *StarBridge*. 1989. Annotated on page 37.

Forward, Robert L. *Camelot 30K*. 1993. Miniature aliens, living on a world that is only 30 degrees above absolute zero, are contacted by humans. Fans of scientific extrapolation in SF will enjoy Forward's forays into physics.

Foster, Alan Dean. *The Dig*. 1997. Annotated on page 5.

Moon, Elizabeth. *Remnant Population*. 1996. Annotated on page 123.

Russell, Mary Doria. *The Sparrow*. 1996. Alternates between the hope-filled days when extraterrestrial music is discovered by Jimmy Quinn and the Jesuit order swings into action outfitting an expedition to the planet Rakhat to the slow drawing out of the horrible outcome from the sole tortured and vilified survivor of the expedition. More on page 105.

> **James Tiptree Jr. Award.**

Saberhagen, Fred. Final Conflict Series.

> *The Arrival.* 1999. This prequel to Gene Roddenberry's television series features the first contact between the Taelons and multibillionaire Jonathan Doors.

Sagan, Carl. *Contact.* 1985. Astrophysicist Ellie Arroway discovers a mathematical message that leads her on a journey to meet an extraterrestrial presence.

Sawyer, Robert J. *Factoring Humanity.* 1998. When a professor finally deciphers alien signals, a new technology is discovered that may transform humankind. Annotated on page 119.

Sawyer, Robert J. *Starplex.* 1996. With the arrival of a mysterious alien vessel at Starplex through a wormhole, an interstellar war could begin. Annotated on page 41.

Stine, G. Harry. *Starsea Invaders: First Action.* 1993. When American personnel start to disappear, an investigating submarine will be the first to encounter an alien race.

Aliens Among Us

Perhaps the aliens are not "out there," but actually living on Earth—perceived or not perceived, ready to take over, ready to help humanity, or perhaps just wanting to survive.

Baird, Wilhelmina. *Psykosis.* 1995. Fifteen years after the Third Alien War, Sword is horrified that the government calls upon him to represent the Earth's military to negotiate a peaceful agreement with the aliens who have returned.

Bear, Greg. *The Forge of God.* 1987. Aliens arrive on Earth with a message of impending doom. The solar system is to become a battleground. And after the self-replicating "Von Neumann machines" get through, little will be left of humankind's home world.

Brown, Frederic. *Martians Go Home.* 1955. Annotated on page 178.

Clarke, Arthur C. *Childhood's End.* 1953. Annotated on page 101.

Clarke, Arthur C. *The Hammer of God.* 1993. Annotated on page 94.

Crichton, Michael. *Sphere.* 1987. When a huge spaceship is found resting on the bottom of the ocean, American scientists rush to the site to study it. To do this, they must descend to the ocean floor and live in a special habitat, accompanied by a top-notch team of navy specialists in underwater survival. Dr. Norman Johnson, a middle-aged psychologist, has been brought on board because of his research concerning how a group might cope when faced with the possibility of meeting representatives of an alien culture for the first time. First contact becomes quite a challenge, however, when a giant green squid begins attacking the habitat.

Douglas, Carole Nelson. *Probe.* 1985. Annotated on page 135.

> *Counterprobe.* 1988. Annotated on page 135.

Heinlein, Robert A. *The Puppet Masters.* 1951. Sluglike creatures take over human hosts and turn them into mindless puppets. Considered by many to be a classic of this type.

Heinlein, Robert A. *The Star Beast.* 1954. Annotated on page 198.

Like, Russel. *After the Blue.* 1998. Annotated on page 189.

Niven, Larry, and Jerry Pournelle. *Footfall.* 1985. Annotated on page 29.

Pratchett, Terry. Bromeliad Series.

> *Truckers.* 1989. The Nomes, truly little people at only four inches high, are also aliens who have been stranded on Earth for 15,000 years, forgetting that they were from an alien world as they struggled to survive on this one. Masklin, the leader of a mostly elderly group that only has ten members left, talks the group into hitching a ride on a truck that delivers them to a store, where they are shocked to discover that they are not the only Nomes still alive.
>
> *Diggers.* 1990. The Nomes' flight into the outside has led them to claim an abandoned quarry as their new home. But Masklin is still wondering about the information that he has heard, that the Nomes are actually from another planet and that a spaceship is still waiting for them, patiently circling the Earth. He and two others head for the airport with the ultimate goal of finding a home that is theirs and theirs alone, that can't be wrested away from them by big, slow-moving, unstoppable humans.
>
> *Wings.* 1990. Masklin, Angelo (the Nome who taught himself to drive a truck and became a mechanical expert), and Gurder (the spiritual leader of the Nomes) are directed by the Thing that is helping them get in touch with their spaceship to take the Concorde to Florida.

Sawyer, Robert J. *Calculating God.* 2000. When a six-legged, two-armed alien lands his shuttle craft in Toronto, the first thing he says (in perfect English, no less) is, "Take me to a paleontologist." He is bringing information that links his planet, our planet, and one other planet to the same five cataclysmic events that may prove the existence of God. More on page 105.

Simak, Clifford D. *Way Station.* 1963. "When Wallace agreed to manage the Way Station, he had been unaware of the greater role for which he was being considered—Earth's sole representative to the Inter-Galactic Council. For more than a century he carried out his duties flawlessly, having become so accustomed to the bizarre and wonderful creatures that passed through his materializer he saw nothing unusual in a plasm that communicated by changing its shape or a beetle that counted by clicking its mandibles. He passed many evenings listening to the fascinating tales of these travelers from the furthest reaches of space."—book jacket.

Hugo Award.

Stewart, Daniel Blair. *Akhunaton: The Extraterrestrial King.* 1995. Annotated on page 107.

Turtledove, Harry. Worldwar Series. Foes at the beginning of World War II become allies when a deadly enemy destroys much of Earth and humanity must unite to survive.

Worldwar: In the Balance: The Alternate History of Alien Invasion. 1994.

Worldwar: Tilting the Balance. 1995.

Worldwar: Upsetting the Balance. 1996.

Worldwar: Striking the Balance. 1996.

Wells, H. G. *The War of the Worlds.* 1898. The inhabitants of Earth panic when the highly organized but loathsome Martians invade. Orson Welles adapted this story for radio, and it created quite a stir when it was first broadcast in 1938.

Wyndham, John. *The Day of the Triffids.* 1951. Annotated on page 95.

Wyndham, John. *The Midwich Cuckoos.* 1958. Annotated on page 98.

Encounters in Space

Bear, Greg. *Legacy.* 1995. Annotated on page 111.

Benford, Gregory. Galactic Center Series

In the Ocean of Night. 1977. A fascinating look at alien encounters by author Benford, a physicist who brings his scientific expertise into his works with a deft touch.

Across the Sea of Suns. 1985. Annotated on page 44.

Great Sky River. 1987. Intelligent machines have become a threat to a human colony located near the core of the galaxy.

Tides of Light. 1989. Annotated on page 74.

Furious Gulf. 1994. The last survivors of Snowglade travel toward the Galactic Center after escaping from the genocidal forces of their home world.

Sailing Bright Eternity. 1995. The violent artificial intelligences known as the mechs have nearly annihilated humankind, but Nigel Walmsley, caught in a space-time anomaly, may be the key to survival.

Budrys, Algis. *Rogue Moon*. 1960. A matter transmitter has been developed that makes it possible to beam humans directly to the moon. But once they arrive, these "men on the moon" are confronted with the existence of a truly frightening alien maze.

Cherryh, C. J. *Brothers of Earth*. 1976. In this novel of the Hanan rebellion, a lone Earthman survives in a world of alien cultures.

Cherryh, C. J. *Cuckoo's Egg*. 1985. The cuckoo in this instance is an ugly child raised by catlike aliens. He discovers when he grows up that he is a human. Characteristically, Cherryh excels at her depiction of alien-human interaction. "Thom was different from his people—ugly in their eyes, strange, sleek-skinned instead of furred, and clawless."

Cherryh, C. J. Faded Sun Trilogy

Kesrith. 1978. The alien Regul are defeated by humans in war and given no choice but to surrender their planet, Kesrith. Unfortunately, this means betraying their allies, the nomadic Mri, a warlike tribe of interstellar nomads who are also fanatical warriors.

Shon'jir. 1978. A human soldier is incredibly accepted by the last of the Mri warriors. He then joins the two as they set out to try to find their long-lost home world.

Kutath. 1979. The concluding volume of the Faded Sun Trilogy. The last of the Mri have found their long-lost home world. But a human space fleet has found their world as well and is debating the issue of whether or not to attack and wipe out the last of the Mri.

Cherryh, C. J. *Finity's End*. 1997. Annotated on page 36.

Cherryh, C. J. Foreigner Series.

Foreigner: A Novel of First Contact. 1994. After accidentally discovering an ecologically suitable planet far beyond known routes, humans decide to try to establish a base there, much to the displeasure of the Atevi who already inhabit the planet. After the human-Atevi wars, the surviving humans are driven off the mainland and settle on Mospheira Island. Only one human is allowed to come into direct contact with the Atevi, the human ambassador to the Atevi. That role has fallen to young Bren Cameron. After an attempt is made on his life, he has to rely on his Atevi bodyguards to save him while trying to find out who was responsible for the assassination attempt and why.

Invader. 1995. After a 200-year absence, the starship *Phoenix* returns, escalating the tensions between the Atevi and the humans.

Inheritor. 1996. After surviving assassination attempts, the paranoia of his own human government (which tried to replace its capable ambassador with an inept stand-in), and a plot against an elite Atevi family that he foiled, Bren has gained the respect of the Assassins guild and a place of honor within the new ruling class. His new challenge is dealing with the two ambassadors sent down to the planet from the starship *Phoenix*. Bren has his hands full—keeping track of the volatile political situation among the Atevi, translating human technical terms into the Atevi language, and coping with the attacks on his friends and family on Mosphiera by the archconservatives there. And on top of everything else, enemy aliens could be on their way.

Precursor. 1999. More than once Bren's survival depended on his Atevi bodyguards. They might not understand the human concept of friendship or liking someone, but they would lay down their lives for their charge, and almost did. In just three short years, since the first appearance of the *Phoenix*, the Atevi have mastered space flight, built a space shuttle, and are ready to start work on the space station. But Bren discovers a conspiracy on the part of the crew to work only with humans, cutting out the Atevi entirely. It seems that the starship captains are paranoid about aliens and do not want to deal with them. But it is the Atevi, not the humans, who have the technology and the skills that the ship needs in this new era of space flight.

Defender. 2001.

Cherryh, C. J. *Forty Thousand in Gehenna*. 1983. Annotated on page 4.

Cherryh, C. J. *Rider at the Gate*. 1995. Annotated on page 134.

Cloud's Rider. 1996. Annotated on page 134.

Dick, Philip K. *A Maze of Death*. 1970. Annotated on page 102.

Kress, Nancy. *Probability Moon*. 2000. The Worlders society is vividly depicted, allowing the reader to see the emotions expressed through their bald scalps and the social manners relating to their neck fur. More on page 7.

Le Guin, Ursula K. *The Left Hand of Darkness*. 1969. Annotated on page 101.

 Hugo, and Nebula Awards.

Lichtenberg, Jacqueline. *Those of My Blood*. 1988. Annotated on page 147.

Dreamspy. 1989. Annotated on page 147.

McCaffrey, Anne. Freedom Trilogy.

Freedom's Landing. 1995. Aliens have invaded the Earth and taken captured humans away to a life of slavery among the stars. Kristin Bjornsen manages to escape her Catteni masters and hide in the jungle for five months. When she sees a Catteni being chased by others of his kind, she goes to his assistance and meets Zainal, an Emassi of extremely high rank. He rewards her for his rescue by trying to rape her, which he considers his right. She knocks him unconscious and returns him to the city, where they are inadvertently swept up in the next shipment of slaves to be dropped on the planet Bounty. Enmity turns to attraction as they adjust to Operation Fresh Start on this beautiful green planet, as well as to the mystery behind the machines and farming techniques of the absent Mech Makers.

Freedom's Choice. 1997. Kris Bjornson and her Catteni lover Zainal were among those deported to the planet Bounty after the takeover of their worlds by the Eosi. Zainal is actually on Bounty by mistake, the victim of an argument with political rivals. But the rule of the Catteni is "once dropped on the planet, you stay." This is fine with him; he's won hard-fought acceptance from the other deportees and fallen in love with Kris. Plus it makes sense for him to stay because he is the Chosen One in his family. If he goes back, he'll be subsumed by the Eosi Overlord his family serves. Together with the other settlers, he explores this new world and succeeds in capturing a couple of Eosi spaceships that land there. With his military expertise and Kris's support, he and Kris begin taking charge of their own lives.

Freedom's Challenge. 1998. Kris and Zainal prepare to face danger and pain, in the final fight for liberty.

McCaffrey, Anne, Elizabeth Ann Scarborough, and Margaret Ball. Acorna Series.

McCaffrey, Anne, and Margaret Ball. *Acorna: The Unicorn Girl*. 1997. Three space prospectors find a strange toddler in a survival pod—and she has incredible powers.

Acorna's Quest. 1998. Acorna, raised by space-faring humans, searches for her people.

McCaffrey, Anne, and Elizabeth Ann Scarborough. *Acorna's People*. 1999. Acorna is reunited with her people.

Acorna's World. 2000. Acorna ships out on a salvage vessel with salvager Becker; his ship's cat, Roadkill; and Aari, a young man of Acorna's race who had been tortured and maimed by the vicious, buglike aliens, the Khleevi. Space opera and romance rolled together.

Acorna's Search. 2002. As Acorna tries to help her people, the Linyaari, rebuild after the devastation of the Khleevi, people start disappearing.

Pohl, Frederik. Heechee Saga.

 Gateway. 1977. Volume 1 of the Heechee Saga. The discovery of alien artifacts leads humans on voyages of space discovery.

> ***Hugo, Nebula, and Locus Awards.***

Beyond the Blue Event Horizon. 1980. Robin Broadhead's wife is abandoned on the "event horizon" of a black hole while he looks to make his fortune by financing an expedition to the "food factory," a Heechee artifact that can transform basic elements into food.

Heechee Rendezvous. 1984. The protagonist of the previous work finally meets the Heechee, his alien benefactors. But there are also some less friendly aliens out there.

The Annals of the Heechee. 1987. The sequel to *Heechee Rendezvous* recounts the struggle by the Heechee and humans to solve the mystery of the alien Assassins. The original protagonist is still present, in the form of a mind stored in a computer.

The Gateway Trip. 1990. Short stories that add to the tale of Heechee.

Russell, Mary Doria. *Children of God*. 1998. In this sequel to *The Sparrow*, Jesuit Emilio Sandoz returns to Rakhat, where enormous changes have taken place, and events that unfolded in the previous book are given a different spin.

Slonczewski, Joan. *The Children Star*. 1998. The highly structured ecosystem of Prokaryon indicates that there must be intelligent life on the planet, but what could it be? An avaricious corporation sees profit in sterilizing the planet and terraforming it, but that would annihilate native sentient life as well as spell an end to the Spirit Brethren colony. Slonczewski's alien life forms are truly alien, with a totally different biological basis than humans, having triple strand DNA and living at a pace so different from humans that it is almost impossible to communicate with them. More on page 130.

Tepper, Sheri S. Marjorie Westriding Trilogy.

Grass. 1989. Humanity is being decimated on every planet by a virulent plague—except on the provincial and isolated Grass, which refuses to allow scientists to come in and conduct studies. The solution is to send ambassadors who will fit in with the "upper crust" of Grass—the seven families, aristocratic descendants of the original settlers—who ride together in brutal hunts. The Yrariers are the perfect choice as ambassadors. Marjorie, Lady Westriding, is a past gold medal winner in the Olympics (equestrian events), and the rest of her family are riders and horse owners as well. But the hunt on Grass is far more dangerous than any she has seen before. When Marjorie's daughter disappears during a hunt, she will not rest until she has found the girl and solved the mystery of this strange planet.

Raising the Stones. 1990. As the children on the pastoral planet Hobbs Land rebuild an ancient shrine left behind by the Owlbrit, the original but seemingly now extinct inhabitants, a strange harmony grows between the residents, while on other planets religion and politics wreak havoc.

Sideshow. 1992. This third work in the Marjorie Westriding trilogy is densely packed, thought-provoking, complex, and rich in philosophical explorations. The new characters are quite interesting, like the Siamese twins Nela and Bertran from Earth. There's also an Enforcer, Zasper Ertigon, who cannot always allow diversity to run its course and so rescues a toddler from the bloody God Molock. Fringe Owldark is a young girl Zasper adopts and sponsors into the Enforcer Academy. Danivon Luze, the boy Zasper saved, also grows up to be an Enforcer. Boarmus, the Provost of Tolerance, knows something is seriously wrong on the Planet Elsewhere, but not how to go about fixing it. So, he sends in the Enforcers, asking Fringe and company to investigate. They discover that the intellectuals who founded the planet have gone into the core and are now insane, bent only on death, destruction, blood, and pain. In the end, it takes great personal sacrifice on the part of Fringe to save the planet and her friends.

Thompson, Amy. *The Color of Distance.* 1995. After being marooned alone on a hostile planet, Juna's only hope for survival is to transform herself into a member of the amphibian Tendu species.

Vinge, Vernor. *A Deepness in the Sky.* 1999. Set 30,000 years before *Fire Upon the Deep.* A civilization of spider-like sentients has been found on a planet where a very strange cycle leaves them in hibernation for years at a time.

 Hugo Award.

White, James. Sector General Series. White's series, set in a hospital that caters to all sentient races, shows some of the diversity possible when one dreams of the different types of life forms that could develop under different conditions.

Hospital Station. 1962.

Star Surgeon. 1963.

Major Operation. 1971.

Ambulance Ship. 1979.

Sector General. 1983.

Star Healer. 1985.

Code Blue: Emergency. 1987.

The Genocidal Healer. 1992.

The Galactic Gourmet. 1996.

Final Diagnosis. 1997.

Mind Changer. 1998.

Double Contact. 1999.

Chapter 5

Genreblending

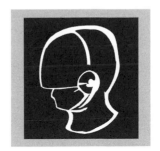

Since its beginning science fiction has often used elements of horror and fantasy to create interesting story blends. Mary Wollstonecraft Shelley's *Frankenstein*, arguably the first science fiction novel, is even more frequently thought of as horror, as is *Relic*, a genetic tampering tale by Douglas Preston and Lincoln Child. Anne McCaffrey's biologically engineered dragons in her Pern series are often considered fantasy along with Marion Zimmer Bradley's Darkover series, which features psionic powers. *Ventus* by Karl Schroeder is most definitely science fiction, with its terraformed planet controlled by artificial intelligence and nanotechnology running rampant, but it has a feel that is very much fantasy-like, with a quest theme and humans who live without technology. In the early days of science fiction, when many of the authors were writing for the pulp magazines of the day, it was profitable to be as prolific as possible, so there is also a tradition of SF writers writing mystery and suspense tales.

The one area that science fiction seemed to avoid for many years was romance. Love and sex were considered very avant-garde topics for the genre when the New Wave movement swept through SF in the 1960s. However, in the 1990s the romance reading world embraced science fiction, bringing the genre to a whole new category of readers. We examine blends of romance and SF in two sections. In "SF Spiced with Romance" the emphasis is on science fiction. In "Romance in a SF World" the stories are decidedly romances, with elements of SF thrown in.

Women's fiction, the genre that deals with relationships and womanly concerns, usually does not intersect with science fiction. There are many women science fiction writers and a number of feminist science fiction titles, but somehow SF just does not combine comfortably with mainstream, literary, or women's fiction genres. Science fiction readers who are interested in more literary works should be directed to titles bearing the "Classics" tag, because many of the genre's earliest and most durable authors were mainstream/literary writers. They may also want to check titles that have won awards. As for readers interested in women's concerns or issues, some titles may be accessed through the subject index, under "female protagonist."

The following sections in this chapter deal with the blending of science fiction with romance, mystery, and humor. Titles that blend SF with inspirational/ Christian, fantasy, and horror are listed at the end of the chapter.

All's Fair in Love and Space

Science Fiction and Romance

The recent trend toward genreblending in all fiction sometimes marries SF and romance. As SF becomes a viable venue for romance stories, romance is creeping into SF. While throughout the history of SF, action and adventure focusing on male heroes was prevalent, the rise of female authors and characters in the genre began to add an emphasis on relationships. This subgenre may have started with the alien abduction tale *Yargo* by Jacqueline Susann, who modeled her eponymous alien hero on Yul Brynner in the 1960s. Many romance readers who stumble across a romance in a science fiction setting discover that they enjoy the unknown backdrop and venture further into science fiction. Time travel is a popular theme in romance fiction, and occasionally time-travel romances have a generous dollop of science fiction. The SF romances that are most clearly science fiction are the ones termed "futuristics" by romance readers.

Readers who enjoy the SF/romance combination will find compatriots on the World Wide Web. The Science Fiction Romance Web Site is at http://members.aol.com/sfreditor/index.htm.

The Sapphire Award, sponsored by the *Science Fiction Romance Newsletter*, includes both science fiction and fantasy. It has been awarded annually since 1995 and has categories for both novel-length and short fiction. Their Web site is at http://www.sfronline.com/sapphire.htm. The 1999 winner was Lois McMaster Bujold's *A Civil Campaign*. The 2000 winner was *Heir to Govandhara* by Saira Ramasastry.

The Prism awards are given by the Futuristic, Fantasy and Paranormal Chapter of the Romance Writers of America. They have categories for Futuristic/Fantasy, Time Travel, Dark Paranormal, and Light Paranormal. The first category is where SF fans may find books of interest. The 2000 winner was Catherine Asaro's *Veiled Web*. The 2001 award, for books published in 2000, announced at the Romance Writers of America conference in July 2001, was *Virtual Desire* by Ann Lawrence.

Science Fiction Spiced With Romance

Novels in this category emphasize SF aspects but add a touch of spice with the romantic entanglements of the characters. Generally, those involved are of human ancestry. Romance is also one of the elements in space opera, and readers may find additional titles in that section in Chapter 1 that they will enjoy.

Asaro, Catherine. *The Phoenix Code.* 2000. Annotated on page 73.

Asaro, Catherine. Saga of the Skolian Empire. In a far distant time and place, politics and romance ensnare genetically enhanced humans in a web of conflict.

Primary Inversion. 1995. Annotated on page 125.

Catch the Lightning. 1996. Annotated on page 125.

The Last Hawk. 1997. Annotated on page 125.

The Radiant Seas. 1999. Annotated on page 126.

Ascendant Sun. 2000. Annotated on page 126.

The Quantum Rose. 2000. A romantic triangle develops when Havyrl Lionstar visits the backwater world of Balumil and runs across Kamoj Quanta Argali, governor of a poor province who is engaged to the unpredictable Jax Ironbridge.

Spherical Harmonic. 2001. Dyhianna coalesces on a forested moon when the psiberweb is destroyed and she must seek her lost husband.

Asaro, Catherine. *Veiled Web.* 1999. A marriage of convenience brings Lucia del Mar, a beautiful world class ballerina, and Rashid al-Jazari, a high-tech Moroccan inventor/businessman, together. More on page 78.

> **Prism Award.**

Asprin, Robert, and Linda Evans. Time Scout Series. Annotated on page 34.

Time Scout. 1995.

Wagers of Sin. 1996.

Ripping Time. 2000.

The House That Jack Built. 2001.

Banks, Iain. *Inversions.* 2000. Annotated on page 11.

Bujold, Lois McMaster. Vorkosigan Saga. Although the entire series has a good deal of romance, the first two listed here, in particular, have enough to satisfy even romance fans. Other titles in the series are listed on page 14.

Shards of Honor. 1986. In a swashbuckling tale of honor, heroism, and love that spans several planets, Betan Commander Cordelia Naismith discovers that her expeditionary force has fled the planet they were surveying after being attacked by Barrayaran forces. While she tries to bury the one crew member left dead in the destroyed camp, Aral Vorkosigan, an injured Barrayaran officer, shows up, plunging them into a relationship that defies both their cultures.

A Civil Campaign. 1999. Both Miles and his clone, Mark, whom he calls brother, seem to be on the path to love. More on page 178.

Brothers in Arms. 1989. The girl Miles has fallen in love with is most definitely not willing to give up a life of danger and adventure to settle down planetside as a "lady," especially not on a planet as hide-bound and restrictive as Barrayar. More on page 15.

Komarr: A Miles Vorkosigan Adventure. 1998. Miles is in love, and this one loves him back—at last! She's taller than he is, but then who isn't? Besides, that doesn't matter to her. She just thinks of him as more "concentrated." More on page 15.

Butler, Octavia E. Patternmaster Series. Annotated on page 134.

Butler, Octavia E. *Wild Seed*. 1980. In this unusual romance, an immortal West African man meets and falls in love with a 300-year-old woman. They emigrate to the new world and become the parents of the super-race found in the author's early Patternist novels.

Dickson, Gordon R. *Wolf and Iron*. 1990. Annotated on page 97.

Dunne, Jennifer. *Raven's Heart*. 2000. Society made them enemies. After all, Raven Armistead is a member of the Auric Rights League, fighting to protect those with genetic gifts from the fear and prejudice of the non-gifted. And Val Tarrant is absolutely the last person she should have anything to do with. He's a policeman, a ruthless agent of the Inter-Continental Police. But circumstances make them allies; like the fact that he is betrayed and she is framed for murder. And destiny, well . . . what do you expect in a romance? From the moment she saves his life and discovers that his aura is now aligned with hers, they are destined to be lovers—provided they live long enough.

Egan, Doris. *The Complete Ivory*. 2001. An omnibus edition of the three Ivory titles.

The Gate of Ivory. 1989. Annotated on page 5.

Two-Bit Heroes. 1992. Theodora, an anthropology scholar from a technologically advanced planet, is finally getting used to the way magic is used on Ivory. Having fallen in love with a nobleman, she has embarked on a complicated and lengthy marriage ritual. More on page 5.

Guilt-Edged Ivory. 1992. Theodora's adventures continue.

Emerson, Jane. *City of Diamond*. 1996. Iolanthe, the greatest beauty of the *City of Pearl* (an intergalactic city ship) is sent to the *City of Diamond* to wed Adrian Mercati, the city ship's Protector. More on page 17.

Finney, Jack. *Time and Again*. 1970. Romance grows out of an encounter that takes place during a government-sponsored time-travel project. Si Morley, a commercial artist, is recruited to travel back in time to New York City in the winter of 1882. Once there, he makes sketches and takes photographs to bring back as proof that he did indeed made the trip. He also falls in love, but how can the course of love run true when one party's presence in the past can alter the present and future? Further time-travel adventures continue in the sequel, *From Time to Time* (1995). Annotated on page 50.

Friesner, Esther. *The Sherwood Game*. 1995. Annotated on page 6.

Gould, Steven. *Jumper.* 1992. When sixteen-year-old Davy discovers that he is a "jumper," that he can teleport to any place that he has actually seen, he runs away to New York. There he falls in love.

Heald, Denise Lopes. *Mistwalker.* 1994. Annotated on page 37.

Lee, Sharon, and Steve Miller. Agent of Change Sequence (a sub-series of the Liaden Universe, has a Web site at http://www.Korval.com/liad.htm).

Partners in Necessity 2000. An omnibus reissue of the following three underground classics.

Conflict of Honors. 1988. Pricilla, an "outcast with a sense of honor is taken in by Shan, a starship Captain who has a habit of caring for strays. While teaching her about the Liaden concept of melant'I, a sort of cross between self esteem and social standing, he also must teach the woman he has come to love that she is worth loving. All while trying to foil the plots of two psychopaths bent on revenge."—Jennifer Dunne, author of *Raven's Heart.*

Agent of Change. 1988. The adventures of Clan Korval continue.

Carpe Diem. 1989. "Val Con [is] a brilliant Scout who has been brainwashed (more like brain folded, spindled and mutilated) to become a covert operative for the mysterious Department of Interior. He meets Miri Robertson, a retired mercenary whose cushy bodyguard job for the wrong man has landed her on the deadly side of vengeance with an intergalactic Mafia. Now the two must struggle to stay alive without killing each other, facing existing enemies and adding scores of new ones with every disastrous attempt to break free of pursuit. Due to a misunderstanding with a clutch of Turtles and a knife, Val Con and Miri are unintentionally married and intentionally lifemated, a pair of complications they'd love to live long enough to figure out."—Jennifer Dunne, author of *Raven's Heart.*

Plan B. 1999. *Plan B* is the stand-alone sequel to the Agent of Change sequence set in the Liaden Universe trilogy: *Conflict of Honors, Agent of Change,* and *Carpe Diem.* Val Con, once an "Agent of Change," has been turned into a killing machine by Liad's Department of the Interior. All that keeps him going is his half-Terran lifemate, Miri Robertson. A former mercenary sergeant, she is almost as deadly in battle as her husband. This is fortunate because Korval has involved Plan B against Liad: retreat strategically, trust no one, and prepare for all-out war. Where there's a war, there'll be Val Con and Miri, fighting to survive.

Pilots Choice. 2001. This omnibus edition of *Local Custom* and *Scout's Progress,* set in the Liaden Universe, is a prequel to *Agent of Change.*

I Dare. 2002. The members of Clan Korval are far flung and out of touch with each other. Val Con yos'Phelium fights for his life in a catastrophe unit while his lifemate finds their link slipping away, but salvation may be in the hands of two giant turtle-like beings. Pat Rin yos'Phelium's adventures on a backward Terran planet are the easiest to follow as he cleverly takes control of the planet with the help of two hired guns.

Like, Russel. *After the Blue*. 1998. After accidentally decimating the Earth, Gruumsbaggians, in an attempt to put it back like it was before they unwittingly caused the end of civilization as we know it, bring in pollution, smog machines, and gridlock plans as they try to reintroduce the humans they have raised on their home planet. A charming romance develops between one of the newly arrived humans and one of the young men from Jamesburg, allowing a skillfully interwoven tale of the history of this world to entwine with the story. More on page 89.

McCaffrey, Anne. All of McCaffrey's titles have a strong emphasis on human interactions, with romance playing a prominent role. Her Partnership series (page 61), Pern series, and Powers That Be series (page 140), some written with co-authors, are all good bets for science fiction readers looking for a little romance.

Moon, Elizabeth. Esmay Suiza Series.

Once a Hero. 1997. Annotated on page 28.

Rules of Engagement. 1998. Annotated on page 28.

Change of Command. 1999. Esmay Suiza and Barin Serrano have fallen in love and want to get married. But they face what at first seem insurmountable odds: his family, her family, Barin's responsibility for the women and children rescued from the New Texas Militia in the previous novel, and Esmay's position as Landbride Suiza.

Nye, Jody Lynn. *The Ship Errant*. 1996. Can a brain and a brawn fall in love and make it work? More on page 62.

Orwell, George. *1984*. 1949. Can love survive in a dystopian world where Big Brother watches everyone and everything? History is rewritten as needed, Big Brother sees all, and the Thought Police make sure everyone behaves. Winston Smith's story of love and tragic betrayal is set in a twisted, horrific world.

Simmons, Dan. *Hyperion*. 1989. Annotated on page 106.

🎗 *Hugo and Locus Awards*.

The Fall of Hyperion. 1990. Annotated on page 106.

Endymion. 1996. Raul Endymion describes the circumstances that led to his imprisonment, in particular his meeting with Aenea, the young girl and supposed messiah he was assigned to protect. More on page 106.

The Rise of Endymion. 1997. Aenea, who was twelve when Raul first rescued her, has now turned sixteen. He is thirty-two and on the verge of falling in love with her. Their lives are in danger, however, because the Church has discovered that Aenea can destroy cruciforms and resurrection, offering true peace to those who die. This makes her an agent of salvation to many, but not to the Church, which is determined to destroy her. Raul is joined by the Shrike in a surprising twist, but the battle to keep Aenea safe is far from assured. Even time travel can offer only temporary refuge for these star-crossed lovers.

Stapledon, Olaf. *Star Maker*. 1937. Annotated on page 107.

Teller, Astro. *Exegesis*. 1997. Annotated on page 80.

Tepper, Sheri S. The Awakeners duology has also been published in one volume as *The Awakeners*. A science fiction romance that takes place along the shores of a mighty river on a distant planet.

> *Northshore*. 1987.

> *Southshore*. 1987.

Tepper, Sheri S. *Beauty*. 1991. A reworking of the Sleeping Beauty tale. Annotated on page 49.

Tyers, Kathy. Firebird Trilogy. Annotated on page 183.

> *Firebird*. 1987.

> *Fusion Fire*. 2000.

> *Crown of Fire*. 2000.

Vinge, Joan D. Snow Queen Universe. On a world where seasons can last centuries, winter gives way to summer with a ritual sacrifice.

> *The Snow Queen*. 1980. Arienrhod, the Queen of Winter, has been using the elixir of life distilled from the slaughtered sea mer to remain the ruler for the past 150 years. But now summer is coming, and she must make way for the Summer Queen. This means that she and her consort Starbuck will be drowned. Arienrhod, however, is not ready to give up control, and plans to sacrifice the clone that is the young Summer Queen in her place.

> ***Hugo and Locus Awards.***

> *World's End*. 1984. Annotated on page 130.

> *The Summer Queen*. 1991. Annotated on page 130.

> *Tangled Up in Blue*. 2000. Can a straight-laced cop make love work with a shapeshifting spy? Set on the planet Tiamat in the city Carbuncle, the same world as Vinge's classic, Hugo-award-winning *Snow Queen*, this noirish mystery tells the story of Hegemonic Police officer Nyx LaisTree, who is the sole survivor of a massacre in a warehouse. Exposed as one of the infamous Nameday Vigilantes, he is stripped of his badge but not his need for justice. Teaming up with Devony, a shapeshifter who is much more than she seems, they find out why his partner and his friends were murdered.

Willis, Connie. *To Say Nothing of the Dog*. 1997. Annotated on page 53.

   ***Hugo and Locus Awards.***

Willis, Connie, and Cynthia Felice. *Promised Land.* 1997. Annotated on page 47.

Zebrowski, George. *The Stars Will Speak.* 1985. The on-again, off-again relationship between college students Lissa and Alek provides the backdrop to a story about humankind striving to understand mysterious messages from the stars.

Romance in a Science Fiction World

Alternative reality romance is a term used by Bontly and Sheridan in their romance guide, *Enchanted Journeys Beyond the Imagination.* Out of all the types of romances they describe (fantasy, time travel, paranormal, and futuristic) the ones that can be considered SF are the futuristics, some of the time travels, and a few of the paranormals. The focus in this section is on romance fiction that has futuristic or alien settings as an exotic backdrop for the relationships. Many of the following titles are published as category romances by paperback romance publishers and quickly go out of print. However, a significant trend toward electronic publishing is becoming evident in this subgenre, probably because of the problems faced when a book goes out of print before demand is engendered by word-of-mouth promotion.

Ballard, Patricia. *By Honor Bound.* 1999. Four thousand years in the future, humanity is striving to recover from centuries of barbarism caused by a mutated virus. The virus was engineered to increase fertility, but it also raises emotions and can be deadly unless the antidote in the form of blood from an infected individual of the opposite gender is administered in a binding ceremony. (Talk about biological imperatives!) Cynnara Kyerrneth, a circus acrobat in twentieth-century America, is the daughter of an anthropologist and a man who has traveled back in time from the distant future. She is kidnapped and taken to her father's era by brawny Raithe Serrodon, second in command of the House Serrodon, to wed his disabled brother and thus preserve his life. In the future the strong rule, and only by an alliance with House Kyerrneth can Raithe hope to save his brother.

Cane, Nancy. *Keeper of the Rings.* 1996. Miami attorney Sarina Bretton was kidnapped by Tier and taken to the Coalition of Sentient Planets, where she is needed to fulfill a prophecy that claims that by her marrying Lord Cam'brii an end to a terrible plague will be found.

Castle, Jayne. *After Dark.* 2000. Lydia Smith, licensed para-archaeologist, is in a world of trouble. Living in a bad neighborhood just outside the walls of the Dead City of Old Cadence, she ekes out a living by working in the somewhat sleazy Shrimpton's House of Ancient Horrors while trying to make it as a consultant on the side. It is all quite a comedown from the time when she was an esteemed member of a university team investigating alien catacombs. She has just signed her first client, Emmett London, when she discovers the murdered body of her friend Chester exhibited in an ancient sarcophagus. After a visit from a particularly nasty ghost, she discovers that Emmett is much much more than he initially appeared and that now she is involved with the "Guild," the planet Harmony's version of organized crime. Lydia's pet, Fuzz, a dust-bunny, is a great sidekick and much more interesting and fierce than most pets inhabiting mystery novels.

Amaryllis. 1996. A psychic detective on a space colony finds hot romance in the midst of a murder investigation.

Orchid. 1998. Orchid Adams, a psychic romance novelist, meets a lone-wolf private investigator who sends her mind and her heart on a tumultuous collision course.

Zinnia. 1997. Zinnia's psionic powers are requested by a casino owner on the space colony of St. Helen's to help find his father's missing journal.

Cozzens, Tracy. *One Perfect Mate*. 1999. Mariss, an emotionally wounded botanist, crash lands in the wilderness on her way to meet the "perfect mate" who had been computer selected for her. Kade Land, a down-on-his-luck space jockey on the run from interstellar cops, agrees to escort Mariss to her destination, but the trek across the beautiful and deadly alien landscape just may change what constitutes her "perfect mate."

Grant, Susan. *The Star King*. 2000. Jasmine's life was once exciting, but now, twenty years after flying planes in the Gulf War, she is just a divorced mother of two young adults. What could be the connection between her and Rom, a minor intergalactic smuggler who visits Earth?

Hall, Chloe. *Last Hope*. 2000. Two couples who have a bizarre tie meet in the Western Mountains where strange manifestations occur. Could they have any relation to the disastrous scientific expedition that cost Arkana Crystal Song her parents; or could they hearken back to the distant past when settlers from Earth crashed on the planet?

Huxman Karin. *Virtual Heart*. 1999. Megan and Jake are trapped in a virtual reality world. Will their love hold up if they are able to find each other in the real world?

Joy, Dara. *Knight of a Trillion Stars*. 1995. Fired from her job and exhausted by her miserable commute, the last thing Deana Jones needs is to find an alien in her living room when she gets home. But how else to explain the man who claims he is from beyond the stars? He says his name is Lorgin and that she is part of his celestial destiny. Deana thinks his reasoning is ridiculous, and she knows he's making an error of cosmic proportions.

Maxwell, Ann. *Dancer's Luck*. 1995. Rheba, a fire dancer, and Kirtn, her warrior-mentor and guardian, have pledged to return a spaceship of freed slaves to their homes; and on a forgotten world at the galaxy's edge, they also find desire and love.

Robb, J. D. Eve Dallas Series. Robb, who is also best-selling romance novelist Nora Roberts, combines romance with science fiction in her futuristic detective series. The titles (to date) are listed on page 172.

A Gumshoe by Any Other Name:
Science Fiction and Mystery

The combination of science fiction and mystery produces galactic policemen and unique private eyes: human, alien, and mechanical. Detection became popular in science fiction novels in the 1950s, following Hal Clement's 1949 novel *Needle*, in which an alien detective comes to Earth and inhabits a human body to catch a malign entity in the body of a young boy's father. Isaac Asimov's R. Daneel Olivaw and Lije Baley, a human and robot detecting team, are the best known detectives in the SF world. As in the standard detective story, there are series detectives in several of the following examples. The first three titles here are short story anthologies that give a delightful glimpse of this type.

Asimov, Isaac, Martin H. Greenberg, and Charles G. Waugh, eds. *The 13 Crimes of Science Fiction*. 1979. A spectrum of story types for a variety of reading tastes. Each of the stories is labeled: Hard-Boiled Detective, Psychic Detective, Spy Story, Analytical Detective, Whodunit, Why-Done-It, Inverted, Locked Room, Cipher, Police Procedural, Trial, and Punishment.

Dozois, Gardner, and Sheila Williams, eds. *Isaac Asimov's Detectives*. Ace Books, 1998. Six stories that were originally published in *Isaac Asimov's Science Fiction Magazine:* "The Barbie Murders" by John Varley, "Cocoon" by Greg Egan, "The Gorgon Field" by Kate Wilhelm, "Rites of Spring" by Lisa Goldstein, "The Backward Look" by Isaac Asimov, and "Fault Lines" by Nancy Kress.

Adams, Douglas. Dirk Gently Series. The adventures of a private investigator who takes on cases as mundane as finding cats and has a theory that it doesn't really matter which car one picks to tail, eventually it will lead to where one needs to be.

Dirk Gently's Holistic Detective Agency. 1987.

The Long Dark Tea-Time of the Soul. 1988.

Anderson, Kevin J., and Doug Beason. *Virtual Destruction*. 1996. A scientist working on a virtual reality project in a top secret lab is murdered.

Asimov, Isaac. Elijah Baley and R. Daneel Olivaw Series. Lije Baley wasn't thrilled to be teamed up with a robot, but against the two of them with their first-rate brains (one organic, one positronic), murderers don't have a chance.

The Caves of Steel. 1954. Annotated on page 73.

The Naked Sun. 1957. Annotated on page 74.

The Robots of Dawn. 1983. Annotated on page 74.

Robots and Empire. 1985. Annotated on page 74.

Banks, Iain. *Feersum Endjinn*. 1994. Annotated on page 82.

Bear, Greg. *Queen of Angels*. 1990. Annotated on page 126.

Bester, Alfred. *The Demolished Man.* 1953. This fascinating murder mystery features Lincoln Powell, a telepathic cop in 2301, on the trail of a man who will do anything to keep from facing "psychic demolition"—including murder.

> *Hugo Award (first winner).*

Biggle, Lloyd Jr. *Watchers of the Dark.* 1966. Jan Darzek, private eye.

Bova, Ben. *Death Dream.* 1994. Annotated on page 83.

Carroll, Jerry Jay. *Inhuman Beings.* 1998. Private Investigator Goodwin Armstrong, formerly a cop, gets involved in a wacky mystery involving a psychic called Princess Dulay who claims that aliens have come to Earth in a bowling ball-sized space craft.

Castle, Jayne. The titles that former librarian Jayne Ann Krentz writes under this pseudonym are all combinations of mystery, science fiction, and romance. They are annotated on page 166.

Cherryh, C. J. *Cyteen.* 1988. For fifty years Ariane Emory, head of a research lab on the planet Cyteen, has been one of the two Councilors from Reseune, consistently elected to represent the most populous entity in the Union—until dissension in the ranks leads to Emory's murder. But Emory is neither gone nor forgotten as an infant replicant of her is activated and begins the education that will put Emory in control of Reseune again. Other books in Cherryh's Merchanter universe are annotated on page 16. Also published as a trilogy under the titles *Cyteen: The Betrayal, Cyteen: The Rebirth,* and *Cyteen: The Vindication,* this modern classic, set in Cherryh's Merchanter Universe, won the Hugo award in 1989.

> *Hugo Award.*

Clement, Hal. *Needle.* 1950. A parasite-police detective ventures to Earth on the trail of a parasite that has invaded the body of a young father.

Dick, Philip K. *Do Androids Dream of Electric Sheep?* 1968. Working for the San Francisco Police Department, Rick Deckard, a Blade Runner, is paid a bounty for every android who has been trying to pass as human that he catches—dead or alive. More on page 74.

Dietz, William C. Sam McCade Series. Wise-cracking, cigar-chomping Sam McCade is an interstellar bounty hunter with a spaceship called *Pegasus.*

Galactic Bounty. 1986. Originally titled *War World.*

Imperial Bounty. 1988.

Alien Bounty. 1990.

McCade's Bounty. 1990.

Dreyfuss, Richard, and Harry Turtledove. *The Two Georges.* 1996. Annotated on page 114.

Dunn, J. R. *This Side of Judgment.* 1994. In the dark future depicted here, a technique has been developed to successfully implant a computer chip in the human brain, which gives these "chipheads" the ability to interact with technology in the virtual realm. But the human brain cannot handle such an information overload for any length of time and begins shutting down, with disastrous results. Page, a "chiphead," has decided to let his murderous impulses run rampant, and Ross Bohlen, an agent for a Computer Strike Force, may be the only one to stop him. Having killed more than his share of chipheads in the past, Bohlen would like to stop killing and start bringing them in from the cold instead.

Foster, Alan Dean. *Cyber Way.* 1990. A Navajo tribal police officer and a Florida cop team up to solve a high-tech murder in the not-too-distant future.

Goulart, Ron. Jake and Hildy Pace Series. A couple of twenty-first-century private eyes will only take on cases considered unsolvable—and for enormous fees. Long out of print, these are not easy to find but are fondly remembered by some readers.

Dr. Scofflaw. 1979.

Hail Hibbler. 1980.

The Big Bang. 1982.

Upside, Downside. 1982.

Gould, Steven. *Blind Waves.* 2000. Patricia Beeman is a well-established entrepreneur who owns a floating block of apartments and a child-care center in a future shaped by rising oceans. But Patricia doesn't just rest on her wealth. She is also a busy underwater salvage operator. When she stumbles across a horrifying sight, she also is forced to go into hiding to evade the powerful INS.

Green, Terence M. *Blue Limbo.* 1997. Fired from the Toronto Police Department, Mitch Helwig decides to fight back against crime. Separated from his cheating wife, he now only cares about his daughter, his father, and a friend still on the force. He has a penchant for high-tech tools, many of them illegal, but now that he's on his own, he is free to use them. In this near-future setting, scientists have developed a technique to bring the dead back to life for a few weeks. The process leaves the subject in a blue void but able to communicate with the living. When Mitch's best friend and former supervisor is gunned down and killed, Mitch bullies the hospital into giving his friend the "Blue Limbo" treatment. Armed with the name of the corrupt cop who murdered his friend, Mitch sets out on a rampage for justice and an attempt to rescue his kidnapped dad.

Gresh, Lois H., and Robert Weinberg. *The Termination Node.* 1999. Annotated on page 77.

Hamilton, Peter F. Greg Mandel series, features a biologically enhanced psychic detective. Hamilton comments on the series at his official Web site: http://freespace.virgin. net/martin.burcombe/greg_by_peter.html.

Mindstar Rising. 1993. Implanted with a biotechnology gland to make him psychic, detective Greg Mandel investigates industrial espionage in a time when England is just beginning to recover from a ruined economy, bad politics, and a devastated global environment.

A Quantum Murder. 1994. Two years after the events in *Mindstar Rising*, Greg investigates a case in the classic locked room tradition. He is called in after a professor is murdered in an English country mansion and the only people there were students.

The Nano Flower. 1995. Greg is called out of retirement when Julia Evans (a character from the previous two books) receives a flower that has alien genes millions of years ahead of terrestrial DNA.

Heinlein, Robert A. *The Door into Summer.* 1957. Annotated on page 53.

Hogan, James P. *Bug Park.* 1997. Annotated on page 81.

Killough, Lee. *Bridling Chaos.* 1998. An omnibus edition of the following three titles that feature the adventures of Detective Sergeant Janna Brill and "Mama" Maxwell, a flamboyant oddball. More information about it can be found at http://www.meishamerlin.com/BridlingChaos.html.

The Doppelgänger Gambit. 1979. "Mama" Maxwell can prove a supposed suicide was actually murder, but by doing so he risks the computer that ensures law and order for an entire country.

Spider Play. 1986. "A vandalized hearse and corpse lead Janna and Mama on a twisted trail from a gang war on Earth...to a citadel of technology in space . . . to a heart-stopping race from a corporate army all too ready to kill to protect its secrets."—Publisher's Web site.

Dragon's Teeth. 1990. A multitude of suspects, witnesses, and clues seem to prove that a series of gang-perpetrated thefts and murders could not have been committed.

Kress, Nancy. *Oaths and Miracles.* 1996. Annotated on page 131.

Lem, Stanislaw. *Tales of Pirx the Pilot.* 1980. A collection of technological detective stories translated from Polish.

Lethem, Jonathan. *Gun, with Occasional Music.* 1994. Annotated on page 129.

MacLean, Katherine. *Missing Man.* 1975. George Sanford, the telepathic private eye, debuted in a Nebula-winning novella of the same title. His talent allows him to assist the New York Police Department.

    Nebula Award.

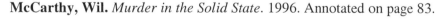

McCarthy, Wil. *Murder in the Solid State.* 1996. Annotated on page 83.

McQuay, Mike. Mathew Swain series. Swain, a Chandleresque private eye, goes up against the corrupt powers that rule the twenty-first century both on Earth and the moon.

Hot Time in Old Town. 1981.

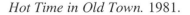

When Trouble Beckons. 1981.

The Deadliest Show in Town. 1982.

The Odds Are Murder. 1983.

Moon, Elizabeth. Heris Serrano Series. Heris keeps coming up against crime as she fulfills her duties as the captain of a luxurious space yacht owned by a wealthy elderly woman.

Hunting Party. 1993. Annotated on page 28.

Sporting Chance. 1994. Annotated on page 28.

Winning Colors. 1995. Annotated on page 29.

Niven, Larry. Hamilton Series. "Gil 'The Arm' Hamilton was one of the top operatives of ARM, the elite UN police force. His intuition was unfailingly accurate, his detective skills second to none, and his psychic powers—esper sense and telekinesis—were awesome."—Book jacket.

The Patchwork Girl. 1980. A woman accused of attempted murder calls on Gil the Arm to prove that she is innocent. Otherwise, she's going to end up in the organ banks.

Flatlander: The Collected Tales of Gil "The Arm" Hamilton. 1995. The ability to transplant organs and other "spare parts" makes theft of body parts a common crime. Gil Hamilton hunts down the organleggers.

Nolan, William F. Sam Space, private eye on Mars. Sam Space series.

Space for Hire. 1971. Sam Space romps through the solar system and parallel worlds to save the life of a beautiful woman and her scientist father.

Look Out for Space. 1985. The further exploits of the Mars-based PI.

3 for Space. 1992. A difficult-to-find collection of three stories featuring Sam Space.

Perriman, Cole. *Terminal Games.* 1994. "The first person to realize what's happening is Marianne Hedison, who stumbles onto a crime scene that looks startlingly familiar: it is identical to the animated murder she had seen the night before on her computer screen. As other subscribers begin to die in increasingly bizarre and violent ways, Marianne begins to see a chilling pattern in the murders—and to have disturbing questions about the mysterious on-screen personality known only as Auggie."—Book jacket. More on page 71.

Robb, J. D. Eve Dallas Series. Eve Dallas is a police lieutenant in twenty-first-century New York.

Naked in Death. 1995. While on the trail of a serial killer, Eve finds herself strangely drawn to Roarke, one of the suspects.

Glory in Death. 1995. Roarke becomes the common link between two murder victims.

Immortal in Death. 1996. Eve Dallas ventures into the world of high fashion when a model is murdered.

Rapture in Death. 1996. Could a virtual reality game be used as a murder weapon?

Ceremony in Death. 1997. Eve questions her own sense of right and wrong.

Vengeance in Death. 1997. A serial killer leaves cryptic riddles for Eve, and once again it looks like Roarke may provide the connection between the victims.

Holiday in Death. 1998. Eve traces the victims of a ritualistic killer to a dating service.

Conspiracy in Death. 1999. Eve pursues a psychotic killer who works with a surgeon's precision.

Loyalty in Death. 1999. Eve goes up against a group of terrorists.

Witness in Death. 2000. A leading man is stabbed to death on center stage in Roarke's new theater and Eve is a witness, as well as the detective in charge.

Judgment in Death. 2000. Eve goes after a cop killer.

"Interlude in Death," a novella in *Out of this World* (2001), sees Eve and Roarke the victims of an attempted murder frame. Why would a contract killer kill a hotel maid?

Betrayal in Death. 2001. Eve is after a vicious killer, and the killer is after Roarke.

Seduction in Death. 2001. Young women are meeting a serial killer in an online poetry chat room.

Reunion in Death. 2002. Eve must stop a female serial killer who has targeted Roarke.

Sawyer, Robert J. *Flashforward.* 1999. Annotated on page 119.

Sawyer, Robert J. *Illegal Alien.* 1997. When a popular scientist, part of the entourage of an alien mission to Earth, is found dead, all evidence points to one of the aliens. The U.S. government, attempting to avoid an interplanetary incident, hires the country's leading civil rights lawyer to defend him, which results in a human and alien courtroom thriller. More on page 148.

Sawyer, Robert J. *The Terminal Experiment.* 1995. Dr. Peter Hobson created three electronic copies of himself to test his theories. One of them turns out to be a killer.

Nebula Winner.

Shatner, William. Tek Series. Jake Cardigan, ex-cop and ex-con, is now a Los Angeles PI in a world devastated by the highly addictive Tek. This series, published under the name of the actor best known as Captain Kirk of the *Enterprise*, was reputedly written by veteran SF-mystery writer Ron Goulart.

TekWar. 1989.

TekLords. 1991.

TekLab. 1992.

Tek Vengeance. 1993.

Tek Secret. 1993.

Tek Power. 1994.

Tek Money. 1995.

Tek Kill. 1996.

Tek Net. 1997.

Shetterly, Will. *Chimera.* 2000. In a future where slavery has returned the chimera, some-times disparagingly called critters, are the slaves, humans derived from animal genes and forced to wear tattoos of their animal antecedents on their foreheads, Max Maxwell, a tough-talking PI, thinks he has a poker hand that can't lose when a beauti-ful woman intrudes on the game asking him to take a case. The ante goes up, she cov-ers his bet, he loses, and is stuck with her for a client—which wouldn't be bad except that he discovers that she is a jaguar chimera disguised as a real human. Her mentor, a famous scientist, has been killed and she is the prime suspect. Before all is said and done Max and Zoe Domingo expose corruption in high places and Max has down and dirty relations with a machine. More on page 132.

Shinn, Sharon. *Wrapt in Crystal.* 1999. The two religious orders on the planet Semay, the ascetic Fideles and the joyous Triumphantes, are being preyed upon by a serial killer who has already murdered a half dozen sisters when Cowen Drake arrives on the planet. A Special Assignment Officer for Interfed, he is extremely well-qualified to investigate the murders. In the course of his investigation, he becomes friends with the heads of both orders. More on page 106.

Stableford, Brian. *Inherit the Earth.* 1998. In a world where long life, if not immortality, has become possible through biomedical nanotechnology, Damon Hart is pitched into a cat-and-mouse game with a terrorist group, Interpol, and a powerful interna-tional corporation.

Vance, Jack. *Galactic Effectuator.* 1980. Sleuth Miro Hetzel, who is an effectuator and likes big fees, high living, and beautiful women, appears in two short stories collected in this volume.

Vinge, Vernor. *Marooned in Realtime.* 1986. Being stranded in real time is tantamount to murder if one must live and die alone. Annotated on page 52.

Vinge, Joan D. *Tangled Up in Blue.* 2000. Annotated on page 165.

Waugh, Charles G., and Martin H. Greenberg, eds. *Sci-Fi Private Eye.* 1997. Nine sci-ence fiction detection stories written by Isaac Asimov, Poul Anderson, Philip José Farmer, Donald E. Westlake, Tom Reamy, Wilson Tucker, Robert Silverberg, Philip K. Dick, and Larry Niven (a Gil Hamilton story).

Werber, Bernard. *Empire of the Ants*. 1998. A family inherits a large basement apartment that comes with a warning: "Above All, Never Go Down into the Cellar!" When the family dog crawls through a crack and disappears, Jonathan ventures down the narrow winding stairs into the dark cellar, and finds its bloody, mangled body. A parallel narrative follows the adventures of members of an ant city who explore, fight invaders, mate, die, and even take part in an expedition to "the end of the world."

Williams, Walter Jon. Drake Maijstral, the world's number one burglar, somehow keeps getting involved in solving crimes.

The Crown Jewels. 1987.

House of Shards. 1988.

Rock of Ages. 1995. Drake is on vacation when a major robbery occurs, and he is the prime suspect. Conversations with a dead dad who can talk back and a bunch of alien Elvis impersonators make this an unforgettable mystery romp.

Williamson, Jack. *The Silicon Dagger*. 1999. When Clay Barstow goes to McAdam, Kentucky, to investigate his half-brother's murder, he discovers a separatist militia armed with technology that may enable them to successfully break away from the United States.

Wolfe, Gene. *Free Live Free*. 1984. Jim Stubb, an out-of-work detective, along with three unlikely companions, seeks the lost treasure of Benjamin Free.

A Funny Thing Happened on the Way to Sirius: Humor and Science Fiction

Humor is in the eye of the beholder! What's funny enough to cause a belly laugh in one reader may only elicit a chuckle—or no reaction at all—in another. That being said, there are some notable examples of humorous writing in the science fiction field that have been enjoyed and appreciated by many, beginning with the inimitable Douglas Adams and his Hitchhiker trilogy—which is no longer a trilogy. Or the adventures of that intrepid scion of a war-faring society, Miles Vorkosigan, who has gotten in and out of so many tight places, just barely avoided disaster again and again, described in lighthearted detail by his creator Lois McMaster Bujold.

Robert Asprin has also made quite a name for himself with humorous fantasy spoofs in his Myth series. Asprin brings a light touch to his science fiction series, which features Phule, wealthy son of a munitions supplier. Phule gets in hot water in the service, is assigned to lead a challenging group of misfits, and succeeds admirably, with the help of his faithful butler, who provides the narrative for his adventures. It's a wonderful spoof of all those action-adventure, high-testosterone, science fiction military adventures. Harry Harrison strikes a similar chord with his *Adventures of Bill the Galactic Hero.*

More zany humor is provided by wacky alien creatures in Frederic Brown's *Martians Go Home* (page 178), Steven Brust's *Cowboy Feng's Space Bar and Grill,* (page 178), and Spider Robinson's *Callahan's Crosstime Saloon* (page 180) and its sequels. The young adult perspective is seen in Paula Danziger's *This Place Has No Atmosphere* (page 197), the adventures of a valley girl forced to go with her family to colonize the moon.

Bimbos of the Death Sun and *Zombies of the Gene Pool* by Sharyn McCrumb will amuse anyone who enjoys science fiction and enjoys a good laugh. Although not strictly SF, these murder mysteries set in science fiction fandom are a delight for fans. What could be more out of this world?

Adams, Douglas. Hitchhiker's trilogy. *The Ultimate Hitchhiker's Guide* is an omnibus edition of the five titles in the "trilogy."

> *The Hitchhiker's Guide to the Galaxy.* 1979. Poor Arthur Dent. One minute he's lying in front of a bulldozer, trying to keep his house from being torn down to make way for an expressway. The next, he's hitchhiking through space with his friend Ford Prefect, a native of Betelgeuse who has been stranded on the Earth for the past fifteen years. Ford is a writer for *The Hitchhiker's Guide to the Galaxy*, and so has the connections to get a ride for himself and his friend when he discovers that the Earth is to be destroyed to make room for an expressway in space. And so begins the zany adventures of Arthur and Ford as they hitchhike through the galaxy, having one madcap adventure after another.

> *The Restaurant at the End of the Universe.* 1980. "Among Arthur's motley shipmates are Ford Prefect, . . . Zaphod Beeblebrox, the three-armed, two-headed ex-president of the galaxy; Tricia McMillan, a fellow Earth refugee who's gone native (her name is Trillian now); and Marvin, the moody android who suffers nothing and no one very gladly. Their destination? The ultimate hot spot for an evening of apocalyptic entertainment and fine dining, where the food (literally) speaks for itself."—Publisher's blurb.

> *Life, the Universe and Everything.* 1982. This third (but not last) in the Hitchhiker's trilogy takes our dauntless hero back in time—to the remote past of the Earth. More hilarious hijinks for Arthur Dent, as he discovers the answer to the "Ultimate Question."

> *So Long, and Thanks for All the Fish.* 1984. Fourth entry in the Hitchhiker trilogy—just one more example of the author's bizarre and appealing sense of humor. Earth was destroyed in book one. Remember those aliens who were putting in an interstellar freeway and were getting rid of all obstructions in their way? And yet Arthur Dent returns home, to an Earth that is still there, despite having been destroyed. His friend and colleague Ford Prefect, however, continues his zany trip through the galaxy.

> *Mostly Harmless.* 1992. The adventures of that intrepid hitchhiking duo continue. Aliens are monitoring the Earth. After a female newspaper reporter interviews an astrologer, she finds herself involved with the hitchhikers. Arthur Dent has a daughter he never knew about. Someone is trying to take over the offices of the *Hitchhiker's*

Guide. And the Vogon decide to destroy planet Earth after all—in this reality. (Talk about the need for a willing suspension of disbelief. But what fun!)

Anthony, Piers. *Prostho Plus.* 1973. Annotated on page 145.

Asprin, Robert. Phule Series.

Phule's Company. 1990. Phule, the son of a mega-millionaire munitions supplier, joins the Legion after a fight with his father. When he strafes a peace conference (an impulsive mistake), he is assigned to a punishment detail, as captain of the Omega Company, an infamous collection of misfits, criminal types, and overt rebels. Accompanied by his ever-present butler Beeker, who is also the narrator of his employer's adventures, Phule comes to the swamp planet where Omega Company is located, takes charge, and transforms this collection of misfits into a force to be reckoned with—able to hold their own even when challenged by the army's elite Red Eagle Unit. First contact with an alien race could have been a disaster, except for Phule's ability to turn almost anything into a financial windfall.

Phule's Paradise. 1992. Phule has been asked to ride herd on a gambling casino, and he does so, coming up with some truly creative solutions to the problems he faces. Once again, his butler, the inimitable Beeker, provides a detailed account of Phule's activities in his journal entries. The villainess is the larger-than-life Maxine Pruet, who controls all of the other casinos and plans to set up an intergalactic casino called the Fat Chance. General Blitzkrieg has given Willard Phule another seemingly impossible assignment, with the fond hope that his bunch of misfits will botch things up completely. And once again Phule and company come through with flying colors.

Asprin, Robert with Peter J. Heck. *A Phule and His Money.* 1999. You've got to hand it to Captain Willard Phule. First, he did the impossible and whipped a bunch of misfits into a company that could hold its own, even against one of the army's elite fighting units. True, a lot of people in military service still considered his company to be a laughingstock, but then he turned them into a crack team — of casino security guards. Now he's been asked to help an underdeveloped planet. What better way than to turn it into one of the biggest galactic playgrounds around?

Phule Me Twice. 2000. This fourth entry in the Phule series takes Captain Phule and his company to the planet Zenobia. The planet has been invaded and the peaceful, dinosaur-like Zenobians want the captain as their military advisor. While the members of his company are busy trying to keep out of the way of their dinosaur employers, Phule has his own problems with a robot double that has suddenly appeared. The Zenobians are faced with two Phules for the price of one. But, as the cover states, "Only the real Phule knows who the real Phule is . . ."

Bethke, Bruce. *Headcrash.* 1995. Annotated on page 82.

Brown, Frederic. *Martians Go Home*. 1955. Our hero, a courageous science fiction author, foils the attack of little green men from Mars. Earth owes a tremendous debt of gratitude to this brave man of letters. On the other hand, if it weren't for him, we wouldn't have been invaded in the first place.

Brust, Steven. *Cowboy Feng's Space Bar and Grille*. 1990. Cowboy Feng's Space Bar and Grille seems to be the focus of nuclear attacks. A strike will occur and the bar will disappear, only to reappear on another planet in another time. This has happened several times already, and everyone present at the time of the strikes has simply gone on with the bar. Now the bar has landed in New Quebec. The narrator, Billy, is a member of the band, a group of folk music specialists. He and the other band members, as well as those who run the bar, are under attack—not nuclear this time, but guns, bombs, etc. The question is, why? And by whom? And where will it all end? At the same time that this is going on, the Hags virus, an AIDS takeoff, is spreading, accompanied by increasing paranoia that soon becomes deadly. The only hope is Feng, a leader from the future.

Bujold, Lois McMaster. *Ethan of Athos*. 1986. Ethan is an obstetrician on a planet with no women. More on page 16.

Bujold, Lois McMaster. *Falling Free*. 1988. Annotated on page 3.

 Nebula Award.

Bujold, Lois McMaster. Vorkosigan Saga. Bujold's wry wit will appeal to those who enjoy comedies of manners and verbal repartee like that of Georgette Heyer and Jane Austen.

Shards of Honor. 1986. Annotated on page 161.

Barrayar. 1991. Annotated on page 14.

The Warrior's Apprentice. 1986. Annotated on page 14.

 The Vor Game. 1990. Annotated on page 14. **Hugo and Nebula Awards.**

Cetaganda. 1995. Annotated on page 15.

Young Miles. 1997. Annotated on page 14.

Borders of Infinity. 1989. Annotated on page 15.

Brothers in Arms. 1989. Annotated on page 15.

 Mirror Dance. 1994. Annotated on page 15. **Hugo and Locus Awards.**

Memory. 1996. Annotated on page 15.

Komarr: A Miles Vorkosigan Adventure. 1998. Annotated on page 16.

 A Civil Campaign. 1999. By hiring her to create an exquisite garden for him, Miles attempts to court the recently widowed Ekaterin Vorsoisson amid the intrigue inherent in the Barrayaran political scene. Meanwhile, as preparations for the royal wedding

advance, will anyone believe that Mark, the clone brother created as an assassin to kill Miles but now a valued member of the family, could fall in
love? He has, with one of the five Koudelka daughters, the one who has stud-
ied on Beta, and now has the knowledge she needs to cope with Mark's multiple personalities. Mark also has a remarkable new product invented by a
mad scientist. He plans to make a fortune selling delicious bug feces, which
he serves at the most hilarious dinner party ever.

Sapphire Award.

Diplomatic Immunity. 2002. Annotated on page 15.

DeChancie, John. *Living with Aliens*. 1995. Annotated on page 192.

Dick, Philip K. *Galactic Pot-Healer*. 1969. Annotated on page 102.

Dick, Philip K. *A Maze of Death*. 1970. Annotated on page 102.

Dick, Philip K. *Now Wait for Last Year*. 1966. A standard space war background becomes something entirely different with the addition of hallucinogenic drugs,
robotic quasi-life, psychological regression, and political chicanery.

Dick, Philip K. *VALIS*. 1981. Annotated on page 102.

Friesner, Esther, and Martin H. Greenberg, eds. *Alien Pregnant by Elvis*. 1994.
A humorous anthology full of stories inspired by tabloid headlines.

Harrison, Harry. *Bill, The Galactic Hero*. 1965. Bill didn't set out to be a galactic
hero, or for that matter, any kind of a hero. But then he was shanghaied into
the intergalactic army. Discipline is ludicrous, to say the very least, and much
of his camaraderie with his fellow soldiers more or less brainless, but he does
become a hero, in spite of everything. This novel is still considered one of the
most effective works of this author. Years after it was published, sequels appeared, co-authored with other SF writers.

Bill, The Galactic Hero on the Planet of Robot Slaves. 1989.

Harrison, Harry, and Robert Sheckley. *Bill, the Galactic Hero on the Planet
of Bottled Brains*. 1990.

Harrison, Harry, and David Bischoff. *Bill, the Galactic Hero on the Planet of
Ten Thousand Bars*. 1991.

Harrison, Harry, and Jack C. Haldeman. *Bill, the Galactic Hero on the Planet
of Zombie Vampires*. 1991.

Harrison, Harry, and David Bischoff. *Bill, the Galactic Hero on the Planet of
Tasteless Pleasure*. 1991.

Harrison, Harry, and David Harris. *Bill, the Galactic Hero: The Final Incoherent Adventure*. 1992.

Like, Russel. *After the Blue*. 1998. Annotated on page 89.

Murphy, Pat. *There and Back Again*. 1999. Annotated on page 20.

Niven, Larry. *Rainbow Mars*. 1999. Hanville Svetz goes back in time on the planet Mars in this humorous and wildly inventive novel. All the most dire predictions for Earth's polluted future have come true. Svetz, who works for the Institute for Temporal Research, is sent back in time by Waldemar the Tenth to recover extinct species for a sadly depleted Earth. But Waldemar the Eleventh is interested in space travel instead and sends him to find out why the Martian canals dried up. So back in time he goes, to the year 1500, at a time of working canals, hostile Martians, and a beanstalk that extends so far out into space it is used as a space elevator. As it turns out, Svetz should have worked harder at discovering just what effect this plant was having on the red planet before working to bring it to Earth.

Pratchett, Terry. Bromeliad Series. Four-inch-tall aliens have made a home on Earth after being stranded here. Annotated on page 151.

> *Truckers*. 1989.
>
> *Diggers*. 1990.
>
> *Wings*. 1990.

Robinson, Spider. Callahan Series. Delightfully zany characters such as Nikola Tesla, Lucky Duck, Fast Eddie, and Ralph Von Wau Wau The Talking Dog drop in and share stories rife with puns.

> *Callahan's Crosstime Saloon*. 1977. The humorous, pun-filled stories in this collection are narrated by customers, both human and alien, who frequent Callahan's famous saloon. The fan following of this book has led to several chat rooms on the Internet being named after it.
>
> ### *Campbell and Skylark Awards.*
>
> *Callahan's Secret*. 1986. The last book set in Callahan's Crosstime Saloon, leading up to an explosive finale.
>
> *Callahan's Lady*. 1989. Lady Sally McGee runs a brothel lovingly called "a house of ill repute with a good reputation" that is regularly visited by BEMs, dimensional travelers, time travelers, and the occasional oddball.
>
> *The Callahan Touch*. 1993. After a minor nuclear explosion takes out Callahan's, Jake Stonebender opens Mary's Place, where all the regulars and some new characters can exchange tall tales.
>
> *Callahan's Legacy*. 1996. Three years after the bar is destroyed, Jake Stonebender tries to re-create the magic of Callahan's by opening another bar.
>
> *The Callahan Chronicles*. 1997. An omnibus edition of the first three titles in the series.
>
> *Callahan's Key*. 2000. The crew from Callahan's ends up in Florida after Mary's Place is closed.
>
> *Time Travelers Strictly Cash*. 2001. An amalgam of collected stories continuing from where *Callahan's Crosstime Saloon* left off.

Stephenson, Neal. *Snow Crash*. 1992. Annotated on page 78.

Vonnegut, Kurt, Jr. *Sirens of Titan*. 1959. Niles Rumford, who was dispersed throughout the galaxy when he went into a chrono-synclastic-infundibula, can rematerialize from time to time. He is scheduled to make an appearance on the moon Titan, where an alien with interesting feet carries a message of huge import across the universe and waits for a necessary spacecraft part.

Willis, Connie. *Bellwether*. 1996. Sociologist Sandra Foster becomes involved with biologist Bennett O'Reilly, a co-worker at HiTek company, when Flip, the office assistant "from hell" mis-delivers a package. Is there any way that Sandra's research into the factors that start fads and trends ties into Bennett's chaos theory investigations? An how do double latte and black lipstick relate to sheepish behavior? Willis is a master at seeing the ridiculous behavior and silliness of contemporary life all around us.

Willis, Connie. *To Say Nothing of the Dog*. 1997. Willis's delightfully wry humor takes us to a future where Lady Shrapnel, a filthy rich American, is funding time travel so that she can rebuild Coventry Cathedral as it was when her great-grandmother experienced an epiphany there. When a time-lagged historian from the future is sent to the Victorian era to escape Lady Shrapnel, he finds love and a problem that could rend the fabric of time. This hilarious romp is not to be missed. More on page 53.

    Hugo and Locus Awards.

Willis, Connie. *Uncharted Territory*. 1994. A clever and witty spoof of what could happen if environmental concerns and government regulations were taken to their not-so-logical extreme. Findriddy and Carson are two explorers engaged in survey activities on the planet Boohte. Their personal bane is the native guide Bult, who spends more time entering fines in his log than helping them explore his planet.

Inspirational or Christian Science Fiction

Although religion has been a popular theme in science fiction since the New Wave, until recently there have not been many titles that appeal to readers looking for stories with a Christian message. Most of the books that combine Christian doctrine with science fiction tend to be apocalyptic, the best known, of course, being the best-selling Left Behind series by LaHaye and Jenkins. Readers who enjoy looking at different concepts of religion and stretching the limits will find titles of interest in the religion section (under "Social Structures") in Chapter 3.

For a more thorough listing of Christian SF, readers should refer to John Mort's *Christian Fiction* (Libraries Unlimited, 2002), which contains a chapter on that subgenre.

LaHaye, Tim, and Jerry B. Jenkins. Left Behind Series. When Rapture happens, the people left on Earth must work out what to do next as evil tries to manipulate events. This best-selling series has been a frequent readers' advisory request, with questions focusing on finding the book that features people disappearing from an airplane over the Atlantic, leaving behind all their clothing and possessions.

Left Behind: A Novel of the Earth's Last Days. 1996. First in the incredibly popular Christian series that describes what happens to those left behind after the Rapture.

Tribulation Force: The Continuing Drama of Those Left Behind. 1997. The Tribulation Force, an underground of penitents who were left behind at the Rapture, now battles the Antichrist.

Nicolae: The Rise of Antichrist. 1997. Pilot Rayford Steele and journalist Buck Williams continue their struggle against the Antichrist, whom they have identified as Nicolae Carpathia, a charming, benevolent leader who turns out to be a cruel and ruthless tyrant in this third entry of the Left Behind series.

Soul Harvest: The World Takes Sides. 1998. After a global earthquake (the wrath of the Lamb), the biblical prophecy of the soul harvest comes true in the form of one of the greatest evangelistic efforts of all time.

Apollyon: The Destroyer Is Unleashed. 1999. In this fifth installment, Apollyon and his plague of locusts are released on the world, attacking all those who do not have the mark of God on their foreheads. Meanwhile the believers gather in Jerusalem for a showdown with the Antichrist.

Assassins: The Great Tribulation Unfolds. 1999. There is a plan to kill the Antichrist, and Rayford Steele is involved. But is that the Christian thing to do?

The Indwelling: The Beast Takes Possession. 2000. Book seven begins with a funeral for the Antichrist. But will he remain dead? According to the prophecies, the tribulation for the people left behind is only just beginning—because Satan will raise the Antichrist from the dead.

The Mark: The Beast Rules the World. 2000. The dawn of the Great Tribulation begins with the return of the Antichrist in book eight. Nicolae Carpathia has risen from the dead and demands that all his followers be subjected to the mark of the beast—branded on the forehead or right hands and vaccinated with a biochip. The choice is simple—the mark or the guillotine.

Lewis, C. S. Perelandra Trilogy. Annotated on page 104. After being abducted by aliens, Dr. Elwin Ransome, a linguist, examines the conflict between science and ethics.

Out of the Silent Planet. 1943.

Perelandra. 1943.

That Hideous Strength. 1945.

Tyers, Kathy. Although science fiction has not been a major venue for Christian publishers, Tyers, who has written several *Star Wars* books, blends faith and romance in a well-developed space opera universe where a privileged young woman falls in love, embraces her husband's faith, and joins those whom her people have sought to annihilate.

Firebird. 1987. Lady Firebird is expendable in her world, so the honorable thing would have been to commit suicide rather than to be captured by the enemy. But her personal spiritual battle leads her into the arms of her captor.

Fusion Fire. 2000. Now pair bonded to her former foe (Sentinel Brennen Caldwell), Firebird, pregnant with twins, becomes a target of her own family.

Crown of Fire. 2000. Unexpectedly called home to be confirmed as heiress, Lady Firebird embarks on an effort to trap an assassin—but her biggest threat may come from a different quarter.

Science Fantasy

The combination of science fiction and fantasy has sometimes been called science fantasy. Readers who like both genres will often enjoy the combination of the two or novels that are SF but have a fantasy "feel" to them. Readers who like the following books will find others in *Fluent in Fantasy* by Diana Tixier Herald (Libraries Unlimited, 1999).

Anthony, Piers. Apprentice Adept Series. Annotated on page 110.

Bradley, Marion Zimmer. Darkover Series. Annotated on page 25.

Burroughs, Edgar Rice. Mars Series. Annotated on page 3.

Cook, Rick. Wiz Zumwalt Series. A computer nerd is shanghaied to a world where magic works.

de Camp, L. Sprague, and Fletcher Pratt. *The Compleat Enchanter: The Magical Misadventures of Harold Shea.* 1975. A couple of psychologists figure out how to travel to parallel worlds.

DeChancie, John. Castle Perilous Series. Come to Castle Perilous through one of its many gateways connected to different realities. Once you arrive, you might just want to stay.

Egan, Doris. *The Gate of Ivory.* 1989. Annotated on page 5.

Two-Bit Heroes. 1992. Annotated on page 5.

Guilt-Edged Ivory. 1992. Annotated on page 162.

Fowler, Karen Joy. *Sarah Canary.* 1991. Annotated on page 146.

Friedman, C. S. Cold Fire Trilogy.

Black Sun Rising. 1991.

When True Night Falls. 1993.

Crown of Shadows. 1995. This is an account of the battle that takes place on the planet Erna, a battle humans wage to keep demonic beings from taking control of all living things. Victory is made possible only by a most unusual partnership; that of a warrior–priest and a zombie sorcerer, who come to understand and appreciate one another in the course of their struggles.

Friesner, Esther. *The Sherwood Game.* 1995. Annotated on page 6.

Gemmell, David. Drenai Tales. These are the adventures of the legendary warriors of the Drenai, including Druss, Captain of the Axe, and feared assassin Waylander the Slayer.

Legend. 1994. The legendary Druss, Captain of the Axe, had retired. But when the barbarian Nadir attacked the Drenai, who could his people call upon to save them but Druss?

The King beyond the Gate. 1995. A mad emperor has seized control of the mighty fortress that Druss the Legend once defended. Now he is sending half-man, half-beast Joinings out to control the land. Oddly enough, it's a half-breed who fights back. Tenaka Khan, hated for his half Nadir, half Drenai parentage, is the one with a plan for bringing down the emperor. With the help of a handful of Drenai heroes, he just might make it happen.

Quest for Lost Heroes. 1995. A peasant boy goes on a quest to rescue a young girl taken by slavers. But he does not go alone as heroes out of legend join him on his quest.

Waylander. 1995. Waylander the Slayer accepted the contract from Kaem the Cruel, but after he made his kill, he was betrayed and had to flee for his life. Now, as Kaem's armies lay waste to the land of the Drenai, Waylander accepts another commission: to bring back the legendary Armor of Bronze from a shadow-haunted land and stop the invasion.

In the Realm of the Wolf. 1998. Waylander the Slayer is a mighty warrior and a feared assassin. But now he is a man on the run, with a fortune in gold offered by his own people for his murder.

The First Chronicles of Druss the Legend. 1999. Druss the Deathwalker had settled down with his beautiful Rowena. But when slavers attacked the village and stole his beloved, Druss set out to rescue her, accompanied only by his powerful, double-bladed ax, Snaga.

The Legend of Deathwalker. 1999. Druss the Deathwalker is called upon to join the warrior Talisman in his search for the stolen Eyes of Alchazzar; twin jewels with the power to save the life of Druss' dying friend and unite the Nadir.

Winter Warriors. 2000. Three Drenai soldiers, Nogusta, Bison, and Kebra, are too old to serve their king, but not too old to protect the young prince, the infant heir to the throne.

Hero in the Shadows. 2000. The hero in the shadows, the mysterious Gray Man, is the assassin, Waylander. Thousands of years ago Kuan Hador was the capital city of an empire ruled by evil sorcerers. They escaped certain defeat by sealing themselves behind a magical doorway. Now the magic is fading, and the sorcerers will soon be free. And when they are, rather than a powerful army, they will face a rag-tag group of adventurers, led by Waylander the Slayer.

Jones, Diana Wynne. *Deep Secret.* 1999. These are the files of young Magid (Magician) Rupert Venables, describing the problems he faces during two important quests. His mentor and friend, the elderly Magid Stan, dies, leaving Rupert with the files of five potential replacements. Because Rupert is so new, Stan gets permission from the Upper Room to return as a disembodied ghost. During this one-year "reprieve," Stan stays in Rupert's house and later his car, close enough to advise him on his quest for a replacement. At the same time, the truly despicable Emperor of the Koyrfonic Empire, who had just executed his only known heir, is assassinated. As the Magid assigned to Earth and the Koyrfonic Empire, Rupert has to help find the new heir before the Empire falls to pieces. There are heirs out there — somewhere. The question is where — and how to protect them from the assassin who killed their father until he can get one of them safely installed as the new Emperor.

Kennealy-Morrison, Patricia. The Keltiad Series.

Silver Branch: A Novel of the Keltiad. 1988. Keltia is a planetary system where magic and spaceships exist side by side. This is a prequel to the following two titles, presenting the early life of Aeron.

The Copper Crown: A Novel of the Keltiad. 1985. This is the first of the books about Aeron, the Queen of Keltia.

The Throne of Scone: A Book of the Keltiad. 1986. The conclusion to the Aeron series. Aeron's journey ties this trilogy and the tales of the Arthur trilogy together.

Hawk's Gray Feather: A Book of the Keltiad. (The Tales of Arthur, Vol. 1) 1990. A most unusual treatment of the King Arthur legend as science fiction, told in journal format. All the major characters are introduced: Merlyn, Arthur, Ygrawn, Uther, Gweniver, and the Bard Taliesin. However, they arc not on Earth, but on a planet far away.

The Oak above the Kings: A Book of the Keltiad. (The Tales of Arthur, Vol. 2). 1994. Taliesin narrates in bardic style the adventures of Arthur, describing how he arrives with an army on Tarra, the home of the traitorous King of the Kelts, and then travels to far off worlds after his victory.

The Hedge of Mist: A Book of the Keltiad. (Tales of Arthur, Vol. 3). 1996. This third volume completes the story of Arthur, set against the backdrop of the Keltian empire. It covers the search for the Graal and concludes with Arthur finding his way to the land where he still resides today.

Blackmantle: A Triumph: A Book of the Keltiad. 1997. Keltia, the space empire founded in the fifth century, is now dominated by the Incomers or Firvolgi. In spite of this, Athyn Cahanagh, the Blackmantle, will become the High Queen. She will also fall in love with the Bard Morric Douglas, only to lose him to Firvolgi poison. Could she possibly be powerful enough to bring him back to life?

The Deer's Cry. 1998. This eighth entry in the Keltiad series tells the story of Brendan mac Fergus, the shepherd. Brendan realized that with Padraic bringing Christianity to Ireland, the Old Ways were doomed. So, in 453 he leads a small band of followers who build starships and then head for a new home in space.

Lee, Tanith. Birthgrave Trilogy.

The Birthgrave. 1975. A woman awakens in a temple in a volcano and has no idea who she is or how she got there. Her search for her identity takes her from healer to warrior to enslaved goddess to reluctant birthgiver.

Vazkor, Son of Vazkor. 1978. Tuvek, raised by adoptive parents, discovers that he is actually the son of warlord/king Vazkor and his bride, the witch/goddess Uastis. The people in the city where his father once reigned mistake the son for his father's reincarnation and imprison him. When he escapes, he discovers the nature of his powers and vows to revenge himself on his mother for killing his father and abandoning him.

Quest for the White Witch. 1978. In this third volume, Tuvek's powers develop as he travels through mystical kingdoms. As the story progresses, vengeance gives way to his journey of discovery.

McCaffrey, Anne. Pern Series. Annotated on page 137.

Norton, Andre. Witch World Series.

Simon Tregarth goes through a portal and finds that he has left all that is familiar behind. Now he is in Estcarp on Witch World, where he helps the native population fight against the invading Kolder. Because these natives possess powerful psi-powers, they are known as witches. This prolific author used the Witch World setting for a number of novels, but the basic Witch World series that started it all is as follows:

Witch World. 1963.

Web of the Witch World. 1964.

Year of the Unicorn. 1965.

Three Against the Witch World. 1965.

Warlock of the Witch World. 1967.

Sorceress of the Witch World. 1968.

Pratchett, Terry. Bromeliad Trilogy. Annotated on page 151.

Tepper, Sheri S. *Beauty.* 1991. Annotated on page 49.

Yolen, Jane. The Pit Dragon Trilogy.

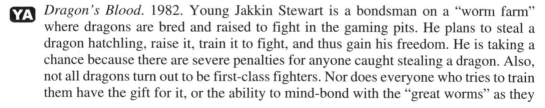 *Dragon's Blood.* 1982. Young Jakkin Stewart is a bondsman on a "worm farm" where dragons are bred and raised to fight in the gaming pits. He plans to steal a dragon hatchling, raise it, train it to fight, and thus gain his freedom. He is taking a chance because there are severe penalties for anyone caught stealing a dragon. Also, not all dragons turn out to be first-class fighters. Nor does everyone who tries to train them have the gift for it, or the ability to mind-bond with the "great worms" as they

are called. Jakkin does obtain a hatchling and he does bond with the baby dragon — to a much higher degree than formerly seen between a dragon and its trainer. In fact, Jakkin and his magnificent dragon, Heart's Blood, are able to communicate in glorious color.

Heart's Blood. 1984. Jakkin is now a Pit Master and Heart's Blood is a successful contestant in the pits of Auster IV. She is also the mother of five hatchlings; baby dragons that Jakkin hopes to be able to imprint in the same manner that he did with Heart's Blood and at the same high level of communication. He has to change his plans, however, when he gets drawn into the political struggle involving a group of rebels. His beloved Akki, who helped him gain his freedom in volume one, disappears into a rebel group, and an off-world politician urges him to follow her, to infiltrate the group and find out what's going on. When an act of violence destroys the pit, all that stands between Jakkin and Akki and an angry mob is Heart's Blood. Even she can do only so much. In the end, they are outcasts, fleeing for their lives with Heart's Blood's hatchlings, wondering what will happen to them and to their world.

A Sending of Dragons. 1987. Now Jakkin and Akki are living in the wild with Heart's Blood's young dragons. Because the two humans hid inside Heart's Blood's body during their escape, their own bodies have undergone a significant change. Now they can communicate with each other mentally in the same way that they can communicate with the dragons, and they can also endure the bitter cold far more easily than before. A helicopter causes them to flee into the caverns of Austar for protection. There they find a society of gray people and gray dragons that depends far too much on the use of dragon's blood. The two young people manage to escape, and in the end, are finally able to return home.

5

Stasheff, Christopher. Rod Gallowglass/Warlock Series. These are the adventures of Rod Gallowglass and his clumsy sidekick, a robot, on the planet Gramarye. This is medieval planet in which magic really works. The following titles in this series are listed according to internal chronology:

The Warlock in Spite of Himself. 1969. Rod Gallowglass is a hardheaded man of science who doesn't believe in magic. So, naturally he lands on a world where elves, witches, goblins and all the other legendary creatures from Earth's Middle Ages actually exist. But not for long — unless Rod can save them.

King Kobold. 1969. Revised and reissued as *King Kobold Revived.* 1986. An insidious mental fog is draining Rod of his powers.

The Warlock Unlocked. 1982. Rod has just started learning the extent of his awesome powers. But are they strong enough to save the world from destruction?

The Warlock Enraged. 1985. This time Rod has to protect his planet from a band of renegade sorcerers.

The Warlock Wandering. 1986. Wandering indeed — into an alternative universe where Rod and his wife are challenged by purple-skinned, fur-kilted natives.

The Warlock Is Missing. 1986. When their parents disappear, Rod's four children combine their mother's power and their father's training to rescue them.

The Warlock Heretical. 1987. The clergy have been tempted by visions of power. Rod must stop their attack on the throne or be burned at the stake.

The Warlock's Companion. 1988. Rod's companion is his faithful cybernetic steed. Fess tells the story of his life to Rod's children, describing the adventures he had with his former masters.

The Warlock Insane. 1989. The work of an evil sorcerer results in an attack on Rod's mind.

The Warlock Rock. 1990. Strange, floating musical crystals have the townspeople of Gramarye under their spell. Will the children be next?

Warlock and Son. 1991. It's time for Magnus, Rod's son, to go off on his own. But Rod follows, for just in case.

M'Lady Witch. 1994. Romance is in the air, but does Rod's daughter Cordelia really want to marry Prince Alain?

Stasheff, Christopher. The Rogue Wizard Series. These are the adventures of the son of Rod Gallowglass, Magnus (aka Gar Pike), and his quest to free lost colony worlds from oppressive local governments.

A Wizard in Bedlam. 1979. Giant Gar, the mysterious stranger no one knows, discovers that Bedlam, an insane asylum, is not the right place to hide if you have telepathic abilities.

A Wizard in Absentia. 1993. His parents are the most powerful sorcerers on the planet. So Magnus Gallowglass leaves the planet and sets off on his own to save the galaxy.

A Wizard in Mind. 1995. On the lost colony world of Petrarch, Magnus and his sentient starship face a warrior prince and a rival from Magnus' past.

A Wizard in War. 1995. Greedy nobles and an arrogant young king are no match for Gar, the mercenary soldier in disguise, who is teaching the serfs how to think for themselves.

A Wizard in Peace. 1997. Gar discovers a planet at peace. But that's because a stern Protector regulates everything and everybody, telling people where they can live, what they can think, even who they can marry. And his liberal use of the torturer's rack kept everyone in line, until Gar arrived.

Wizard in Chaos. 1998. A planet founded by anarchists has regressed to a backward state of perpetual war — until Gar arrives.

A Wizard and a Warlord. 2000. Gar and his companion land on a world of simple peasants, a world with no formal government and no problems, except those that are handled by the mysterious Scarlet Companions.

Wizard in the Way. 2001. This time Gar faces a tyrannical wizard and downtrodden serfs.

A Wizard in a Feud. 2002. Gar Pike, the Rogue Wizard, and his traveling companion bring peace to a planet of feuding clans.

Wolfe, Gene. *Book of the New Sun* Tetralogy. While Wolfe's other *Sun* series are SF, this series is a hybrid of science fiction and fantasy, of interest to fans of both genres.

Wolfe, Gene. *Free Live Free.*

Zelazny, Roger. *The Chronicles of Amber.* There are actually two linked series about Amber: one featuring Corwin, and one featuring his son, Merlin. Amber is a central reality that contains a number of "Shadow" realities, one of which is the Earth. When the series begins, Corwin is on the Earth, suffering from amnesia. Only gradually does he discover that he is one of the sons of Oberon; that he can travel back to his home world, where danger lies in waiting; and that eventually he can bring peace. The novels about Corwin are as follows:

Nine Princes in Amber. 1970. Corwin wakes up in a hospital on Earth with no memory of his past. As enemies try to kill him, he begins to piece together the puzzle of his existence and discovers that he is more than mortal and heir to the throne — if he survives.

The Guns of Avalon. 1972. Prince Corwin's struggles against those trying to keep him from his place on the throne continue.

Sign of the Unicorn. 1975. The royal family's secret ability to travel to other worlds through Shadow is out — courtesy of a traitor.

The Hand of Oberon. 1976. It is going to take all the superhuman powers that Corwin and the remaining princes of Amber have to defeat their traitorous brother.

The Courts of Chaos. 1978. Corwin must travel to the Courts of Chaos to save his world from destructive forces that could change the universe.

The novels about Corwin's son, Merlin, are as follows:

Trumps of Doom. 1985. Merle Corey, a California computer hacker, discovers that he is Merlin, son of Prince Corwin of Amber. Could this be why an unknown assailant attacks him every April 30th?

Blood of Amber. 1986. Captured by enemies, Merle has to trust a beautiful shapeshifter to restore balance.

Sign of Chaos. 1987. This time Merle is trapped beyond the Looking Glass, where he meets characters like Mad Hatter and Cheshire Cat as well as an enemy — a dead girlfriend.

Knight of Shadows. 1989. Merle continues his search for his missing father and must choose between the Patterns of Amber or of Chaos.

Prince of Chaos. 1991. In the tenth and final book, Merle faces murderous discord between Amber and Chaos and can at last free his captive royal father from a villain's spell.

It's Horrific: Science Fiction and Horror

Horror is the stuff of nightmares: monsters, ghosts, vampires, and other paranormal beings. Usually, horror is closer to fantasy than to science fiction, but occasionally the horror is created by science or brought to light by contact with alien beings. Depending on one's definition of horror, most of the tales in the "Future Is Bleak" section of Chapter 3, as well as several other titles throughout this book, could be considered horror. Science fiction and horror are more often blended in film than in novels, for example, in movies such as *Invasion of the Body Snatchers, Alien*, and *The Fly*.

Castle, Jayne. *After Dark.* 2000. Annotated on page 166.

Friedman, C. S. Coldfire Trilogy. Annotated on page 183.

Friedman, C. S. *Madness Season.* Reissue edition Nov. 1991. The reptilian Tyr has subjugated humanity for hundreds of years, but now Daetrin, a vampire, fights back.

Gerrold, David. *Under the Eye of God.* 1993. Humankind has been subjugated by genetically engineered killing machines.

   A Covenant of Justice. 1994.

Heinlein, Robert A. *Puppet Masters.* 1951.

Lichtenberg, Jacqueline. *Those of My Blood.* 1988. Annotated on page 147.

   Dreamspy. 1989. Annotated on page 147.

Nix, Garth. *Shade's Children.* 1997.

Preston, Douglas, and Lincoln Child. *Mount Dragon.* 1996.

Preston, Douglas, and Lincoln Child. *Relic.* 1995.

   Reliquary. 1997.

Preston, Richard. *The Cobra Event.* 1998.

Shelley, Mary Wollstonecraft. *Frankenstein.* 1818.

Wyndham, John. *The Day of the Triffids.* 1951. Annotated on page 95.

Chapter 6

The Golden Age of Science Fiction Is—Twelve

Young Adult Science Fiction

According to well-known critic and author David Hartwell, science fiction's golden age is twelve. He says this because it is around the age of twelve that many readers discover and "get hooked" on SF. Teens reading science fiction are frequently reading adult books—and quite comfortable in doing so. But there is also a wealth of books written, in the past and today, that are targeted specifically for teens and children. Young readers may be drawn to well-loved classics, familiar and not-so-familiar authors, brand new titles, and sometimes quite challenging works in the world of SF. The best and the brightest, it has frequently been said, are reading science fiction and its companion genre, fantasy. The best and the brightest indeed—so many worlds—so much reading entertainment! The books in this section are of particular interest to readers aged 12–18.

Robert A. Heinlein's thirteen "juveniles," published mostly in the 1950s, remain some of the most remembered and beloved SF tales. Many adult SF readers attribute their love of the genre to the entertaining escapism they found in his books as young readers. Those titles are now published as adult books. Tor Books, with its Jupiter series, is attempting to bring SF adventure novels to the forefront for teen readers with original works of science fiction written by prominent authors. The goal is to bring back the virtues of the classics for today's teen readers: colorful characters, fast-paced adventure, thought-provoking ideas, and scientific accuracy.

Youthful Protagonists

Science fiction has a long tradition of adolescent characters. Perhaps more than in any other genre, teenagers are acceptable protagonists for SF novels. Perhaps science fiction writers don't consciously aim for a young adult audience, but the typical SF adventure of journeying to new frontiers takes idealism and bravado. It's a young person's game, and this is reflected in the youthful characters of SF.

Asimov, Isaac, and Robert Silverberg. *The Ugly Little Boy.* 1992. A Neanderthal boy is catapulted into the twenty-first century. Annotated on page 52.

Barnes, John *Orbital Resonance.* 1991. At thirteen, Melpomene Murphy is one of the first generation to be born and raised in a space colony. Annotated on page 34.

Bear, Greg. *Anvil of Stars.* 1992. Annotated on page 44. The children of Earth are seeking revenge.

Bradley, Marion Zimmer. *Hawkmistress!* 1982. During the Ages of Chaos on Darkover, Romilly, who has the ability to communicate with and control animals, struggles and fails to gain her father's approval. After running away, she is caught in the ongoing Civil War and winds up tending Sentry Birds for the king. The Free Amazons offer her a place of refuge, but she finds them as restrictive and narrow in their ways as the ruling class males. Besides, her laran is beginning to stir, and untrained, she is a danger to herself and to others.

Card, Orson Scott. *Ender's Game.* 1985. A six-year-old boy may hold the only hope for the survival of Earth. Annotated on page 22.

  Hugo, Nebula, and Locus Awards.

Ender's Shadow. 1999. Annotated on page 22.

Shadow of the Hegemon. 2000. Annotated on page 23.

Card, Orson Scott. Homecoming Series. Although the protagonist of this series is young, the situations and social mores of his planet are for mature teen readers. Annotated on page 122.

The Memory of Earth. 1992.

The Call of Earth. 1992.

The Ships of Earth. 1994.

Earthfall. 1995.

Earthborn. 1995.

DeChancie, John. *Living with Aliens.* 1995. "Zorg and Flez are aliens and they're the best friends a thirteen-year-old can have. They have made Drew smarter, they helped him get a girlfriend, and on his first date, they took him to Minneapolis, Egypt, and Mars. It was all really cool, until Blog showed up."—Arapahoe Library catalog copy.

Feintuch, David. *Midshipman's Hope*. 1994. Features a youthful hero, Nicholas Seafort. Annotated on page 24.

> *Challenger's Hope*. 1995. Nicholas Seafort is still young here, only twenty when the novel opens. He's in charge of the same youthful crew he worked with on the ill-fated *Hibernia*, plus some sixty passengers and forty-two teen transpops (members of Earth's homeless transient population). Society has developed a new program for its homeless, sending some of the younger ones out to a new life among the stars. More on page 24.

Gould, Steven. *The Helm*. 1998. Annotated on page 122.

Gould, Steven. *Jumper*. 1992. Davy, abused by his father and nearly raped by a burly trucker after he runs away from home, discovers a talent for teleportation. More on page 135.

Gould, Steven. *Wildside*. 1996. Annotated on page 112. An 18-year-old inherits an entire world.

Lethem, Jonathan. *Girl in Landscape*. 1998. Annotated on page 136.

McCaffrey, Anne. *Decision at Doona*. 1969. Annotated on page 8.

McCaffrey, Anne. Talents Series. Physical disabilities don't keep these psionically gifted teens from excelling. Annotated on page 139.

> *To Ride Pegasus*. 1973.
>
> *Pegasus in Flight*. 1990.
>
> *Pegasus in Space*. 2000.

Panshin, Alexei. *Rite of Passage*. 1968. Annotated on page 46.

Thornley, Diann. Unified Worlds Saga

> *Ganwold's Child*. 1995. Tristan has grown up in an alien culture, so he finds life as a hostage in a human dictatorship extremely strange.

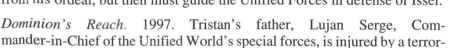

> *Echoes of Issel*. 1996. Reunited with his parents, Tristan begins to recover from his ordeal, but then must guide the Unified Forces in defense of Issel.
>
> *Dominion's Reach*. 1997. Tristan's father, Lujan Serge, Commander-in-Chief of the Unified World's special forces, is injured by a terrorist bomb.

Vinge, Joan D. *Psion*. 1982. Cat, a sixteen-year-old half-human and half-Hydran delinquent, has been on his own since he was four. A latent telepath, he has no knowledge of how he wound up in Oldcity. Circumstances have forced him to fight for his existence all his life. Then he is conscripted for labor and his psi abilities are discovered. This lands him in a special psi training program, where he receives the preliminary training he will need to battle an evil psi genius trying to take over civilization. Cat becomes both victim and hero as he is swept along at breakneck speed toward the final confrontation with the villain in an action-filled, many-layered tale of discrimination, coming of age, and coming to terms with what life has dealt.

Written for Young Adults

The science fiction titles written for young adults tend to focus on psionic powers or survival in post-apocalyptic settings. Publishers who market books for young adults know that SF is a favorite genre of teen readers. Most of the titles in this section are more popular with the 12–15 age range. Although some trilogies and series are published for this segment of the population, most of the titles are single works, exploring a different situation with different characters in each book.

Ames, Mildred. *Anna to the Infinite Power.* 1981. Anna, age twelve, is a genius at mathematics, but also a budding kleptomaniac and a potential sociopath, with no feelings for anyone but herself. When her older brother Rowan takes her to a museum exhibit, they meet her double, after which their mother admits that Anna is part of a classified government program. Anna Zimmerman, a brilliant physicist, died while working on a replicator and was cloned several times. When a new music teacher brings up memories of Auschwitz in Anna, she loses her hard edge. But after the government takes her and the other clones away for "testing," she learns that they are all scheduled for termination as part of a failed experiment.

Anderson, Kevin J., and Rebecca Moesta. Young Jedi Knights Series. The following is merely a sampling of action-packed adventure titles in an engaging series that appeals to younger teen readers.

Jedi Bounty. 1997.

Return to Ord Mantell. 1998.

Trouble on Cloud City. 1998.

Crisis at Crystal Reef. 1998.

The Emperor's Plague. 1998.

Baird, Thomas. *Smart Rats.* 1990. In the ecologically impoverished future, Laddie Grayson, age seventeen, keeps trying unsuccessfully to find a job. With his test scores he ought to be in Council School, but his parents won't allow it. In addition, Laddie is the only surviving member of the Smart Rats, a secret club he had formed with three of his friends. The others are dead. One was deported (i.e., killed) after being accused of theft; one was sent off with the new progeny program (drowned at sea) by the government to keep families down to one child; and one tried to escape and was mutilated and displayed as a warning. Now Laddie has been selected to join the new progeny program, but he's decided he's not going.

Butts, Nancy. *The Door in the Lake.* 1998. A barefoot boy enters a convenience store and collapses after seeing a picture on the back of a milk carton of himself as a missing boy. After two years Joseph Patrick Finney, wearing the same clothes he disappeared in and exactly the same age he was when he disappeared, has returned home. But he can't provide an answer to where he's been or what has happened to him. Then the seizures begin.

Chetwin, Grace. *Collidescope.* 1990. Shot down by an enemy over Manhattan, an android (whose job is to locate and record oxygen-type planets in the Intergalactic Register so they can be protected) manages to travel backwards in time to prevent wholesale destruction. He rescues Sky-Fire-Trail, a Native American teen, and they travel forward in time to present-day Manhattan, where they meet a teenage girl who joins their effort to save the Earth from an alien takeover.

Christopher, John. Tripods Series. This popular series about teens fighting alien invaders was also a British television show.

The White Mountains. 1967. Will Parker manages to escape the capping ceremony that is forced on humans by the alien Tripods when they turn fourteen. Having been told that there is a human resistance force in the White Mountains, Will decides to go there, the only way he can to remain free and continue to fight against the aliens who have taken over the Earth.

The City of Gold and Lead. 1967. Book two of the original Tripods Trilogy continues the story of Will and his friends as he joins a cadre of boys in training for the annual Games, the winners of which will be carried off by the Tripods. Will infiltrates the Tripods' city and learns terrible things about the fate of humanity. Panic strikes when he learns that the Tripods have a four-year plan, at the end of which the atmosphere on Earth will be converted to the poison gas that the aliens breathe. Will or Fritz must escape to warn the resistance.

The Pool of Fire. 1968. In the final volume of the Tripods Trilogy, Will and his friends succeed in capturing a Tripod driven by one of the Masters. This leads to an assault on all three Tripod cities. Heroism, sacrifice, and triumph mark the conclusion of a trilogy that has become a modern classic.

When the Tripods Came. 1988. The prequel to the Tripods Trilogy describes the arrival on Earth of the Tripods, three-legged, three-tentacled machines. Using subliminal television cartoons and mind-control caps, they begin their mission to take over the human race. An English school boy and his family realize what is going on just in time.

Cooper, Susan. *King of Shadows.* 1999. Orphan Nat Field has been selected to join the Company of Boys, a theater group chosen from schools and youth theaters all over the United States to go to London. There the company will present two plays, *Julius Caesar* and *A Midsummer Night's Dream*, in the newly reconstructed Globe Theatre on the banks of the Thames. Nat is a talented gymnast and actor, just perfect for the part of Puck. When he becomes deathly ill and is rushed to the hospital in the middle of the night, he is diagnosed with bubonic plague and put in isolation. The next morning he wakes up, feeling fit as a fiddle. But he is no longer in the twentieth century. He has traveled back in time to 1599 and is a guest member in Shakespeare's troop, playing Puck under the tutelage of Shakespeare himself in a special performance before the queen. How long will he remain in Elizabethan England? And who has taken his place and is lying in a hospital bed in contemporary London?

Crispin, A. C., with Deborah A. Marshall. *Serpent's Gift*. 1992. Eleven-year-old Heather is the youngest student ever admitted to StarBridge Academy, an institution dedicated to the education of the young of all sentient species, with the goal of bringing about greater understanding and peace. Brilliant and precocious, Heather is also an abused foster child with a penchant for getting into trouble, especially when Heather discovers that she can merge her mind with the central computer and control it.

Cross, Gillian. *New World*. 1995. Miriam and Stuart, two fourteen-year-olds, are hired to play a new experimental computer game—one last trial before the marketing blitz. What neither of them knows is that the game has been rigged to play on their fears and that the designer's son, Will, is also playing.

Danziger, Paula. *This Place Has No Atmosphere*. 1986. It is 2057, and Aurora has just learned that her family is moving—to the moon! Aurora must leave her friends behind for the duration of the five-year-contract her parents have signed. Miserable at first, she gradually begins to accept her new situation and make friends, including a new boyfriend.

Dexter, Catherine. *Alien Game*. 1995. At Oak Hill, everyone who wants to can play the annual Elimination Game. You can only be captured when you're not holding on to two others. So everyone playing goes around in chains of threes, until they are tricked into letting go. Zoe Brook, an eighth grader, and her friends weren't particularly interested in the game last year. But this year, everything's different. For one thing, there's Christina, a new girl in school, who looks like a model but copies everything that Zoe does. Then there are the blinking lights outside Zoe's house, and Zoe's strange feeling of being watched. Finally, Norton's uncle sees something in an abandoned school and is struck by lightning. And why does Christina, who is so eager to play the game, dissolve in a shower of fireflies standing in front of her locker?

Dickinson, Peter. *Eva*. 1989. Annotated on page 88.

Engdahl, Sylvia. *Children of the Star*. 2000. An omnibus reprint of the classic trilogy. Benign aliens rule the world with religion.

This Star Shall Abide. 1972. (Published in the UK as Heritage of the Star.)

Beyond the Tomorrow Mountains. 1973.

The Doors of the Universe. 1981.

Farmer, Nancy. *The Ear, the Eye, and the Arm.* 1995. This unusual work of science fiction opens in the compound of General Amadeus Matsika in Zimbabwe in 2194. The general has three children, who have been raised behind barbed wire, have never ridden a bus, been to the market, or seen a subway. But now thirteen-year-old Tendai wants to earn a boy scout badge, and to do so, he must go on a trip. He manages to sneak out of the compound, but he doesn't go alone. His younger sister and brother have insisted on going with him. They are kidnapped by the Great She Elephant for a stint of slave labor in her plastics mine, the first of several adventures, each more dangerous than the last. Through it all, the Ear, the Eye, and the Arm—mutant detectives whose special abilities will ensure their success if only the children will just stay in one place—are on their trail.

Gilmore, Kate. *The Exchange Student.* 1999. Daria runs her own personal zoo as one of Earth's youngest licensed breeders of endangered species. Then one day her mother, a famous author, proudly announces that an exchange student is coming to live with them—an exchange student from outer space. One of nine Chelans, Fen is tall, skinny, and gray (except when he changes color in reaction to what is going on around him). Like all Chelans, he is passionate about animals, but he tries to hide what being around all these living creatures means to him.

Haddix, Margaret Peterson. *Among the Hidden.* 1998. Luke is a third child in an overpopulated future where the penalty for having more than two children in a family is death. So he hides in the attic, all day, every day. But everything changes when he sees a face in the window of one of the new houses next door. Sneaking over, he meets Jen, who is also a third child. She has been in contact with third children all over the country and has invited them to a rally on the president's lawn as part of a plan to force the president to disband the Population Police and let all of the third children come out of hiding. She wants Luke to come along, but he's not sure this is a good idea. Once the Population Police find out about the rally, they have the legal right to kill all the third children. It would be safer to stay among the hidden.

Among the Imposters. 2001. Luke has been taken to an isolated private school under the assumed identity of Lee, a wealthy boy, who was legal and had died. At the school he wanders around in a daze, eventually finding a door that leads to the outside of the windowless building. There he finds a forest where he can plant a tiny garden with sprouts and potato eyes sneaked out of the cafeteria. Tormented by another boy in his eight-bed dorm room, he discovers that others are sneaking out of the building and that they are other thirds also hiding under false identities.

Hautman, Pete. *Hole in the Sky.* 2001. In a not-so-distant future, the human population has been decimated by a deadly flu. The only people left are the few who were not infected and the few who survived but lost their hair and suffered other permanent damage.

Hautman, Pete. *Mr. Was.* 1996. As a boy Jack Lund stood by helplessly while his father, in an alcoholic rage, killed his mother. Before that he was almost choked to death by his dying grandfather to the refrain of, "Kill you. Kill you. Kill you again." In between these two events Jack discovers a door at Bogg's End, his grandfather's house, a door that leads into the past—fifty years into the past, to be exact. That's where he meets Scud, who becomes his best friend and later tries to kill him, and Andie, the girl he falls in love with and follows across time.

Heinlein, Robert A. *Have Space Suit—Will Travel.* 1958. Annotated on page 6.

Heinlein, Robert A. *The Star Beast.* 1954. John Thomas, the eleventh generation of a distinguished space-faring family, has a most unusual pet, Lummox, a star beast brought to Earth generations ago from who knows where as a tiny stowaway on the spaceship *Trailblazer.* As the years have passed, Lummox has grown until now he is the size of a small dinosaur. Small wonder, considering his voracious appetite, which has led him to devour hay, metal, steel, trees, vicious dogs, and even prize rose bushes, which is where the trouble begins. Declared by the authorities to be a dangerous threat to humanity, the termination order is signed and sealed. John Thomas, who was supposed to be getting ready for college, winds up fleeing into the wilderness with Lummox instead, accompanied by his girlfriend Betty, who insists on going along to help. What no one realizes is that an interstellar incident of major proportions is brewing.

Hogan, James P. *Outward Bound.* 1999. Annotated on page 7. (Jupiter series)

Hoover, H. M. *The Winds of Mars.* 1995. The narrator, Annalyn, is the seventeen-year-old daughter of the president of Mars. Her mother was a starship commander whose ship left Mars orbit just months after Annalyn's birth. Once she's old enough to go to military academy, Annalyn receives a priceless gift from her mother—Hector Protector, her very own personal security robot. And it's a good thing, because Annalyn soon finds that her stepmother is plotting something terrible and that her father, suffering from paranoid delusions, is ready to destroy Mars. It's daughter against father (and stepmother) for the fate of an entire world, ably assisted by Hector Protector.

Howarth, Lesley. *Maphead.* 1994. Maphead is twelve, in his Dawn of Power year, but before he can gather and complete himself, he must meet his mother. That is why he and his father, Powers, have come to Rubytown. His mother, a woman from Earth, now has another son, Kenny, who is Maphead's age. Maphead needs to meet her, and he will, even if it means going to school with Kenny to do so.

Hughes, Monica. *The Crystal Drop.* 1993. The hole in the ozone layer, the greenhouse effect, and a lack of rain have set up a grim scenario for thirteen-year-old Megan. On her drought-stricken farm, she must bury her mother and the infant she died giving birth to. Then Megan and her ten-year-old brother leave, heading west to look for Uncle Greg. He left years ago to establish a settlement at the head of a river, near a waterfall. There is a picture of that waterfall in an old calendar hanging on the wall in their house. The two children risk life and limb to find it. Read this one with a tall glass of ice water on hand, because the future is bleak indeed, and incredibly dry.

Jacobs, Paul Samuel. *Born into Light.* 1988. Roger Westwood, an octogenarian, looks back on what happened seventy years before, in the spring of 1913. There was a bright flash, a barren burned spot in the woods, and a naked wild boy that his family raised. The local doctor helps treat the boy and brings the family a girl as well. Ben and Nell learn quickly, but they are also different. They age more quickly, are extremely fragile, and are driven to complete a mission before their early deaths. This first novel is a gentle reflective tale of living with the "aliens" among us.

Johnson, Annabel, and Edgar Johnson. *The Danger Quotient.* 1984. Casey's real name is K/C-4 (SCI). He's a boy from the future, genetically engineered to be the best and the brightest of the small group of humans who survived the conflagration and now live in tunnels deep beneath major population centers. But eighteen-year-old Casey only has six more months to live unless he can spark his longevity factor. All KCs burn out fast, but right before 3 died, she discovered something about 4 that could mean the salvation of humanity. Now, 4 is ready to travel—back in time to 1981.

Lawrence, Louise. *Calling B for Butterfly.* 1982. Four young teens, passengers on the spaceship *Sky Rider*, are headed for Omega Five. Glynn, who signed on as a steward, is an angry young man who has nothing to look back on or forward to. Ann and her father are hoping to build a new life together after the death of her mother. Sonja is spoiled rotten, a rich little "princess" who resents being dragged away from all the parties on Earth because of the ambassadorship awaiting her father on Omega 5. And Matthew, a quiet, intellectual boy with a passion for butterflies, is looking forward to studying new species on Omega 5. Under normal circumstances these four young people would have had nothing to do with each other. But after the ship is hit by an asteroid, they are the only survivors, along with a hyperactive three-year-old girl and her five-month-old baby brother. But their lifeboat is set on a collision course toward Jupiter, and it will take a miracle to save them.

Lawrence, Louise. *Dream-Weaver.* 1996. A spaceship from a severely overpopulated Earth heads toward the planet Arbroth, loaded with thousands of colonists who will awaken after seven years in cryogenic sleep to colonize the planet. During a waking period, seventeen-year-old Troy Morrison, a junior biotechnician on the flight, sees a ten-year-old girl with long dark hair and tangerine eyes standing in the corridor. Then she vanishes. That girl is Eth, a Dream-Weaver from the planet Arbroth.

Lawrence, Louise. *Keeper of the Universe.* 1992. Ben Harran, the only Galactic Controller who believes in free will and a policy of nonintervention for the planets in his charge, is on trial for genocide and culpable neglect because one of his planets blew itself up. In his defense, he tries an experiment, putting two inhabitants from his free-choice worlds with a girl from a completely controlled world. He hopes that the behavior of these test subjects will prove to the other Controllers that his is the best approach—but the cards are stacked against him.

Lawrence, Louise. *Moonwind.* 1986. The man in the moon is actually a woman, or in this case a young girl who was stranded when her spaceship broke down 10,000 years ago. Bethkahn passes centuries alone in oblivion until a star base is constructed on the moon, and her ship wakes her up. Soon she will meet a human, seventeen-year-old Gareth, who won a trip to the moon with his poetry.

Lawrence, Louise. *The Patchwork People.* 1994. This dual narrative contrasts the working-class Hugh, one of many indigent youths caught in the welfare trap, with Helena, a privileged daughter of the upper class whose soul is as deprived of nourishment as Hugh's body is of food. From two different social levels, they nevertheless find comfort and healing in each other's company. Their love is doomed, however, by a strike and by Hugh's refusal to sell his soul to the mining company. But then the Patchwork People—environmentalists looking for young people to work hard and make a difference—arrive, which changes everything.

Levitin, Sonia. *The Cure.* 1999. In a world ruled by uniformity, masked inhabitants recite the mantra: "Conformity begets Harmony begets Tranquility begets Peace begets Universal Good." When Gemm 16884 starts having dreams, hears music and rhythm all around him, and finally breaks free to express himself, he faces death—unless he is willing to take the cure. Gemm chooses the cure and finds himself in Strasbourg inhabiting the body of Johannes, a young Jew, in a time when Jews are being blamed for the spread of the black plague.

Lipsyte, Robert. *The Chemo Kid*. 1992. Fred gets icy-cold prickles, hormonal rushes, sensory enhancement, and almost enough strength to leap tall buildings. Using his special abilities he becomes a champion, fighting the evil chemical dumping plant in his home town. But he gets these powers because he has cancer. After the lump on his neck is removed, the chemical infusion he is given for chemotherapy turns him into the "Chemo Kid."

Lowry, Lois. *The Giver*. 1993. Jonas has been selected to be the next Receiver of Memory, a position of great honor. Now The Giver passes his memories on to Jonas, who must take over the role of protector of the community. The memories are glorious and wonderful at times, excruciatingly painful at others. Jonas can stand the pain. It's the discovery of his society's secrets that he can't stand—especially the discovery of what happens to those who are different and what it means to be released.

> *Newbery Award.*

Gathering Blue. 2000. This companion novel to *The Giver* is set in a future totalitarian dystopian world where technology has been left behind. Kira has just lost the mother who fought for her life when she was born lame. But the embroidering skills her mother taught her, as well as her phenomenal talent, gain her a place in life far removed from the dingy gathering of huts where she has lived with her mother. Kira is chosen to restore the cloak, embroidered with the history of the people, that the Singer wears in an annual ceremony.

Lubar, David. *Hidden Talents*. 1999. Edgeview Alternative School is the end of the line for kids with behavioral problems who can't cut it in regular schools. Martin Anderson has an uncanny knack for irritating everyone he comes in contact with, until he hooks up with a group of misfits in a boarding school full of misfits: his roommate Torchie and other kids called Trash, Lucky, Cheater, and Flinch. Martin discovers that they all have hidden talents.

McCaffrey, Anne. Harper Hall Trilogy. Set concurrently with McCaffrey's Pern saga, this series written for teens focuses on adolescents who tame tiny fire lizards that quickly carry messages by traveling "between."

Dragonsong. 1976. Menolly (age 15), youngest daughter of the leader of Half Circle Hold, is a talented musician whose fascination with all things musical enrages her mother and father. Forbidden all music, Menolly runs away. Life is dangerous outside the Hold, but she survives, and for the first time is made to feel welcome. Menolly would gladly spend the rest of her life with the Dragonriders. But the Masterharper has other plans.

Dragonsinger. 1977. Menolly's dream of training to be a Harper has come true, but she discovers that she will need more than musical talent and a facility with words.

Dragondrums. 1979. Piemur, Menolly's young friend and a golden-voiced soprano, loses his voice in adolescence. Master Robinton eases the boy's pain at this loss by making him his special assistant. He wants the boy to be able to attend gathers, listen, and pick up tidbits of information, so he assigns him to the drummers to learn drum language and be ready for special missions.

Nix, Garth. *Shade's Children.* 1997. Annotated on page 98.

O'Brien, Robert C. *Z for Zachariah.* 1975. Everything is barren and dead outside the valley where Ann lives as the sole survivor after a nuclear war. Luckily for her, the winds have blown the deadly radiation away from her refuge. From a picture book she used in Sunday School, *The Bible Letter Book*, she learned that "A is for Adam," "B is for Benjamin," and "C is for Christian," all the way to "Z is for Zachariah." Because Ann knew Adam was the first man, she assumed Zachariah must be the last man. Then she sees a stranger coming across the barren waste toward her valley. Could this be Zachariah?

Oppel, Kenneth. *Dead Water Zone.* 1993. The future is a bleak place, especially after Paul's brother Sam disappears. Then Paul gets a call from his brother, asking him to come down to the Dead Water zone, where Sam has made an important discovery. When Paul gets there, instead of Sam he meets Monica, who doesn't drink the water herself but has inherited some of its special attributes from her Waterdrinker mother.

Pace, Sue. *The Last Oasis.* 1993. In this grim future, water is so scarce that it has become a precious commodity, while exposure to the sun without sunscreen is life threatening. There is a rumor, however, that there are still hydroponics labs in Idaho, a last oasis for the human race. Phoenix, a hard-working, sympathetic young man, cares for his failing mother with love and compassion. Madonna, an amoral, me-first, do-any-thing-to-survive young girl, hides in the mall as long as she can. The two make a most unlikely pair as they set out for the Snake River and a series of adventures that they hope will lead them to a place where there is plenty of water for everyone.

Paulsen, Gary. *The Transall Saga.* 1998. On a solo camping trip, Mark sees a strange light. It sucks him in, then disgorges him on a world with red foliage, yellow skies, and strange critters. He spends many months learning alien survival skills and discovering his own strengths and inner resourcefulness. This pulp-like SF adventure breaks no new ground but is an entertaining diversion.

Pournelle, Jerry. *Starswarm.* 1998. (Jupiter Series) Kip, who lives on an interstellar colony, hears a voice in his head—but it isn't imaginary. A chip, embedded in him, is being used by an artificial intelligence to guide him.

Pratchett, Terry. Bromeliad Series. Tiny aliens from another planet have lived underfoot for eons. Annotated on page 151.

Truckers. 1989.

Diggers. 1990.

Wings. 1990.

Rubinstein, Gillian. *Galax-Arena.* 1995. Stolen children are forced to perform dangerous gymnastic routines before the alien Vexa in a specially designed structure, the Galax-Arena. Hythe only wanted the talented Peter and Liane, but he couldn't take them without Joella, who is not a gymnast like her brother and sister. But it is Joella who manages to escape from the cell where she is being kept as an alien's pet. Now she must warn the others of what she has discovered: the horrifying secret behind the Galax-Arena.

Rubinstein, Gillian. *Space Demons.* 1988. Andrew can't read the instructions or understand the warnings on the *Space Demons* game his father brought back from Japan. But he can figure out how to get started, and he does. He is so engrossed in the game he doesn't even realize that his parents have separated. Nor does he see the first signs of space demons actually appearing in real life. When his two friends become too frightened to play the game any more, he tricks a bully into joining him, not realizing that the space demons are getting stronger, and only one of them will make it back out of the game.

Sargent, Pamela. *Alien Child.* 1988. Nita grew up in a special institute watched over by a Guardian, a place where embryos are frozen and preserved until parents are ready for them. In Nita's case, however, her parents had changed their minds and never came back for her. At age fifteen, Nita discovers that she's not alone. Sven has had access to the library and is horrified at what he has learned about humanity—its irrational pursuit of war and the final destruction of the Earth. Now they must decide whether to revive other children.

Sargent, Pamela. *Earthseed.* 1983. The earthseed are human children, traveling on a spaceship to a habitable planet. They do not know they are on a ship, nor do they understand the nature of their mission. It is the ship's responsibility to prepare them, mentally and physically, for their competitions with each other and for the rigors of establishing a colony on a suitable planet. Then a group of adults wakes up and tries to take over.

Schmitz, James H. The Telzey Amberdon Series. Annotated on page 141.

Schmitz, James H. *The Witches of Karres.* 1966. Young Captain Pausert is a pretty nice guy, so when he runs across three little girls being held as slaves he buys them to free them and return them to their home planet. What he didn't bargain for was the fact that Goth, Maleen, and the Leewit are talented teleports!

A Web site that features several of the different covers, artwork, and jacket copy is at http://www.white-crane.com/Schmitz/Witches_novel.htm.

Scott, Michael. *Gemini Game*. 1994. Gemini Corporation markets and sells sophisticated, wildly popular virtual reality games. The creators of these games are fifteen-year-old twins, who inherited the corporation after their parents' untimely deaths. Their latest game, *Night's Castle*, seems to have sent a dozen people into virtual reality comas while playing it. The police are investigating, and the only way for the twins to clear themselves is to go into the game to find out what is wrong with it firsthand; such an action may have deadly consequences.

Sheffield, Charles. *Billion Dollar Boy*. 1997. (Jupiter Series). Because he is so rich, Shelby Cheever V thinks he can do whatever he wants to do. This lands him on a mining ship twenty-seven light years from Earth, where being one of the wealthiest people in the twenty-second century doesn't really count.

Sheffield, Charles. *The Cyborg from Earth*. 1998. (Jupiter Series). Notorious as a screwup in his powerful military family, Jeff Kopal is sent into deep space to deal with some rebellious cyborgs.

Sheffield, Charles. *Putting Up Roots*. 1997. (Jupiter Series). Fourteen-year-old Josh, abandoned after his mother leaves him to pursue her acting career, heads for his uncle's farm in Oregon. Unfortunately, in the past eight years his loving, warm-hearted aunt has died. His uncle's new wife doesn't want Josh around, and she would also like to get rid of his cousin Dawn, an autistic girl Josh's age who does not react "normally" to life—human life, that is. Dawn does a fine job of establishing rapport with pets and alien creatures. After being sold into service to Foodlines, a company that has a farming franchise on habitable planets, the two teens discover that there's a plot to turn the planet Solerino over to Unimine, with potentially deadly consequences.

Sheffield, Charles, and Jerry Pournelle. *Higher Education*. 1996. (Jupiter Series). After being expelled from school, Rick Luban, age sixteen, gains a position as an asteroid miner trainee. Then he discovers just how dangerous corporate espionage in space can be.

Shusterman, Neal. *The Dark Side of Nowhere*. 1997. Jason Miller, a natural leader, lives a rather bland life in a Norman Rockwell-style town. After one of his best friends dies mysteriously, he is given a weird, glovelike weapon by the school janitor. This starts Jason on a path of self-discovery in the midst of a scheme for the alien conquest of Earth.

Shusterman, Neal. Star Shards Trilogy.

> *Scorpion Shards*. 1995. Six tormented teens are the victims of a star that exploded when they were born. The star sent shards of its soul into them, which later attracted foul, tentacled aliens that invaded their bodies. Dillon can see patterns and he can cause devastation to those around him. Deanna is tortured by intense fear. Winston

seems to be shrinking away to nothing. Tory, hideously deformed by the disease eating away at her, sickens those she touches. Lourdes, who hasn't eaten in weeks, is massively obese to the point where her weight could smother someone. Michael, irresistible to girls, exudes an aura that makes boys hate him, while his kisses steal the souls of his girl victims. These teens are attracted to one another because only by joining forces can they defeat the aliens trying to destroy the universe.

Thief of Souls. 1999. The Bringer has escaped the prison that held him for thousands of years, and he has the power to destroy the world. Only the combined efforts of the survivors of *Scorpion Shards* can stop him.

Skurzynski, Gloria. *Cyberstorm.* 1995. Eleven-year-old Darcy Kane has moved to a new neighborhood, one with no kids in it. The only bright spot is her small dog Chip, but now someone has complained about his barking, and the Animal Control People are going to take Chip from her. She thinks her elderly neighbor, eighty-five-year-old Evelyn Galloway, complained, but when she and her father talk to the woman, they discover it was just a misunderstanding. Meanwhile the man installing the Virtual Reality Rent a Memory machine for Evelyn's week of reliving Happy Memories mentions to the guard that the dog's barking is interfering with the proper functioning of his machine. The Animal Control People won't listen to reason, so Darcy and Chip try to hide inside the machine. But Chip's barking sets it off, and soon Darcy is reliving her neighbor's memories—trapped inside the machine.

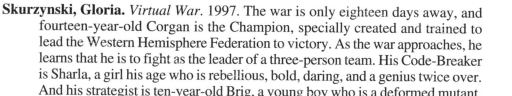

Skurzynski, Gloria. *Virtual War.* 1997. The war is only eighteen days away, and fourteen-year-old Corgan is the Champion, specially created and trained to lead the Western Hemisphere Federation to victory. As the war approaches, he learns that he is to fight as the leader of a three-person team. His Code-Breaker is Sharla, a girl his age who is rebellious, bold, daring, and a genius twice over. And his strategist is ten-year-old Brig, a young boy who is a deformed mutant, but a genius three times over. The war is for a true prize, an island that is the last piece of uncontaminated land in the world. Together they have a good chance of winning, but first Corgan must learn how to ignore the blood and gore and the cries and screams of the virtual deaths he causes.

Sleator, William. *The Boxes.* 1998. Annie's mysterious uncle leaves her with two boxes and instructions to keep them apart and unopened. She can't stand the suspense for long, so she opens a box in the basement and accidentally lets a strange buglike creature escape. In a few days it has grown, reproduced, and started talking to her telepathically. Annie is compelled to open the other box. When an evil developer, who wants to raze the neighborhood to build a mall, gets wind of Annie's discoveries, he tries to interfere.

Marco's Millions. 2001. Marco, fascinated by numbers, goes through an opening in the basement to a world where time and gravity are very different. By the time he returns, his sister has grown up, had a child, and died. A prequel to *The Boxes*.

Sleator, William. *House of Stairs*. 1974. Five young orphans suddenly find themselves transported to a mysterious house of stairs. No explanation of why they are there or what they are to do is given. Each simply finds himself or herself stranded on the stairs and left to wander around, trying to figure out what they are supposed to do. The five teens form an uneasy alliance as they explore their environment, an alliance that is ultimately shattered. This futuristic novel is a very somber, almost Kafkaesque treatment of the human condition.

Sleator, William. *Interstellar Pig*. 1984. A vacation at the beach is boring for Barney until the new tenants move in next door. They invite him, a teenager, to compete in their mysterious game, *Interstellar Pig*. It's a really exciting game, with possession of The Piggy as its ultimate goal. Players risk their lives trying to save their planets from annihilation by getting possession of The Piggy. Things get serious when Barney discovers that there actually is a Piggy, which means the game must be real, too—and Joe, Manny, and Zena are not what they appear to be.

Sleator, William. *The Night the Heads Came*. 1996. Best friends Leo and Tim have an up-close-and-personal encounter with a UFO. They are driving on an isolated road in the middle of the night when lights appear in the sky, the car dies, and something begins scratching at the window. Soon they're being propelled toward amber lights, taken up into the sky, and examined by tall thin creatures and crawling heads. Leo is returned and for the next two days tries to convince people, including the authorities, a hypnotist, and Tim's parents, that he is not responsible for Tim's disappearance. Two days later when Tim returns, he is a couple of years older and has some bizarre drawings that he made during his abduction—drawings that he says must be kept away from the Others (shapeshifting aliens on Earth) at all costs.

Sleator, William. *Others See Us*. 1993. Sixteen-year-old Jared was looking forward to summer at the beach with his family, in particular spending time with his beautiful cousin Annelise. But then a bike accident in the swamp near his house dumps him in water that used to be a toxic waste dump. At the party that night his head begins to buzz, and suddenly he discovers that he can hear other people's thoughts. That's how he learns that Cousin Annelise is not what she seems to be. She must be stopped, but how?

Sleator, William. *Singularity*. 1985. When the sixteen-year-old twins, Barry and Harry, visit the estate their uncle left to their family, they begin to hear strange rumors about their eccentric uncle. Then they find his diary, in which he talks about "it" progressing, hoping the walls will be strong enough to keep "it" from getting out. This seems to be connected with the mysterious playhouse, a double-walled structure that could serve as an emergency bunker. But inside this playhouse, time is different.

Slepian, Jan. *Back to Before*. 1993. Lenny and Hilary, two unhappy eleven-year-olds, find a tarnished, oversized ring in an abandoned house. Riding a bike through a heavy storm clutching the ring, they are transported back in time to just a few days before the death of Lenny's mother and the departure of Hilary's father. Maybe this is their chance to change the future.

Stevermer, Caroline. *River Rats*. 1992. Fifteen years ago the Flash resulted in nuclear Armageddon. Now *The River Rat*, an ancient Mississippi steamboat, has been liberated by a group of kids who call themselves The River Rats. It provides them with a home and transportation as they work their way up and down the river, delivering mail and giving rock concerts at various ports of call. The Mississippi River has become a stream of polluted sludge, but there's still enough water to keep them moving from port to port. To protect themselves, they absolutely never take on passengers, but then one day they break this rule to save a man's life.

Tolan, Stephanie S. *Welcome to the Ark*. 1996. The ark is a Global Family Group Home project, established to give researchers free rein in their work with a small group of extremely bright but mentally unstable children. The point of the experiment is connection: intense human connection within the therapeutic family and electronically around the world. Miranda, a young girl pursuing a doctorate in Romance languages and literature, was sent to Laurel Mountain at age sixteen when she began claiming she was an alien. Elijah is an eight-year-old black boy who felt the growl of violence growing, then experienced his mother's death and shut down completely. Sixteen-year-old Doug, a computer whiz and gifted flute player in a family of hunters, is sent to the home after attempting suicide. Nine-year-old Taryn, whose mother built "The Church of St. Taryn" around her mixed-daughter's mystical qualities, was sent to live with her aunt and four brutish male cousins after her mother's death. Their treatment drove the child toward schizophrenia and ultimately into the ark. Once she arrives, Taryn is the catalyst that brings them all together. The four connect, then reach out to other gifted children, forming a network that astonishingly can control violence in the world. But jealous Dr. Turnbull intervenes, drugs Taryn, and breaks the connection, with long-lasting and far-reaching results. Elijah's story continues in *Flight of the Raven*.

Ure, Jean. *Plague*. 1991. Fran returns after a month in a wilderness survival class to find a barricade around London and two kids outside it wearing surgical masks. Fran gets through the barricade, but when she gets home she finds the moldering bodies of her parents—dead from the plague. An acquaintance from school offers to help her get out of the city, but then he comes down with the plague. Their survival now depends on the formerly shy, irresolute Fran.

Vande Velde, Vivian. *User Unfriendly*. 1991. A group of kids who are used to gaming together get their hands on a pirated copy of a state-of-the-art interactive game that requires carefully controlled preparation and constant monitoring during play. Being eighth graders, they dive in and begin playing with no safeguards at all. The narrator is Arvin Rizalli, who is also an elf in the game—Harek Longbow of the Silver Mountains Clan. Play is complicated for Arvin/Harek when Felice, a serving wench, joins the game. He soon discovers that she is his mother, and that her headaches are a sign that something is seriously wrong. In fact, she is in danger of having a stroke in real life before the game ends. To make matters worse, the program gets a glitch, begins to loop in spots, and with no cleric to raise the dead, they are all in danger of losing their lives for real.

Weaver, Will. *Memory Boy*. 2001. Miles Newell, a teen inventor, creates a vessel that will take his family away from the dangers and shortages in Minneapolis after volcanic activity has devastated life as we know it.

Williams, Sheila, ed. *The Loch Moose Monster: More Stories from Isaac Asimov's Science Fiction Magazine*. 1993. The title story is from Janet Kagan's *Mirabile*, laced with humor and featuring a strong female protagonist. Others include a family that goes into a television—literally; water as a scarce commodity; what's in store for those who are different; paying a debt to a childhood friend, only to find there is no end to retribution; a real ghost who plays Shakespeare; human dependence on robots; the eternal battle; a visitor from another planet searching for a lost artifact; and a typical American tall tale—on Mars.

Zelazny, Roger. *A Dark Traveling*. 1987. James Wiley is a fourteen-year-old boy whose parents work for the Transit Foundation, an organization that monitors and at times participates in what is going on in the other bands. These can be lightbands, the site of normal human endeavors; darkbands, the location of the home of the enemy; or deadbands, destroyed by the incorrect use of technology, either accidentally or due to deliberate sabotage by darkband infiltrators. After an attack on a transit station, James's father disappears, leaving behind only a trace of blood. James activates the Golem guardian (a soft-skinned robot) and then calls on his adopted sister Becky, a witch, for help. The two, joined by exchange student Barry, a trained assassin and karate expert, use magic to help them teleport to alternate worlds to search for their father. To further complicate matters, James, who has reached puberty and takes after his uncle, is in the process of becoming a werewolf.

Children's

Many readers discover science fiction at a young age. When fans of the genre are queried as to what got them started, it is not uncommon to hear fond reminisces of first encounters with *A Wrinkle in Time* or *The Wonderful Flight to the Mushroom Planet* and how that led to a lifelong habit of looking for those little rocket ship genre spine stickers with every library visit.

The books in this section are for children who read chapter books. Many science fiction fans tend to be intellectually precocious, so they are undaunted by lengthy books or challenging ideas. Grades 3–5 seem to be peak years for children to begin reading SF.

Applegate, K. A. Animorphs Series. Jake, Marco, Tobias, Rachel, and Cassie use their abilities to "morph" into different animal shapes so they can defend the world against an interplanetary takeover. There are more than 50 titles in the series. A television show and a video game have also resulted from the popularity of these books.

Brennan, Herbie, and Neal Layton. *Zartog's Remote.* 2001. Eight-year-old alien Zartog visits Earth, where he inadvertently switches his remote control with one that belongs to an eight-year-old Earthling, a child who has been the target of bullies.

Cameron, Eleanor. Mushroom Planet Series. David and Chuck embark on a series of adventures with their small spaceship after answering a newspaper ad that takes them to Mr. Tyco M. Bass.

The Wonderful Flight to the Mushroom Planet. 1954.

Stowaway to the Mushroom Planet. 1956.

Mr. Bass's Planetoid. 1958.

A Mystery for Mr. Bass. 1960.

Time and Mr. Bass. 1967.

Engdahl, Sylvia. *Enchantress from the Stars.* 1970. (Reissued, 2001.) This is an absolutely fascinating treatment of the perils involved in preserving a culture during first contact. Elana has come to the medieval planet Andrecia as a stowaway. Her father is the leader of a Federation Anthropological Service team that is trying to preserve the planet's culture. This is made difficult because the planet is being invaded by the Imperial Exploration Corps. The Imperials are getting the planet ready for colonization, which will include shipping all the residents to reservations. But Apprentice Medical Officer Jorel is unhappy at the brutal way the natives are being treated by the Imperials. The natives are represented by Georyn, who is headed toward the Imperial camp, on a quest with his brother to slay the dragon (the heavy equipment the Imperials are using to tear up the surface of the planet). Elana's father makes her an official member of the Anthropological team by giving her the Oath of the Federation. He then has her play the role of Enchantress to Georyn and his brother, in this way helping them on their quest. Once Georyn learns to control his innate mental abilities and can demonstrate them to the invaders, the Imperials will have to acknowledge that the native population is human; not animals, which means that they will have to pack up and look for another planet to settle. Before it's all over, the two young people have fallen in love, even though they both know that in the end the Enchantress must return to the stars.

Newbery Honor Book Award.

Klause, Annette Curtis. *Alien Secrets.* 1993. Puck's parents are studying the alien Showa, one of the species enslaved by the tyrannical Grakk. After a twenty-year war, Earth has defeated the Grakk and the Showa are going home to Aurora. Puck is going home, too, after having been kicked out of boarding school. In the spaceport before departure, she sees two men fighting. One of these men is dead. The other is a passenger on her ship. And now it seems than an ancient Showan artifact has been stolen.

L'Engle, Madeleine. Time Quartet.

 A Wrinkle in Time. 1962. Meg and Charles Wallace Murray, along with their friend Calvin, go off on a journey through space and time to find their missing father.

Newbery Award.

The Wind in the Door. 1973. Charles Wallace sees dragons in the garden, and Meg and Calvin go off on a galactic journey to fight evil.

A Swiftly Tilting Planet. 1978. Now fifteen years old, Charles Wallace must go back in time to stop a dictator and avert a nuclear war in the present.

Many Waters. 1986. Sandy and Dennys, the twins in the Murray family, didn't notice the note on the door to their mother's lab. On the resulting sojourn back in time, they encounter Noah.

Lindbergh, Anne. *Nick of Time.* 1994. Thirteen-year-old Jericho and his friends are students at Mending Wall, a small boarding school that encourages independence and creative thinking. Mending Wall students study the three C's: Cognizance, Culture, and Conscience. Then Nick appears, walking right through the kitchen wall in his stocking feet. He has come from the future, where their school has become a monument and a regular site for tours and lectures about life "in the good old days." Nick invites Jericho and his friends to come with him for a visit and they discover truths about their lives and the future.

Norton, Andre, and Dorothy Madlee. *Star Ka'at.* 1976. Illustrated by Bernard Colonna. This novel features two endearing characters, or four if you count the Ka'ats. Ka'ats are aliens whose mission is to strive to save fellow aliens. At the same time they must cope with the strange bond that each has developed with a human child.

Peck, Richard. Cyberspace Series.

Lost in Cyberspace. 1995. Josh, a sixth grader, isn't fazed when his best friend Aaron announces that he can time-travel with his computer. But when Aaron actually microprocesses himself into cyberspace, unexpected visitors from the past teach the boys more about their school's history than they ever wanted to know.

The Great Interactive Dream Machine. 1996. The two sixth grade protagonists of *Lost in Cyberspace* are back, and this time they can actually move in both space and time, courtesy of computer geek Aaron's state-of-the-art microsystem workstation. In this comedy of errors, Aaron has created a new formula that he hopes will get him into computer camp for the summer. Josh, who's facing the perils of soccer camp alone, changes the formula slightly so that it won't work, only to discover instead that he has made it interactive. Aaron has created a great interactive dream machine that fulfills the wishes of dogs as well as people. Now virtually anything can happen.

Service, Pamela E. *Stinker from Space.* 1988. When an alien pursued by enemies crash lands on Earth, his body is fatally injured, so he must take the first body passing by. That's how he becomes—a skunk! Now he is an alien in a skunk's body who needs human help to fix his spaceship and return to his own world. Fortunately, he can communicate telepathically, which is how he gets two children to help him. After impersonating a tame skunk, doing tricks so that he'll be allowed to stay with a suspicious family, the alien gets his two young friends to help him hijack the space shuttle. But those aliens who chased him to Earth are still waiting.

Service, Pamela. *Stinker's Return.* 1993. The alien skunk is back for another adventure on Earth. It seems that when he arrived home, he was not given a hero's welcome. His visit to Earth had not been authorized. To get back into the good graces of the ruler in charge of Earth's sector of space, Tsynq Yr (or Stinker as he's known to his two young Earth friends) must retrieve a souvenir. So the skunk and his two young companions head for Washington, D.C. and the costume museum containing Dorothy's ruby slippers. Once NASA finds out, of course, the chase is on in this humorous sequel.

Sleator, William. *Boltzmon!* 1999. Chris is ostracized at school, in large part because his popular older sister really has it in for him. When he goes upstairs to break up a party on the instructions of his mom, he finds a darting, glowing blob that he quickly pockets. The blob can take on any form that it wants. It's "Boltzmon," the remnant of a black hole from the future, which when perturbed moves into other places. Boltzmon takes Chris to Arteria, a parallel world forty years farther down the time continuum, and Chris learns a few things about the future—and the present.

Sleator, William. *The Green Futures of Tycho.* 1981. Tycho Tithonus, the youngest child in a family of "super-achievers," accidentally discovers a silver egg while digging up ground for a garden. While trying to keep the egg hidden from his family, Tycho discovers that with the egg's magic powers he can visit the past and the future, and if he likes, he can make changes. What he doesn't realize is that when changes are made, there are serious consequences.

Sleator, William. *Rewind.* 1999. After being killed by running out in front of a car, eleven-year-old Peter gets the chance to come back and do things differently. But time is running out, and he keeps running out—into the same street at the same time.

Slote, Alfred. *My Robot Buddy.* 1975. On his tenth birthday, Jack gets the friend he always wanted, in the form of a robot.

Chapter 7

Short Stories

One of the best ways to become acquainted with the characteristics of authors in the science fiction genre, and particularly with the work of new authors, is through anthologies. Both the theme anthologies and the critical and historical collections may have stories from all periods, although some suffer from repetition of much-anthologized pieces. The short story is a very popular form in both science fiction and fantasy. Though the following listing of anthologies is long, it is by no means exhaustive.

The essential reference tool for contending with the massive number of short stories is William F. Contento's *Index to Science Fiction Anthologies and Collections*, which after 1984, became part of an annual published by Locus Press called *Science Fiction, Fantasy, and Horror*. The entire run is available on a CD-ROM from Locus Press.

Ballard, J. G. *Love and Napalm*. Grove Press, 1972. This is the American title for Ballard's *The Atrocity Exhibition* first published in Great Britain in 1970 by Jonathan Cape and reissued in 1990 by Re/Search Publications, a collection of 15 avant-garde short stories that have as their central character a doctor who appears to be suffering from a nervous breakdown.

Bisson, Terry. *Bears Discover Fire*. Tor, 1993. Nineteen stories by an SF innovator. The title story won Nebula, Hugo, Locus, and Theodore Sturgeon awards.

Bisson, Terry. *In the Upper Room and Other Likely Stories*. Tor, 2000. Sixteen stories.

Brown, Frederic. *The Best of Frederic Brown*. Doubleday, 1977. Published posthumously and edited by Robert Bloch, this collection of short stories confirms Brown's reputation as the wittiest American writer of "short-shorts." Many of the pieces are quite brief, gleaned from magazine stories that were published in the 1940s, 50s and 60s. It also includes an assortment of those that are more substantial in length, including the classic "Arena," which depicts a duel between a human and an alien. It does not contain "The Waverlies," the story considered by many to be his finest. That story can be found in the collection *Angels and Spaceships*, published in 1954.

Delany, Samuel R. *Driftglass*. Signet, 1971. Ten science fiction short stories that represent the 1960s New Wave movement in America at its best. Two are Nebula award winners: "Aye, and Gomorrah" (1967) and "Time Considered as a Helix of Semi-Precious Stones" (1968).

   Nebula Award.

Dick, Philip K. *The Collected Stories of Philip K. Dick: We Can Remember It for You Wholesale*. Citadel, 1990. All of Dick's short works are availible now in collections. The title story in this particular collection was the basis of the Arnold Swartnegger movie, *Total Recall*.

Ellison, Harlan. *I Have No Mouth and I Must Scream: Stories*. Pyramid, 1967. This collection consists of seven stories that appeared in science fiction magazines in the late 1950s and early 1960s. The title story won the Hugo award in 1968. Also included are "Delusion for a Dragon Slayer" and "Pretty Maggie Moneyeyes."

Gibson, William. *Burning Chrome*. Arbor House, 1986. Ten stories from one of the progenitors of cyberpunk including "Johnny Mnemonic" that was made into a movie starring Keanu Reeves.

Sterling, Bruce. *A Good Old-Fashioned Future*. Bantam, 1999. Seven stories by the one-time chronicler of cyberpunk.

General Anthologies

The following anthologies give an overview of the genre and are a wonderful way to become acquanted with a wide variety of styles and writers important in the genre.

Bear, Greg, ed. *New Legends*. Tor, 1995. An anthology of 15 original stories by various major authors in the genre.

Boucher, Anthony, ed. *A Treasury of Great Science Fiction*. Doubleday, 1959. Two volumes. Short stories and novellas by Anthony Boucher, John Wyndham, Richard Deming, Ray Bradbury, Robert A. Heinlein, Philip K. Dick, Henry Kuttner and C. L. Moore, C. M. Kornbluth, Theodore Sturgeon, George P. Elliott, Poul Anderson, Malcolm Jameson, Oscar Lewis, Judith Merril, George O. Smith, Arthur C. Clarke, Nelson S. Bond, E.B. White, Mildred Clingerman, and Alfred Bester.

Bova, Ben, et al. *Future Quartet: Earth in the Year 2042, a Four-Part Invention*. Avon Books, 1994. Four stories and four articles written by Ben Bova, Frederik Pohl, Jerry Pournelle, and Charles Sheffield.

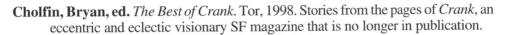

Card, Orson Scott, ed. *Masterpieces: The Best Science Fiction of the Century.* Ace, 2001. Twenty-nine classic stories in the genre.

Cholfin, Bryan, ed. *The Best of Crank.* Tor, 1998. Stories from the pages of *Crank*, an eccentric and eclectic visionary SF magazine that is no longer in publication.

Datlow, Ellen, ed. *Omni Visions.* Omni Books, 1993. Stories that originally appeared in the pages of *Omni* magazine.

Dozois, Gardner, ed. *Modern Classics of Science Fiction.* St. Martin's Press, 1993. Anthology of 26 stories published after 1955.

Ellison, Harlan, ed. *Again, Dangerous Visions.* Doubleday, 1972. Forty-six original stories. Ellison's two *Dangerous Visions* anthologies are essential reading for anyone who wants a good background in SF, although they tend to be on the dark side. They contain stories once considered unpublishable, often because of their sexual content.

Ellison, Harlan, ed. *Dangerous Visions.* Doubleday, 1967. Thirty-three original stories.

Greenberg, Martin H., ed. *My Favorite Science Fiction Story.* DAW, 1999. Seventeen favorite stories selected and commented upon by popular authors including Arthur C. Clarke, Anne McCaffrey, and Joe Haldeman. Stories by Theodore Sturgeon, Keith Laumer, Frederik Pohl, Gordon R. Dickson, Roger Zelazny, and others.

Gunn, James, ed. *Road to Science Fiction:* Volume 1. *From Gilgamesh to Wells.* New American Library, 1979. Volume 2. *From Wells to Heinlein.* New American Library, 1979. Volume 3. *From Heinlein to Here.* New American Library, 1979. Volume 4. *From Here to Forever.* Mentor, 1982. Volume 5. *The British Way.* Borealis, 1998 Volume 6. *Around the World.* White Wolf, 1998. Earlier volumes have been reissued by White Wolf. The first four volumes document the history of science fiction through the short story.

Harrison, Harry, and Brian W. Aldiss, eds. *The Astounding Analog Reader.* Doubleday, 1972. Stories that originally appeared in *Astounding* magazine.

Hartwell, David G. and Milton T. Wolf, eds. *Visions of Wonder: The Science Fiction Research Association Anthology.* TOR, 1996. This is the third anthology of contemporary speculative fiction endorsed by this international organization of teachers and scholars devoted to science fiction. In the 1970s and 1980s these works reflected the current concerns of SF and were used by succeeding generations of teachers. In the 1990s, it's a mixture of fantasy and science fiction, accompanied by essays to illuminate the fiction. Only a few of these stories are more than ten years old. The authors include masters like Anne McCaffrey, Andre Norton, and Robert Jordan as well as those who are beginning to have considerable influence in the field. The essays, added at the request of teachers, are ones that are important and yet difficult to obtain,

7

which makes this work useful for classroom work as well as independent reading. The stories themselves are challenging, engaging, and provocative, but, above all, they are fun to read.

Lapine, Warren, and Stephen Pagel, eds., *Absolute Magnitude.* Tor, 1997. Stories reprinted from the pages of *Absolute Magnitude* magazine.

Le Guin, Ursula K., and Brian Attebery, eds. *The Norton Book of Science Fiction: North American Science Fiction, 1960–1990.* W.W. Norton, 1993.

Mohan, Kim, ed. *More Amazing Stories.* Tor, 1998. Fifteen stories that would have appeared in the next issue of *Amazing* (but it ceased publication) and five stories that were reprinted from earlier years.

Pohl, Frederik, ed. *The SFWA Grand Masters.* Tor. Vol. 1, 1999; Vol. 2, 2001; Vol. 3, 2001. The Science Fiction Writer's of America have awarded the Grand Master Award fifteen times. This collection features works by the greats who have won this most prestigious of SF awards.

Pohl, Frederik, Martin Harry Greenberg, and Joseph Olander, eds. *The Great Science Fiction Series.* Harper, 1980. Twenty-one stories, each introduced by its author. Series following a character or theme are among the most popular types of science fiction.

Pringle, David, ed. *The Best of Interzone.* St. Martin's, 1997. Twenty-nine stories reprinted from *Interzone,* a British science fiction magazine.

Rusch, Kristine Kathryn, ed. *The Best of Pulphouse: The Hardback Magazine.* St. Martin's Press, 1991.

Rusch, Kristine Kathryn, and Edward L. Ferman, eds. *The Best from Fantasy & Science Fiction: A 45th Anniversary Anthology.* St. Martin's Press, 1994.

The Science Fiction Hall of Fame. Doubleday, 1970, 1973. 3 vols. Selections chosen by the Science Fiction Writers of America as the best in the genre.

Shippey, Tom, ed. *The Oxford Book of Science Fiction Stories.* Oxford University Press, 1992. Thirty stories from a 1903 story by H. G. Wells to a 1990 story by David Brin.

Silverberg, Robert, ed. *Far Horizons: All New Tales from the Greatest Worlds of Science Fiction.* Eos, 1999. Stories set in the worlds created in their novels: *The Ekumen*, Ursula K. Le Guin; *The Forever War*, Joe Haldeman; *The Ender* series, Orson Scott Card; *The Uplift Universe*, David Brin; *Roma Eterna*, Robert Silverberg; *The Hyperion Cantos*, Dan Simmons; *The Sleepless*, Nancy Kress; *Tales of the Heechee*, Frederik Pohl; *The Galactic Center* series, Gregory Benford; *The Ship Who Sang*, Anne McCaffrey; *The Way*, Greg Bear.

Williams, Sheila, ed. *The Loch Moose Monster: More Stories from Isaac Asimov's Science Fiction Magazine.* Delacorte, 1993. Annotated on page 208.

Wynorski, Jim, ed. *They Came from Outer Space: 12 Classic Science Fiction Tales That Became Major Motion Pictures.* With a Special Introduction by Ray Bradbury. Doubleday, 1980.

Theme Anthologies

These anthologies provide an intriguing introduction to the imaginative variety of themes explored and to the authors in the genre. Themes are noted in the following list, unless the title is self-explanatory. A useful guide for older classic stories is *Index to Stories in Thematic Anthologies for Science Fiction*, edited by Marshall B. Tymn, Martin H. Greenberg, L.W. Currey, and Joseph D. Olander; with an introduction by James Gunn (G.K. Hall, 1978).

Another access to reading by theme can be found through the "Checklist of Themes" in *The Science Fiction Encyclopedia*, edited by Peter Nicholls (see "Encyclopedias," p. 223, for a thorough description). For each theme, the encyclopedia article provides definition, history, and criticism of the treatment of the theme in general literature as well as in science fiction, including the key works (both short stories and novels). Some of the themes listed are black holes, clones, communications, cosmology, cryonics, discovery and invention, genetic engineering, mathematics, metaphysics, mutants, politics, psychology, reincarnation, terraforming, time paradoxes, war, and weather control.

Asimov, Isaac, et al., eds. *Machines That Think: The Best Science Fiction Stories About Robots and Computers*. Holt, 1983. Republished as *War with the Robots*. Wings, 1992.

Asimov, Isaac, Martin H. Greenberg, and Charles G. Waugh, eds. *The 13 Crimes of Science Fiction*. Doubleday, 1979. Each of the stories is labeled: Hard Boiled Detective; Psychic Detective; Spy Story; Analytical Detective; Whodunit; Why Done It; Inverted; Locked Room; Cipher; Police Procedural; Trial; Punishment.

Bujold, Lois McMaster, ed. *Women at War*. Tor, 1997.

Dann, Jack, and Gardner Dozois, eds. *Genometry*. Ace, 2001. Eleven stories of genetic engineering.

Datlow, Ellen, ed. *Alien Sex: 19 Tales by Masters of Science Fiction and Dark Fantasy*. Dutton, 1990.

Dozois, Gardner, and Sheila Williams. *Isaac Asimov's Detectives*. Ace, 1998.

Dozois, Gardner. *The Furthest Horizon: SF Adventures to the Far Future*. Griffin, 2000.

The Good New Stuff: Adventure SF in the Grand Tradition. Griffin, 1999.
The Good Old Stuff: Adventure SF in the Grand Tradition. Griffin, 1998.

Dozois, Gardner, and Sheila Williams, eds. *Roads Not Taken: Tales of Alternate History*. Del Rey, 1988.

Drake, David and Billie Sue Mosiman, eds. *Armageddon*. Baen, 1998. The end of the world.

Elliot, Elton, ed. *Nanodreams.* Baen, 1995.

Friesner, Esther and Martin H. Greenberg. *Alien Pregnant by Elvis.* DAW, 1994. Humorous tabloid style stories by Dennis McKiernan, Lawrence Watt-Evans, Barry Malzberg, James Brunet, Laura Resnick, Karen Haber, Deborah Wunder, Allen Steele, Mark Tiedemann, and Kristine Kathryn Rusch

Greeley, Andrew M., and Michael Cassuth, eds. *Sacred Visions.* Tor, 1991.

Greenberg, Martin Harry, ed. *Dinosaurs.* Donald I. Fine, 1996.

Griffith, Nicola and Stephen Pagel, eds. *Bending the Landscape: Science Fiction.* Overlook Press, 1998. Gay and lesbian themes.

Hartwell, David G., ed. *Christmas Stars.* Tor, 1992.

Hartwell, David G., and Kathryn Cramer, eds. *The Ascent of Wonder: The Evolution of Hard SF.* Tor, 1994.

Manson, Cynthia, and Charles Ardai, eds. *Aliens and UFOs: Extraterrestrial Tales from Asimov's Science Fiction and Fact.* Smithmark, 1993.

Preiss, Byron, and Robert Silverberg, eds. *The Ultimate Dinosaur: Past, Present, Future.* Bantam, 1992.

Rucker, Rudy, ed. *Mathenauts.* Arbor House, 1987.

Smith, David Alexander, ed. *Future Boston: The History of a City, 1990–2100.* Tor, 1994.

Thomas, Sheree R. ed., *Dark Matter: A Century of Speculative Fiction from the African Diaspora.* Aspect, 2000. Forty stories (some reprints and some original) spanning more than 100 years of writing by authors of African ancestry. Authors include Charles W. Chesnutt, W.E.B. Du Bois, George S. Schuyler, Samuel R. Delany, Charles R. Saunders, Octavia E. Butler, Derrick Bell, Henry Dumas, Ishmael Reed, Amiri Baraka, Anthony Joseph, Linda Addison, Steven Barnes, Nalo Hopkinson, Ama Patterson, Leone Ross, Nisi Shawl, Tananarive Due, Robert Fleming, Jewelle Gomez, Akua Lezli Hope, Honorée Fanonne Jeffers, Kalamu ya Salaam, Kiini Ibura Salaam, Evie Shockley, and Darryl A. Smith.

Turtledove, Harry, Elizabeth Moon, and Roland Green, eds. *Alternate Generals.* Pocket, 1998.

Waugh, Charles, and Martin H. Greenberg. *Space Wars.* Tor, 1988.

Chapter 8

Resources for Librarians and Readers

Science fiction is a genre that seems to be under-appreciated and under-read by many librarians. The following resources can aid librarians and others in finding information for both readers' advisory and collection development.

Journals

One of the best resources for book reviews is *Locus* magazine, which reviews or at least lists almost everything published in science fiction, fantasy, and horror. Some titles are reviewed by several different reviewers, providing alternate perspectives. Other worthwhile journal resources specific to SF are *Science Fiction Chronicle* and the *New York Review of Science Fiction*. *Booklist* does an excellent job of reviewing mostly hardcover releases. *Library Journal, Publishers Weekly*, and *Kirkus* all review some SF. *VOYA: Voice of Youth Advocates,* which reviews books for teens, does a commendable job of reviewing paperback original SF since many teen readers read SF published for adults as well as SF published for young adults. Science fiction magazines such as *Interzone, Fantasy and Science Fiction, Asimov's Science Fiction Magazine*, and *Analog* all feature a limited number of reviews.

Locus. P.O. Box 13305, Oakland, CA 94661
http://www.locusmag.com

Published monthly, *Locus* lists all SF and fantasy published in English. Seven accomplished reviewers discuss book-length fiction and short stories. It also includes author interviews, news of events and personalities, bibliographies, and the highly respected *Locus Poll*, which make it very useful.

Science Fiction Chronicle. P.O. Box 022730, Brooklyn, NY 11202-0056
http://www.dnapublications.com/sfc/

Monthly publication of reviews and science fiction news. It is also a good source for up-to-date information on awards.

VOYA: Voice of Youth Advocates. Scarecrow Press. 4720A Boston Way, Lanham, MD 20706
http://www.voya.com

A bimonthly that reviews books for young adults, this journal has remarkably good coverage of science fiction, fantasy, graphic novels and horror paperback originals.

New York Review of Science Fiction. Dragon Press
P. O. Box 570, Pleasantville, NY 10570
http://ebbs.english.vt.edu/olp/nyrsf/nyrsf.html

Essays and articles in addition to reviews.

Online Resources

There are an incredible number of Web sites devoted to science fiction. Most organizations related to SF and most publishers dealing with SF have Web sites, as do many individual authors. Online booksellers provide reviews and lists of science fiction on their Web sites. The following is just a sampling that demonstrates the wealth of information available. A Web page of links from this guide is online at http://www.sff.net/people/dherald/, so users can merely click to follow the links rather than typing in the sometimes lengthy URLs.

Bowling Green State University Popular Culture Library Science Fiction, Fantasy, and Related Collections (http://www.bgsu.edu/colleges/library/pcl/pcl9.html). The collection has approximately 25,000 titles related to SF and related genres.

Eidolon Online (http://www.eidolon.net/ezine/) provides the "scoop" on Australian SF, publishing reviews, interviews, news, and short stories.

Foundation: The International Review of Science Fiction (http://www.rdg.ac.uk/~lhsjamse/fnd.htm).

Interzone (http://www.sfsite.com/interzone/), a British magazine, features both science fiction and fantasy and is edited by David Pringle, one of the most knowledgeable minds in all SF.

Genreflecting.com (http://www.genreflecting.com) is the home page of the Genreflecting Readers' Advisory Series. It features annotated lists by genre.

The Genrefluent Page (http://www.genrefluent.com) reviews science fiction and other genres. Includes genre descriptors.

The Locus Index to Science Fiction (1994-1998), by Charles N. Brown & William G. Contento (http://www.locusmag.com/index/0start.html), lists just about all SF published in English.

Locus Online (http://www.locusmag.com) includes excerpts of reviews of featured books as well as other topical SF information.

The Merril Collection of Science Fiction, Speculation and Fantasy at the Toronto Public Library (http://www.tpl.toronto.on.ca/merril/home.htm) is the home of one of the finest collections open to the public.

The Science Fiction Foundation Collection Home Page (http://www.liv.ac.uk/ ~asawyer/ sffchome.html). The collection is housed in Special Collections at the University of Liverpool Library. It contains 20,000 fiction monographs and 1,600 critical works. Perusing the online catalog is a fascinating journey into the SF world.

Science Fiction and Fantasy Research Database (http://access-co2.tamu. edu/hhall/) allows the searcher to locate articles and monographs using Boolean searches. An excellent resource for researchers, it indexes articles in journals and monographs.

Science Fiction Weekly (http://www.scifi.com/sfw/) reviews new titles and gives them a letter grade.

The SF Site (http://www.sfsite.com/) is another good online resource for reviews and also offers a wealth of information and links to conventions and authors.

University of California Riverside Library Eaton Collection (http://library. ucr.edu/ spcol/eaton.shtml) is the largest collection of SF in the world; it not only houses 65,000 volumes but also collects the literary papers of several prominent SF authors.

Bibliographies, Biographies, and Indexes

Ash, Brian. *Who's Who in Science Fiction.* Taplinger, 1976. Brief bio-bibliographical listings with critical evaluations of characteristics of a science fiction writer. Prefaced with a "Chronological Guide: 100 Leading Writers and Editors in Their Main Periods of Production," from 1800 to the 1970s. Although this work is dated in bibliographic terms, it does a good job on early SF and remains available in libraries.

Barron, Neil, ed. *Anatomy of Wonder: A Critical Guide to Science Fiction.* 4th ed. Bowker, 1994. Critically annotated author listings are grouped by period or type with introductory essays: "The Emergence of Science Fiction: The Beginnings to the 1920s," by Thomas Clareson; "Science Fiction between the Wars: 1918–1938," by Brian Stablefield; "The Modern Period: 1938–1980," by Joe De Bolt and John R. Pfeiffer; "Children's Science Fiction," by Francis J. Molson; and "Foreign Language Science Fiction," by several authors, covering German, French, Russian, Italian, Japanese and Chinese. "Research Aids" includes chapters on indexes, bibliographies, history and criticism, author studies, film and television, illustration, classroom aids, magazines, library collections, and a core collection checklist.

Barron, Neil, ed. *What Fantastic Fiction Do I Read Next? A Reader's Guide to Recent Fantasy, Horror and Science Fiction.* Gale, 1998. Non-critical, this describes books released in the specified time span of 1989 to 1997. It includes indexes for characters, settings, and key words.

Bloom, Harold. *Classic Science Fiction Writers*. Chelsea House, 1995. A useful resosurce for research.

Bontly, Susan W., and Carol J. Sheridan. *Enchanted Journeys Beyond the Imagination, Vols. 1 and 2: An Annotated Bibliography of Fantasy, Futuristic, Supernatural, and Time Travel Romances*. Blue Diamond Publications, 1996. Bontly and Sheridan have identified romance books that fall into the science fiction, fantasy, and supernatural areas. They have managed to categorize this diverse and unusual but wildly popular area with panache. They list time-travel romances written by more than ninety authors, identifying times and destinations, grouping the books by American West, American Revolution/Frontier, America, Contemporary, Europe, Old South/Civil War, and Regency England, and have a category for time-travel romances that don't fit elsewhere. Other classifications include fantasy (myth and legend—futuristic, categorized by Earth-related, Other Worlds, and UFOs); supernatural romance—with angels, ghosts, vampires, and magic; and more. This unique bibliography is a boon to readers' advisors, both in libraries and bookstores, offering access to some of the most popular subgenres of romance fiction. Readers of these genres will be delighted to find old favorites and discover new. It includes listings of pseudonyms and listings by category and series. Author/title index.

Burgess, Michael. *Reference Guide to Science Fiction, Fantasy, and Horror*. Libraries Unlimited, 1992. A comprehensive guide to secondary materials. Burgess critically annotates 551 resources. Core collections for different types of libraries are also recommended.

Clarke, I. F., comp. *The Tale of the Future from the Beginning to the Present Day*. Library Association, 1978. The following subtitle tells it all: An annotated bibliography of those satires, ideal states, imaginary wars and invasions, coming catastrophes and end-of-the-world stories, political warnings and forecasts, interplanetary voyages, and scientific romances, all located in an imaginary future period, that have been published in the United Kingdom between 1644 and 1976.

Kunzel, Bonnie and Suzanne Manzuk. *First Contact: A Reader's Selection of Science Fiction and Fantasy*. Scarecrow Press, 2001. Instead of a comprehensive selection tool, this is a beginning readers' advisory book that groups science fiction and fantasy titles together under a series of thematic headings: *Alien Contact; All Creatures Great and Small; Alternate Reality; Biotechnology; Brain Power; Brave New World; Double, Double, Toil and Trouble; Endangered Earth; Hackers and Droids; Here There Be Dragons; Imagination's Other Place; In Legendary Camelot; A Matter of Belief; Metamorphoses; Once Upon a Time; Postapocalypse; Space Opera; A Story, A Story; Time Warp; To a Galaxy Far, Far Away;* and *To Be Continued*. The titles included in each section are favorites of the authors. This includes classics, as well as current titles that are popular with both younger and older teens. In-depth annotations of the entries are provided, as well as an author/title index.

Hall, Hal W., ed. *Science Fiction and Fantasy Reference Index, 1985–1991: An International Author and Subject Index to History and Criticism*. Libraries Unlimited, 1993. *Science Fiction and Fantasy Reference Index, 1992–1995: An International Subject and Author Index to History and Criticism*. Libraries Unlimited, 1997. Definitive listings of secondary materials. http://access-co2.tamu.edu/hhall/

Pringle, David. *Science Fiction: The 100 Best Novels.* 2d ed. Carroll & Graf, 1997. The titles are presented chronologically, each with a full and very readable story analysis and critical evaluation. Michael Moorcock's foreword (to the first edition) suggests that while anyone might quarrel with some of the selections, most readers would agree on at least fifty, "an excellent percentage."

Pringle, David. *The Ultimate Guide to Science Fiction.* 2d ed. Ashgate Press, 1995. Science fiction enthusiasts will enjoy paging through Pringle's work. It provides brief synopses of all the the major (and some of the minor) science fiction novels and short stories written in English since the term *science fiction* was coined (approximately 1929). In the introduction, Pringle pokes fun at science fiction clichés and outlines the beginnings of science fiction writing. He explains the structure of every entry and evaluates each work. Where appropriate, he includes the names of sequels, related works, film versions, and author pen names. Occasionally he also inserts quotations from other science fiction critics. The A-to-Z list contains nearly 3,500 entries. Works are arranged alphabetically by title. To enable readers to quickly find an entry, Pringle uses two types of cross-references: variant titles for the same books and parent novels of series or related works.

Reginald, R. *Science Fiction and Fantasy Literature: A Checklist, 1700–1974.* Gale, 1979.

Science Fiction and Fantasy Literature, 1975–1991: A Bibliography of Science Fiction, Fantasy, and Horror Fiction Books and Nonfiction Monographs. Gale, 1993. Cites approximately 22,000 monographs. Lists series titles, awards, and other topics of interest to readers.

Encyclopedias

Clute, John. *Science Fiction: The Illustrated Encyclopedia.* Dorling Kindersley, 1995. A magnificent treatment of science fiction, done in the inimitable Dorling Kindersely style. In addition to the wealth of illustrations, both color and black-and-white, that adorn every page, the text is lively, informative, and accessible to readers of all ages. Clute provides a picture of how science fiction fits into modern or contemporary times; discusses major authors and books; uses timelines to good effect to provide a historical perspective; and goes on to cover magazines, movies, radio, and television programs and even world events. A wealth of information is woven into just 312 colorful pages. The result is a visual and an intellectual delight.

Clute, John, and Peter Nicholls, eds. *The Encyclopedia of Science Fiction.* St. Martin's, 1995. This essential guide for science fiction lists trends, authors, titles, terminology, and much more for science fiction in written and visual forms. It contains 4,360 entries. Alphabetical arrangement of themes, biographies, and other topics, with many cross-references. Historical and critical, with extensive bibliographical material. Biographical listings for many little-known authors. Many of the articles are extended critical essays.

Gunn, James, ed. *The New Encyclopedia of Science Fiction*. Viking-Penguin, 1988. Summaries, criticism, and bibliographical and historical information on people, books, topics, trends, and films in science fiction.

Dictionaries

Colburn, Jeff. *The Writer's Dictionary of Science Fiction, Fantasy, Horror and Mythology*. Madison Books, 1999. This most unusual dictionary provides a strict alphabetical listing of terms, phrases, and concepts that might be of use to authors who write science fiction, fantasy, and horror. It also draws together mythological terms from the world's cultures. As a result, you can find juxtapositions such as A.I. (Artificial Intelligence) and ATLAS (Atmospheric Laboratory for Applications and Science—a Spacelab aboard the Space Shuttle) along with definitions for Abbey and the Abominable Snowman. A separate section provides subject listings and a variety of tables, including Gods, Manned Space Flight, the Planets, and Space Walks. It's hard to put humor into a dictionary, but the author managed to achieve a light touch in a work that is both interesting and useful.

Rogow, Roberta. *FutureSpeak: A Fan's Guide to the Language of Science Fiction*. Paragon House, 1991. Although not exactly a dictionary, this is an overall survey of the world of science fiction, from books to movies to fandom.

Stableford, Brian M. ed. *The Dictionary of Science Fiction Places*. Fireside, 1999. The history, geography, and inhabitants of more than 1,500 imaginary places that were created by 250 authors.

History

Science fiction history may start either in classical literature or in the nineteenth century, depending on an author's definition of the genre. Many of the following books are critical to the point of being controversial. They are written by authors of the genre and by fans, both lay and academic. In addition to the following books, the reader will find considerable historical material in encyclopedias (see p. 223) and criticism (see p. 225).

Ackerman, Forrest J. *Forrest J. Ackerman's World of Science Fiction*. General Publishing Group, 1997. A highly personalized view of the history of science fiction, written by the fan who coined the term sci-fi.

Alkon, Paul K. *Science Fiction Before 1900: Imagination Discovers Technology*. Twayne, 1994.

Landon, Brooks. *Science Fiction After 1900: From the Steam Man to the Stars*. Twayne Publishers, 1997.

Perret, Patti. *The Faces of Science Fiction: Photographs*. Bluejay Books, 1984.

Sanders, Joe, Ed. *Science Fiction Fandom*. Greenwood Press, 1994.

Criticism

The quantity of critical exposition on science fiction is daunting. The quality varies from the popular fandom to the academic obscurant, with, fortunately, some lively and imaginative discussion in between, both by authors of the genre and fans in the academic world. The following is merely a sampling to show the wealth of commentary available.

Asimov, Isaac. *Asimov's Galaxy: Reflections on Science Fiction.* Doubleday, 1989. Essays published as editorials in *Isaac Asimov's Science Fiction Magazine.*

Bleiler, Everett F., ed. *Science Fiction Writers: Critical Studies of the Major Authors from the Early Nineteenth Century to the Present Day.* Scribner's, 1982. Seventy-six authors analyzed in essays by various writers.

Bloom, Harold, ed. *Classic Science Fiction Writers.* Chelsea House, 1995. History, criticism, and bio-bibliography of Edward Bellamy, Edgar Rice Burroughs, Sir Arthur Conan Doyle, Aldous Huxley, C. S. Lewis, Jack London, H. P. Lovecraft, George Orwell, Edgar Allan Poe, Mary Shelley, Olaf Stapledon, and H. G. Wells.

Disch, Thomas M. *The Dreams Our Stuff Is Made of: How Science Fiction Conquered the World.* Free Press, 1998.

Fletcher, Marilyn P., ed. *Readers' Guide to Twentieth-Century Science Fiction.* American Library Association, 1989.

Hartwell, David G. *Age of Wonders: Exploring the World of Science Fiction.* Tor, 1996. A classic on the history and development of SF, updated for the 1990s, which describes both the literature of science fiction and the subculture (fandom) the nourishes it.

Hassler, Donald M., and Clyde Wilcox, eds. *Political Science Fiction.* University of South Carolina Press, 1997.

Landon, Brooks. *Science Fiction After 1900: From the Steam Man to the Stars.* Twayne Publishers, 1997.

Le Guin, Ursula K., ed. *The Language of the Night: Essays on Fantasy and Science Fiction.* HarperCollins, 1992.

McCaffery, Larry. *Across the Wounded Galaxies: Interviews with Contemporary American Science Fiction Writers.* University of Illinois Press, 1990. Gregory Benford, William S. Burroughs, Octavia E. Butler, Samuel R. Delany, Thomas M. Disch, William Gibson, Ursula K. Le Guin, Joanna Russ, Bruce Sterling, and Gene Wolfe.

Sobczak, A. J., and T. A. Shippey, eds. *Magill's Guide to Science Fiction and Fantasy Literature.* Salem Press, 1996. Four volumes: v. 1. The absolute at large—Dragonsbane; v. 2. Dream—The lensman series; v. 3. Lest darkness fall—So love returns; v. 4. Software and wetware—Zotz!

Spinrad, Norman. *Science Fiction in the Real World.* Southern Illinois University Press, 1990.

Writing Guides

The following are meant to instruct writers in their craft but are also illuminating for the reader of the science fiction genre.

Bova, Ben. *The Craft of Writing Science Fiction That Sells*. Writer's Digest Books, 1994.

Card, Orson Scott. *How to Write Science Fiction and Fantasy*. Writer's Digest Books, 1990.

Costello, Matthew J. *How to Write Science Fiction*. Paragon House, 1992.

Dozois, Gardner, ed. *Writing Science Fiction and Fantasy*. St. Martin's Press, 1991.

Gerrold, David. *Worlds of Wonder: How to Write Science Fiction and Fantasy*. Writer's Digest Books, 2001.

Gunn, James. *The Science of Science Fiction Writing*. Scarecrow Press, 2000. In addition to invaluable information on writing SF, Gunn also includes a good deal of history, criticism, and several author profiles.

Ochoa, George, and Jeffrey Osier. *The Writer's Guide to Creating a Science Fiction Universe*. Writer's Digest Books, 1993.

Scott, Melissa. *Conceiving the Heavens: Creating the Science Fiction Novel*. Heinemann, 1997.

Sheffield, Charles. *Borderlands of Science: How to Think Like a Scientist and Write Science Fiction*. Beanstalk, 1999.

Spinrad, Norman. *Staying Alive: A Writer's Guide*. Donning, 1983.

Publishers

For years, science fiction was published most extensively in paperback, with a few of the "big" authors and major anthologies coming out in hardcover. As the acceptance (and commercial success) of science fiction grew, hardcover publication increased. The advantage to publishing in hardcover is that the books have a better chance of being reviewed and thus a better chance of reaching a mainstream audience. However, science fiction fans really do seem to prefer the paperback versions. It is not uncommon to read on the Internet correspondence from a reader questioning whether a specific title is so essential to read immediately that it should be purchased in hardcover; the reader will usually wait for the paperback edition. Science fiction readers have also been know to donate hardcover copies of a title when the paperback is released because they can then purchase the size that keeps their collection consistent.

Anthologies appear widely in both forms. Critical works, which formerly were issued largely in hardcover, are now appearing regularly in both formats. Illustrated science fiction novels (as well as fantasy) are published in both formats, but, notably, in greater numbers in paperback originals.

As major publishers merge and smaller publishing houses are bought and sold, it seems that the number of houses publishing science fiction would decline, but the Internet has made it possible for small publishers and e-publishers to make a go of it. There are numerous publishers who publish only one science fiction title in a year or over a number of years. The following list includes publishers that regularly issue SF titles and a few that are not active now but have had a major impact on SF.

Ace is an imprint of Penguin Putnam that publishes a newsletter on the Internet at http://www.penguinputnam.com/clubppi/news/ace/index.htm.

Baen (http://www.baen.com/) is known for militaristic science fiction, publishing Lois McMaster Bujold, David Weber, and David Drake. It does, however, also publish many other types of science fiction and fantasy. It also publishes e-books, making its titles available for downloading slightly before they appear in bookstores.

Big Engine (http://www.bigengine.co.uk/) is a British publisher of both new and vintage SF.

DAW is an imprint of Penguin Putnam (http://www.penguinputnam.com/ clubppi/ news/daw/index.htm).

Easton Press publishes beautifully bound collector's editions of science fiction. Its "Science Fiction Masterpieces" series features titles from James Gunn's "Basic Science Fiction Library," which appeared in the November 15, 1988, issue of *Library Journal*.

Eos is the SF imprint of HarperCollins.

Firebird is a paperback imprint of Penguin Putnam, specializing in SF and fantasy for YA's.

Gollancz publishes SF in the UK.

Gregg Press. Historically speaking, the Gregg Press Hardcover Editions, published from 1975 to 1981, brought a plentitude of some of the best SF originally published in paperback or reissues of out-of-print works to libraries. For serious collectors of SF, David G. Hartwell has a checklist of the Gregg titles at http://ebbs.english.vt.edu/ exper/kcramer/gregg.html.

HarperCollins (http://www.harpercollins.com/hc/features/eos/) publishes science fiction under the Eos imprint, which replaced HarperPrism and AvoNova.

Ibooks, Inc. (http://www.ibooksinc.com/) publishes electronic editions of new titles in cooperation with the hard copy publisher, as well as reprints.

Meisha Merlin published one new hardcover title and six paperbacks in 2000. Some were omnibus editions of several titles previously published individually.

NESFA, the New England Science Fiction Association (http://www. nesfa.org/press/) publishes collections of stories and essays by guests of honor at its conference and other major SF conferences. It also publishes hardcover reprints of important classic SF titles that have gone out of print and books about science fiction. In 2000 it published three hardcover titles, two originals and one reprint.

Orb is the Tor imprint that publishes trade paperback reprints of classic and award-winning science fiction.

Orbit (http://www.orbitbooks.co.uk/) is the UK Science Fiction and Fantasy imprint of Little Brown.

Orion is a UK publisher of SF.

Penguin Putnam (http://www.penguinputnam.com/catalog/fiction/books/browse_cat5_pg1.html) now publishes Ace, DAW, and Roc.

Pocket, an imprint of Simon & Schuster, publishes the *Star Trek* books.

Random publishes science fiction under the Spectra and Del Rey imprints. Its authors include Harry Turtledove and Julian May. It also publishes the Star Wars series. DRIN, the Del Rey Internet Newsletter, can be read on the Web or received via e-mail.

Roc is an imprint of Penguin Putnam (http://www.penguinputnam.com/clubppi/news/roc/index.htm).

The Science Fiction Book Club (http://www.sfbc.com/) publishes book club hardcover editions of new science fiction published elsewhere in hardcover or paperback. It also frequently publishes omnibus editions of titles in series. In 2000 it published eighty-seven science fiction and fantasy titles in hardcover.

Starscape is a paperback imprint of Tor, specializing in SF for young adult and middle grade readers.

Tor (http://www.tor.com/tor.html) is the major publisher of SF in the United States. For fourteen years running, it has won the Locus Poll award for best SF publisher. Under the Orb imprint it reprints classic and award-winning science fiction in trade paperback format. In 2000 it published 139 science fiction, fantasy, and horror titles, including 51 new hardcover titles.

Voyager is the SF imprint of HarperCollins Australia (http://www.voyageronline.com.au/).

Voyager is the HarperCollins SF imprint in the UK (http://www.fireandwater.com/imprints/index.htm).

Warner Aspect publishes in both hardcover and paperback.

Organizations and Conventions

Fans and writers form many associations and hold innumerable conventions, usually combining science fiction and fantasy, and often adding horror and the supernatural. "Con" is usually part of the conference name. The conferences are listed in science fiction magazines and on the Internet. The SF Site at http://www.sfsite.com/home.htm does an exceptionally good job of listing conventions.

British Science Fiction Association
Started by a group of authors, publishers, booksellers, and fans in 1958, it has a Web site at http://members.aol.com/tamaranth/index.htm.

European Science Fiction Society
Formed in 1972, it has a membership of fans from several European countries and meets at an annual convention.

Science Fiction & Fantasy Writers of America
Founded in 1965 by Damon Knight, who also served as the first president, the group was originally the Science Fiction Writers of America. The name was changed to include fantasy in 1992, better reflecting the entwining and close relationship of the two genres. Membership is only open to writers of published science fiction or fantasy. It sponsors the annual "Nebula" awards for several categories of science fiction writing. Its motto is "The Future Isn't What It Used to Be" (http://www.sfwa.org/).

SF Canada
Formerly called the Speculative Writers' Association of Canada, membership is open only to published authors (http://www.sfcanada.ca/).

World Science Fiction Convention ("WorldCon")
The first was held in 1939; the sixtieth is slated for San Jose in 2002 (http://www.conjose.org).

Awards

There are several good places on the World Wide Web to find information about science fiction awards. One of the more recent ones is The Locus Index to Science Fiction Awards (http://www.locusmag.com/SFAwards/index.html). Other good sources are Award Web (http://dpsinfo.com/awardweb/index.shtml) and the SF Site: Science Fiction and Fantasy Awards (http://www.sfsite.com/depts/awd01.htm).

Arthur C. Clarke Award
Awarded for the best science fiction novel the previous year. Sponsored by Arthur C. Clarke and chosen by a jury.

Compton Crook Award
British science fiction and fantasy award. Awarded annually by the British Science Fiction Association. (http://www.sfsite.com/depts/awd01.htm)

Ditmar Awards
The Australian Science Fiction Achievement award is voted on by members of the Australian National Science Fiction Convention.

Hugo Awards

Named after Hugo Gernsback, who is considered by many to be the "father" of science fiction. The eligible works are nominated and voted on by the membership of the World Science Fiction Convention. One of the most prestigious awards, it is a reflection of fan opinion.

James Tiptree Jr. Award

Named for Alice Sheldon, who wrote under the male pseudonym, this award is presented for science fiction and fantasy that looks at gender in a different way. The James Tiptree Jr. Award is "given to the work of science fiction or fantasy published in one year which best explores or expands gender roles."

John W. Campbell Award

Awarded annually by the World Science Fiction Convention to the best new science fiction writer of the year.

John W. Campbell Memorial Award

Named for the editor often credited with inventing science fiction; the award committee discusses titles eligible for the year and comes to a consensus decision. It was first awarded in 1973 (http://falcon.cc.ukans.edu/~sfcenter/campbell.htm).

Locus Poll of Best Science Fiction Ever

(Compiled in 1987.) Most science fiction aficionados will have already read most of the books in the list, which can be found online at http://www.sff.net/locus/poll/list87.html#ALLT1.

Locus Poll

The Locus polls provide a terrific window on what American science fiction readers really enjoy. To be eligible to vote in the poll does not require publication credits like the Nebula nor a large chunk of money to support the annual WorldCon like the Hugo, even though many of the voters in the Locus poll probably also vote in one or both of the other major awards.

Nebula Awards

Awarded by the Science Fiction and Fantasy Writers of America. Membership in SFWA is only open to published authors in the field, making this a prestigious award of peers that reflects high literary merit.

Philip K. Dick Award

Awarded to a science fiction or fantasy book published in paperback. It is administered by the Philadelphia SF society.

Prix Aurora Award

Awarded for best in Canadian science fiction and fantasy.

Prometheus Award

A gold coin award, given since 1982 by the Libertarian Futurist Society to provide encouragement to science fiction writers whose books examine the meaning of freedom.

Sapphire Award

Awarded for Best SF Romance of the Year and sponsored by the SF Romance Newsletter (http://members.aol.com/sfreditor/bestsfr.htm).

The SFWA Hall of Fame (The Grand Masters)

The Grand Master Award is presented by the Science Fiction Writers of America. It is not awarded every year. The year listed is the year the award was given.

Robert A. Heinlein 1974 (deceased)

Jack Williamson 1975

Clifford D. Simak 1976 (deceased)

L. Sprague de Camp 1978

Fritz Leiber 1981 (deceased)

Andre Norton 1984

Arthur C. Clarke 1986

Isaac Asimov 1987 (deceased)

Alfred Bester 1988 (deceased)

Ray Bradbury 1989

Lester del Rey 1991 (deceased)

Frederik Pohl 1992

Damon Knight 1994

A. E. van Vogt 1995

Jack Vance 1996

Poul Anderson 1997 (deceased)

Hal Clement 1998

Brian W. Aldiss 1999

Philip Jose Farmer 2000

Sidewise Awards

"The Sidewise Awards for Alternate History were conceived in late 1995 to honor the best 'genre' publications of the year. The award takes its name from Murray Leinster's 1934 short story 'Sidewise In Time,' in which a strange storm causes portions of Earth to swap places with their analogs from other timelines. The first Sidewise Awards were announced in summer 1996."—Sidewise Award Web site.

Theodore Sturgeon Award

Awarded annually for a science fiction short story. Nominations are made by a large group of editors and reviewers, with final selection made by a small committee of experts.

Appendix

Award-Winning Titles, Best Authors, and Best Works

Hugo Award

Note: There were no Hugo awards for novels in 1954 or 1958. In 1966 and 1993 the final outcome resulted in a tie and two winners. In 2001, the Hugo was awarded to a fantasy novel; the first time a children's novel has ever been awarded the Hugo award.

2001—Rowling, J. K. *Harry Potter and the Goblet of Fire.*

2000—Vinge, Vernor. *A Deepness in the Sky.*

1999—Willis, Connie. *To Say Nothing of the Dog.*

1998—Haldeman, Joe. *The Forever Peace.*

1997—Robinson, Kim Stanley. *Blue Mars.*

1996—Stephenson, Neal. *The Diamond Age.*

1995—Bujold, Lois McMaster. *Mirror Dance.*

1994—Robinson, Kim Stanley. *Green Mars.*

1993—Vinge, Vernor. *A Fire upon the Deep.*

1993—Willis, Connie. *Doomsday Book.*

1992—Bujold, Lois McMaster. *Barrayar.*

1991—Bujold, Lois McMaster. *The Vor Game.*

1990—Simmons, Dan. *Hyperion.*

1989—Cherryh, C. J. *Cyteen.*

1988—Brin, David. *The Uplift War.*

1987—Card, Orson Scott. *Speaker for the Dead.*

1986—Card, Orson Scott. *Ender's Game.*

1985—Gibson, William. *Neuromancer.*

1984—Brin, David. *Startide Rising.*

1984—(novella award). Bear, Greg. *Blood Music.*

1983—Asimov, Isaac. *Foundation's Edge.*

1982—Cherryh, C. J. *Downbelow Station.*

1981—Vinge, Joan D. *The Snow Queen.*

1980—Clarke, Arthur C. *The Fountains of Paradise.*

1979—McIntyre, Vonda. *Dreamsnake.*

1978—Pohl, Frederik. *Gateway.*

1977—Wilhelm, Kate. *Where Late the Sweet Birds Sang.*

1976—Haldeman, Joe. *The Forever War.*

1975—Le Guin, Ursula K. *The Dispossessed.*

1974—Clarke, Arthur C. *Rendezvous with Rama.*

1973—Asimov, Isaac. *The Gods Themselves.*

1972—Farmer, Philip José. *To Your Scattered Bodies Go.*

1971—Niven, Larry. *Ringworld.*

1970—Le Guin, Ursula K. *The Left Hand of Darkness.*

1969—Brunner, John. *Stand on Zanzibar.*

1968—Zelazny, Roger. *Lord of Light.*

1967—Heinlein, Robert A. *The Moon Is a Harsh Mistress.*

1966—Zelazny, Roger. *And Call Me Conrad.*

1966—Herbert, Frank. *Dune.*

1965—Leiber, Fritz. *The Wanderer.*

1964—Simak, Clifford D. *Way Station.*

1963—Dick, Philip K. *The Man in the High Castle.*

1962—Heinlein, Robert A. *Stranger in a Strange Land.*

1961—Miller, Walter M., Jr. *A Canticle for Leibowitz.*

1960—Heinlein, Robert A. *Starship Troopers.*

1959—Blish, James. *A Case of Conscience.*

1957—Leiber, Fritz. *The Big Time.*

1956—Heinlein, Robert A. *Double Star.*

1955—Clifton, Mark, and Frank Riley. *The Forever Machine.*

1953—Bester, Alfred. *The Demolished Man.*

Nebula Award Winners

2000—Bear, Greg. *Darwin's Radio.*

1999—Butler, Octavia E. *Parable of the Talents.*

1998—Haldeman, Joe. *The Forever Peace.*

1997—McIntyre, Vonda. *The Moon and the Sun.*

1996—Griffith, Nicola. *Slow River.*

1995—Sawyer, Robert J. *The Terminal Experiment.*

1994—Bear, Greg. *Moving Mars.*

1993—Robinson, Kim Stanley. *Red Mars.*

1992—Willis, Connie. *Doomsday Book.*

1991—Swanwick, Michael. *Stations of the Tide.*

1990 (fantasy)—Le Guin, Ursula K. *Tehanu: The Last Book of Earthsea.*

1989 (fantasy)—Scarborough, Elizabeth Ann. *The Healer's War.*

1988—Bujold, Lois McMaster. *Falling Free.*

1987—Murphy, Pat. *The Falling Woman.*

1986—Card, Orson Scott. *Speaker for the Dead.*

1985—Card, Orson Scott. *Ender's Game.*

1984—Gibson, William. *Neuromancer.*

1983—Brin, David. *Startide Rising.*

1983—Bishop, Michael. *No Enemy But Time.*

1981—Wolfe, Gene. *The Claw of the Conciliator.*

1980—Benford, Gregory. *Timescape.*

1979—Clarke, Arthur C. *The Fountains of Paradise.*

1978—McIntyre, Vonda. *Dreamsnake.*

1977—Pohl, Frederik. *Gateway.*

1976—Pohl, Frederik. *Man Plus.*

1975—Haldeman, Joe. *The Forever War.*

1974—Le Guin, Ursula K. *The Dispossessed.*

1973—Clarke, Arthur C. *Rendezvous with Rama.*

1972—Asimov, Isaac. *The Gods Themselves.*

1971—Silverberg, Robert. *A Time of Changes.*

1970—Niven, Larry. *Ringworld.*

1969—Le Guin, Ursula K. *The Left Hand of Darkness.*

1968—Panshin, Alexei. *Rite of Passage.*

1967—Delany, Samuel R. *The Einstein Intersection.*

1966—Keyes, Daniel. *Flowers for Algernon.*

1966—Delany, Samuel R. *Babel-17.*

1965—Herbert, Frank. *Dune.*

Locus Poll Award

The Locus Poll is one of the few awards that has different categories for science fiction, horror, and fantasy, so all titles listed here are science fiction.

2001—Ursula K. Le Guin. *The Telling.*

2000—Neal Stephenson. *Cryptonomicon.*

1999—Connie Willis. *To Say Nothing of the Dog.*

1998—Dan Simmons. *The Rise of Endymion.*

1997—Kim Stanley Robinson. *Blue Mars.*

1996—Neal Stephenson. *The Diamond Age.*

1995—Lois McMaster Bujold. *Mirror Dance.*

1994—Kim Stanley Robinson. *Green Mars.*

1993—Connie Willis. *Doomsday Book.*

1992—Lois McMaster Bujold. *Barrayar.*

1991—Dan Simmons. *The Fall of Hyperion.*

1990—Dan Simmons. *Hyperion.*

1989—C.J. Cherryh. *Cyteen.*

1988—David Brin. *The Uplift War.*

1987—Orson Scott Card. *Speaker for the Dead.*

1986—David Brin. *The Postman.*

1985—Larry Niven. *The Integral Trees.*

1984—David Brin. *Startide Rising.*

1983—Isaac Asimov. *Foundation's Edge.*

1982—Julian May. *The Many-Colored Land.*

1981—Joan D. Vinge. *The Snow Queen.*

1980—John Varley. *Titan.*

1979—Vonda N. McIntyre. *Dreamsnake.*

1978—Frederik Pohl. *Gateway.*

1977—Kate Wilhelm. *Where Late the Sweet Birds Sang.*

1976—Joe Haldeman. *The Forever War.*

1975—Ursula K. Le Guin. *The Dispossessed.*

1974—Arthur C. Clarke. *Rendezvous with Rama.*

1973—Isaac Asimov. *The Gods Themselves*.

1972—Ursula K. Le Guin. *The Lathe of Heaven*.

1971—Larry Niven. *Ringworld*.

James Tiptree Jr. Award

The Tiptree Award is given by a panel of five judges at WisCon, a feminist-oriented science fiction convention, for "science fiction or fantasy that explores and expands the roles of women and men for work by both women and men."

2000—*Wild Life*. Molly Gloss.

1999—*The Conqueror's Child*. Suzy McKee Charnas.

1998—"Congenital Agenesis of Gender Ideation by K. N. Sirsi and Sandra Botkin." Raphael Carter.

1997—*Black Wine*. Candas Jane Dorsey. "Travels With the Snow Queen." Kelly Link.

1996—"Mountain Ways." Ursula K. Le Guin. *The Sparrow*. Mary Doria Russell.

1995—*Waking the Moon*. Elizabeth Hand. *The Memoirs of Elizabeth Frankenstein*. Theodore Roszak.

1994—"The Matter of Seggri." Ursula K. Le Guin. *Larque on the Wing*. Nancy Springer.

1993—*Ammonite*. Nicola Griffith.

1992—*China Mountain Zhang*. Maureen F. McHugh.

1991—*A Woman of the Iron People*. Eleanor Arnason. *White Queen*. Gwyneth Jones.

Sidewise Award for Alternate History

2000—Mary Gentle. *Ash: A Secret History*. (Published in United States as *A Secret History, Carthage Ascendant, The Wild Machines,* and *Lost Burgundy*.)

1999—DuBois, Brendan. *Resurrection Day*.

1998—Fry, Stephen. *Making History*.

1997—Harry Turtledove. *How Few Remain*.

1996—Stephen Baxter. *Voyage*.

1995—Paul J. McAuley. *Pasquale's Angel*.

Sapphire Award Winners

2000—Saira Ramasastry. *Heir to Govandhara*.

1999—Lois McMaster Bujold. *A Civil Campaign*.

1998—Patricia White. *A Wizard Scorned*.

1997—Catherine Asaro. *Catch the Lightning*.

1996—Laurell K. Hamilton. *Bloody Bones*.

1995—Dara Joy. *Knight of a Trillion Stars*.

"Best" Authors and Their Best

A list of "best" authors and their best works is impossible to compile except on an eccentric basis. Included here are most of the winners of Hugo and Nebula awards, and their award-winning titles. Many of these authors are listed as examples in this book. Most of the following authors are currently writing or appear regularly on lists of the "best." Many more titles could be listed for most of these authors. The ones listed are those most often cited. The few authors listed without titles are those whom critics and fans consider important for the influence of the author's work as a whole.

James Wallace Harris maintains a wonderful Web site at http://www.scifan.com/classics/ (accessed 2/19/02), where he has compiled a ranked list from seven critical works, six fan polls, and five award lists. Harris's Web site also features his essays on what constitutes a classic. He analyzes classics in several different ways, presenting charts on age (i.e., date published). James Gunn has a "Basic Science Fiction Library" list, complete with annotations, at http://falcon.cc.ukans.edu/~sfcenter/sflib.htm (accessed 2/19/02).

The following list takes into consideration award winners, lists of "bests," and availability in public libraries. It is intended as a starting point for libraries that want to maintain a collection including classics in the genre. It also works as a general list for readers trying to broaden their scope within the genre.

Adams, Douglas. *Hitchhiker's Guide to the Galaxy*. 1979.

Aldiss, Brian. *The Long Afternoon of Earth*. 1960.

Anderson, Poul. *Tau Zero*. 1970.

Asimov, Isaac. *The Gods Themselves*. 1972. The Foundation Trilogy.

Barnes, John. *Mother of Storms*. 1994.

Bear, Greg. *Darwin's Radio*. 1999. *Moving Mars*. 1993.

Bester, Alfred. *The Demolished Man*. 1953. *The Stars My Destination*. 1956.

Bishop, Michael. *No Enemy But Time*. 1982.

Blish, James. *Cities in Flight*. 1970 *A Case of Conscience*. 1958.

Boucher, Anthony. *The Compleat Werewolf*. 1969.

Bradbury, Ray. *The Martian Chronicles*. 1950. *Fahrenheit 451*. 1953.

Brin, David. *Startide Rising*. 1983. *The Uplift War*. 1987.

Brunner, John. *Stand on Zanzibar*. 1968.

Budrys, A. J. *Rogue Moon*. 1960. *Who?* 1958.

Bujold, Lois McMaster. *The Vor Game*. 1990. *Barrayar*. 1991. *Mirror Dance*. 1994.

Burgess, Anthony. *A Clockwork Orange*. 1962.

Butler, Octavia. *Parable of the Sower*. 1993. *Parable of the Talents*. 1998.

Card, Orson Scott. *Ender's Game*. 1985.

Cherryh, C. J. *Downbelow Station*. 1981. *Cyteen*. 1988.

Clarke, Arthur C. *Rendezvous with Rama*. *Childhood's End*. 1953. *The City and the Stars*. 1956.

Clement, Hal. *Mission of Gravity*. 1954

Davidson, Avram. *Or All the Seas with Oysters*. 1962

Delany, Samuel R. *Nova*. 1968. *Babel-17*. *Dhalgren*. 1977.

Dick, Philip K. *Do Androids Dream of Electric Sheep?* 1968. *Ubik*. 1969. *The Man in the High Castle*. 1962.

Dickson, Gordon R. *Soldier Ask Not*. 1967. *Dorsai!* 1986.

Disch, Thomas M. *334*. 1972.

Ellison, Harlan. *I Have No Mouth and I Must Scream*. 1967. *The Beast Who Shouted Love at the Heart of the World*. 1968.

Farmer, Philip José. *To Your Scattered Bodies Go*. 1971.

Gibson, William. *Neuromancer*. 1984.

Griffith, Nicola. *Slow River*. 1995.

Haldeman, Joe. *The Forever War*. 1974. *Forever Peace*. 1997.

Harrison, Harry. *Bill, the Galactic Hero*. 1965. *Make Room! Make Room!* 1966.

Heinlein, Robert A. *Time for the Stars*. 1956. *Double Star*. 1956. *Starship Troopers*. 1959. *Stranger in a Strange Land*. 1961. *The Moon Is a Harsh Mistress*. 1966.

Herbert, Frank. *Dune*. 1965.

Huxley, Aldous. *Brave New World*. 1932.

Keyes, Daniel. *Flowers for Algernon*. 1966.

Kornbluth, C. M. *The Syndic*. 1953.

Kress, Nancy. *Beggars in Spain*. 1991.

Lafferty, R. A. *Past Master*. 1968.

Le Guin, Ursula K. *The Left Hand of Darkness*. 1969. *The Dispossessed*. 1974.

Leiber, Fritz. *The Wanderer*. 1965. *A Specter Is Haunting Texas*. 1969. *The Big Time*. 1961.

Malzberg, Barry N. *Beyond Apollo*. 1972.

Matheson, Richard. *I Am Legend*. 1954.

May, Julian. *The Many-Colored Land*. 1981.

McCaffrey, Anne. *Dragonflight*. 1968. *Restoree*. 1967. *The Ship Who Sang*. 1969.

McIntyre, Vonda N. *Dreamsnake*. 1978.

Miller, Walter M., Jr. *A Canticle for Leibowitz*. 1961.

Niven, Larry. *Ringworld*. 1970. *The Integral Trees*. 1984.

Orwell, George. *1984*.

Pangborn, Edgar. *A Mirror for Observers*. 1954. *Davy*. 1964.

Panshin, Alexei. *Rite of Passage*. 1976.

Pohl, Frederik. *Man Plus.* 1975. *Gateway.* 1977.

Pohl, Frederik, and C. M. Kornbluth. *The Space Merchants.* 1953.

Robinson, Kim Stanley. *Red Mars.* 1992. *Green Mars. Blue Mars.* 1996.

Russ, Joanna. *The Female Man.* 1975.

Shute, Nevil. *On the Beach.* 1957.

Silverberg, Robert. *Dying Inside.* 1972.

Simak, Clifford D. *Way Station.* 1963. *City.* 1952.

Simmons, Dan. *Hyperion.* 1989. *The Rise of Endymion.* 1997.

Smith, Cordwainer. *Norstrilia.* 1975.

Spinrad, Norman. *The Iron Dream.* 1972.

Stapledon, Olaf. *Last and First Men.* 1930.

Stephenson, Neal. *Snow Crash.* 1992. *The Diamond Age.* 1995.

Sturgeon, Theodore. *More Than Human.* 1953.

Tepper, Sheri. *The Gate to Women's Country.* 1988.

Tiptree, James, Jr. *Brightness Falls From The Air.* 1985.

van Vogt, A. E. *Slan.* 1946.

Verne, Jules. *20,000 Leagues Under the Sea.* 1870.

Vinge, Joan D. *The Snow Queen.* 1980. *Psion: A Novel of the Future.* 1982.

Vinge, Vernor. *A Fire Upon the Deep.* 1992. *A Deepness in the Sky.* 1999.

Vonnegut, Kurt, Jr. *Sirens of Titan.* 1959. *Slaughterhouse Five.* 1969. *Cat's Cradle.* 1963.

Wells, H. G. *The Time Machine.* 1895. *War of the Worlds.* 1898.

Wilhelm, Kate. *Where Late the Sweet Birds Sang.* 1976.

Williamson, Jack. *The Humanoids.* 1949.

Willis, Connie. *The Doomsday Book.* 1992. *To Say Nothing of the Dog.* 1997.

Wolfe, Gene. *The Claw of the Conciliator.* 1981. *The Citadel of the Autarch.* 1983.

Wyndham, John. *The Midwich Cuckoos.* 1958. *The Day of the Triffids.* 1951.

Zelazny, Roger. *Lord of Light.* 1967. *The Isle of the Dead.* 1969. *Dream Master.* 1966. *The Doors of His Face, the Lamps of His Mouth.* 1971.

Author/Title Index

Subject Index

Character Index